CAPTAIN AMERICA

ROAD TO REBORN

"SENTINEL OF LIBERTY"
ART: Marcos Martin
COLOR ASSIST: Muntsa Vicente
LETTERER: VC's Joe Caramagna

ISSUES #49-50
WRITER: Ed Brubaker
PENCILS: Luke Ross
INKS: Rick Magyar
COLOR ART: Frank D'Armata
COVER ART: Steve Epting

ISSUES #600
WRITERS: Ed Brubaker, Roger Stern,
Mark Waid & Paul Dini
ARTISTS: Butch Guice, Howard Chaykin, Rafael
Albuquerque, David Aja. Mitch Breitweiser,
Kalman Andrasofszky, Dale Eaglesham & Alex Ross
COLOR ART: Frank D'Armata, Edgar Delgado, Matt Hollingsworth,
Mitch Breitweiser, Marte Gracia & Paul Mounts
LETTERERS: VC's Joe Caramagna, Chris Eliopoulos & Todd Klein

"PASSING THE TORCH"
STORY & ART: Fred Hembeck
COLORS: Chris Giarrusso

ISSUES #601
WRITER: Ed Brubaker
ART: Gene Colan
COLOR ART: Dean White
LETTERER: Artmonkeys'
Dave Lanphear

ASSOCIATE EDITOR: Jeanine Schaefer
EDITOR: Tom Brevoort
Captain America created by Joe Simon & Jack Kirby

Collection Editor: Jennifer Grünwald • **Assistant Editors:** Alex Starbuck & John Denning
Editor, Special Projects: Mark D. Beazley • **Senior Editor, Special Projects:** Jeff Youngquist
Senior Vice President of Sales: David Gabriel

Editor in Chief: Joe Quesada • **Publisher:** Dan Buckley • **Executive Producer:** Alan Fine

CAPTAIN AMERICA: ROAD TO REBORN. Contains material originally published in magazine form as CAPTAIN AMERICA #49-50 and #600-601. First printing 2009. Hardcover ISBN# 978-0-7851-4174-7. Softcover ISBN# 978-0-7851-4175-4. Published by MARVEL PUBLISHING, INC., a subsidiary of MARVEL ENTERTAINMENT, INC. OFFICE OF PUBLICATION: 417 5th Avenue, New York, NY 10016. Copyright © 2009 Marvel Characters, Inc. All rights reserved. Hardcover: $24.99 per copy in the U.S. (GST #R127032852). Softcover: $19.99 per copy in the U.S. (GST #R127032852). Canadian Agreement #40668537. All characters featured in this issue and the distinctive names and likenesses thereof, and all related indicia are trademarks of Marvel Characters, Inc. No similarity between any of the names, characters, persons, and/or institutions in this magazine with those of any living or dead person or institution is intended, and any such similarity which may exist is purely coincidental. **Printed in the U.S.A.** ALAN FINE, EVP - Office Of The Chief Executive Marvel Entertainment, Inc. & CMO Marvel Characters B.V.; DAN BUCKLEY, Chief Executive Officer and Publisher - Print, Animation & Digital Media; JIM SOKOLOWSKI, Chief Operating Officer; DAVID GABRIEL, SVP of Publishing Sales & Circulation; DAVID BOGART, SVP of Business Affairs & Talent Management; MICHAEL PASCIULLO, VP Merchandising & Communications; JIM O'KEEFE, VP of Operations & Logistics; DAN CARR, Executive Director of Publishing Technology; JUSTIN F. GABRIE, Director of Publishing & Editorial Operations; SUSAN CRESPI, Editorial Operations Manager; ALEX MORALES, Publishing Operations Manager; STAN LEE, Chairman Emeritus. For information regarding advertising in Marvel Comics or on Marvel.com, please contact Mitch Dane, Advertising Director, at mdane@marvel.com. For Marvel subscription inquiries, please call 800-217-9158. **Manufactured between 9/7/09 and 10/7/09 (hardcover), and 9/7/09 and 1/6/10 (softcover), by R.R. DONNELLEY, INC., SALEM, VA, USA.**

10 9 8 7 6 5 4 3 2 1

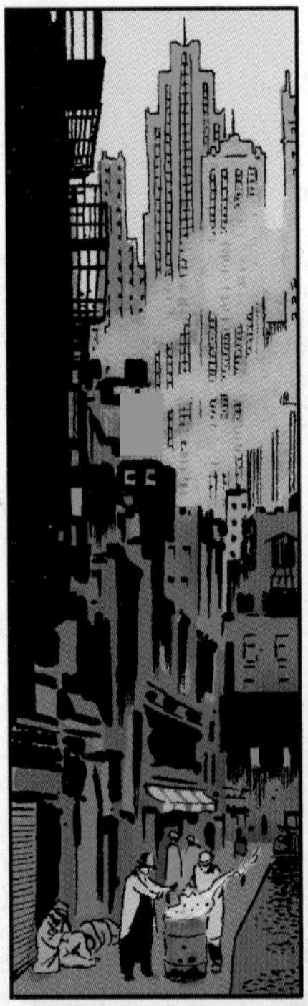

1940! And as the clouds of war gathered in Europe, army reject Steve Rogers became the first test subject of Project: Rebirth, whose goal was to elevate a man to the peak of human physical perfection, thus creating the ultimate soldier!

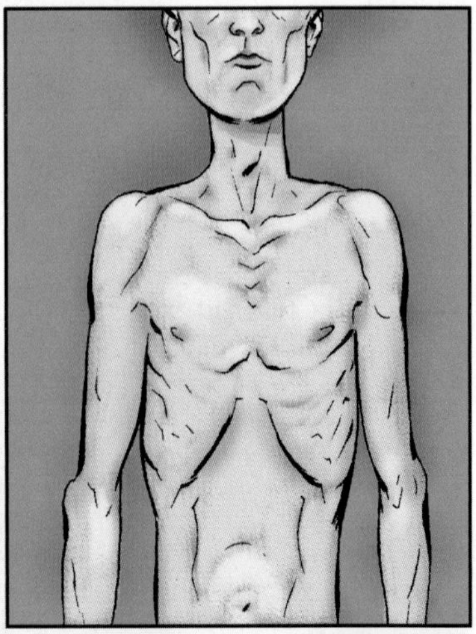

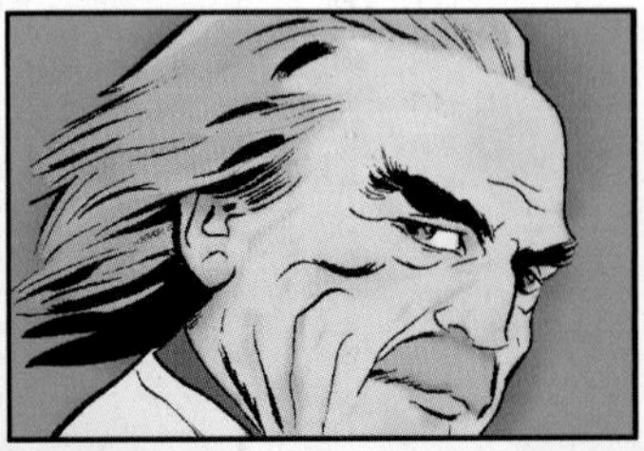

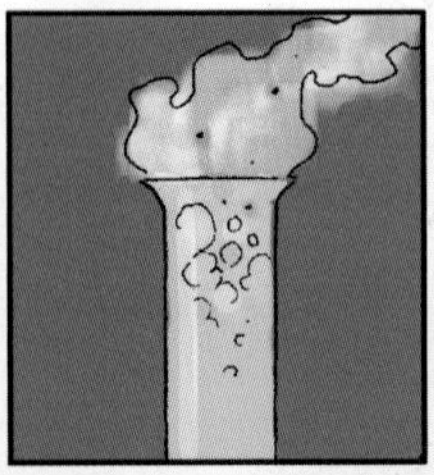

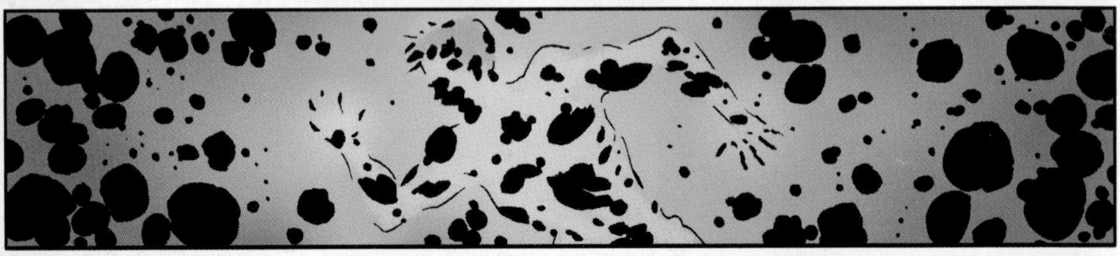

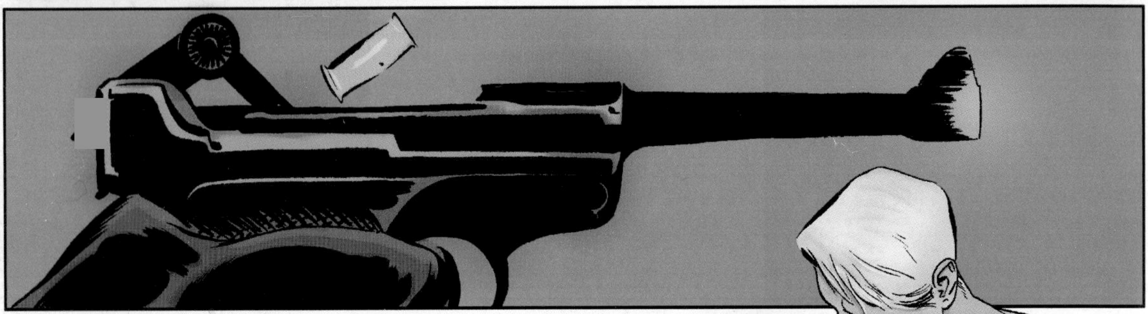

But a single gunshot from a Nazi saboteur insured that there would never be more than a single American prototype!

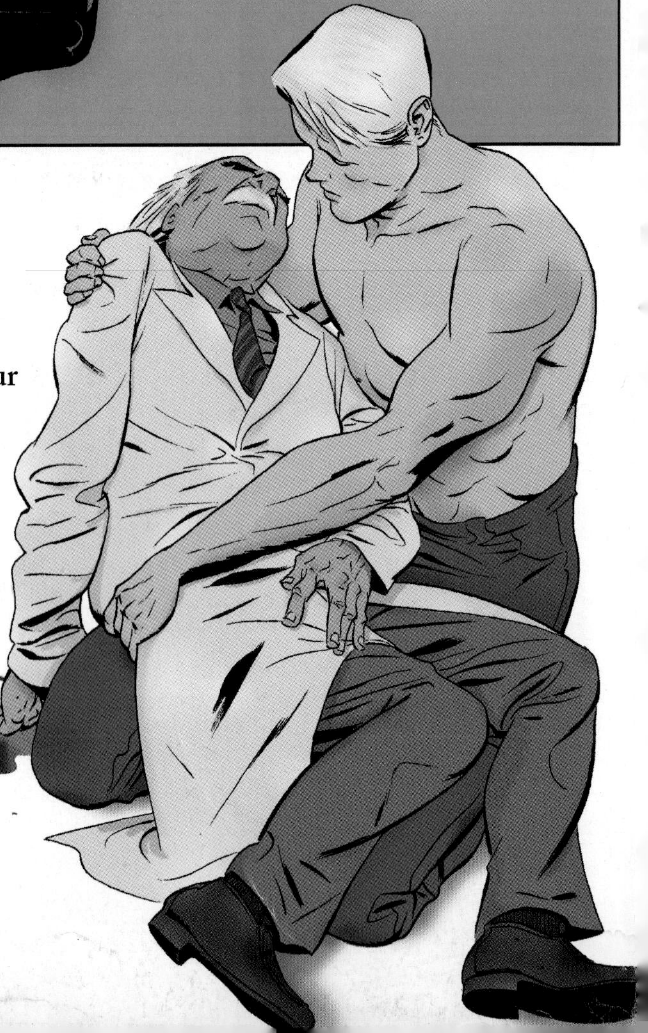

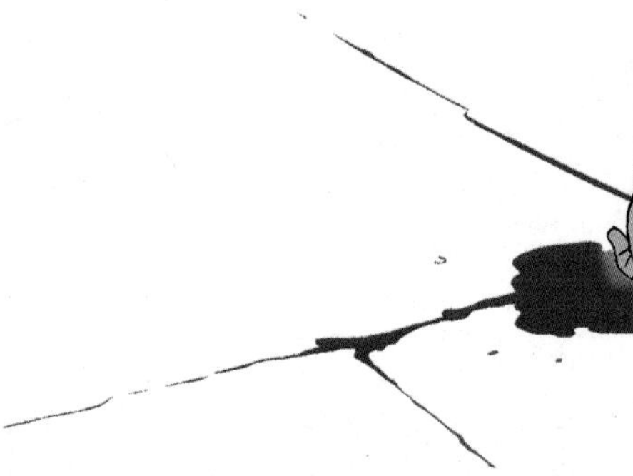

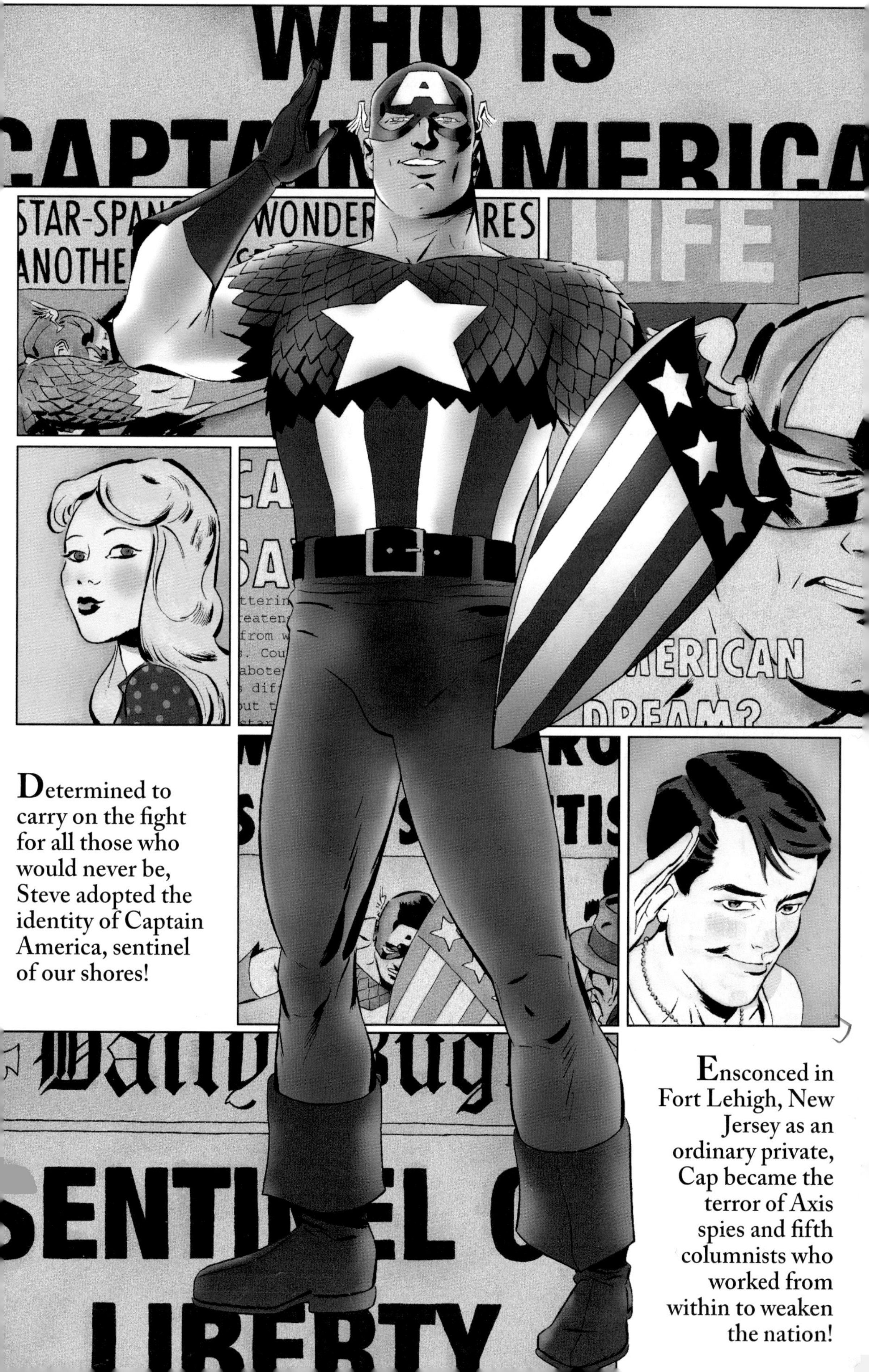
WHO IS
LIFE
Determined to carry on the fight for all those who would never be, Steve adopted the identity of Captain America, sentinel of our shores!
Ensconced in Fort Lehigh, New Jersey as an ordinary private, Cap became the terror of Axis spies and fifth columnists who worked from within to weaken the nation!

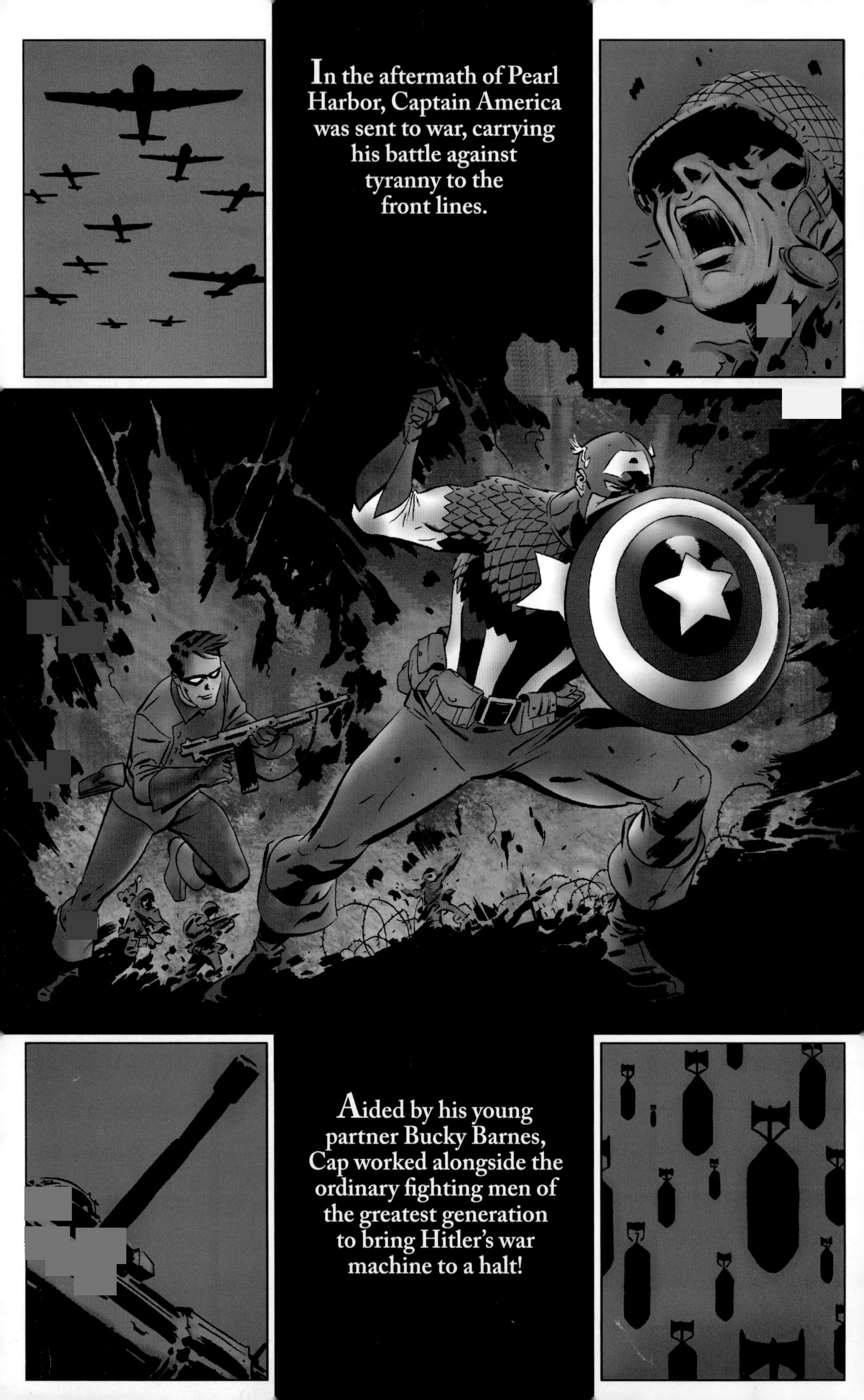
In the aftermath of Pearl Harbor, Captain America was sent to war, carrying his battle against tyranny to the front lines.
Aided by his young partner Bucky Barnes, Cap worked alongside the ordinary fighting men of the greatest generation to bring Hitler's war machine to a halt!

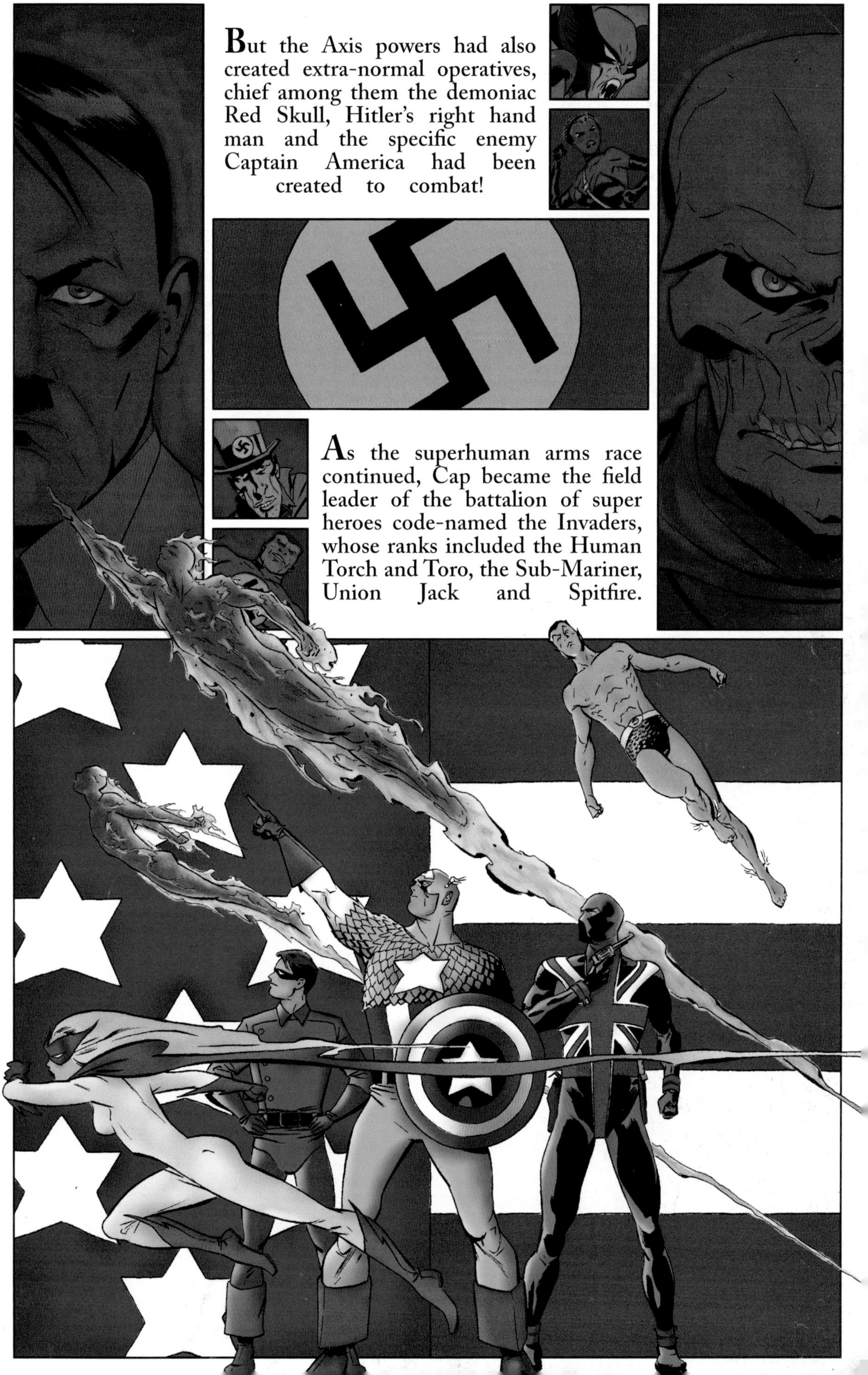
But the Axis powers had also created extra-normal operatives, chief among them the demoniac Red Skull, Hitler's right hand man and the specific enemy Captain America had been created to combat!
As the superhuman arms race continued, Cap became the field leader of the battalion of super heroes code-named the Invaders, whose ranks included the Human Torch and Toro, the Sub-Mariner, Union Jack and Spitfire.

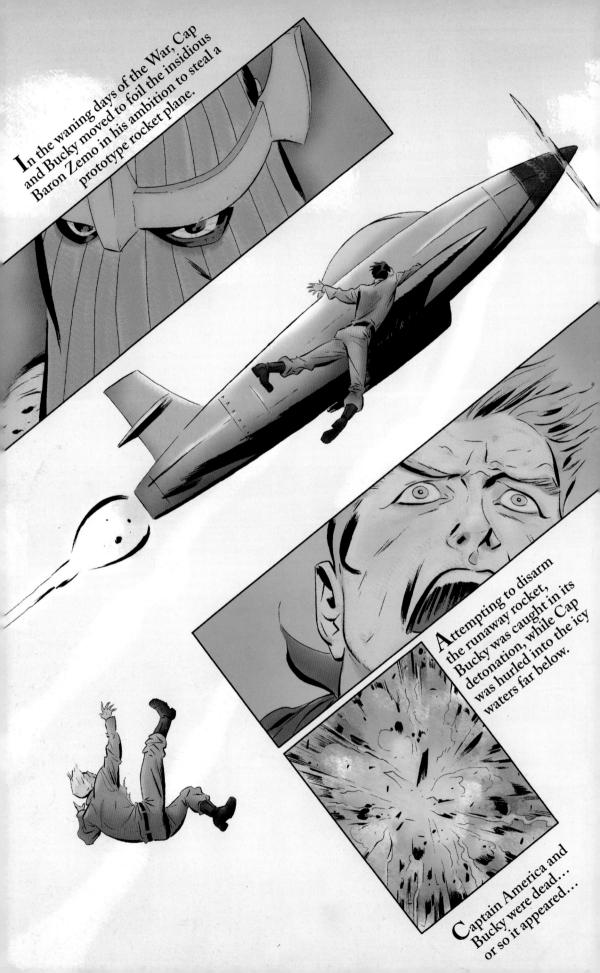

In the waning days of the War, Cap and Bucky moved to foil the insidious Baron Zemo in his ambition to steal a prototype rocket plane.

Attempting to disarm the runaway rocket, Bucky was caught in its detonation, while Cap was hurled into the icy waters far below.

Captain America and Bucky were dead... or so it appeared...

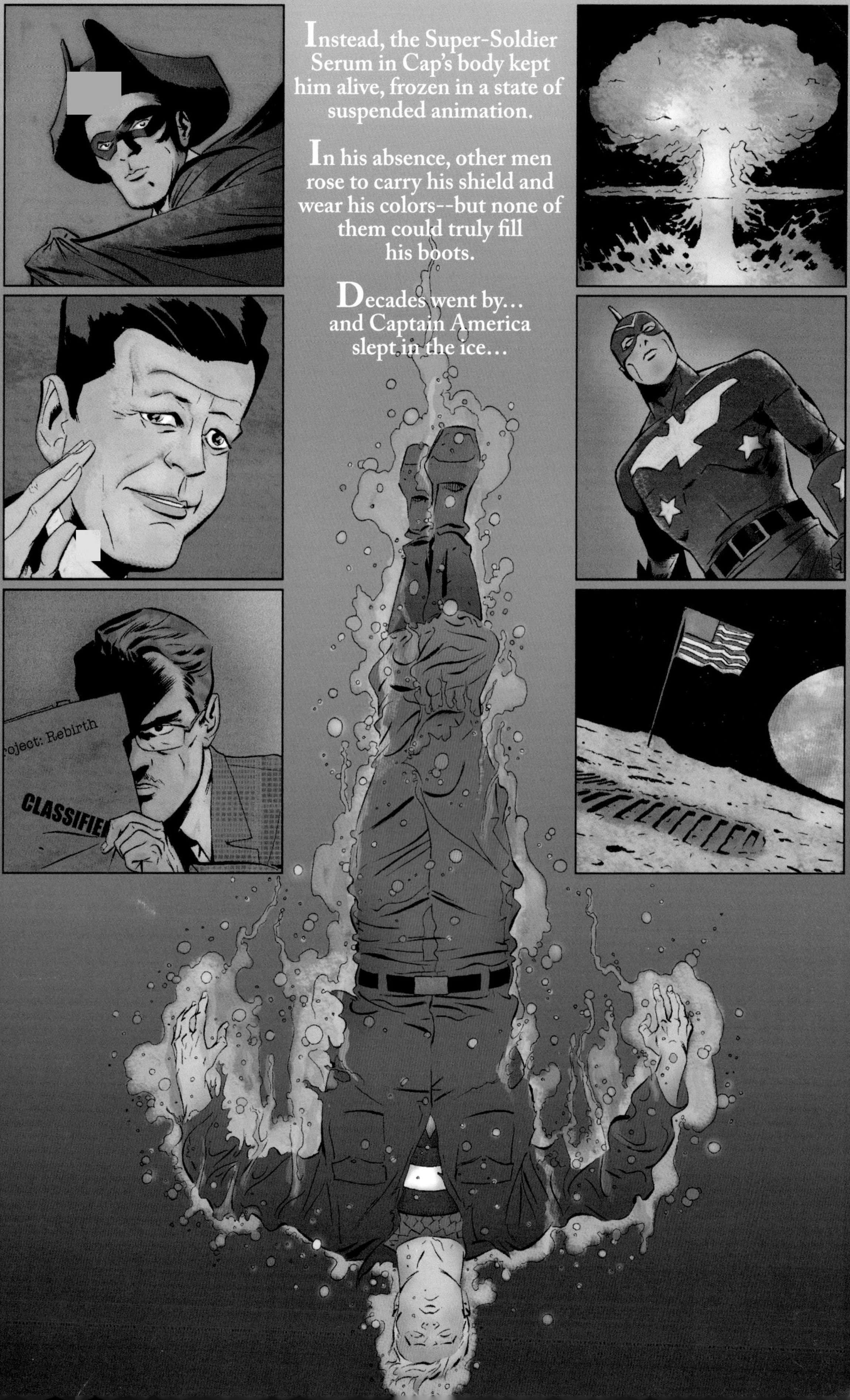
Instead, the Super-Soldier Serum in Cap's body kept him alive, frozen in a state of suspended animation.
In his absence, other men rose to carry his shield and wear his colors--but none of them could truly fill his boots.
Decades went by... and Captain America slept in the ice...
roject: Rebirth
CLASSIFIE

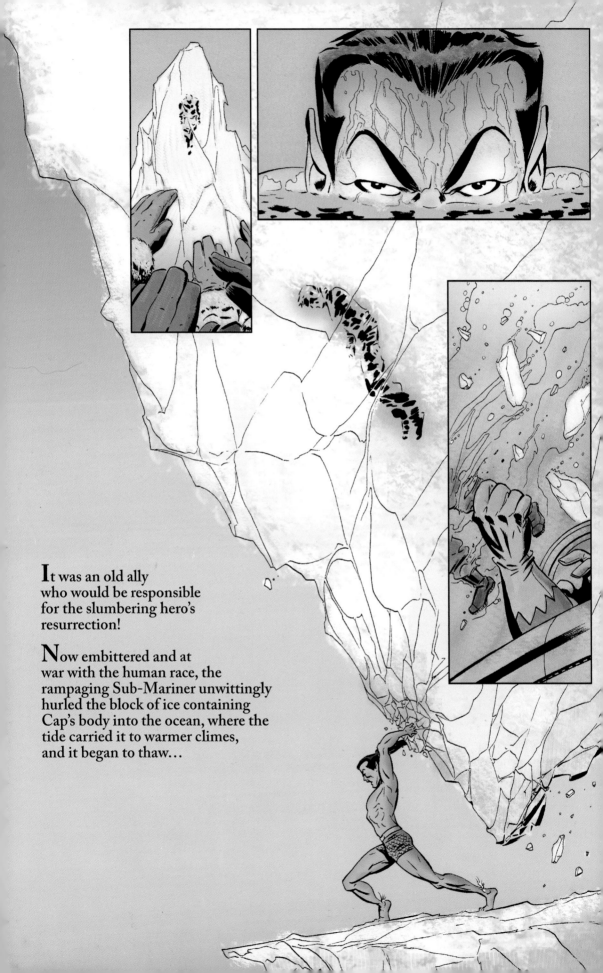

It was an old ally who would be responsible for the slumbering hero's resurrection!

Now embittered and at war with the human race, the rampaging Sub-Mariner unwittingly hurled the block of ice containing Cap's body into the ocean, where the tide carried it to warmer climes, and it began to thaw…

Cap's comatose body was recovered and revived by the Avengers, Earth's Mightiest Heroes!

With his partner Bucky dead and the life he once knew a distant memory, the Avengers gave Cap a purpose in this brave new world. He quickly became their most stalwart member!

And when the founding Avengers went their separate ways, it was entrusted to Captain America to ride herd over a team of new recruits and keep the Avengers legacy alive!

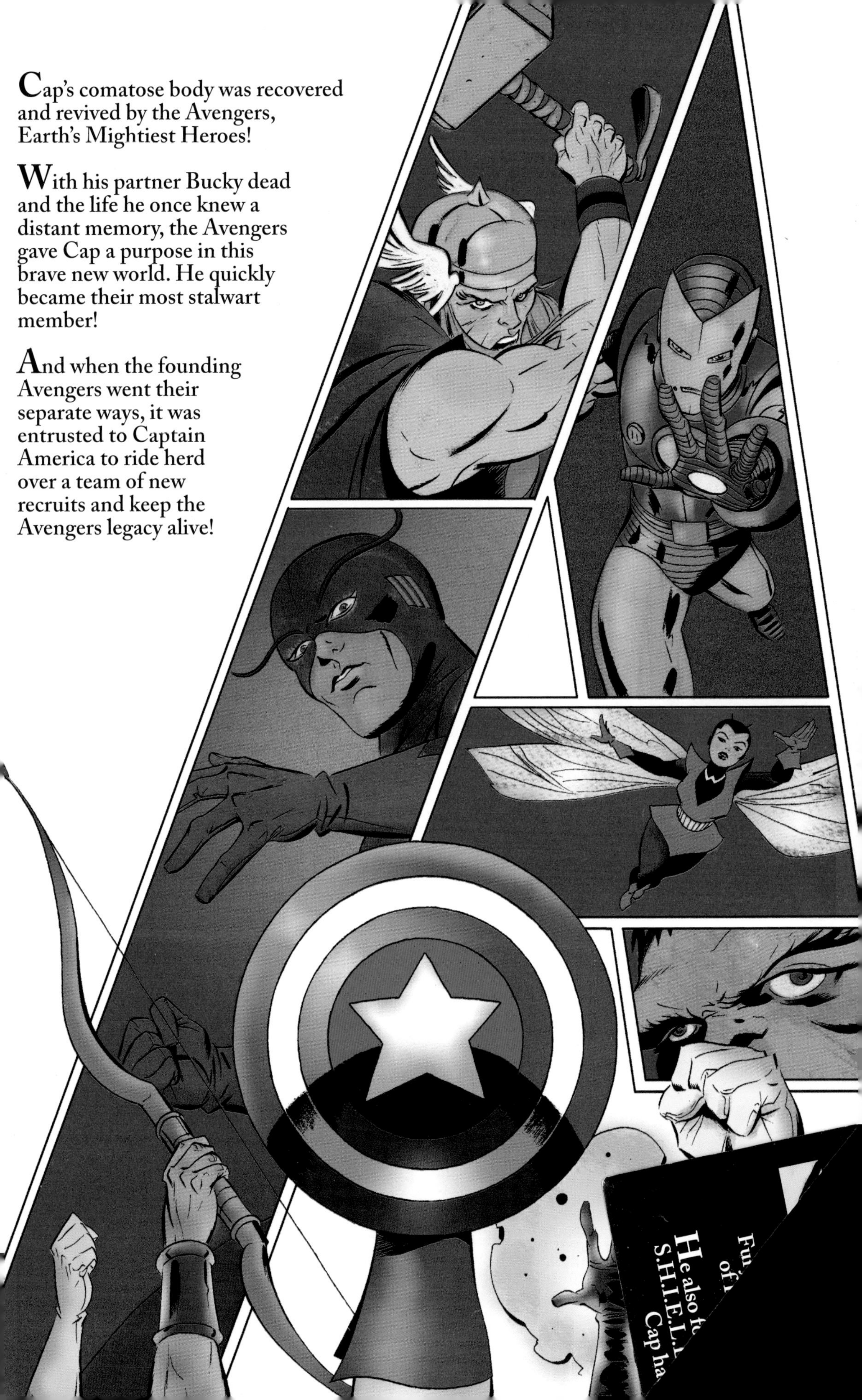

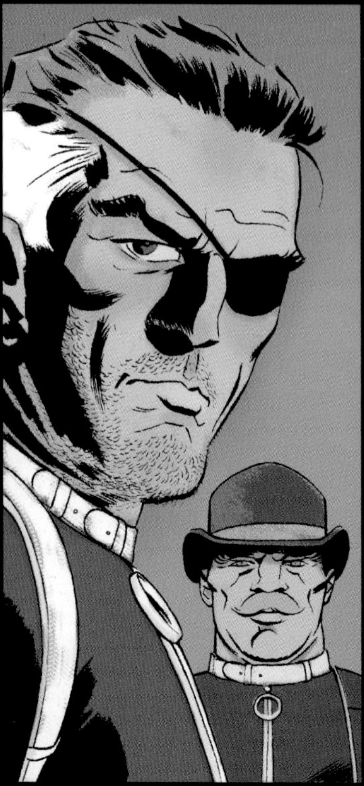

Cap also contacted his wartime ally Nick Fury, now head of the global peace-keeping organization called S.H.I.E.L.D., and offered his services.

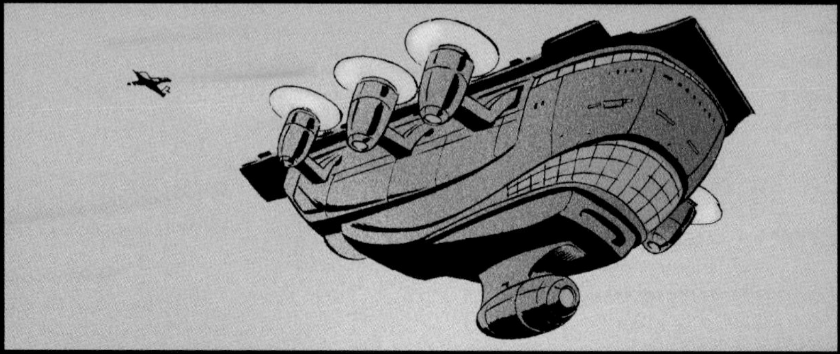

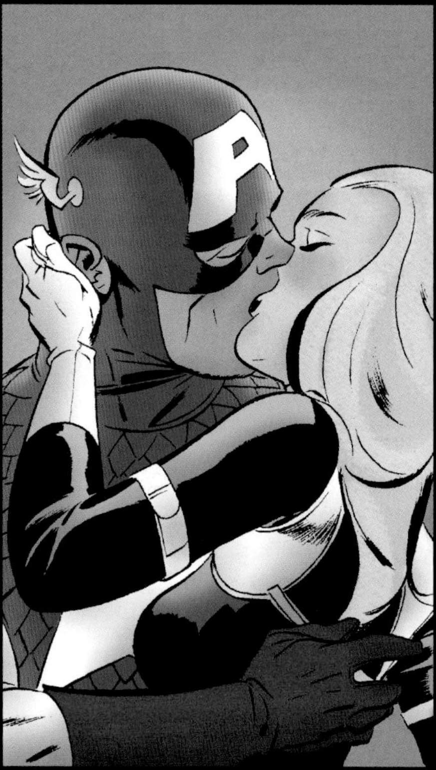

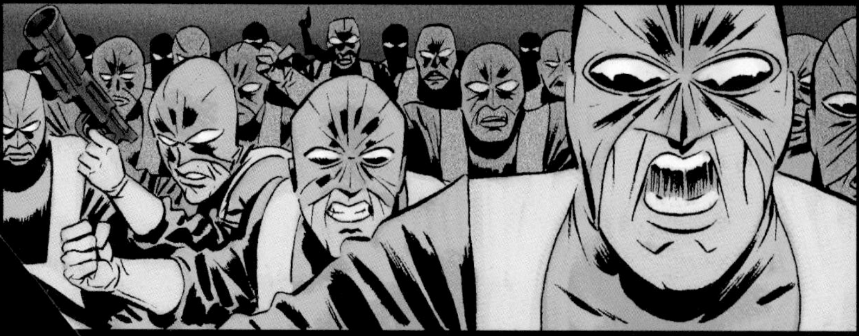

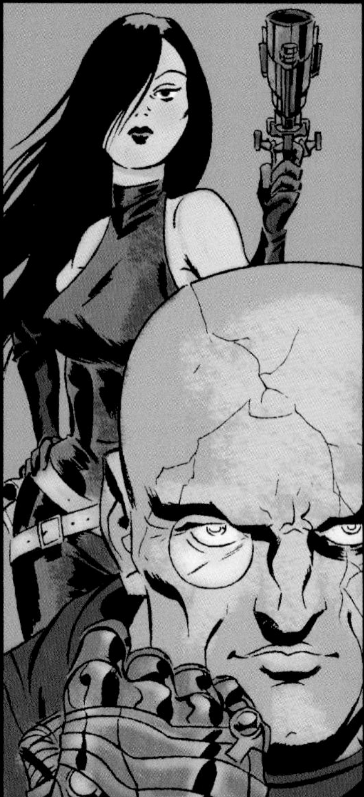

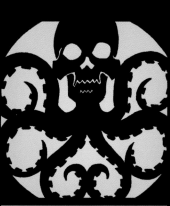

As an operative for S.H.I.E.L.D., Cap joined ry's ongoing struggle against the terrorist hordes Hydra, led by the notorious Baron Strucker.

found romance in the arms of Sharon Carter, D. Agent 13, who was the niece of the girl d loved and lost during the War.

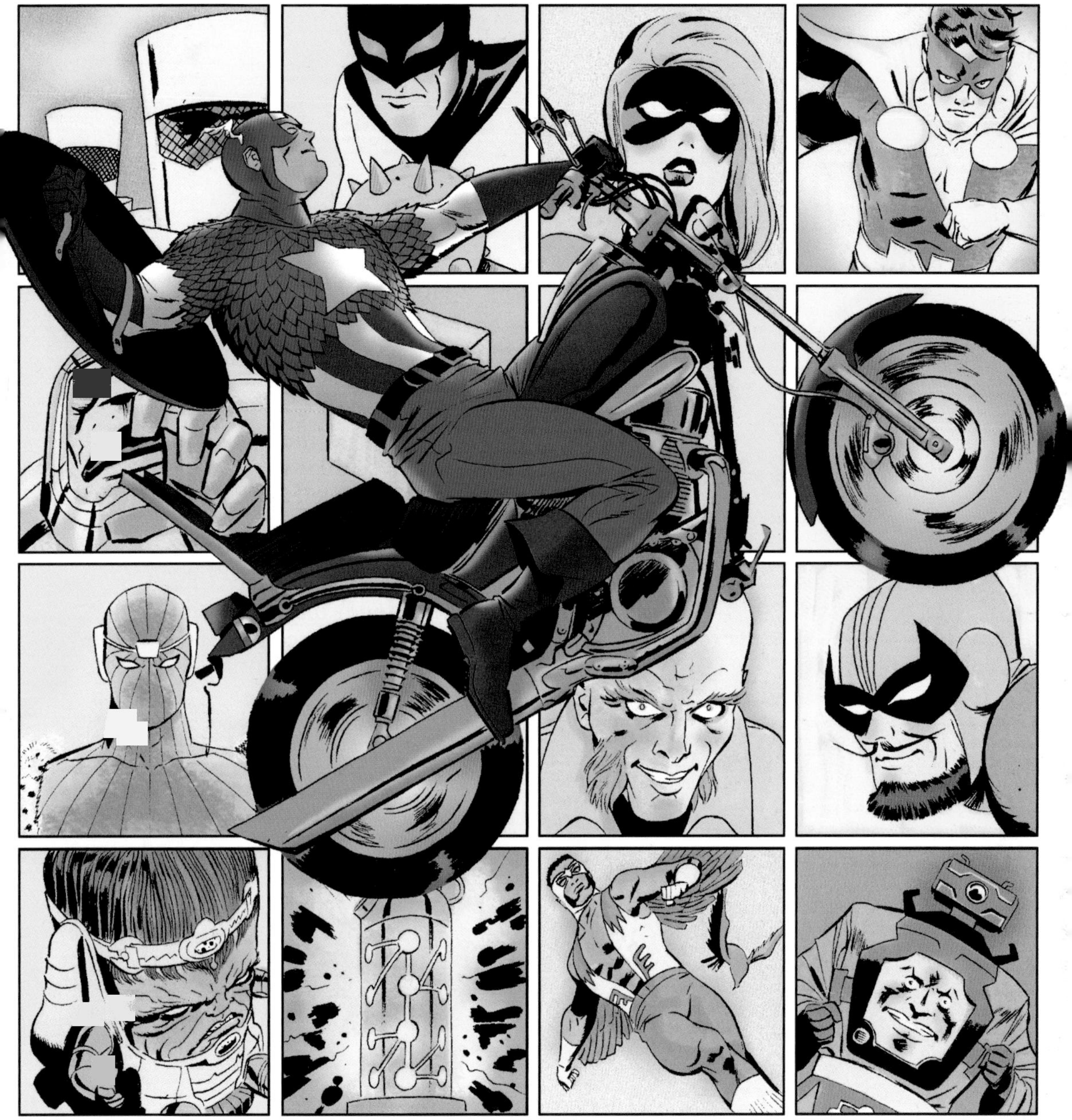

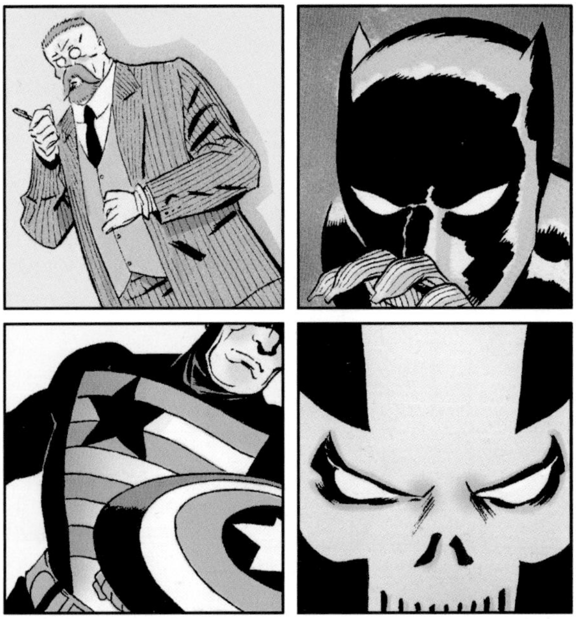

Whether as a member of the Avengers, alongside S.H.I.E.L.D., or on his own, Captain America hurled himself into action time and again on behalf of the Free World.

He became an inspiration to a whole generation of modern super heroes, such as the high-flying Falcon, and an ever-present scourge feared by villains across the globe!

His most enduring sorrow remained the loss of his young partner, Bucky.

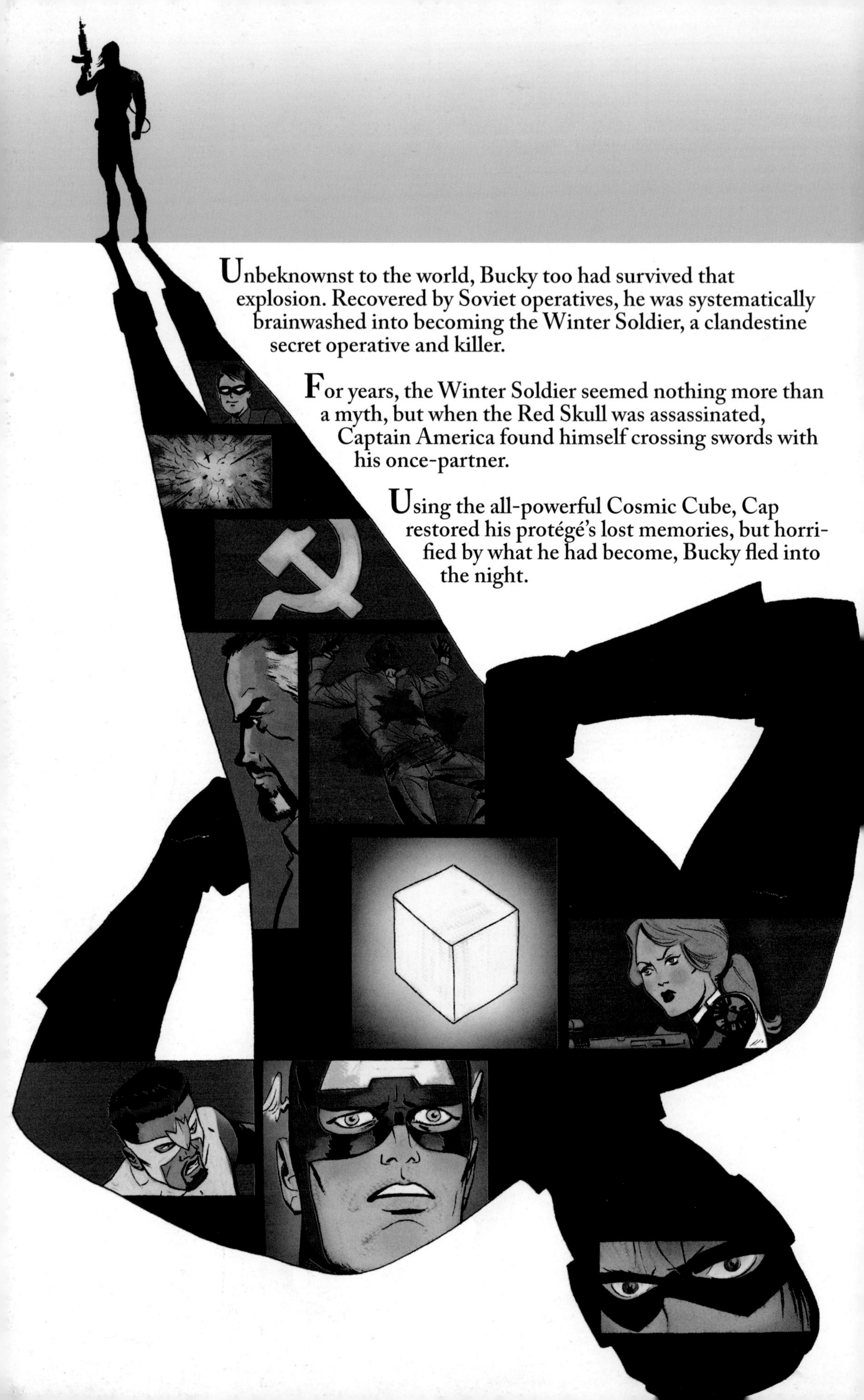

Unbeknownst to the world, Bucky too had survived that explosion. Recovered by Soviet operatives, he was systematically brainwashed into becoming the Winter Soldier, a clandestine secret operative and killer.

For years, the Winter Soldier seemed nothing more than a myth, but when the Red Skull was assassinated, Captain America found himself crossing swords with his once-partner.

Using the all-powerful Cosmic Cube, Cap restored his protégé's lost memories, but horrified by what he had become, Bucky fled into the night.

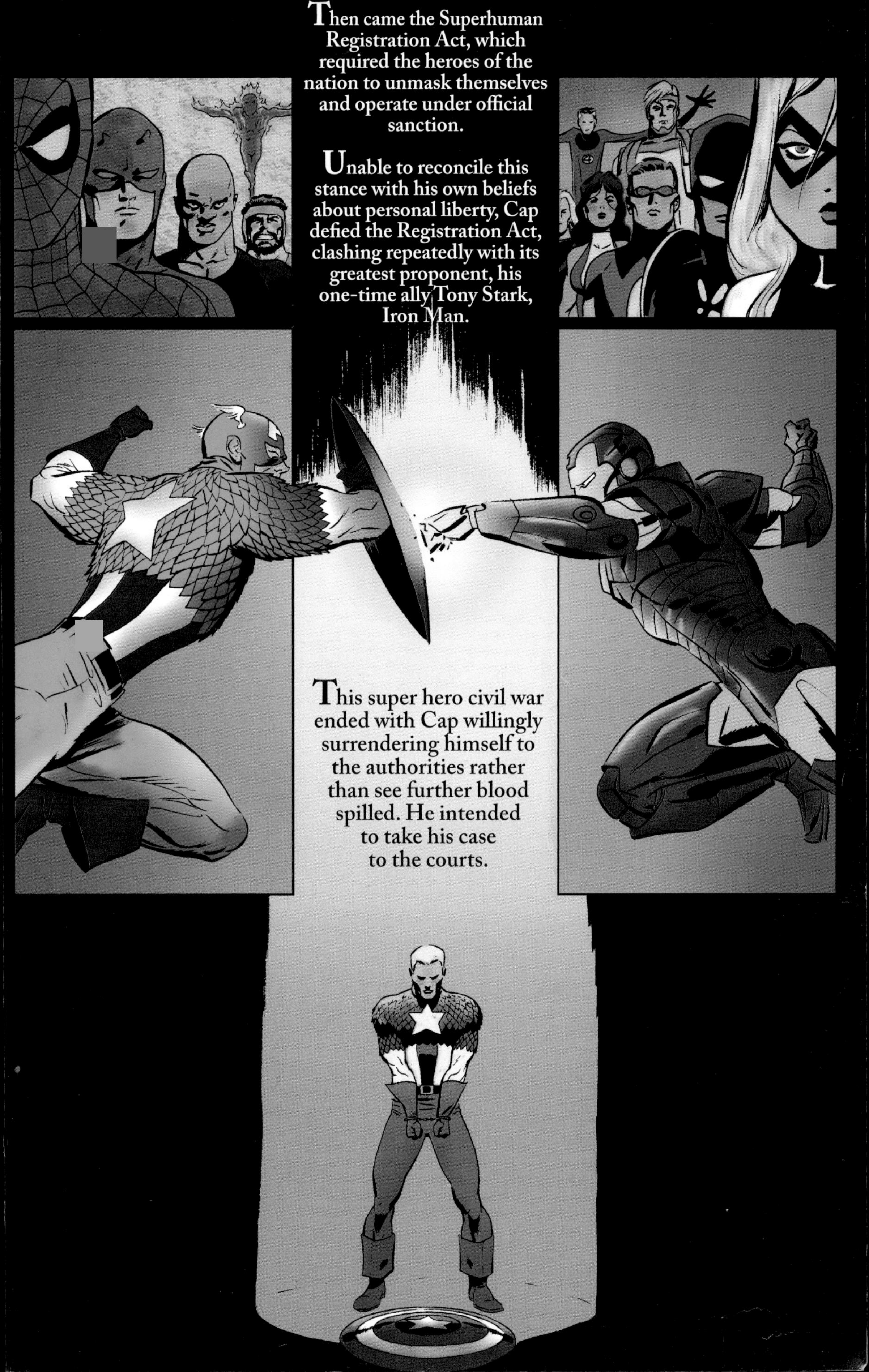
Then came the Superhuman Registration Act, which required the heroes of the nation to unmask themselves and operate under official sanction.
Unable to reconcile this stance with his own beliefs about personal liberty, Cap defied the Registration Act, clashing repeatedly with its greatest proponent, his one-time ally Tony Stark, Iron Man.
This super hero civil war ended with Cap willingly surrendering himself to the authorities rather than see further blood spilled. He intended to take his case to the courts.

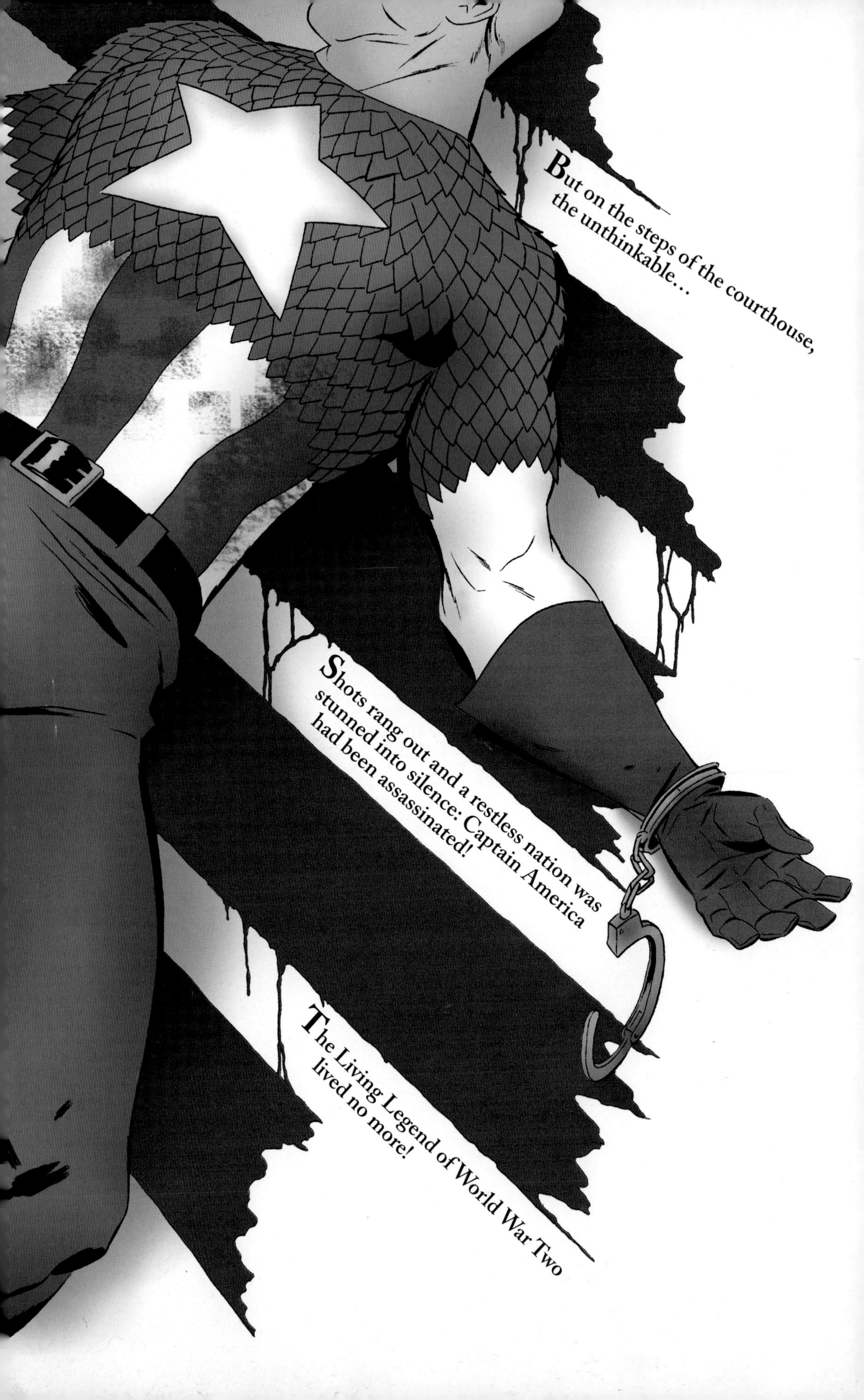
But on the steps of the courthouse, the unthinkable...
Shots rang out and a restless nation was stunned into silence: Captain America had been assassinated!
The Living Legend of World War Two lived no more!

Now the head of S.H.I.E.L.D., Tony Stark sought out Bucky Barnes, and gave him Cap's indestructible shield and the mantle that Rogers had carried so long and so proudly.

D... ...ed to carry on in... ...memory, Bucky ... ...one for his dark stru... ...g up to an ideal ... ...han any one man!

T... ...Rogers has fa... ...tain America

SENTINEL OF LIBERTY

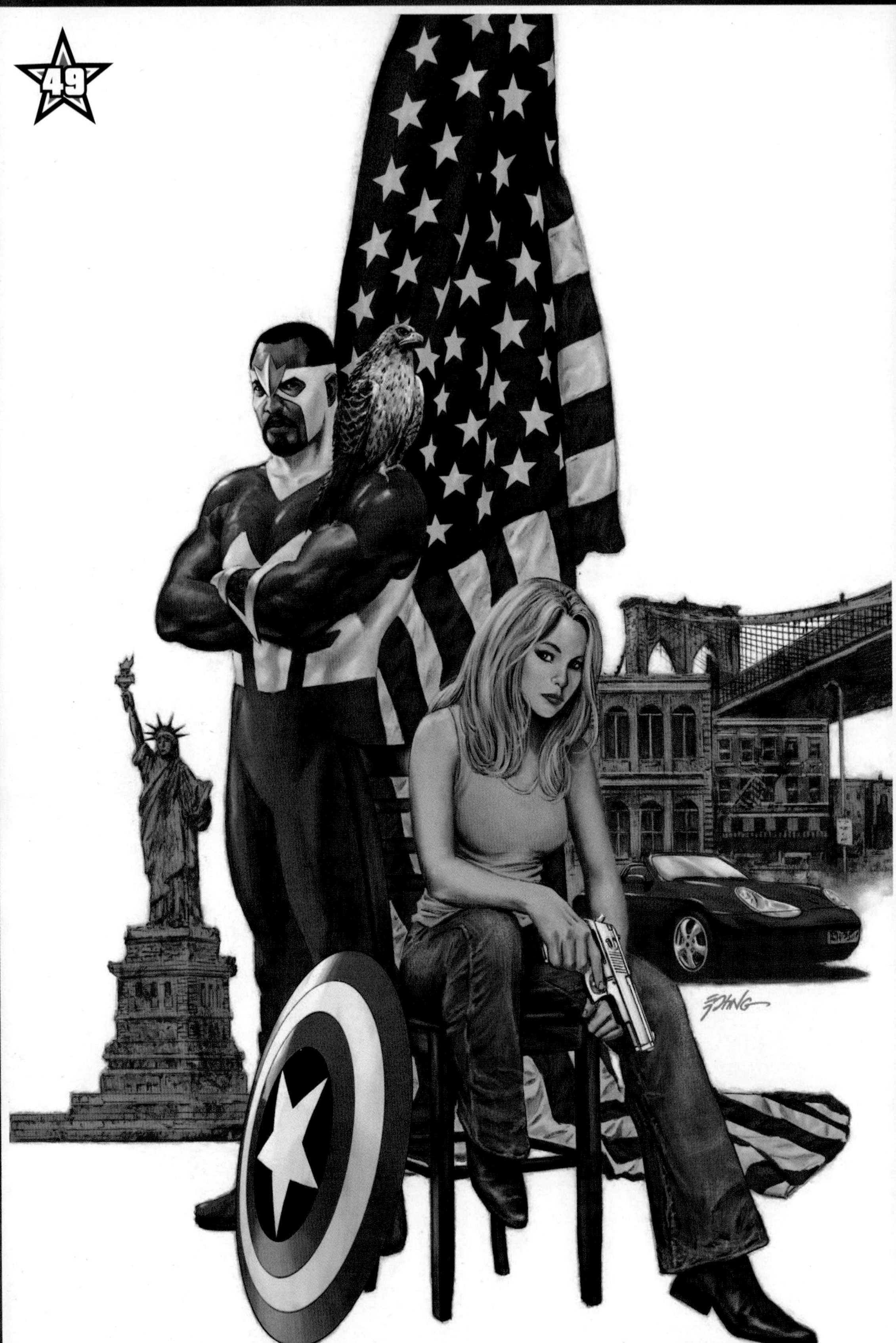
49

THE DAUGHTER OF TIME

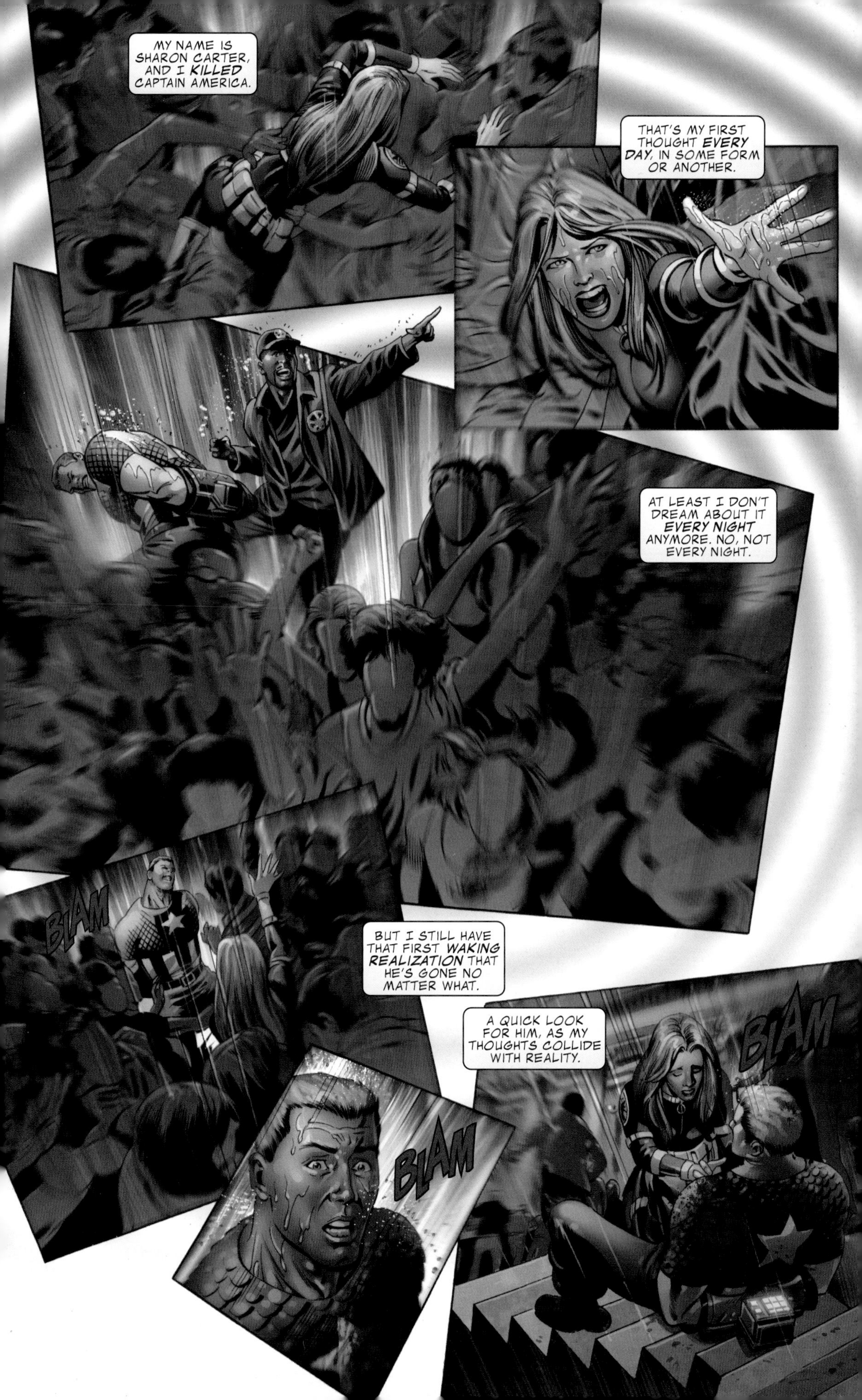
MY NAME IS SHARON CARTER, AND I KILLED CAPTAIN AMERICA.
THAT'S MY FIRST THOUGHT EVERY DAY, IN SOME FORM OR ANOTHER.
AT LEAST I DON'T DREAM ABOUT IT EVERY NIGHT ANYMORE. NO, NOT EVERY NIGHT.
BLAM
BUT I STILL HAVE THAT FIRST WAKING REALIZATION THAT HE'S GONE NO MATTER WHAT.
A QUICK LOOK FOR HIM, AS MY THOUGHTS COLLIDE WITH REALITY.
BLAM
BLAM

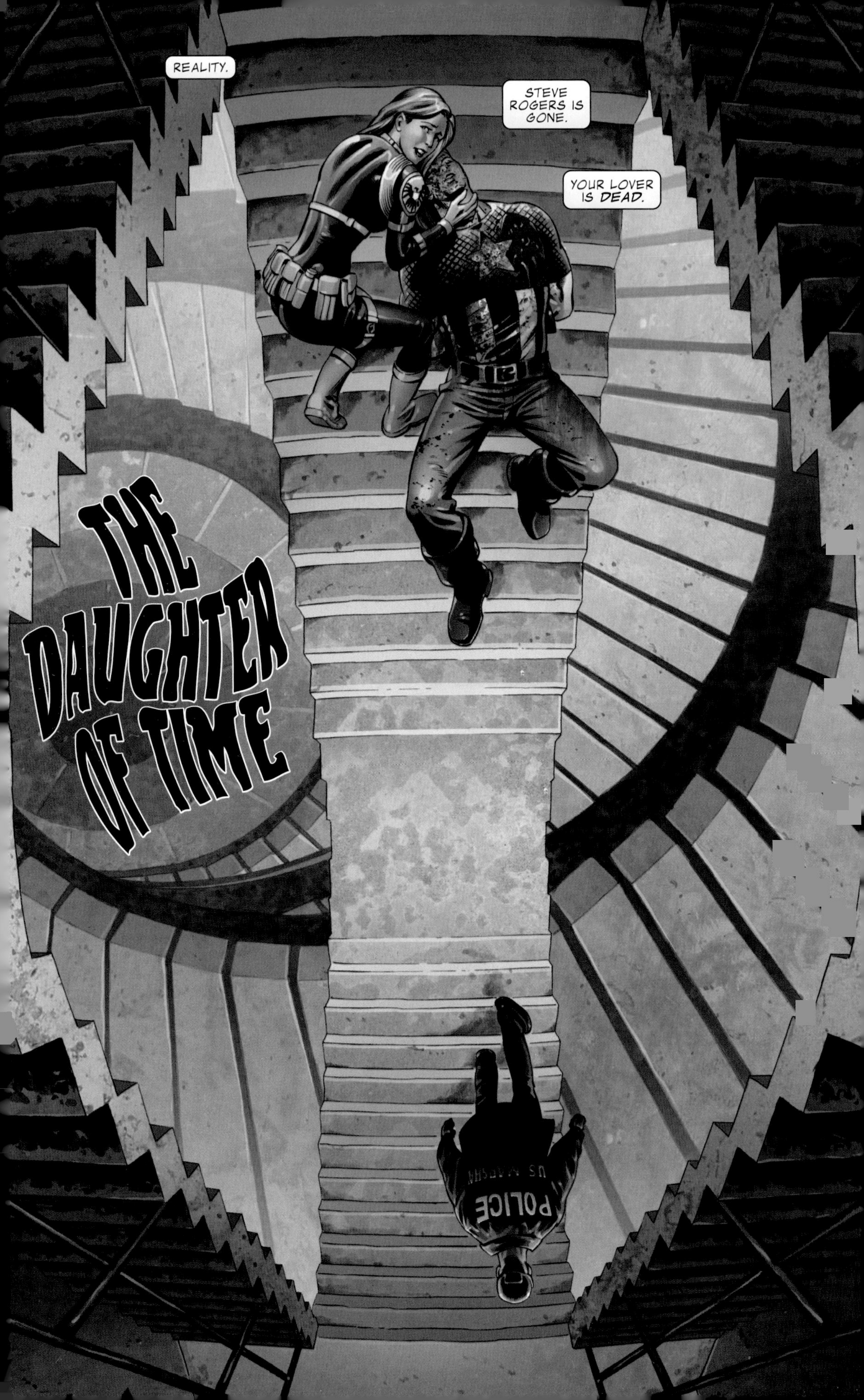
REALITY.
STEVE ROGERS IS GONE.
YOUR LOVER IS DEAD.
THE DAUGHTER OF TIME
POLICE

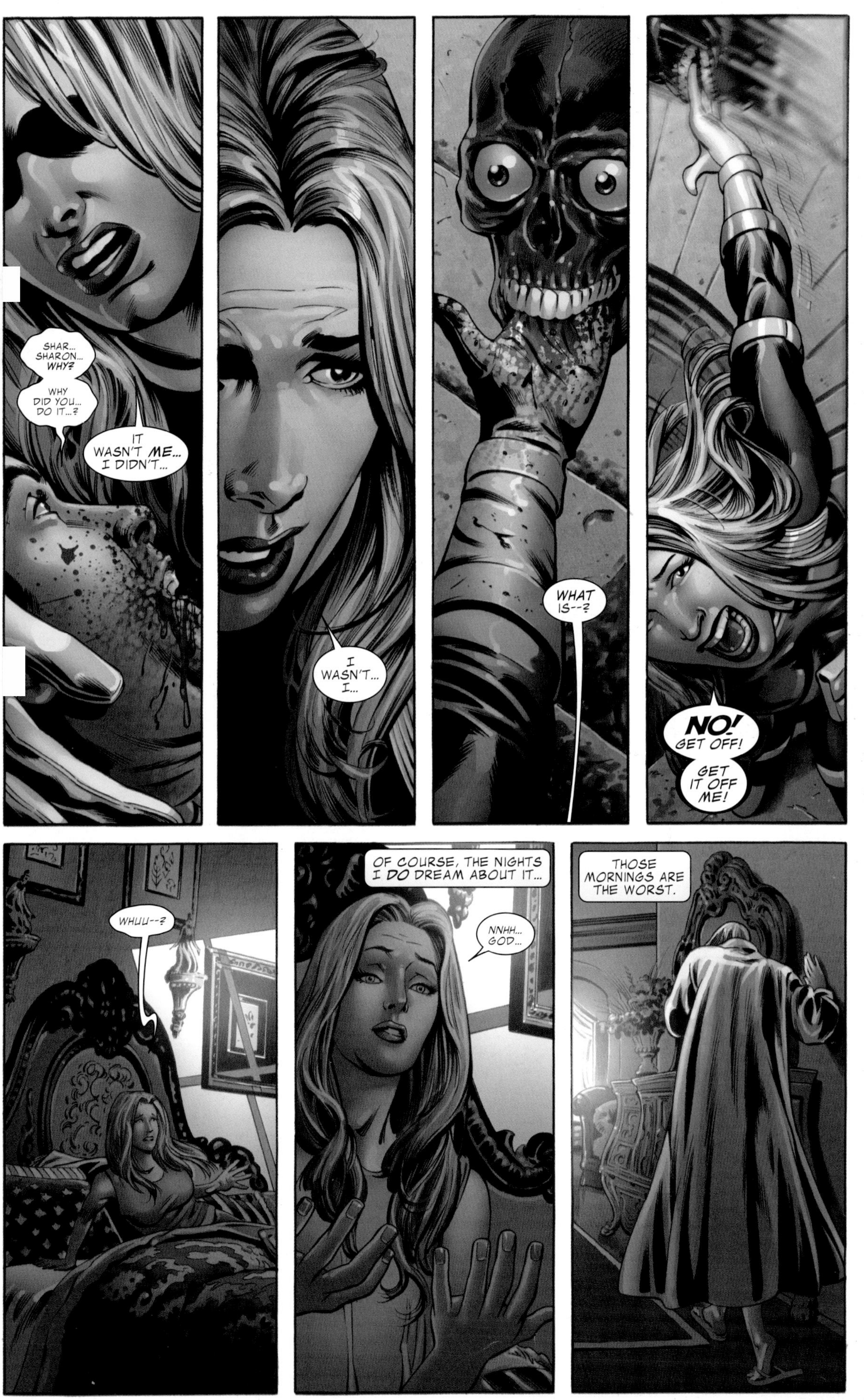
SHAR... SHARON... WHY?
WHY DID YOU... DO IT...?
IT WASN'T ME... I DIDN'T...
I WASN'T... I...
WHAT IS--?
NO! GET OFF!
GET IT OFF ME!
WHUU--?
OF COURSE, THE NIGHTS I DO DREAM ABOUT IT...
NNHH... GOD...
THOSE MORNINGS ARE THE WORST.

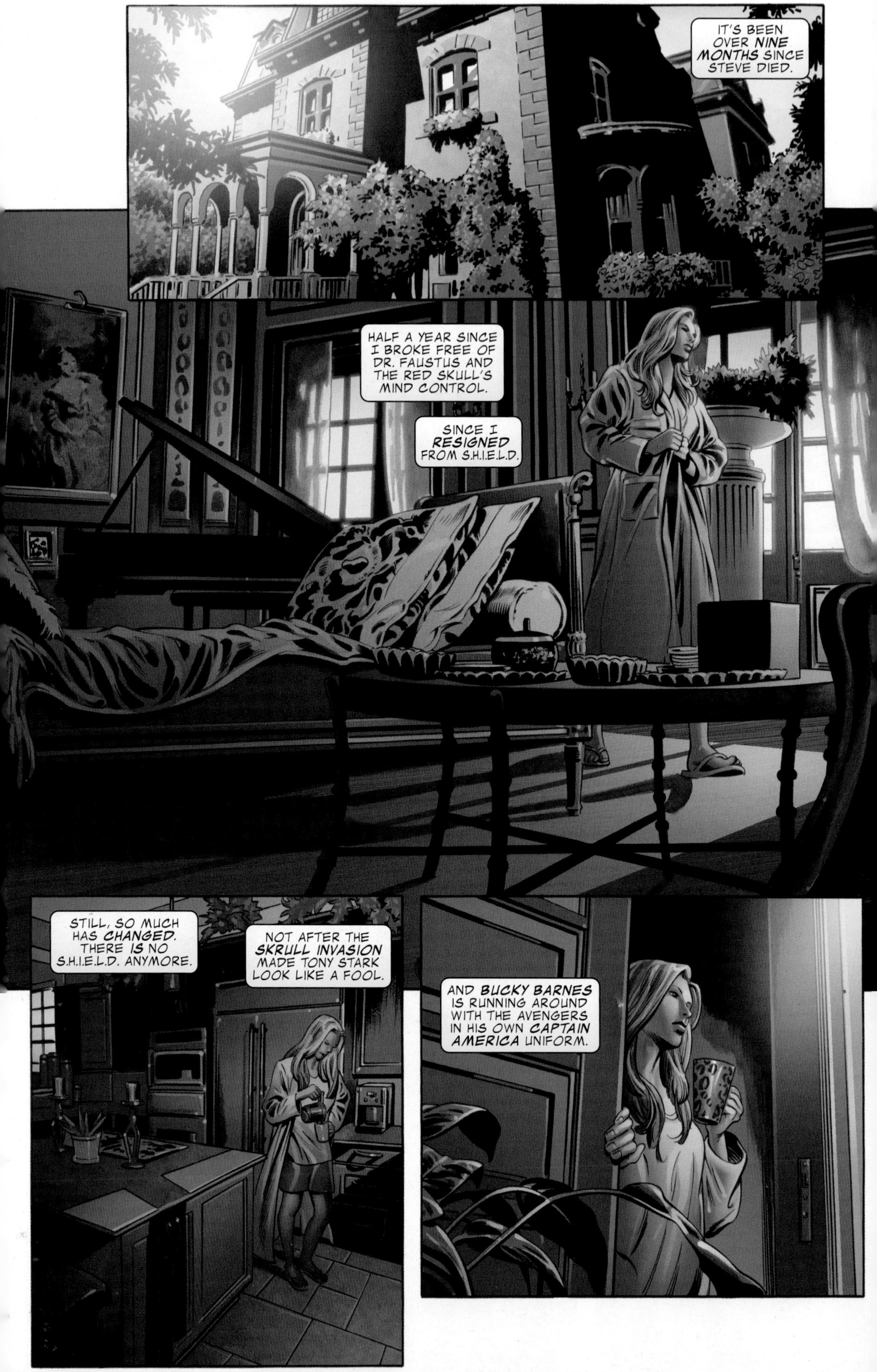
IT'S BEEN OVER NINE MONTHS SINCE STEVE DIED.
HALF A YEAR SINCE I BROKE FREE OF DR. FAUSTUS AND THE RED SKULL'S MIND CONTROL.
SINCE I RESIGNED FROM S.H.I.E.L.D.
STILL, SO MUCH HAS CHANGED. THERE IS NO S.H.I.E.L.D. ANYMORE.
NOT AFTER THE SKRULL INVASION MADE TONY STARK LOOK LIKE A FOOL.
AND BUCKY BARNES IS RUNNING AROUND WITH THE AVENGERS IN HIS OWN CAPTAIN AMERICA UNIFORM.

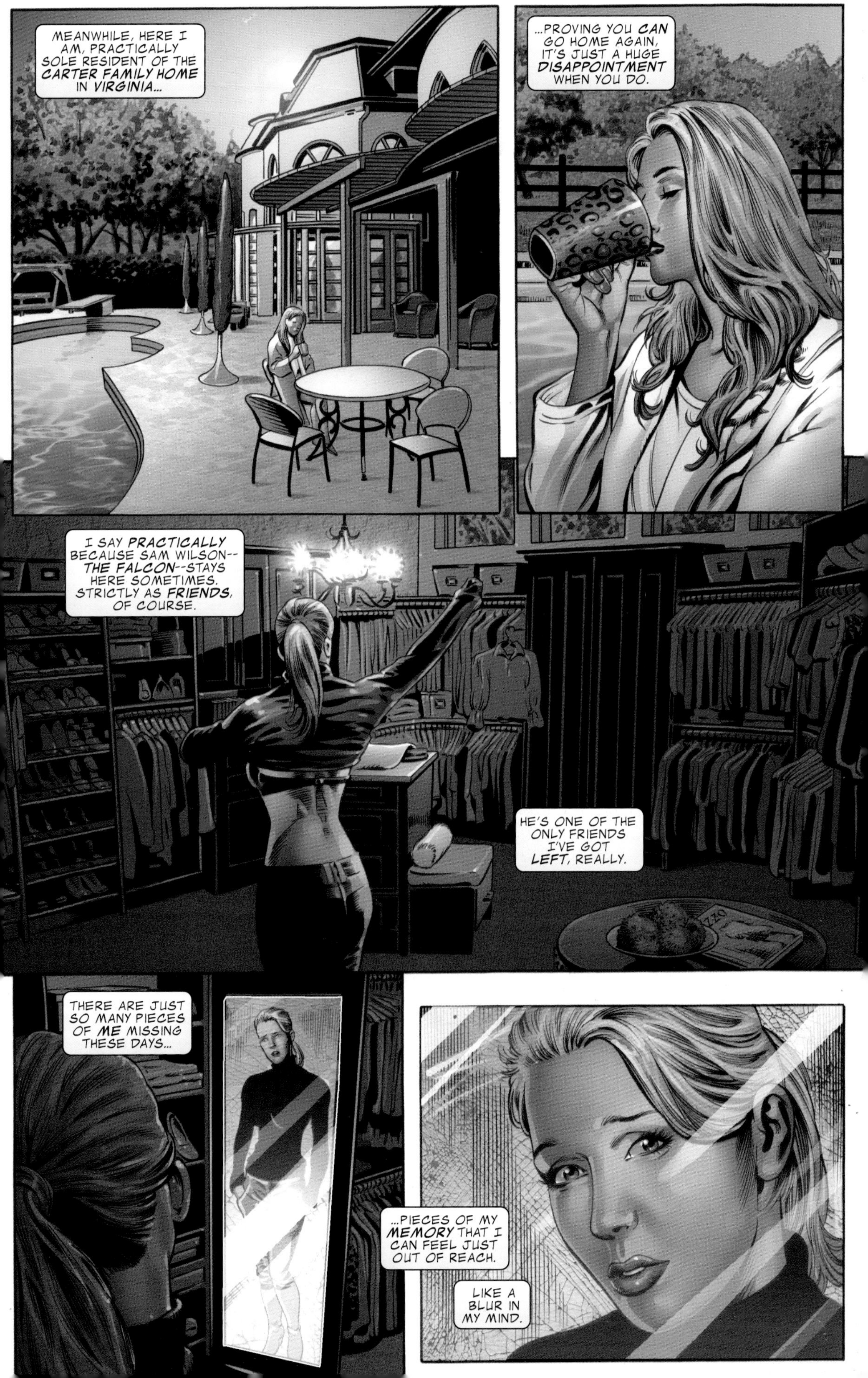
MEANWHILE, HERE I AM, PRACTICALLY SOLE RESIDENT OF THE CARTER FAMILY HOME IN VIRGINIA...
...PROVING YOU CAN GO HOME AGAIN, IT'S JUST A HUGE DISAPPOINTMENT WHEN YOU DO.
I SAY PRACTICALLY BECAUSE SAM WILSON-- THE FALCON--STAYS HERE SOMETIMES. STRICTLY AS FRIENDS, OF COURSE.
HE'S ONE OF THE ONLY FRIENDS I'VE GOT LEFT, REALLY.
THERE ARE JUST SO MANY PIECES OF ME MISSING THESE DAYS...
...PIECES OF MY MEMORY THAT I CAN FEEL JUST OUT OF REACH.
LIKE A BLUR IN MY MIND.

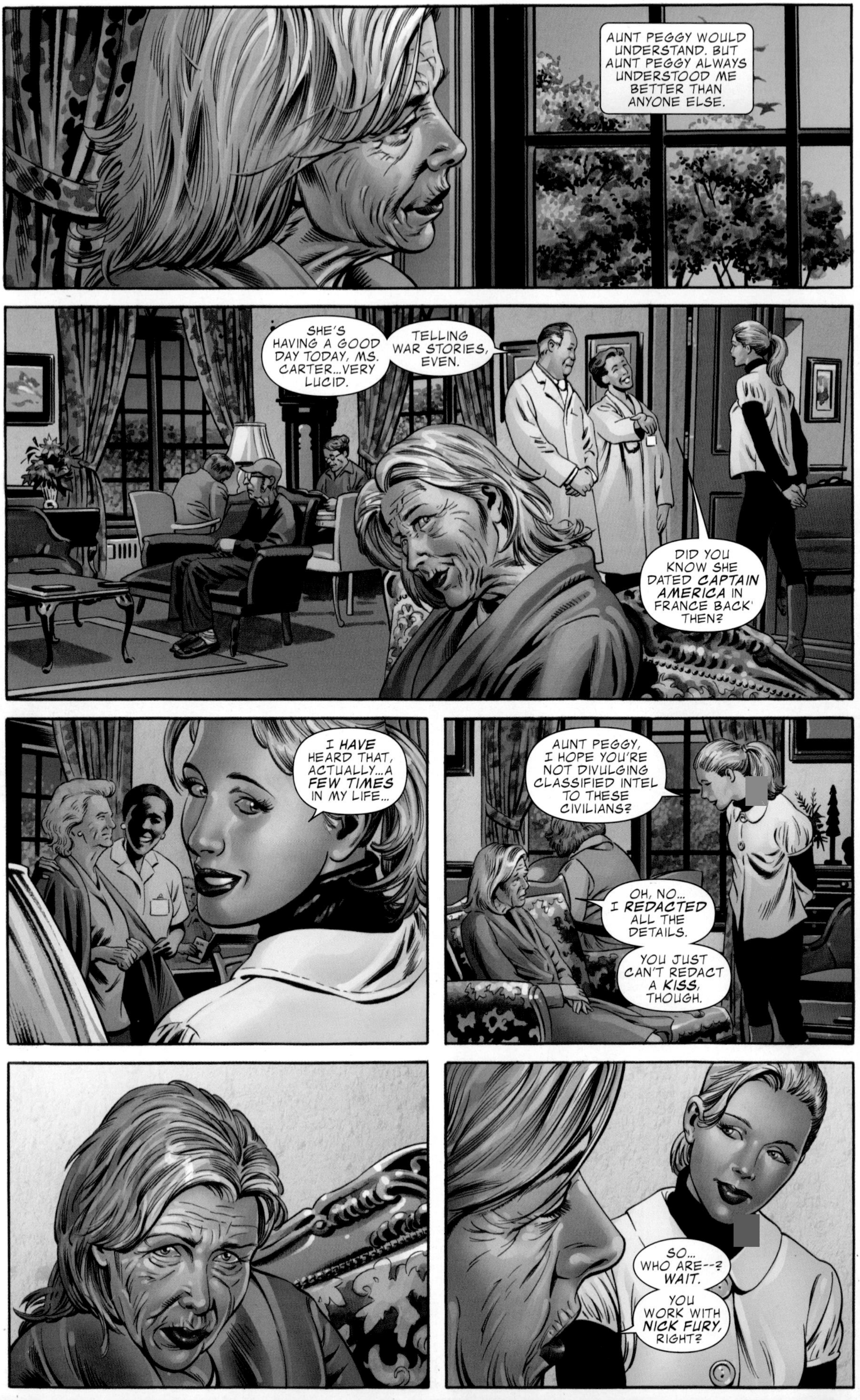
AUNT PEGGY WOULD UNDERSTAND. BUT AUNT PEGGY ALWAYS UNDERSTOOD ME BETTER THAN ANYONE ELSE.
SHE'S HAVING A GOOD DAY TODAY, MS. CARTER...VERY LUCID.
TELLING WAR STORIES, EVEN.
DID YOU KNOW SHE DATED **CAPTAIN AMERICA** IN FRANCE BACK' THEN?
I ***HAVE*** HEARD THAT, ACTUALLY...A ***FEW TIMES*** IN MY LIFE...
AUNT PEGGY, I HOPE YOU'RE NOT DIVULGING CLASSIFIED INTEL TO THESE CIVILIANS?
OH, NO... I ***REDACTED*** ALL THE DETAILS.
YOU JUST CAN'T REDACT A ***KISS***, THOUGH.
SO... WHO ARE--? ***WAIT.***
YOU WORK WITH ***NICK FURY***, RIGHT?

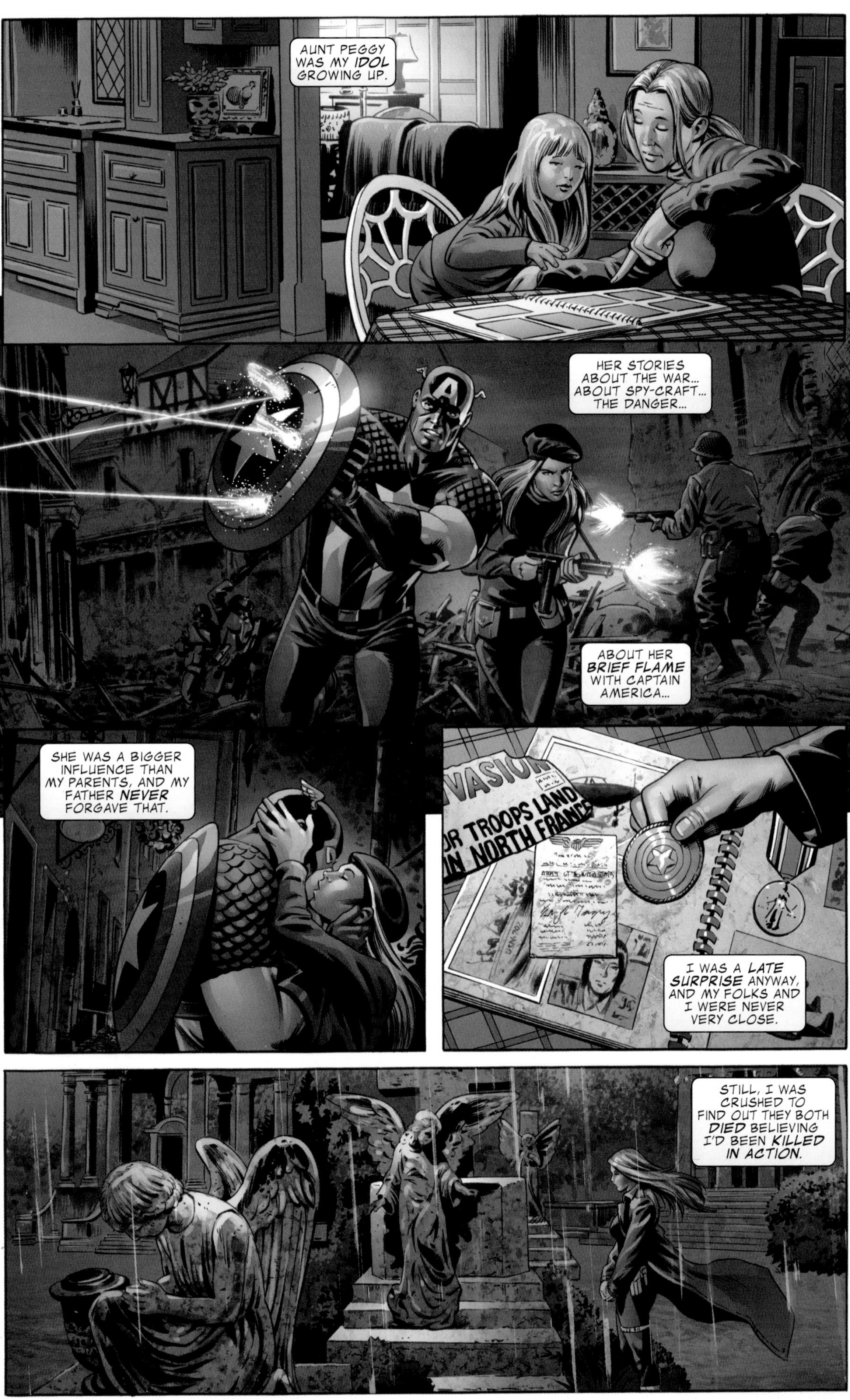
AUNT PEGGY WAS MY IDOL GROWING UP.
HER STORIES ABOUT THE WAR... ABOUT SPY-CRAFT... THE DANGER...
ABOUT HER BRIEF FLAME WITH CAPTAIN AMERICA...
SHE WAS A BIGGER INFLUENCE THAN MY PARENTS, AND MY FATHER NEVER FORGAVE THAT.
INVASION
OR TROOPS LAND IN NORTH FRANCE
I WAS A LATE SURPRISE ANYWAY, AND MY FOLKS AND I WERE NEVER VERY CLOSE.
STILL, I WAS CRUSHED TO FIND OUT THEY BOTH DIED BELIEVING I'D BEEN KILLED IN ACTION.

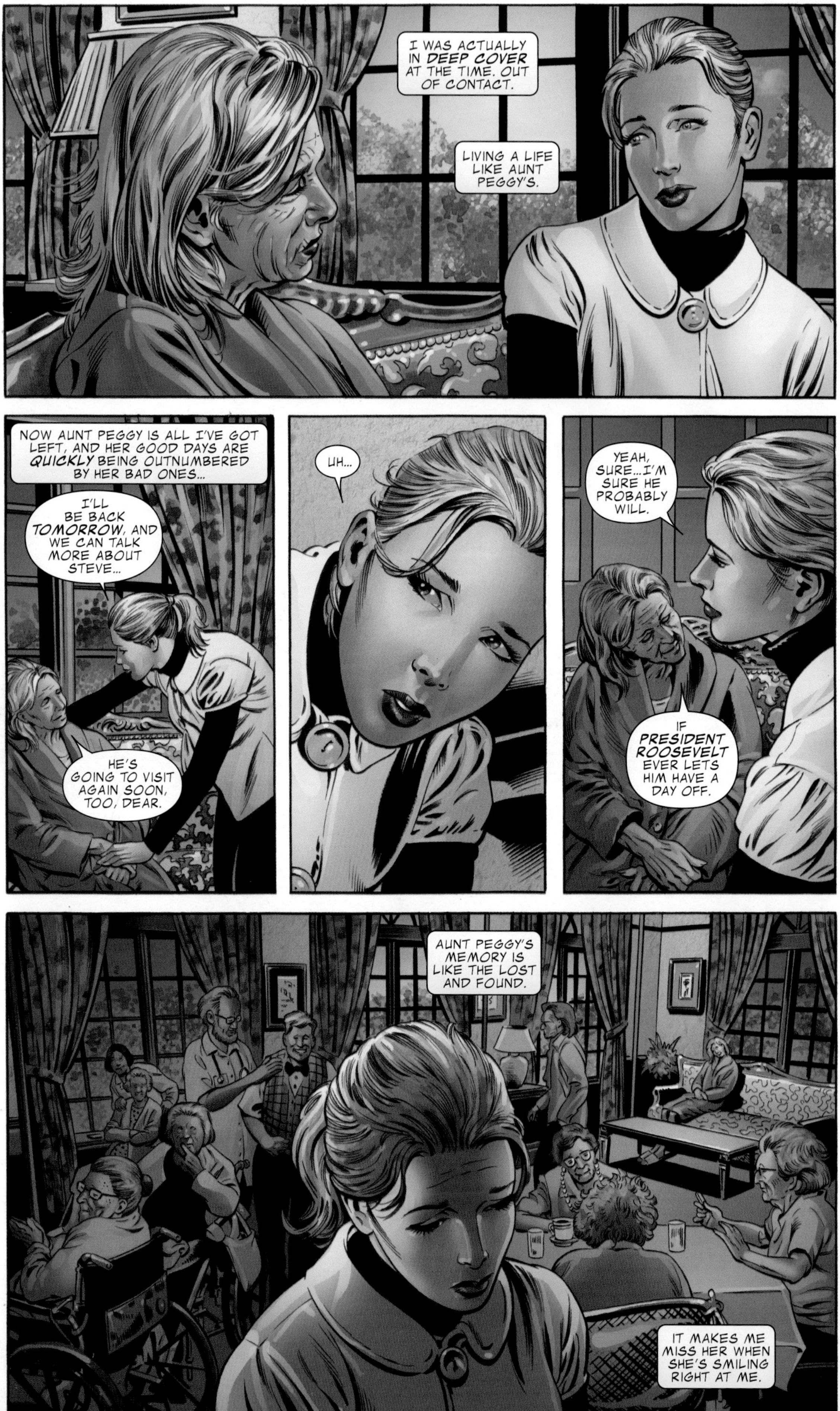
I WAS ACTUALLY IN DEEP COVER AT THE TIME. OUT OF CONTACT.
LIVING A LIFE LIKE AUNT PEGGY'S.
NOW AUNT PEGGY IS ALL I'VE GOT LEFT, AND HER GOOD DAYS ARE QUICKLY BEING OUTNUMBERED BY HER BAD ONES...
I'LL BE BACK TOMORROW, AND WE CAN TALK MORE ABOUT STEVE...
HE'S GOING TO VISIT AGAIN SOON, TOO, DEAR.
UH...
YEAH, SURE...I'M SURE HE PROBABLY WILL.
IF PRESIDENT ROOSEVELT EVER LETS HIM HAVE A DAY OFF.
AUNT PEGGY'S MEMORY IS LIKE THE LOST AND FOUND.
IT MAKES ME MISS HER WHEN SHE'S SMILING RIGHT AT ME.

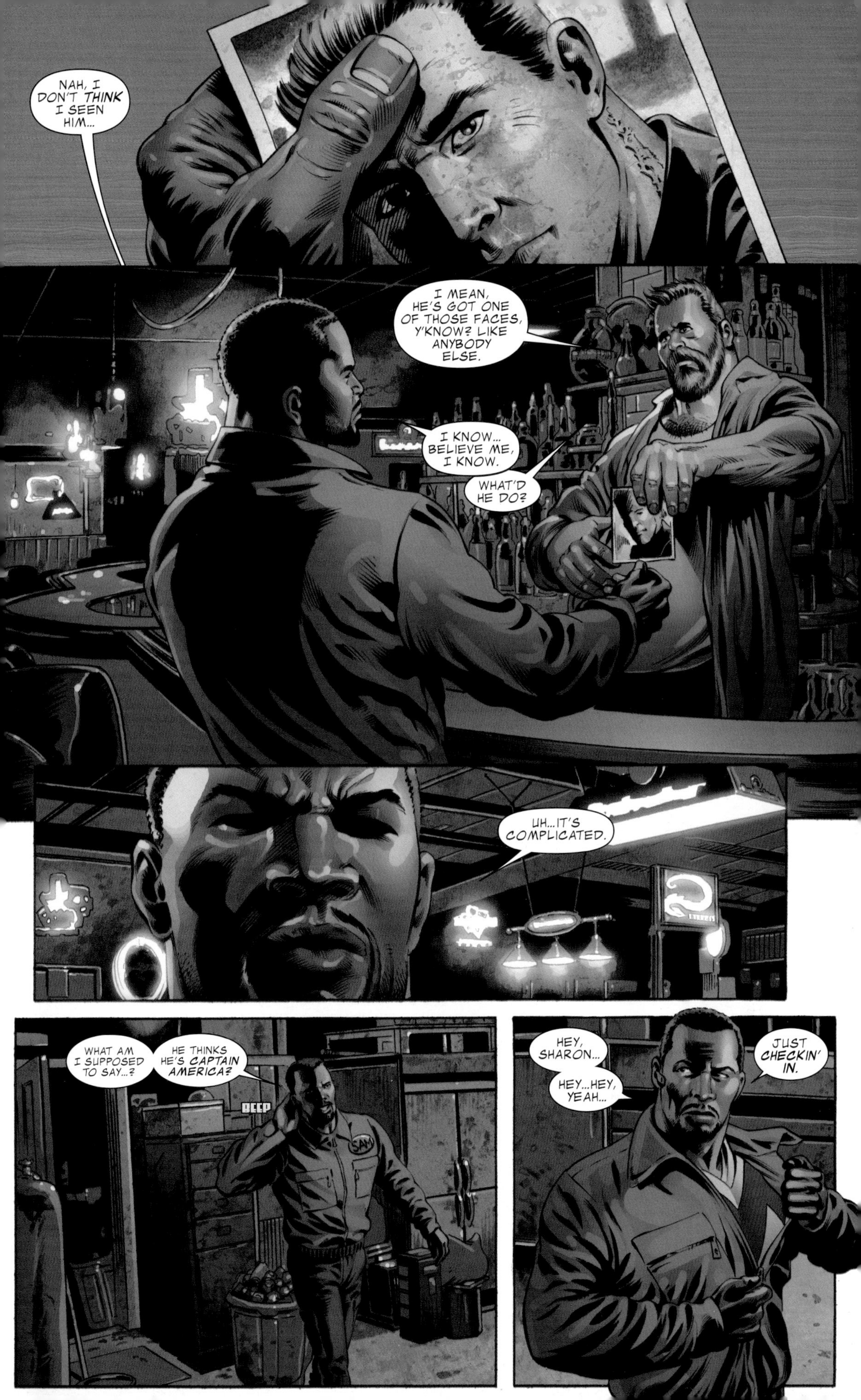
NAH, I DON'T THINK I SEEN HIM...
I MEAN, HE'S GOT ONE OF THOSE FACES, Y'KNOW? LIKE ANYBODY ELSE.
I KNOW... BELIEVE ME, I KNOW.
WHAT'D HE DO?
UH...IT'S COMPLICATED.
WHAT AM I SUPPOSED TO SAY...?
HE THINKS HE'S CAPTAIN AMERICA?
BEEP
SAM
HEY, SHARON...
HEY...HEY, YEAH...
JUST CHECKIN' IN.

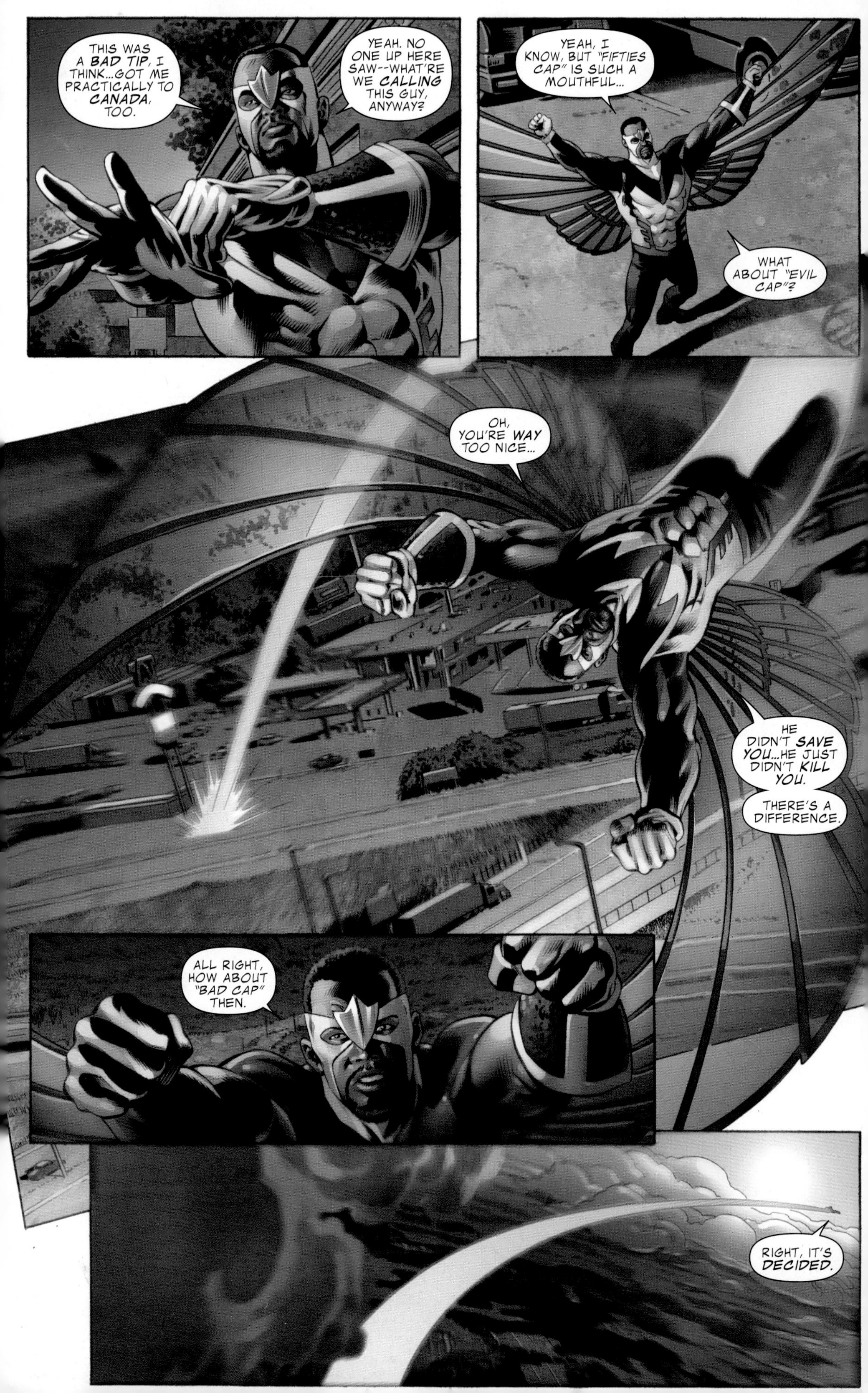
THIS WAS A BAD TIP, I THINK...GOT ME PRACTICALLY TO CANADA, TOO.
YEAH. NO ONE UP HERE SAW--WHAT'RE WE CALLING THIS GUY, ANYWAY?
YEAH, I KNOW, BUT "FIFTIES CAP" IS SUCH A MOUTHFUL...
WHAT ABOUT "EVIL CAP"?
OH, YOU'RE WAY TOO NICE...
HE DIDN'T SAVE YOU...HE JUST DIDN'T KILL YOU.
THERE'S A DIFFERENCE.
ALL RIGHT, HOW ABOUT "BAD CAP" THEN.
RIGHT, IT'S DECIDED.

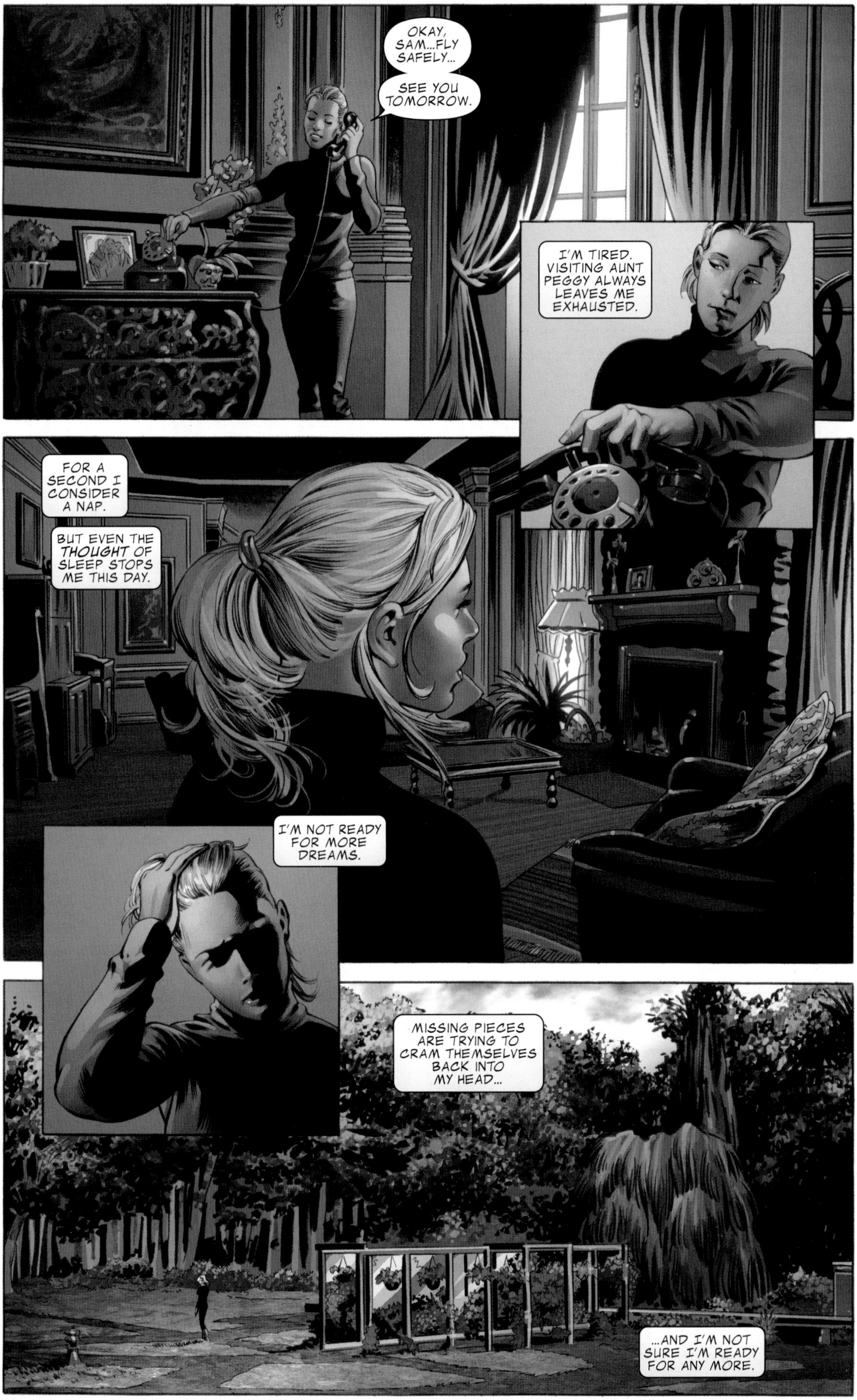
OKAY, SAM...FLY SAFELY...
SEE YOU TOMORROW.
I'M TIRED. VISITING AUNT PEGGY ALWAYS LEAVES ME EXHAUSTED.
FOR A SECOND I CONSIDER A NAP.
BUT EVEN THE *THOUGHT* OF SLEEP STOPS ME THIS DAY.
I'M NOT READY FOR MORE DREAMS.
MISSING PIECES ARE TRYING TO CRAM THEMSELVES BACK INTO MY HEAD...
...AND I'M NOT SURE I'M READY FOR ANY MORE.

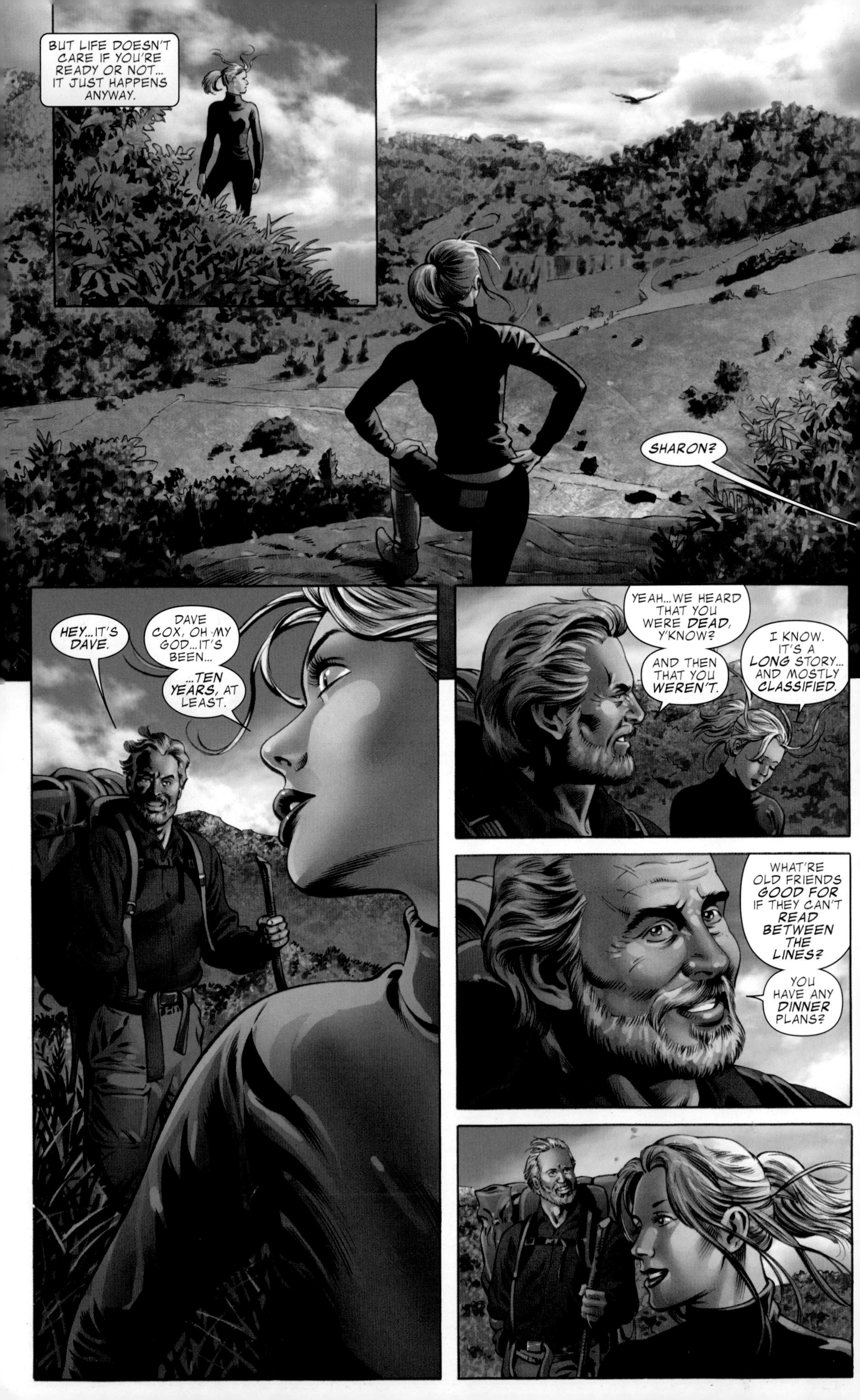
BUT LIFE DOESN'T CARE IF YOU'RE READY OR NOT... IT JUST HAPPENS ANYWAY.
SHARON?
HEY... IT'S DAVE.
DAVE COX, OH MY GOD... IT'S BEEN...
...TEN YEARS, AT LEAST.
YEAH... WE HEARD THAT YOU WERE DEAD, Y'KNOW?
AND THEN THAT YOU WEREN'T.
I KNOW. IT'S A LONG STORY... AND MOSTLY CLASSIFIED.
WHAT'RE OLD FRIENDS GOOD FOR IF THEY CAN'T READ BETWEEN THE LINES?
YOU HAVE ANY DINNER PLANS?

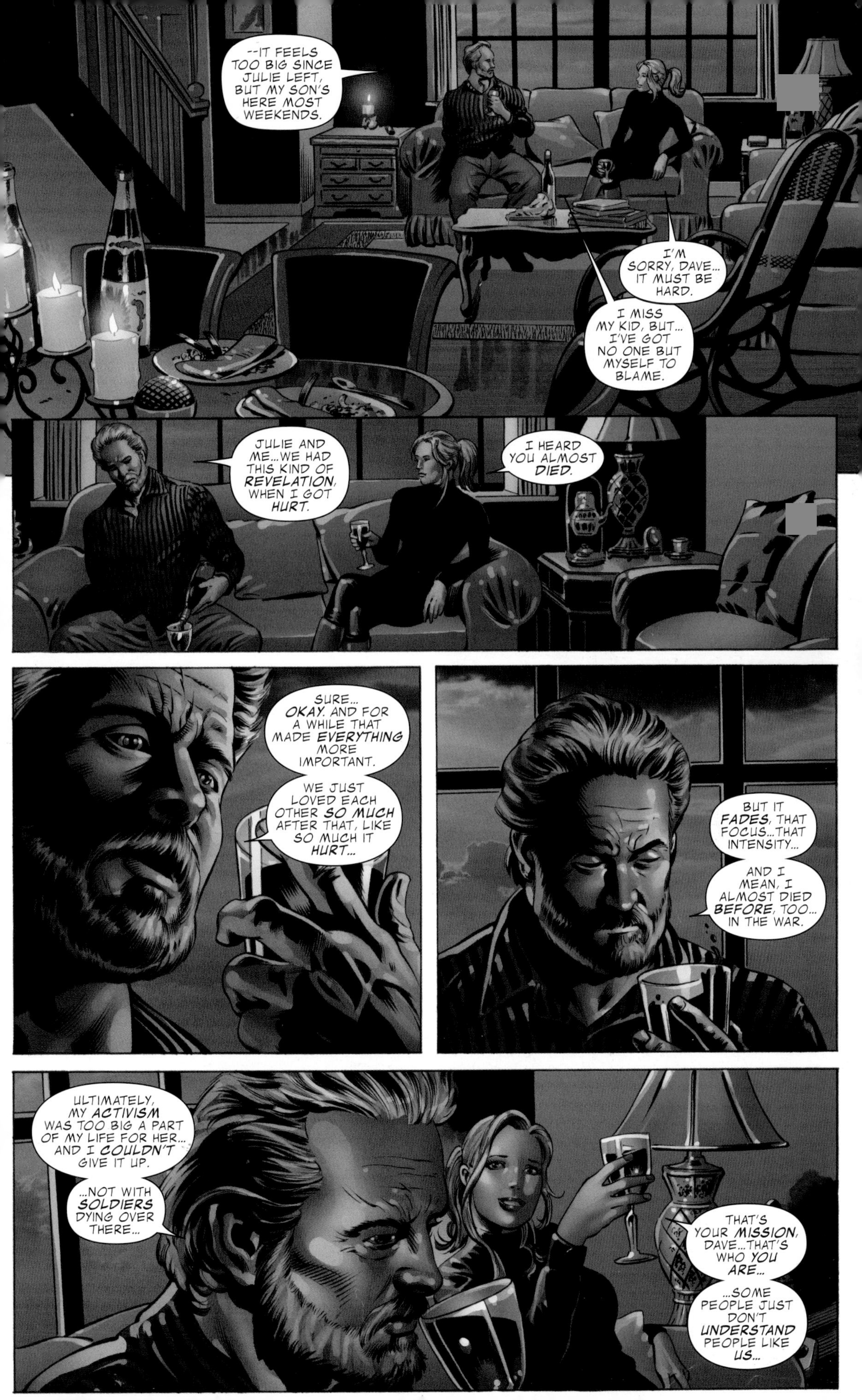
--IT FEELS TOO BIG SINCE JULIE LEFT, BUT MY SON'S HERE MOST WEEKENDS.
I'M SORRY, DAVE... IT MUST BE HARD.
I MISS MY KID, BUT... I'VE GOT NO ONE BUT MYSELF TO BLAME.
JULIE AND ME...WE HAD THIS KIND OF REVELATION, WHEN I GOT HURT.
I HEARD YOU ALMOST DIED.
SURE... OKAY. AND FOR A WHILE THAT MADE EVERYTHING MORE IMPORTANT.
WE JUST LOVED EACH OTHER SO MUCH AFTER THAT, LIKE SO MUCH IT HURT...
BUT IT FADES, THAT FOCUS...THAT INTENSITY...
AND I MEAN, I ALMOST DIED BEFORE, TOO... IN THE WAR.
ULTIMATELY, MY ACTIVISM WAS TOO BIG A PART OF MY LIFE FOR HER... AND I COULDN'T GIVE IT UP.
...NOT WITH SOLDIERS DYING OVER THERE...
THAT'S YOUR MISSION, DAVE...THAT'S WHO YOU ARE...
...SOME PEOPLE JUST DON'T UNDERSTAND PEOPLE LIKE US...

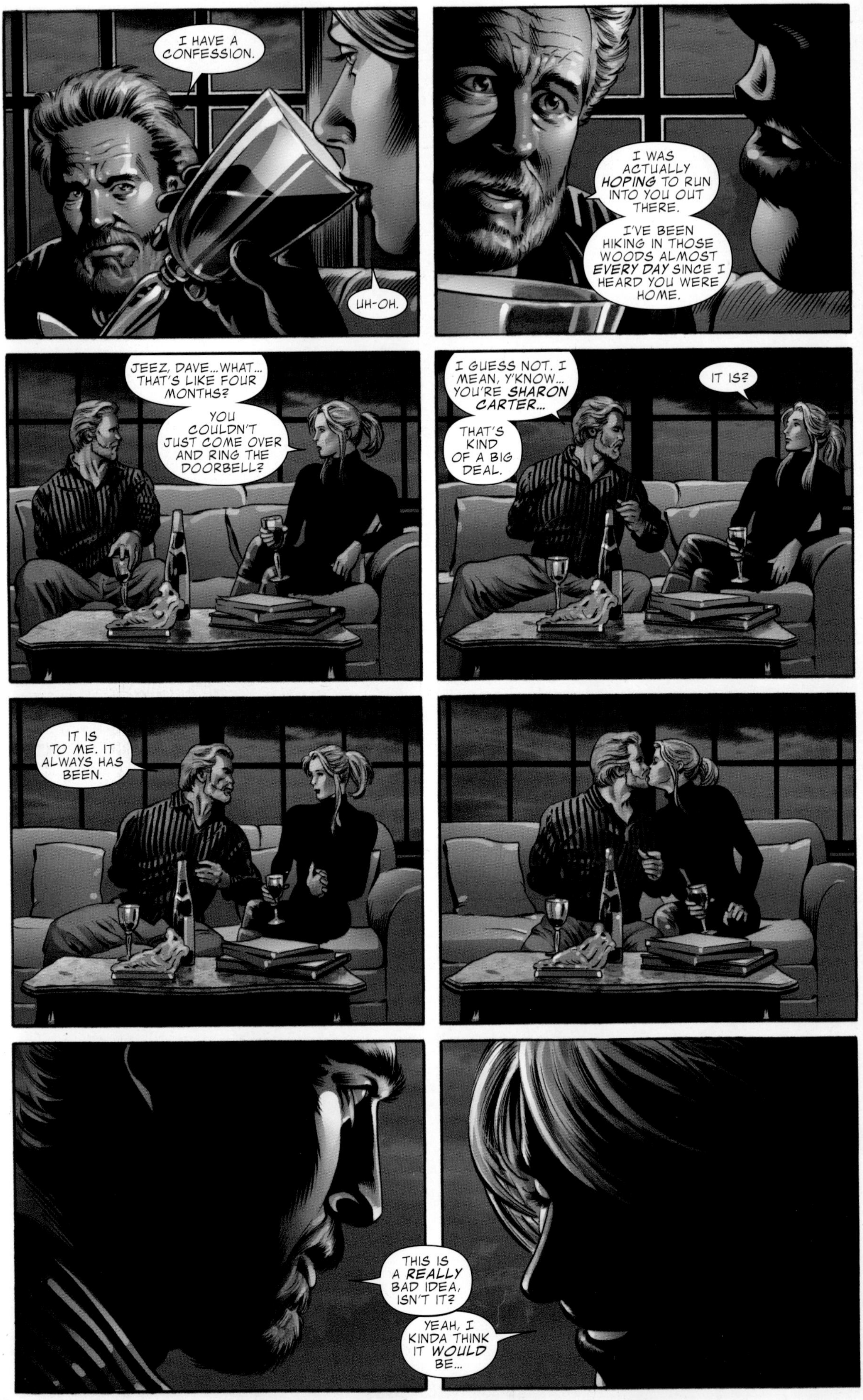
I HAVE A CONFESSION.
UH-OH.
I WAS ACTUALLY HOPING TO RUN INTO YOU OUT THERE.
I'VE BEEN HIKING IN THOSE WOODS ALMOST EVERY DAY SINCE I HEARD YOU WERE HOME.
JEEZ, DAVE... WHAT... THAT'S LIKE FOUR MONTHS?
YOU COULDN'T JUST COME OVER AND RING THE DOORBELL?
I GUESS NOT. I MEAN, Y'KNOW... YOU'RE SHARON CARTER...
THAT'S KIND OF A BIG DEAL.
IT IS?
IT IS TO ME. IT ALWAYS HAS BEEN.
THIS IS A REALLY BAD IDEA, ISN'T IT?
YEAH, I KINDA THINK IT WOULD BE...

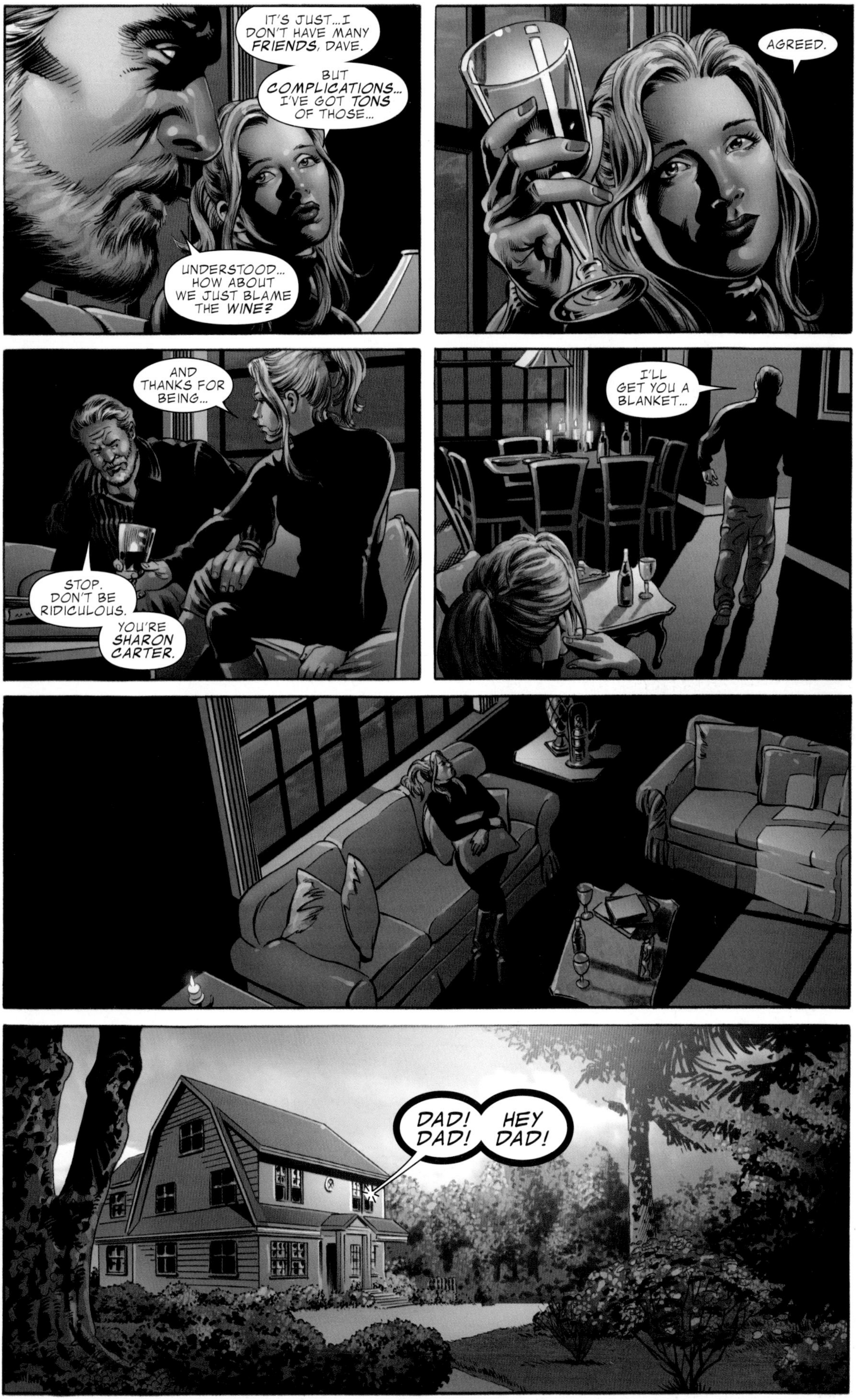
IT'S JUST...I DON'T HAVE MANY FRIENDS, DAVE.
BUT COMPLICATIONS... I'VE GOT TONS OF THOSE...
UNDERSTOOD... HOW ABOUT WE JUST BLAME THE WINE?
AGREED.
AND THANKS FOR BEING...
STOP. DON'T BE RIDICULOUS.
YOU'RE SHARON CARTER.
I'LL GET YOU A BLANKET...
DAD! DAD!
HEY DAD!

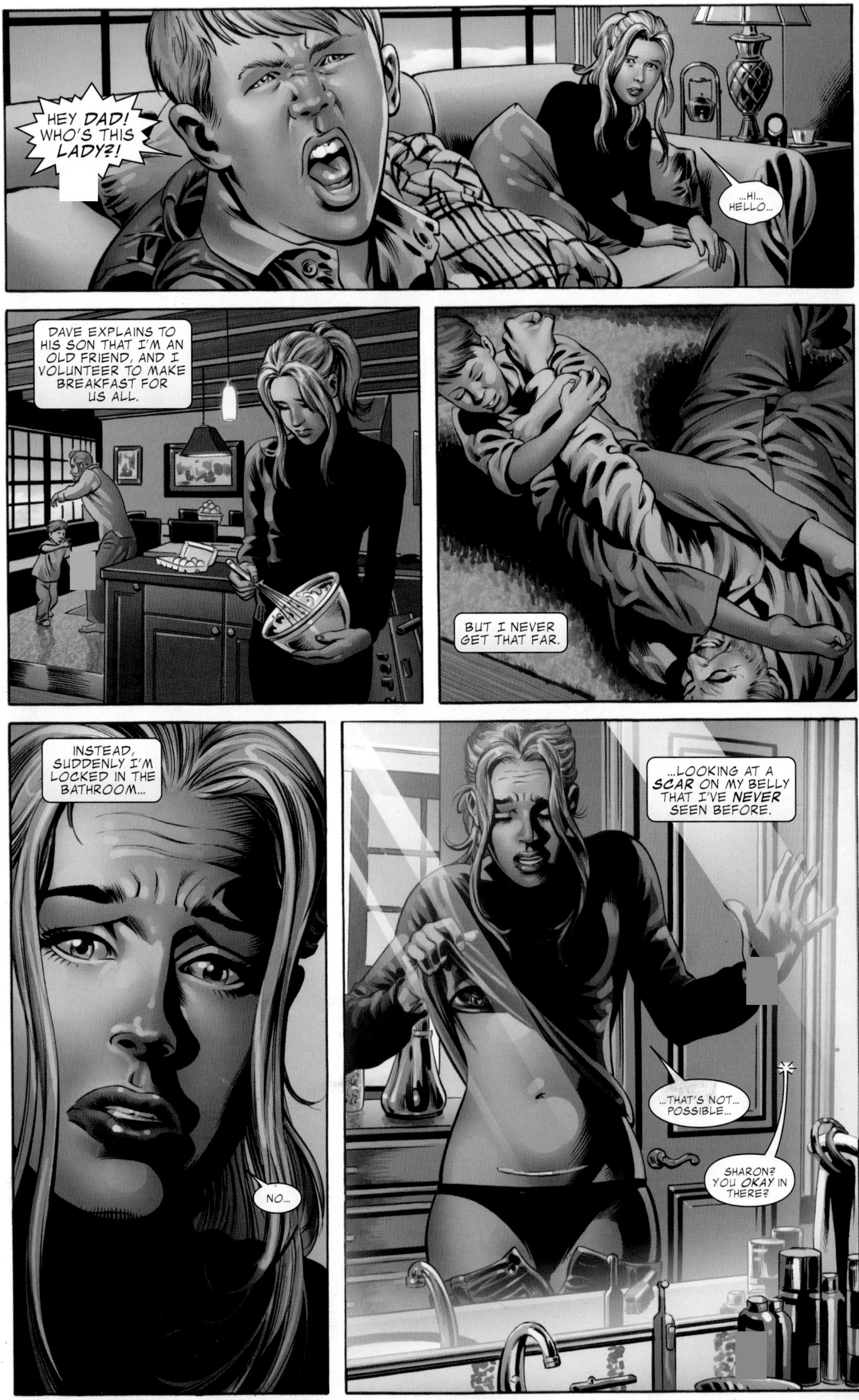
HEY DAD! WHO'S THIS LADY?!
...HI... HELLO...
DAVE EXPLAINS TO HIS SON THAT I'M AN OLD FRIEND, AND I VOLUNTEER TO MAKE BREAKFAST FOR US ALL.
BUT I NEVER GET THAT FAR.
INSTEAD, SUDDENLY I'M LOCKED IN THE BATHROOM...
NO...
...LOOKING AT A SCAR ON MY BELLY THAT I'VE NEVER SEEN BEFORE.
...THAT'S NOT... POSSIBLE...
SHARON? YOU OKAY IN THERE?

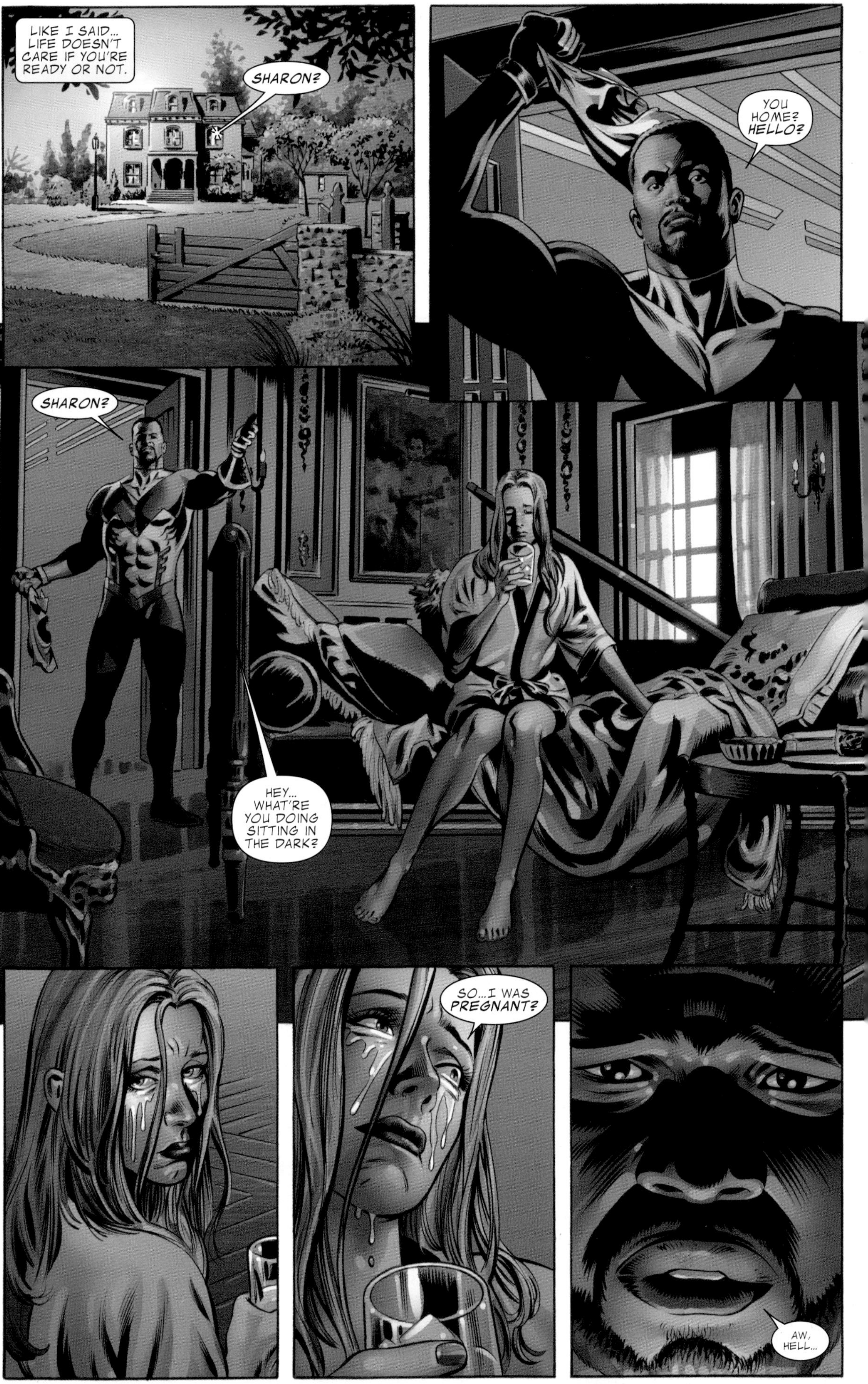
LIKE I SAID... LIFE DOESN'T CARE IF YOU'RE READY OR NOT.
SHARON?
YOU HOME? HELLO?
SHARON?
HEY... WHAT'RE YOU DOING SITTING IN THE DARK?
SO...I WAS PREGNANT?
AW, HELL...

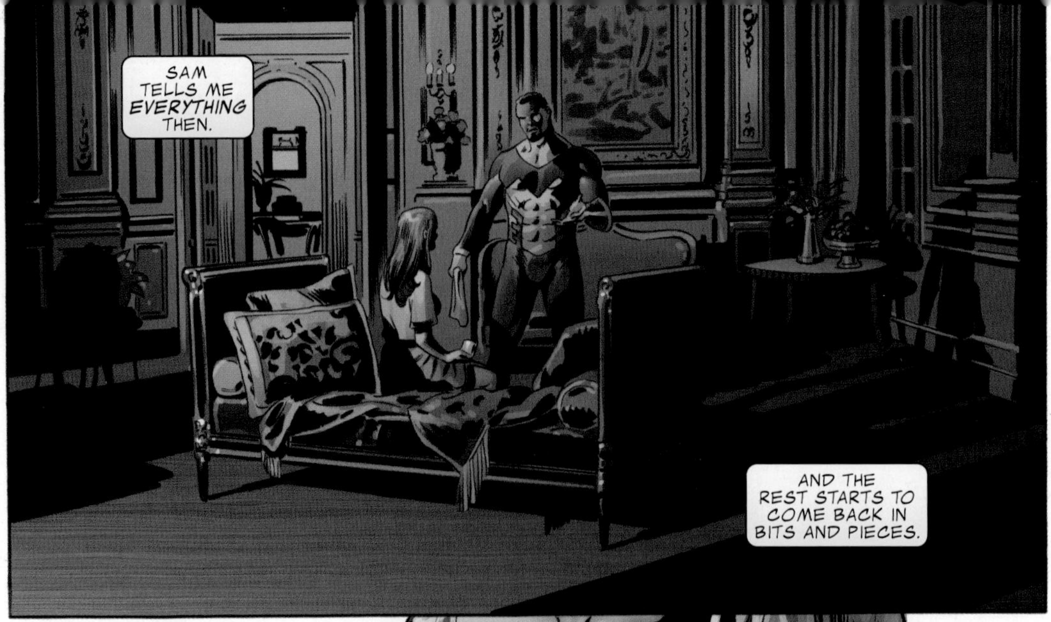
SAM TELLS ME EVERYTHING THEN.
AND THE REST STARTS TO COME BACK IN BITS AND PIECES.
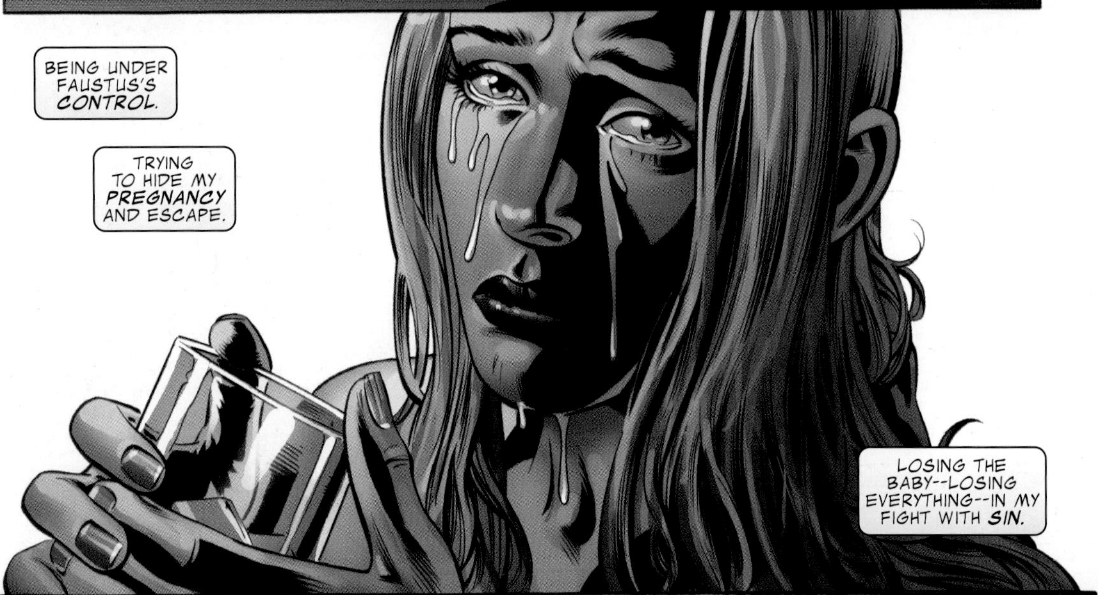
BEING UNDER FAUSTUS'S CONTROL.
TRYING TO HIDE MY PREGNANCY AND ESCAPE.
LOSING THE BABY--LOSING EVERYTHING--IN MY FIGHT WITH SIN.
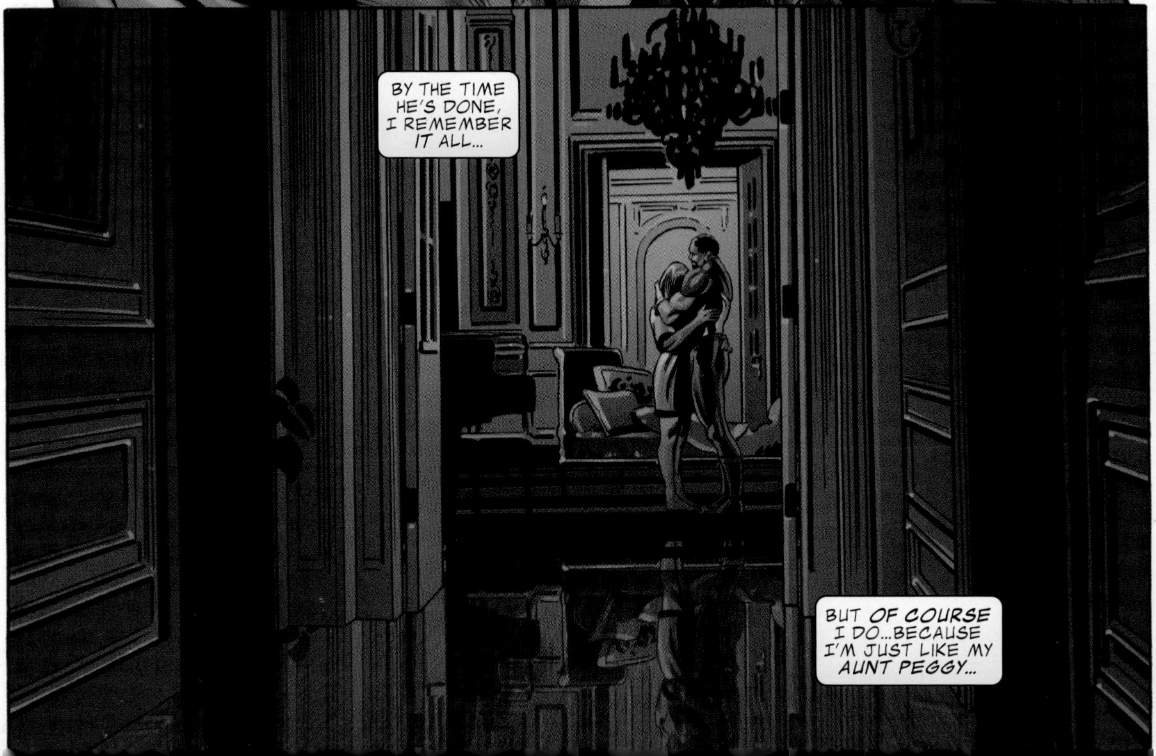
BY THE TIME HE'S DONE, I REMEMBER IT ALL...
BUT OF COURSE I DO...BECAUSE I'M JUST LIKE MY AUNT PEGGY...

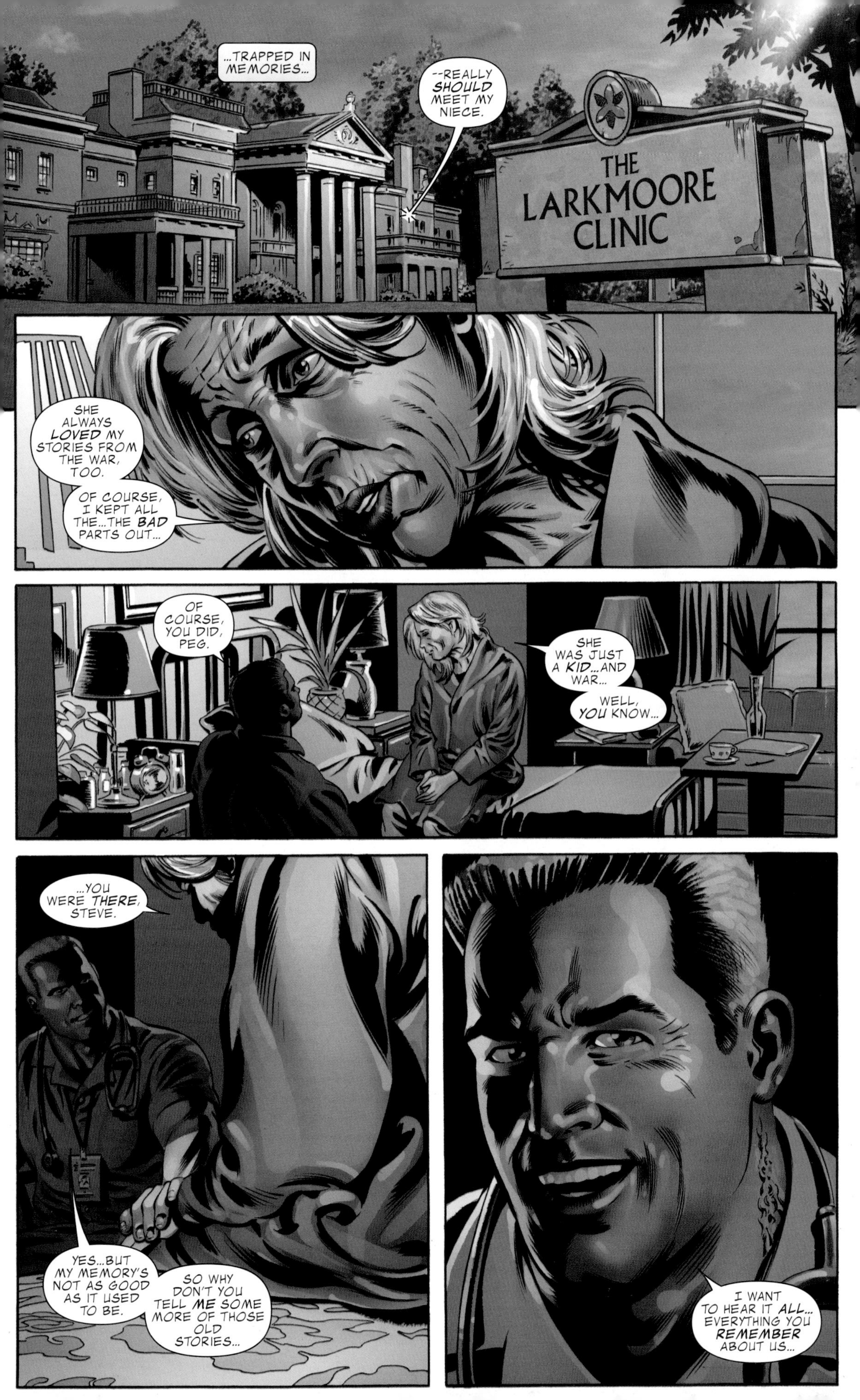

...TRAPPED IN MEMORIES...
--REALLY SHOULD MEET MY NIECE.
THE LARKMOORE CLINIC
SHE ALWAYS LOVED MY STORIES FROM THE WAR, TOO.
OF COURSE, I KEPT ALL THE...THE BAD PARTS OUT...
OF COURSE, YOU DID, PEG.
SHE WAS JUST A KID...AND WAR...
WELL, YOU KNOW...
...YOU WERE THERE, STEVE.
YES...BUT MY MEMORY'S NOT AS GOOD AS IT USED TO BE.
SO WHY DON'T YOU TELL ME SOME MORE OF THOSE OLD STORIES...
I WANT TO HEAR IT ALL... EVERYTHING YOU REMEMBER ABOUT US...

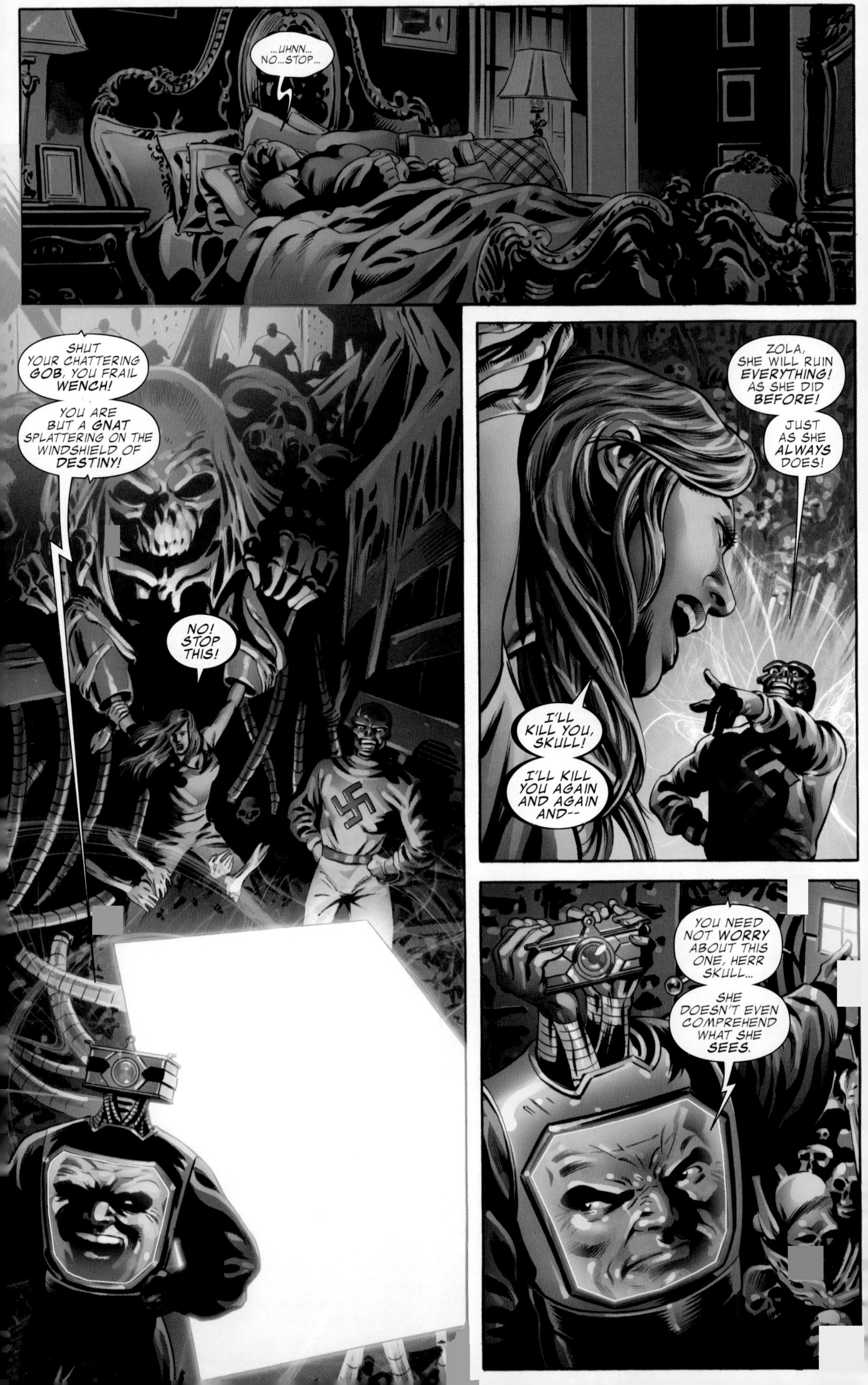
...UHNN... NO...STOP...
SHUT YOUR CHATTERING GOB, YOU FRAIL WENCH!
YOU ARE BUT A GNAT SPLATTERING ON THE WINDSHIELD OF DESTINY!
NO! STOP THIS!
ZOLA, SHE WILL RUIN EVERYTHING! AS SHE DID BEFORE!
JUST AS SHE ALWAYS DOES!
I'LL KILL YOU, SKULL!
I'LL KILL YOU AGAIN AND AGAIN AND--
YOU NEED NOT WORRY ABOUT THIS ONE, HERR SKULL...
SHE DOESN'T EVEN COMPREHEND WHAT SHE SEES.

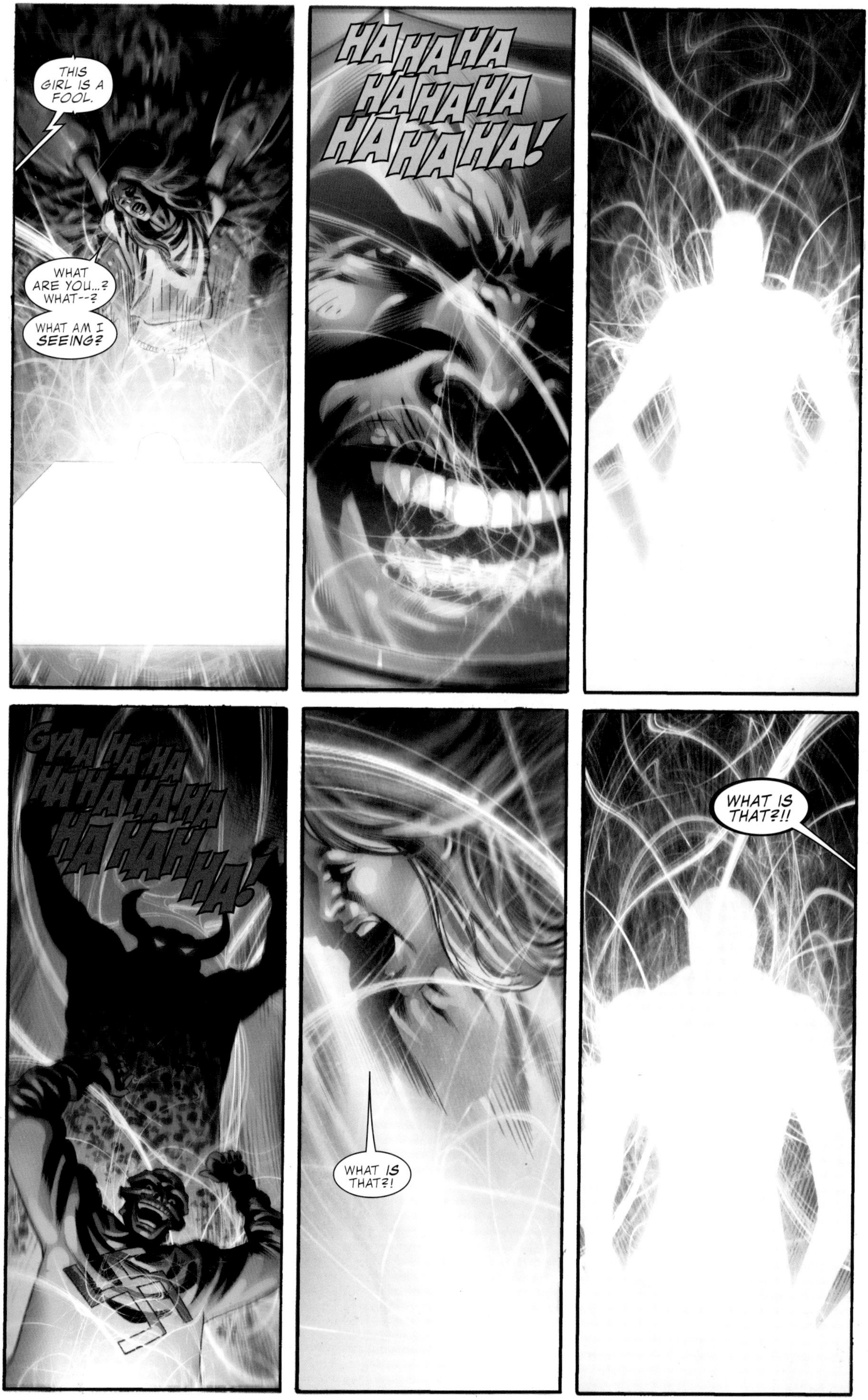
THIS GIRL IS A FOOL.
WHAT ARE YOU...? WHAT--?
WHAT AM I SEEING?
HAHAHA HAHAHA HAHAHA!
GYAA HA HA HA HA HA HA HA HA HA HA HA!
WHAT IS THAT?!
WHAT IS THAT?!!

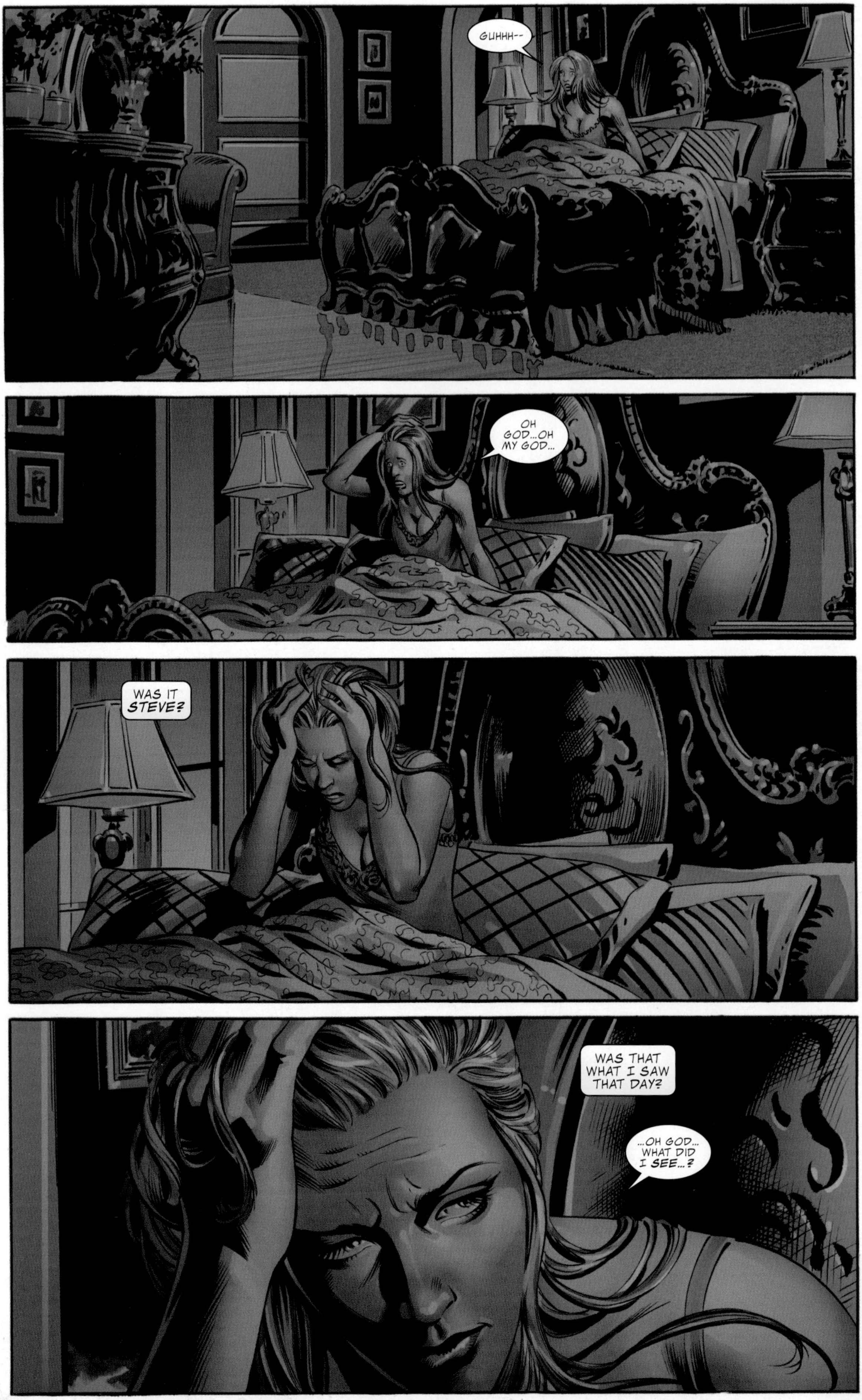
GUHHH--
OH GOD...OH MY GOD...
WAS IT STEVE?
WAS THAT WHAT I SAW THAT DAY?
...OH GOD... WHAT DID I SEE...?

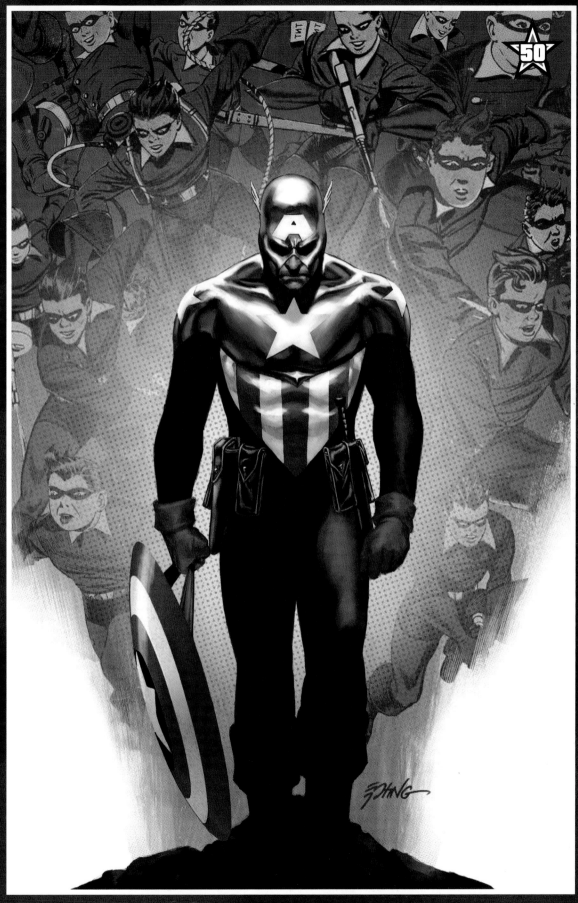

DAYS GONE BY

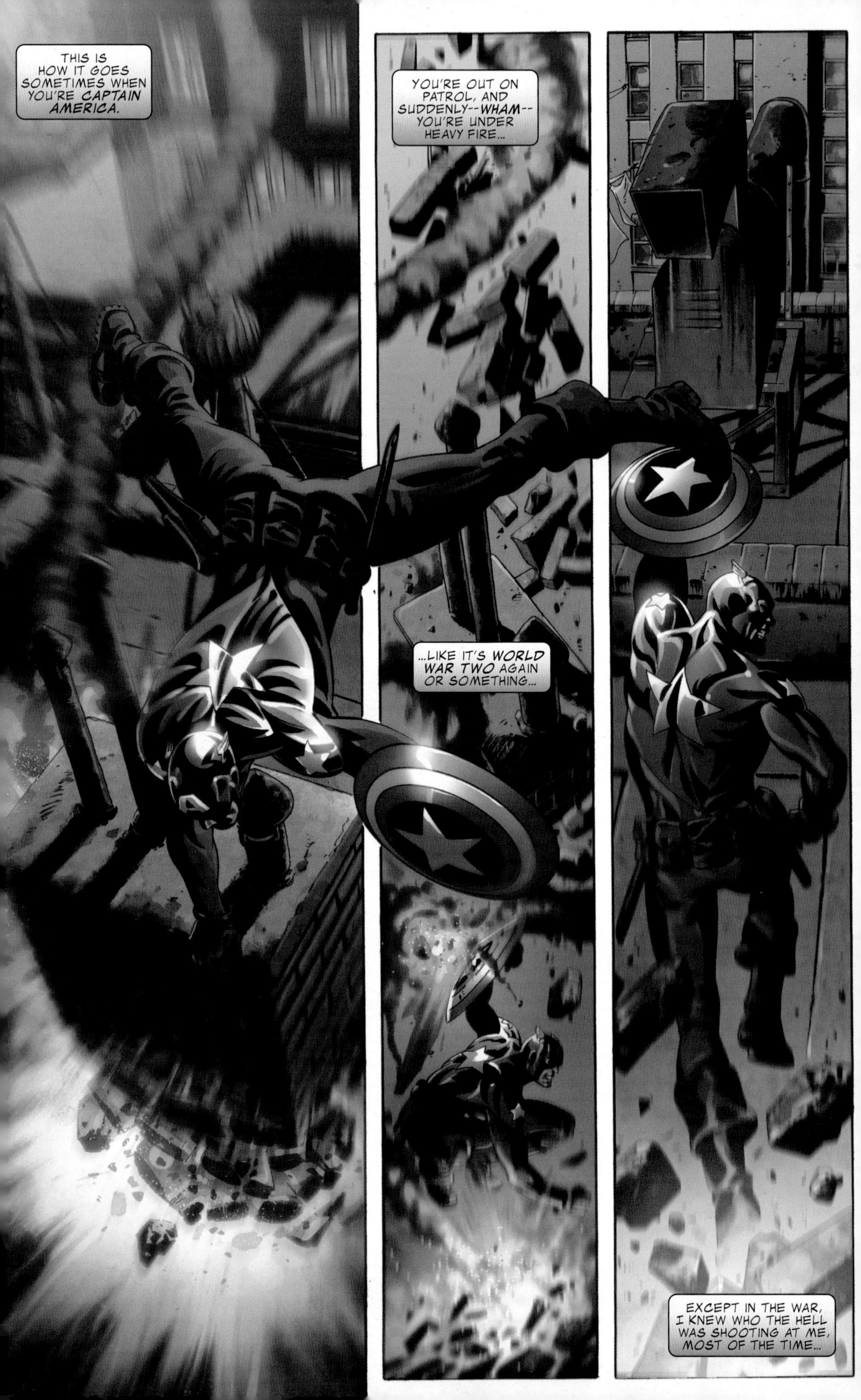
THIS IS HOW IT GOES SOMETIMES WHEN YOU'RE CAPTAIN AMERICA.
YOU'RE OUT ON PATROL, AND SUDDENLY--WHAM--YOU'RE UNDER HEAVY FIRE...
...LIKE IT'S WORLD WAR TWO AGAIN OR SOMETHING...
EXCEPT IN THE WAR, I KNEW WHO THE HELL WAS SHOOTING AT ME, MOST OF THE TIME...

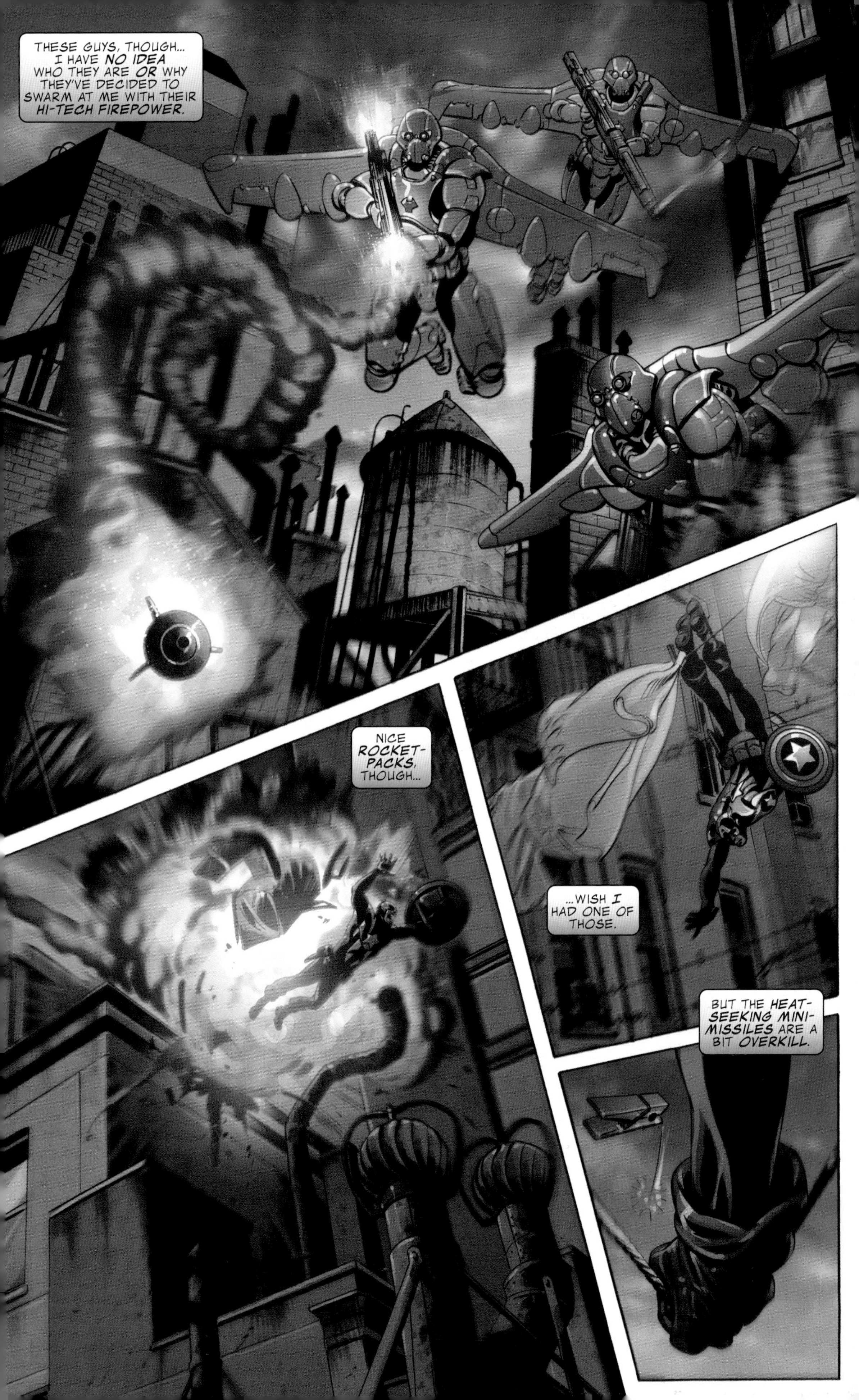
THESE GUYS, THOUGH... I HAVE NO IDEA WHO THEY ARE OR WHY THEY'VE DECIDED TO SWARM AT ME WITH THEIR HI-TECH FIREPOWER.
NICE ROCKET-PACKS, THOUGH...
...WISH I HAD ONE OF THOSE.
BUT THE HEAT-SEEKING MINI-MISSILES ARE A BIT OVERKILL.

AND TO TOP IT ALL OFF, IT'S MY BIRTHDAY, AND THIS IS HOW I GET TO SPEND IT...
...FIGHTING.
STILL, WHY SHOULD THIS BIRTHDAY BE ANY DIFFERENT THAN THE ONES THAT CAME BEFORE?
DAYS GONE BY

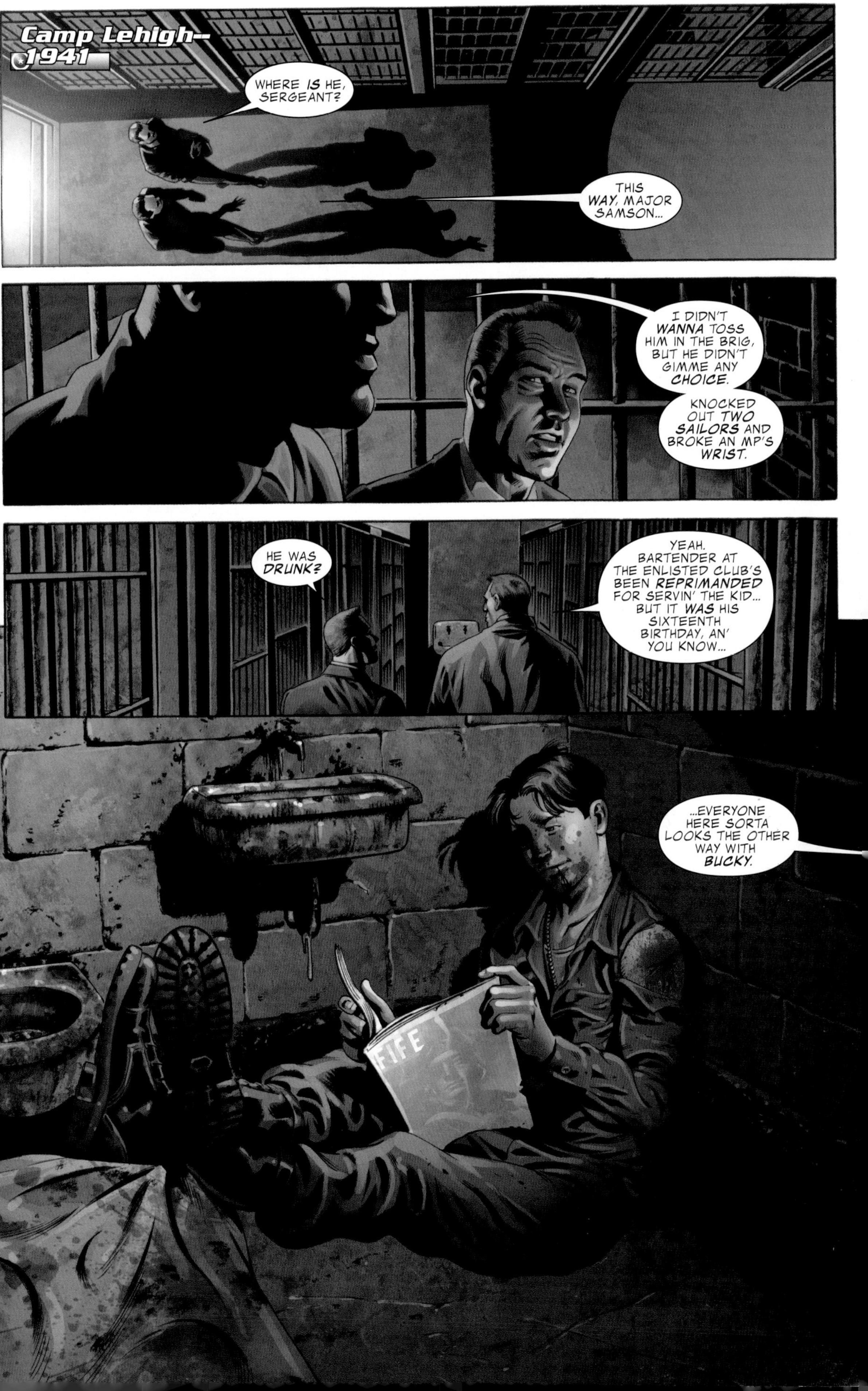
Camp Lehigh--
1941
WHERE IS HE, SERGEANT?
THIS WAY, MAJOR SAMSON...
I DIDN'T WANNA TOSS HIM IN THE BRIG, BUT HE DIDN'T GIMME ANY CHOICE.
KNOCKED OUT TWO SAILORS AND BROKE AN MP'S WRIST.
HE WAS DRUNK?
YEAH. BARTENDER AT THE ENLISTED CLUB'S BEEN REPRIMANDED FOR SERVIN' THE KID... BUT IT WAS HIS SIXTEENTH BIRTHDAY, AN' YOU KNOW...
...EVERYONE HERE SORTA LOOKS THE OTHER WAY WITH BUCKY.

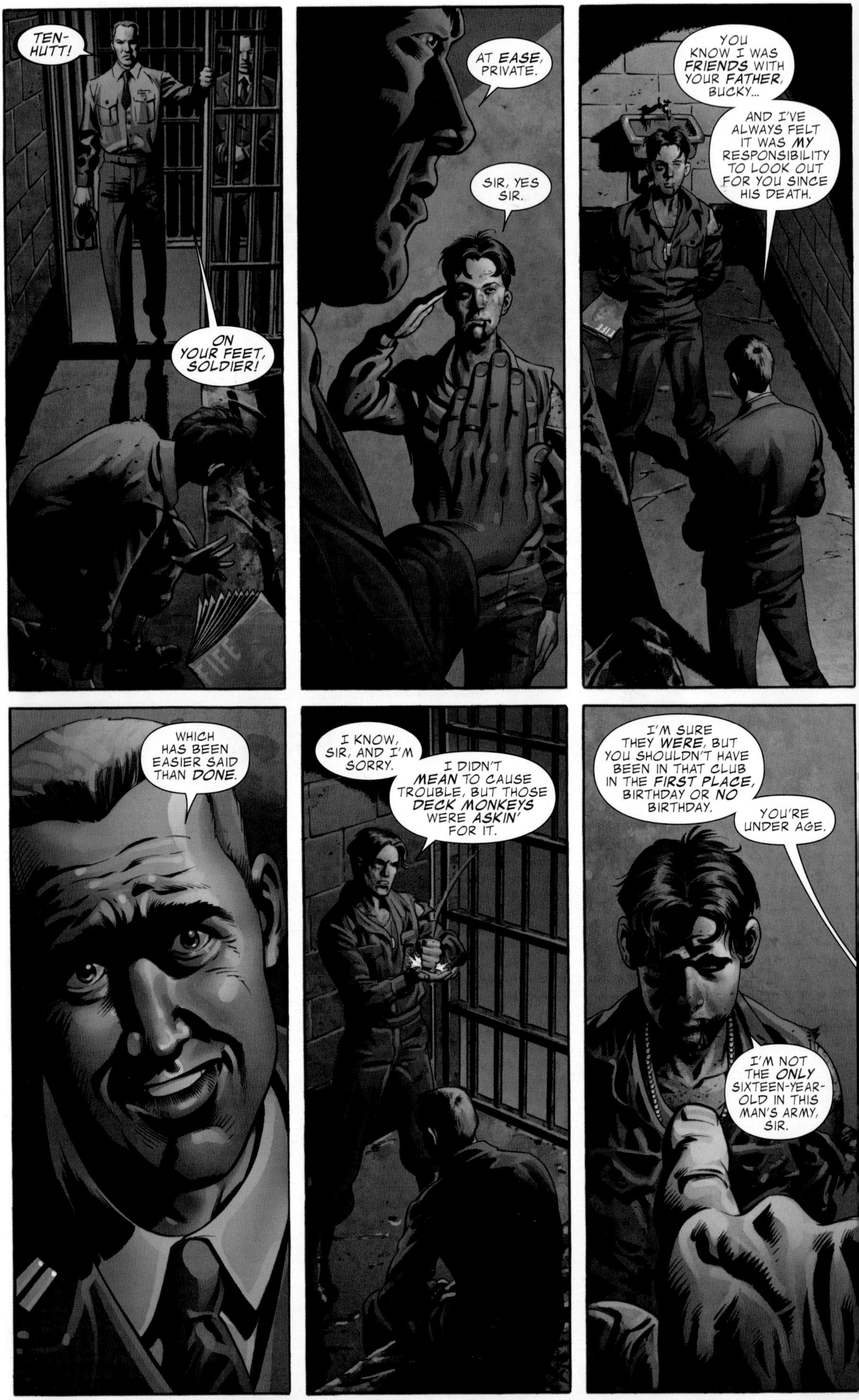
TEN-HUTT!
ON YOUR FEET, SOLDIER!
AT EASE, PRIVATE.
SIR, YES SIR.
YOU KNOW I WAS FRIENDS WITH YOUR FATHER, BUCKY...
AND I'VE ALWAYS FELT IT WAS MY RESPONSIBILITY TO LOOK OUT FOR YOU SINCE HIS DEATH.
WHICH HAS BEEN EASIER SAID THAN DONE.
I KNOW, SIR, AND I'M SORRY.
I DIDN'T MEAN TO CAUSE TROUBLE, BUT THOSE DECK MONKEYS WERE ASKIN' FOR IT.
I'M SURE THEY WERE, BUT YOU SHOULDN'T HAVE BEEN IN THAT CLUB IN THE FIRST PLACE, BIRTHDAY OR NO BIRTHDAY.
YOU'RE UNDER AGE.
I'M NOT THE ONLY SIXTEEN-YEAR-OLD IN THIS MAN'S ARMY, SIR.

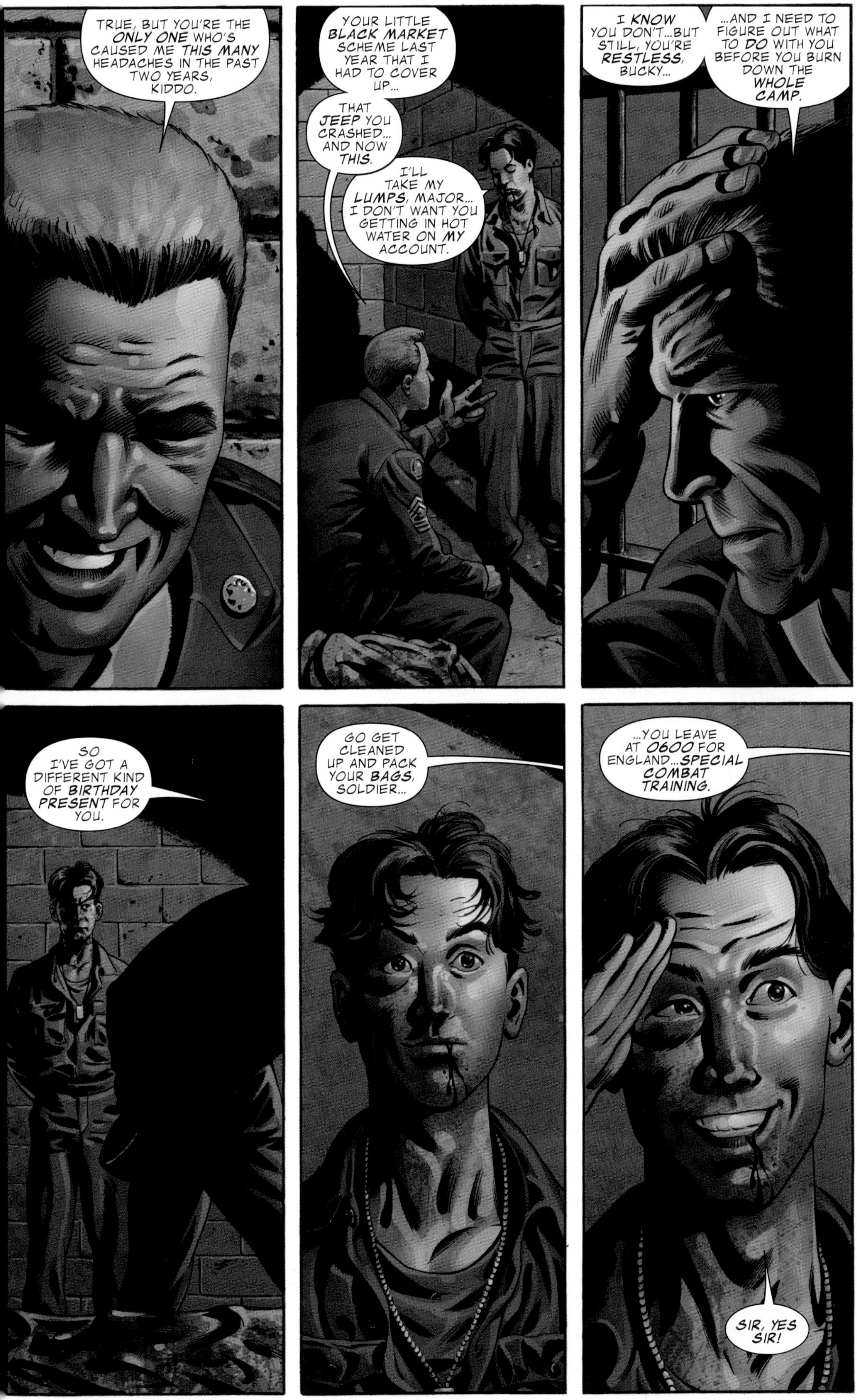
TRUE, BUT YOU'RE THE ONLY ONE WHO'S CAUSED ME THIS MANY HEADACHES IN THE PAST TWO YEARS, KIDDO.
YOUR LITTLE BLACK MARKET SCHEME LAST YEAR THAT I HAD TO COVER UP...
THAT JEEP YOU CRASHED... AND NOW THIS.
I'LL TAKE MY LUMPS, MAJOR... I DON'T WANT YOU GETTING IN HOT WATER ON MY ACCOUNT.
I KNOW YOU DON'T...BUT STILL, YOU'RE RESTLESS, BUCKY...
...AND I NEED TO FIGURE OUT WHAT TO DO WITH YOU BEFORE YOU BURN DOWN THE WHOLE CAMP.
SO I'VE GOT A DIFFERENT KIND OF BIRTHDAY PRESENT FOR YOU.
GO GET CLEANED UP AND PACK YOUR BAGS, SOLDIER...
...YOU LEAVE AT 0600 FOR ENGLAND...SPECIAL COMBAT TRAINING.
SIR, YES SIR!

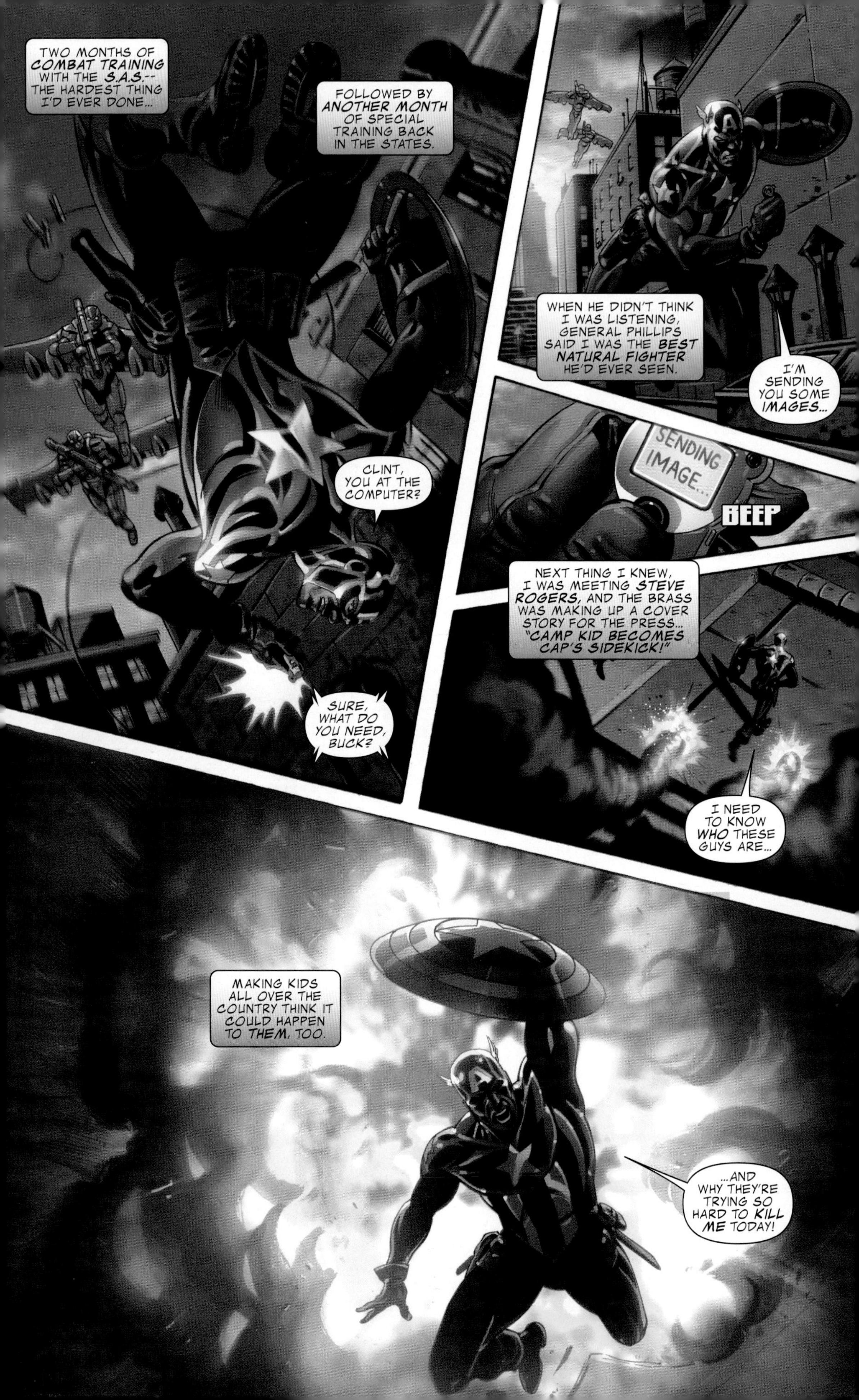
TWO MONTHS OF COMBAT TRAINING WITH THE S.A.S.-- THE HARDEST THING I'D EVER DONE...
FOLLOWED BY ANOTHER MONTH OF SPECIAL TRAINING BACK IN THE STATES.
CLINT, YOU AT THE COMPUTER?
SURE, WHAT DO YOU NEED, BUCK?
WHEN HE DIDN'T THINK I WAS LISTENING, GENERAL PHILLIPS SAID I WAS THE BEST NATURAL FIGHTER HE'D EVER SEEN.
I'M SENDING YOU SOME IMAGES...
SENDING IMAGE...
BEEP
NEXT THING I KNEW, I WAS MEETING STEVE ROGERS, AND THE BRASS WAS MAKING UP A COVER STORY FOR THE PRESS... "CAMP KID BECOMES CAP'S SIDEKICK!"
I NEED TO KNOW WHO THESE GUYS ARE...
MAKING KIDS ALL OVER THE COUNTRY THINK IT COULD HAPPEN TO THEM, TOO.
...AND WHY THEY'RE TRYING SO HARD TO KILL ME TODAY!

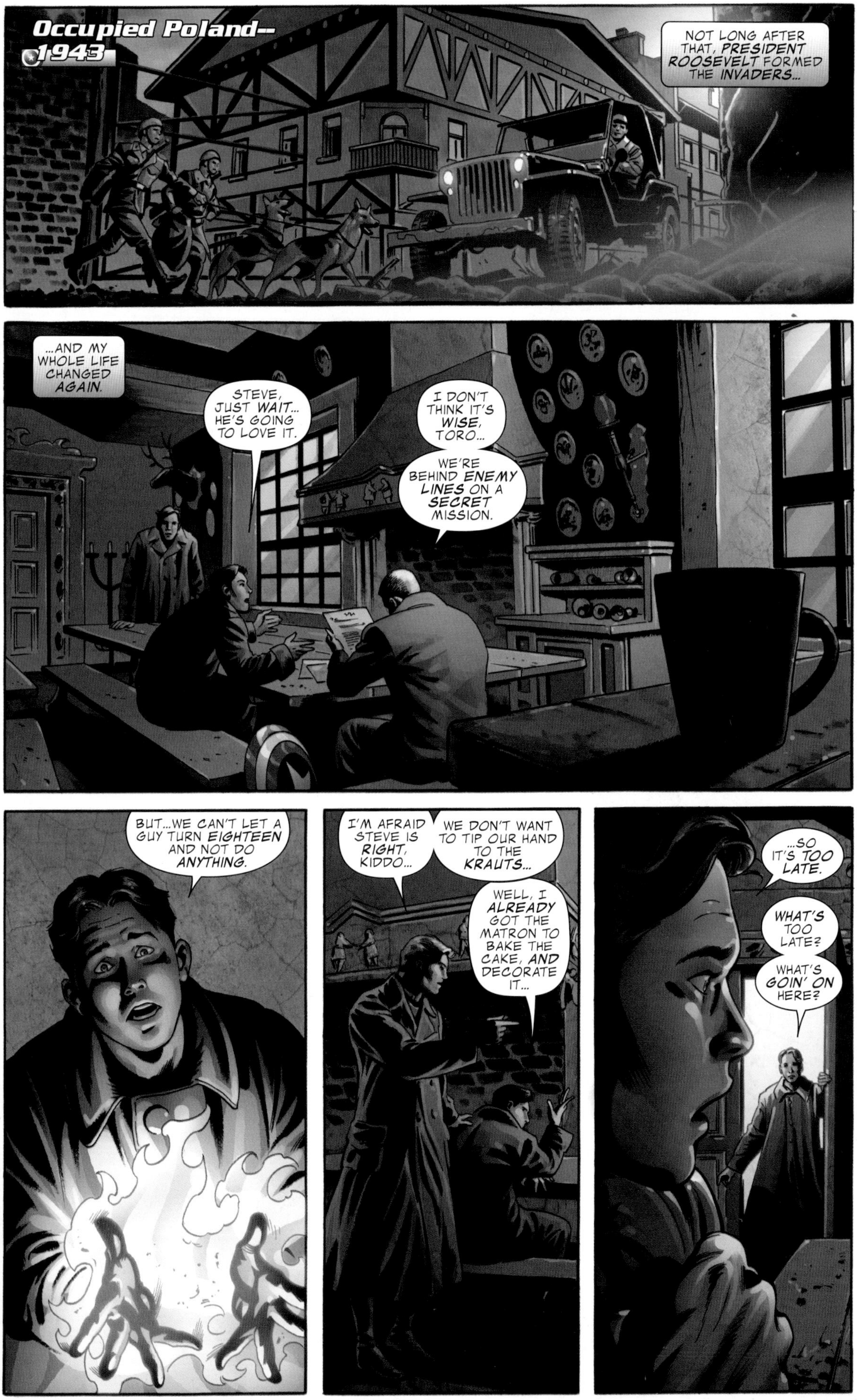
Occupied Poland--1943
NOT LONG AFTER THAT, PRESIDENT ROOSEVELT FORMED THE INVADERS...
...AND MY WHOLE LIFE CHANGED AGAIN.
STEVE, JUST WAIT... HE'S GOING TO LOVE IT.
I DON'T THINK IT'S WISE, TORO...
WE'RE BEHIND ENEMY LINES ON A SECRET MISSION.
BUT...WE CAN'T LET A GUY TURN EIGHTEEN AND NOT DO ANYTHING.
I'M AFRAID STEVE IS RIGHT, KIDDO...
WE DON'T WANT TO TIP OUR HAND TO THE KRAUTS...
WELL, I ALREADY GOT THE MATRON TO BAKE THE CAKE, AND DECORATE IT...
...SO IT'S TOO LATE.
WHAT'S TOO LATE?
WHAT'S GOIN' ON HERE?

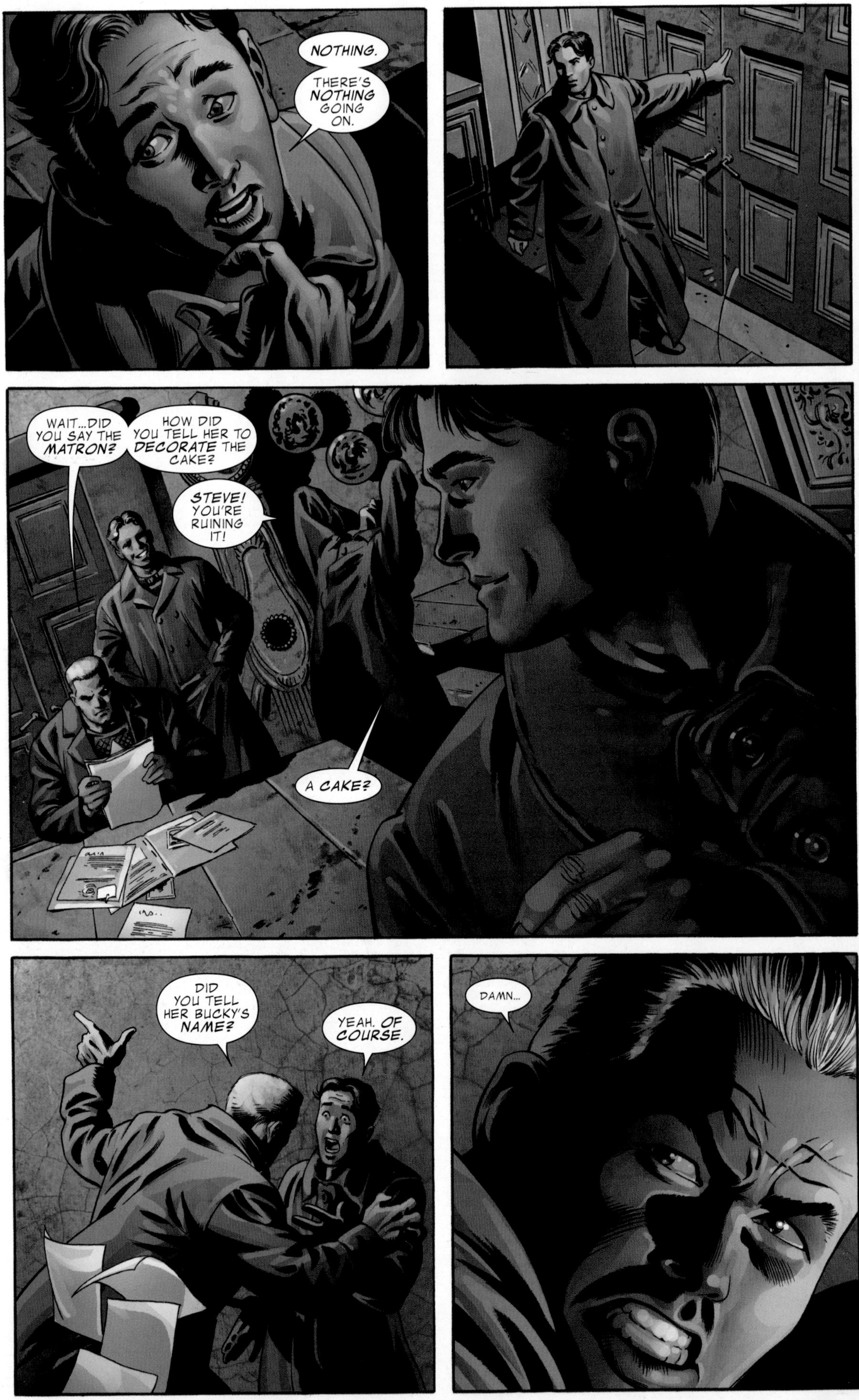
NOTHING.
THERE'S NOTHING GOING ON.
WAIT...DID YOU SAY THE MATRON?
HOW DID YOU TELL HER TO DECORATE THE CAKE?
STEVE! YOU'RE RUINING IT!
A CAKE?
DID YOU TELL HER BUCKY'S NAME?
YEAH. OF COURSE.
DAMN...

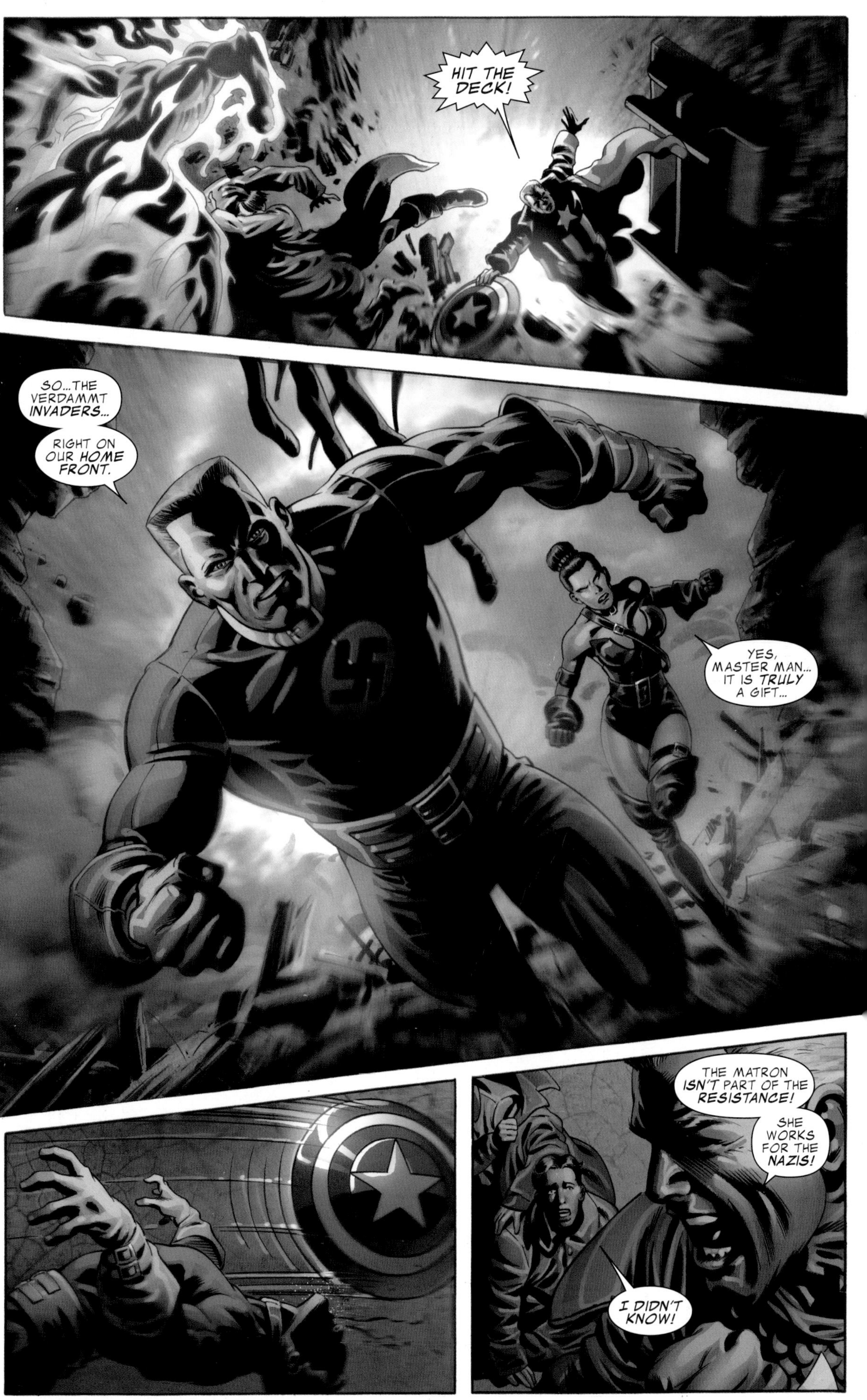

HIT THE DECK!
SO...THE VERDAMMT INVADERS...
RIGHT ON OUR HOME FRONT.
YES, MASTER MAN... IT IS TRULY A GIFT...
THE MATRON ISN'T PART OF THE RESISTANCE!
SHE WORKS FOR THE NAZIS!
I DIDN'T KNOW!

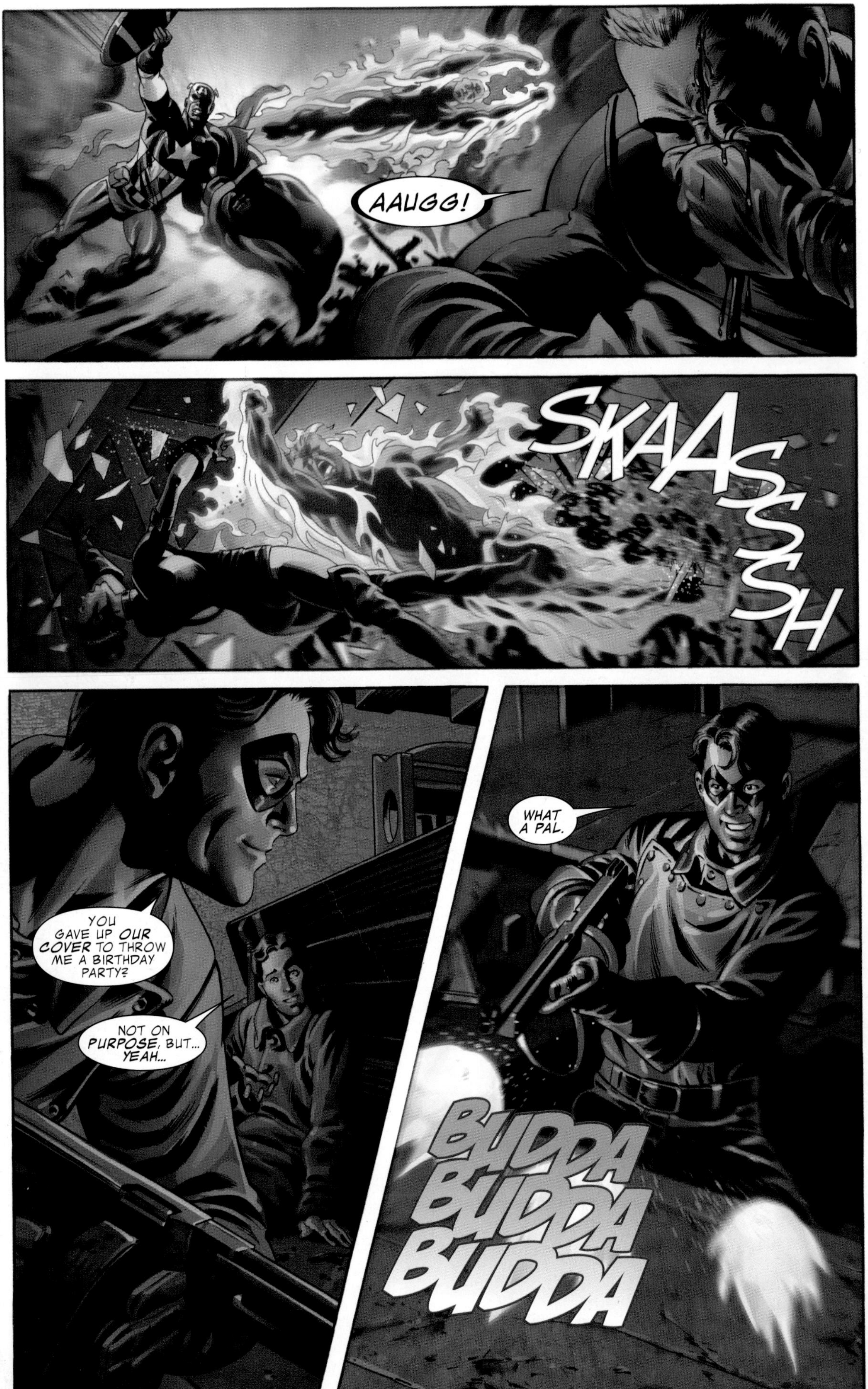
AAUGG!
SKAASSSH
YOU GAVE UP OUR COVER TO THROW ME A BIRTHDAY PARTY?
NOT ON PURPOSE, BUT... YEAH...
WHAT A PAL.
BUDDA BUDDA BUDDA

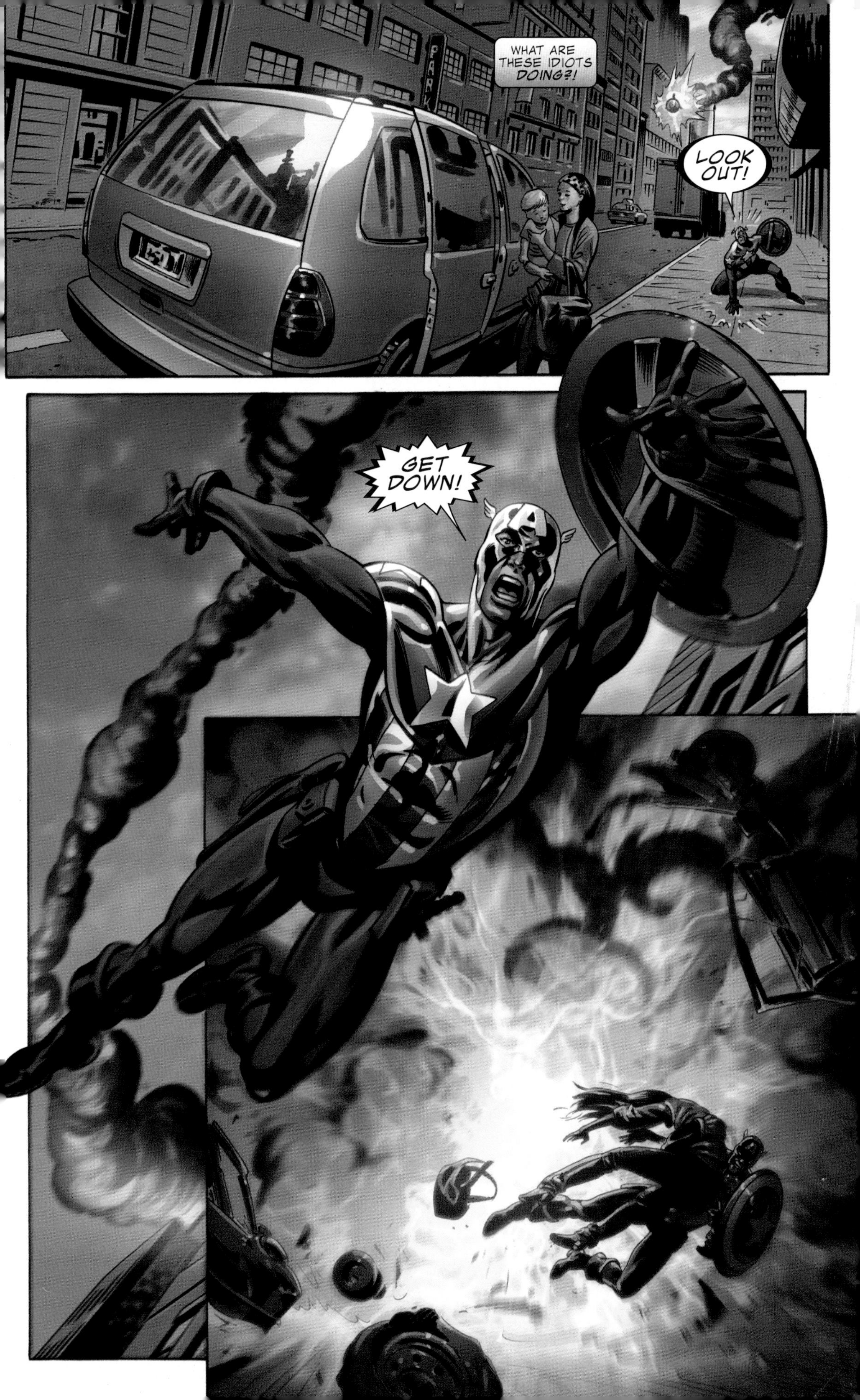
WHAT ARE THESE IDIOTS DOING?!
LOOK OUT!
GET DOWN!

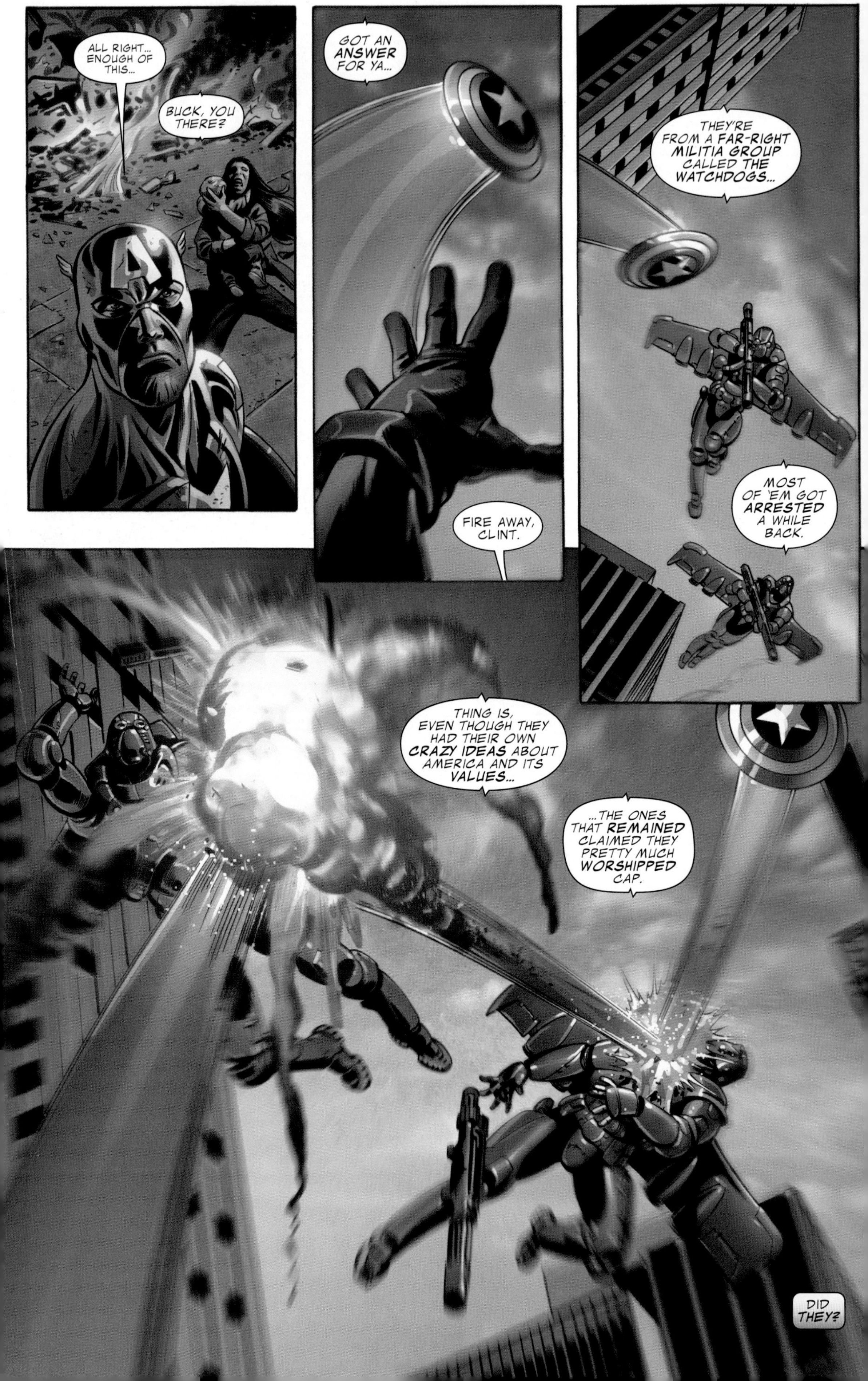
ALL RIGHT... ENOUGH OF THIS...
BUCK, YOU THERE?
GOT AN ANSWER FOR YA...
FIRE AWAY, CLINT.
THEY'RE FROM A FAR-RIGHT MILITIA GROUP CALLED THE WATCHDOGS...
MOST OF 'EM GOT ARRESTED A WHILE BACK.
THING IS, EVEN THOUGH THEY HAD THEIR OWN CRAZY IDEAS ABOUT AMERICA AND ITS VALUES...
...THE ONES THAT REMAINED CLAIMED THEY PRETTY MUCH WORSHIPPED CAP.
DID THEY?

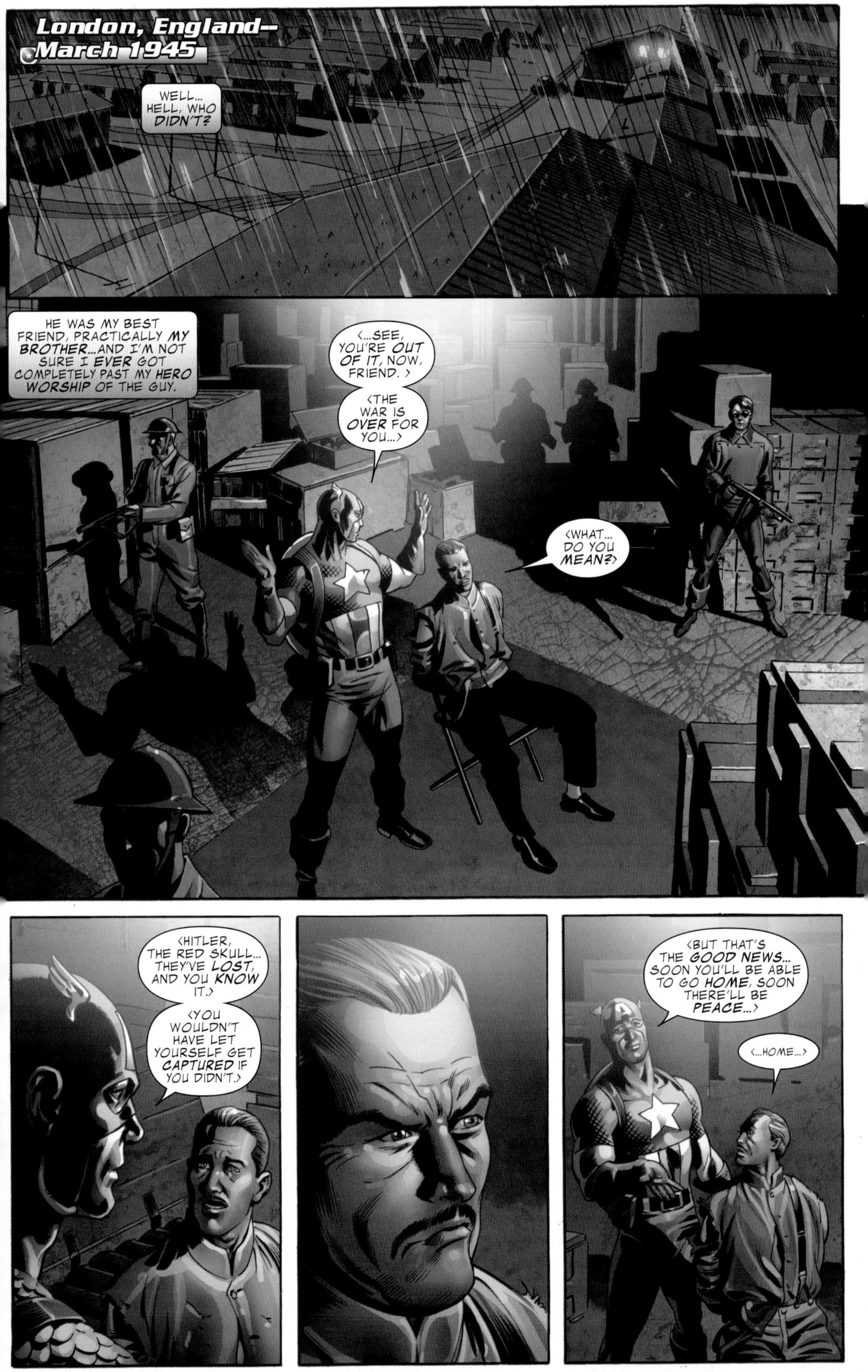
London, England--
March 1945
WELL... HELL, WHO DIDN'T?
HE WAS MY BEST FRIEND, PRACTICALLY MY BROTHER...AND I'M NOT SURE I EVER GOT COMPLETELY PAST MY HERO WORSHIP OF THE GUY.
‹...SEE, YOU'RE OUT OF IT, NOW, FRIEND.›
‹THE WAR IS OVER FOR YOU...›
‹WHAT... DO YOU MEAN?›
‹HITLER, THE RED SKULL... THEY'VE LOST, AND YOU KNOW IT.›
‹YOU WOULDN'T HAVE LET YOURSELF GET CAPTURED IF YOU DIDN'T.›
‹BUT THAT'S THE GOOD NEWS... SOON YOU'LL BE ABLE TO GO HOME, SOON THERE'LL BE PEACE...›
‹...HOME...›

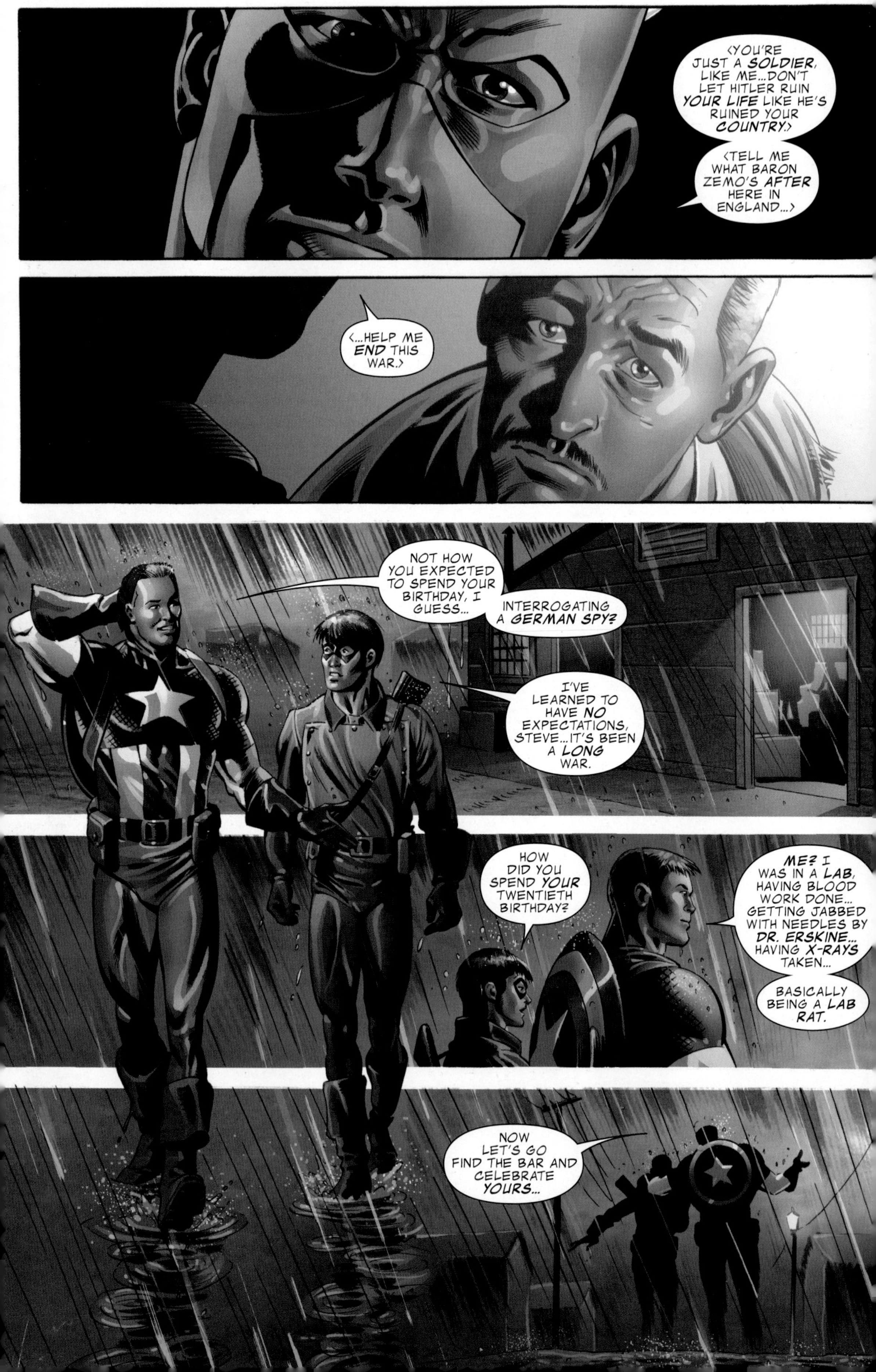
<YOU'RE JUST A SOLDIER, LIKE ME...DON'T LET HITLER RUIN YOUR LIFE LIKE HE'S RUINED YOUR COUNTRY.>
<TELL ME WHAT BARON ZEMO'S AFTER HERE IN ENGLAND...>
<...HELP ME END THIS WAR.>
NOT HOW YOU EXPECTED TO SPEND YOUR BIRTHDAY, I GUESS...
INTERROGATING A GERMAN SPY?
I'VE LEARNED TO HAVE NO EXPECTATIONS, STEVE...IT'S BEEN A LONG WAR.
HOW DID YOU SPEND YOUR TWENTIETH BIRTHDAY?
ME? I WAS IN A LAB, HAVING BLOOD WORK DONE... GETTING JABBED WITH NEEDLES BY DR. ERSKINE... HAVING X-RAYS TAKEN...
BASICALLY BEING A LAB RAT.
NOW LET'S GO FIND THE BAR AND CELEBRATE YOURS...

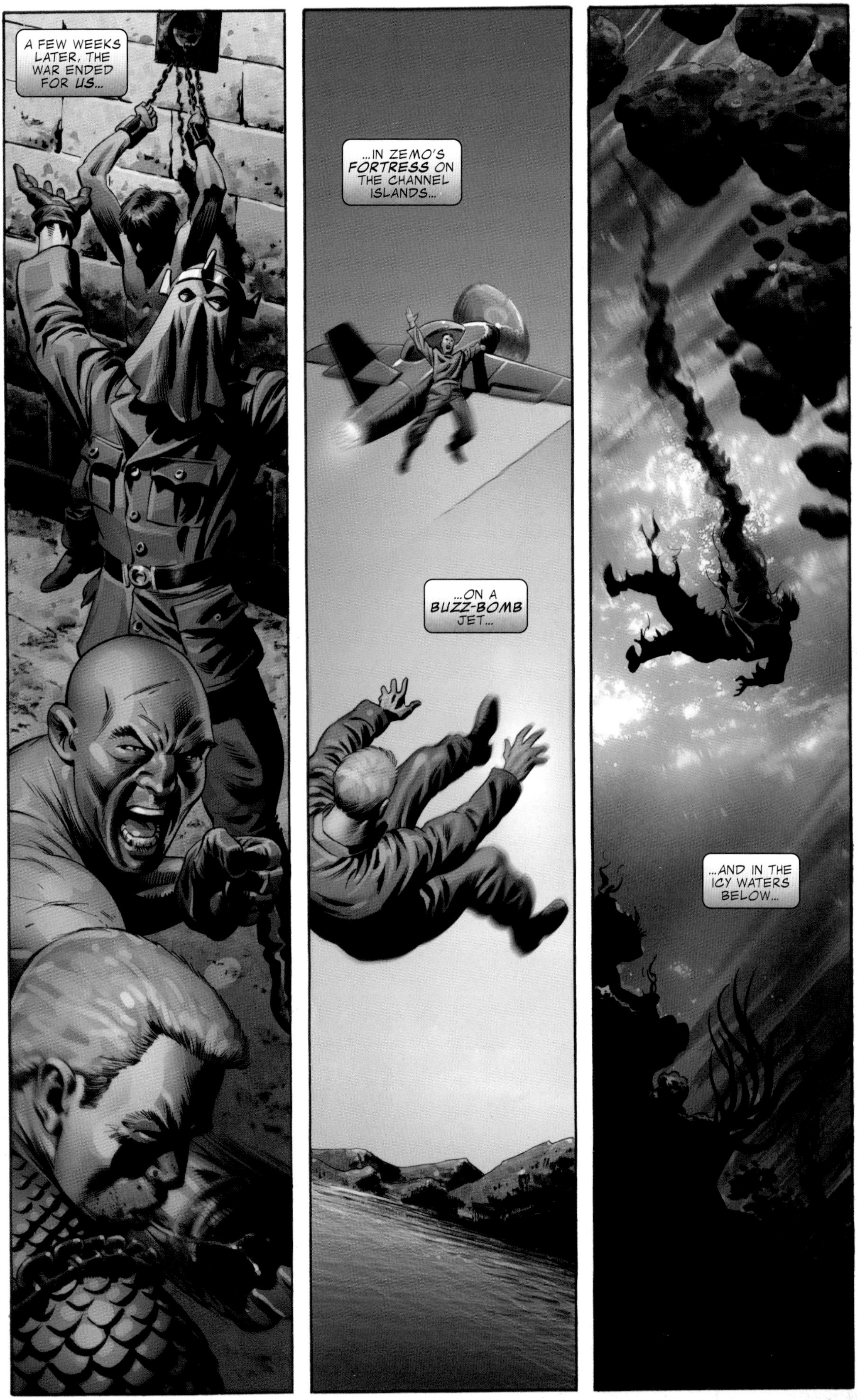
A FEW WEEKS LATER, THE WAR ENDED FOR US...
...IN ZEMO'S FORTRESS ON THE CHANNEL ISLANDS...
...ON A BUZZ-BOMB JET...
...AND IN THE ICY WATERS BELOW...

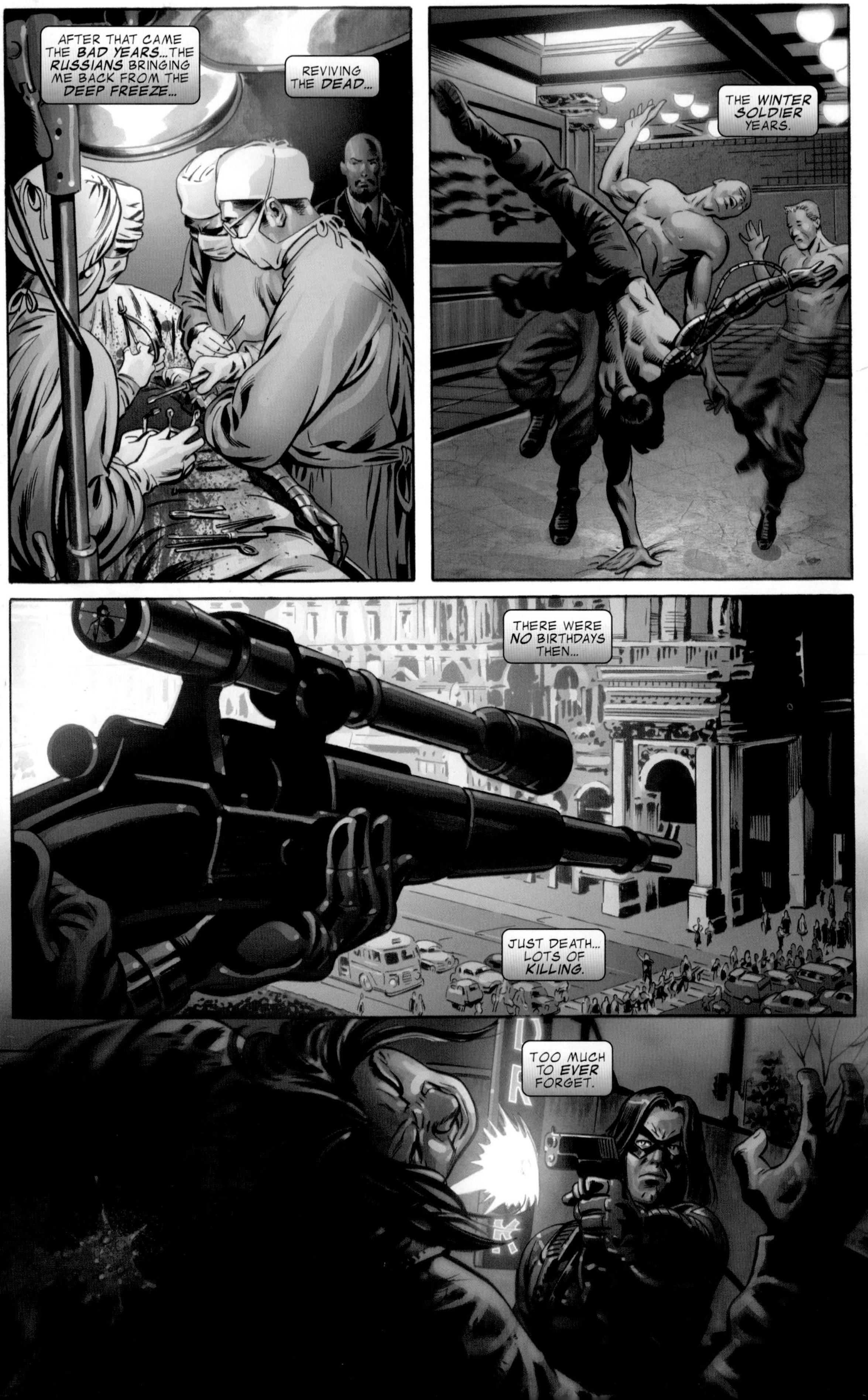
AFTER THAT CAME THE BAD YEARS... THE RUSSIANS BRINGING ME BACK FROM THE DEEP FREEZE...
REVIVING THE DEAD...
THE WINTER SOLDIER YEARS.
THERE WERE NO BIRTHDAYS THEN...
JUST DEATH... LOTS OF KILLING.
TOO MUCH TO EVER FORGET.

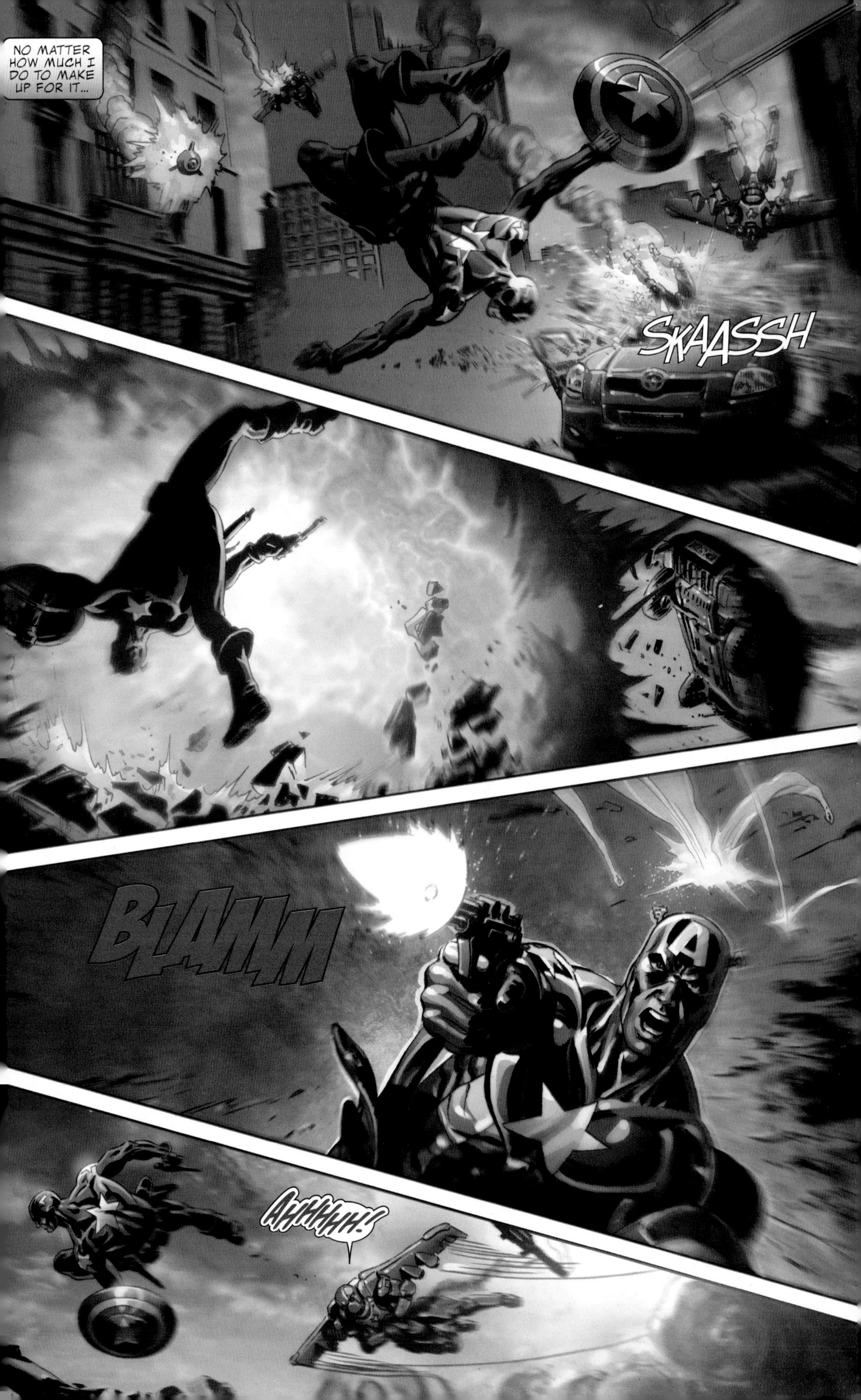
NO MATTER HOW MUCH I DO TO MAKE UP FOR IT...
SKAASSH
BLAMM
AHHHHH!

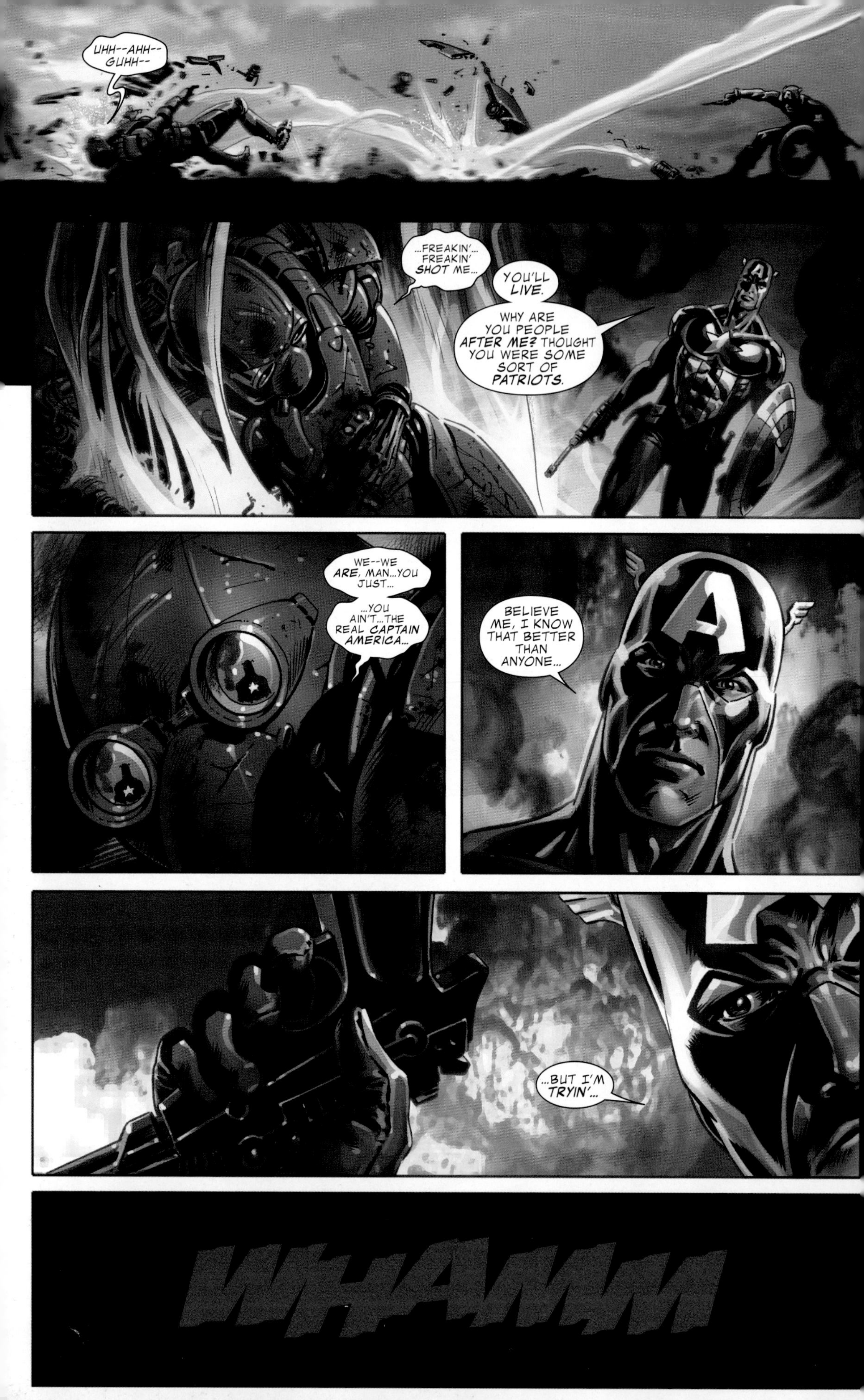
UHH--AHH--GUHH--
...FREAKIN'... FREAKIN' SHOT ME...
YOU'LL LIVE.
WHY ARE YOU PEOPLE AFTER ME? THOUGHT YOU WERE SOME SORT OF PATRIOTS.
WE--WE ARE, MAN...YOU JUST...
...YOU AIN'T...THE REAL CAPTAIN AMERICA...
BELIEVE ME, I KNOW THAT BETTER THAN ANYONE...
...BUT I'M TRYIN'...
WHAMM

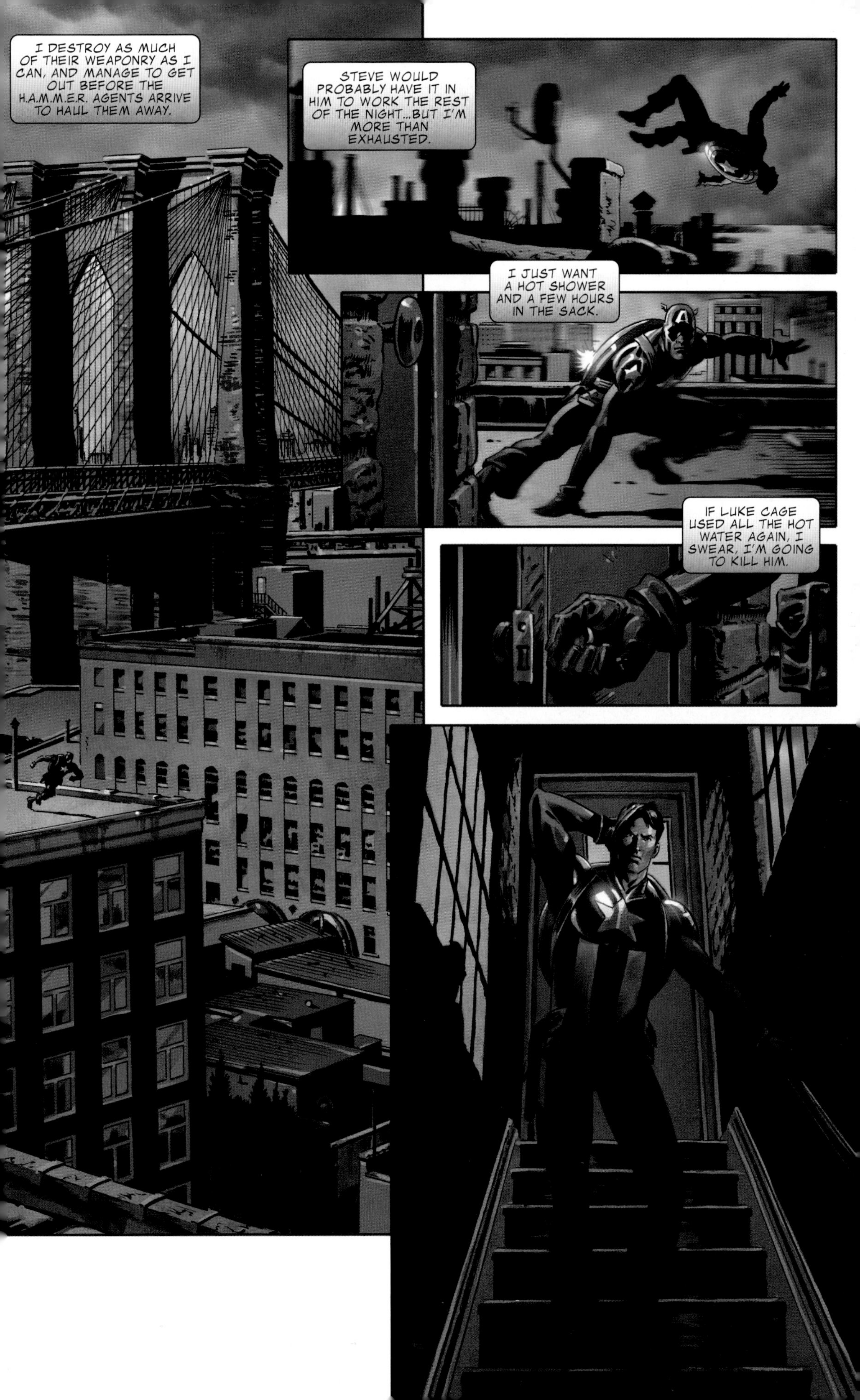
I DESTROY AS MUCH OF THEIR WEAPONRY AS I CAN, AND MANAGE TO GET OUT BEFORE THE H.A.M.M.E.R. AGENTS ARRIVE TO HAUL THEM AWAY.
STEVE WOULD PROBABLY HAVE IT IN HIM TO WORK THE REST OF THE NIGHT...BUT I'M MORE THAN EXHAUSTED.
I JUST WANT A HOT SHOWER AND A FEW HOURS IN THE SACK.
IF LUKE CAGE USED ALL THE HOT WATER AGAIN, I SWEAR, I'M GOING TO KILL HIM.

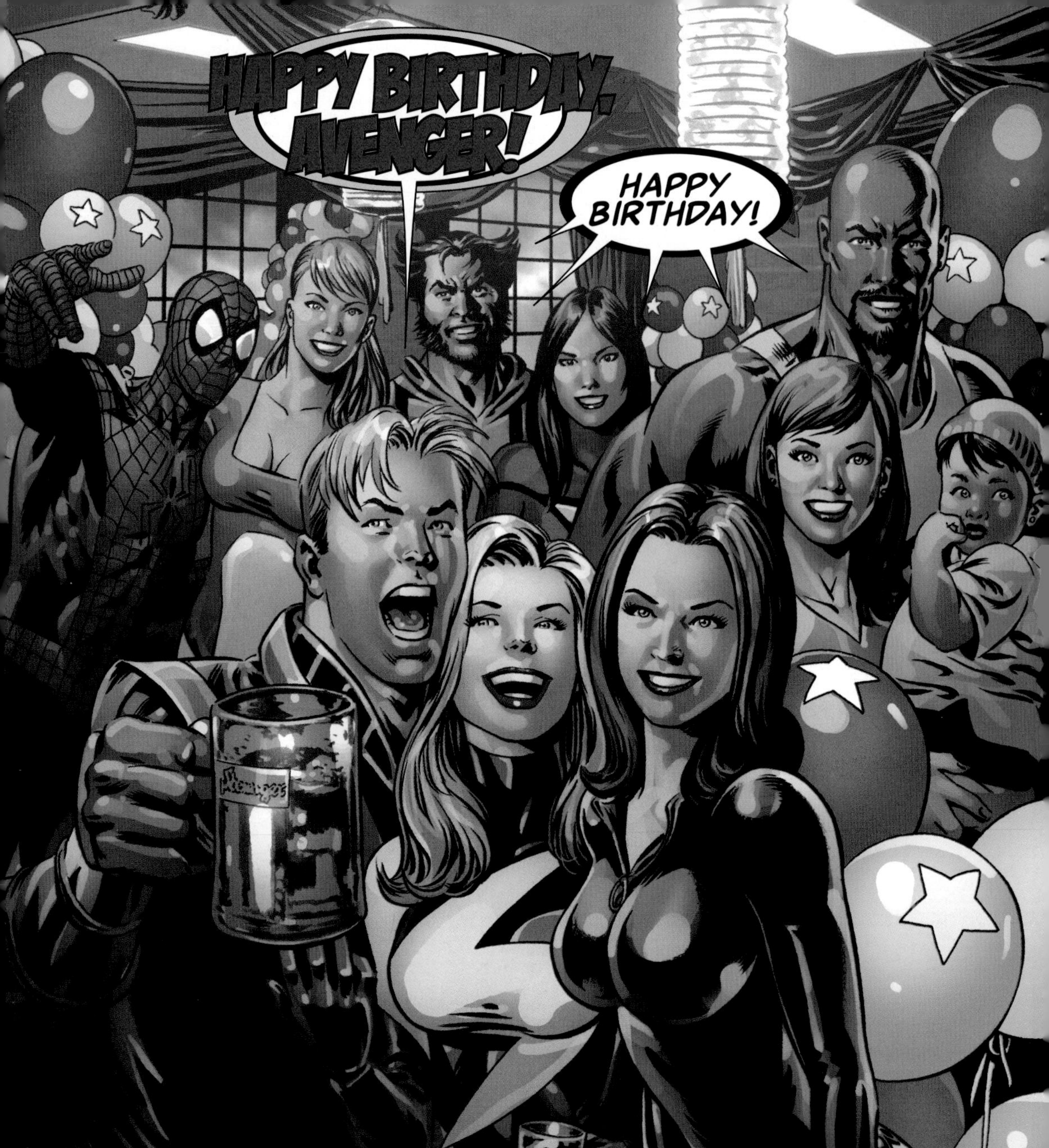
HAPPY BIRTHDAY, AVENGER!
HAPPY BIRTHDAY!

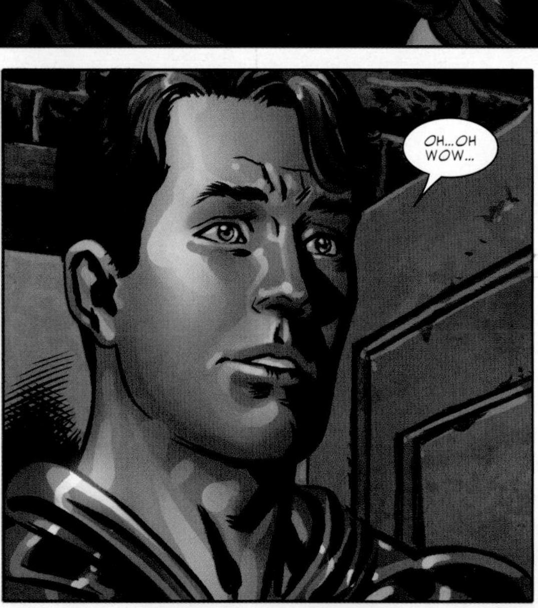
OH...OH WOW...

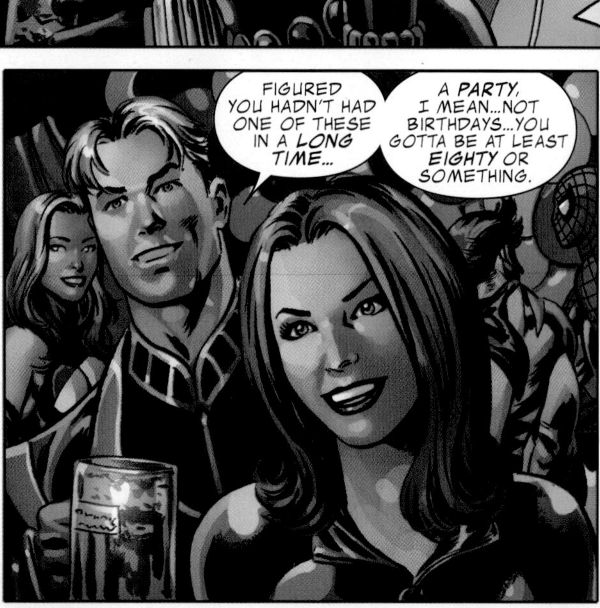
FIGURED YOU HADN'T HAD ONE OF THESE IN A LONG TIME...
A PARTY, I MEAN...NOT BIRTHDAYS...YOU GOTTA BE AT LEAST EIGHTY OR SOMETHING.

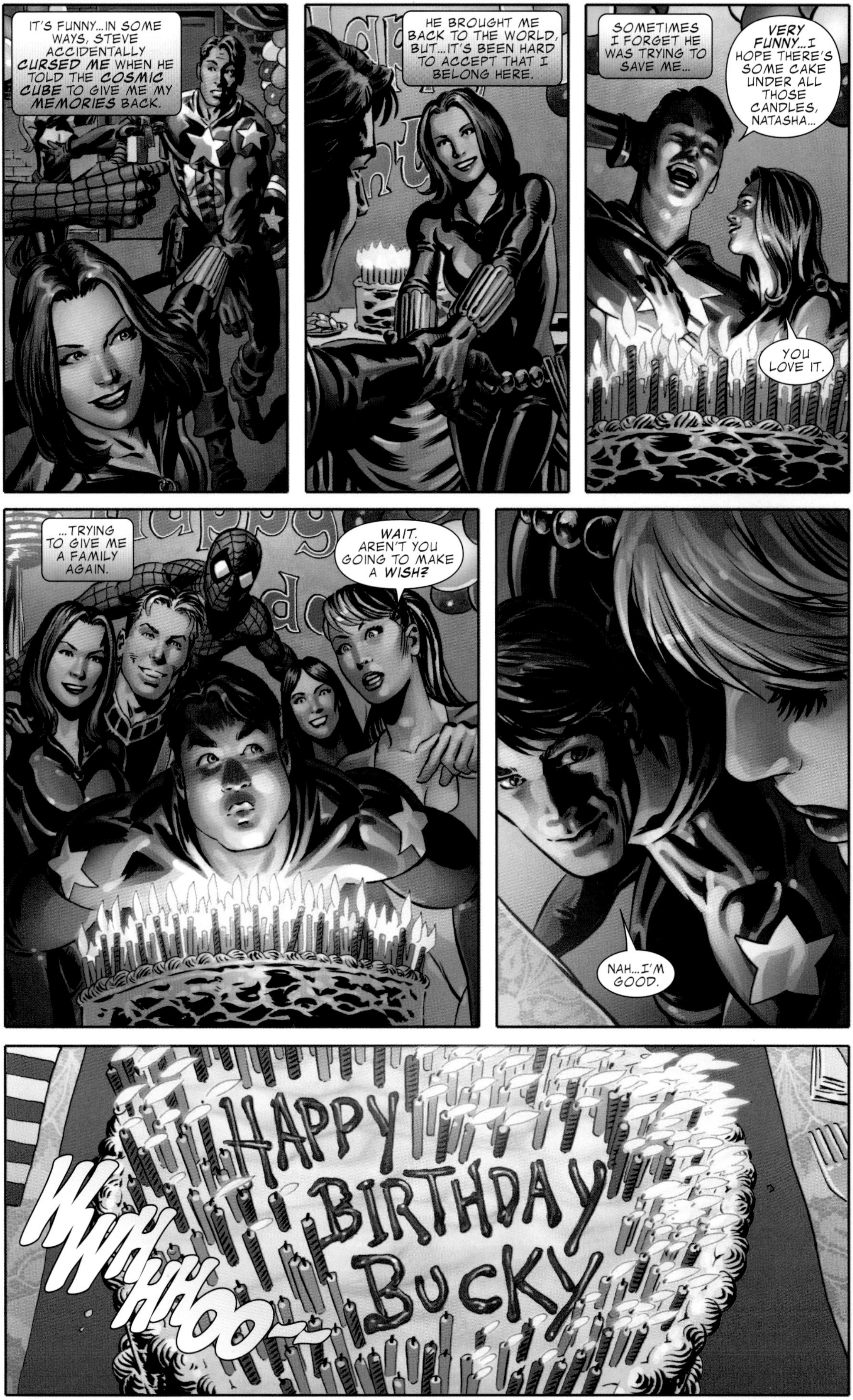
IT'S FUNNY...IN SOME WAYS, STEVE ACCIDENTALLY CURSED ME WHEN HE TOLD THE COSMIC CUBE TO GIVE ME MY MEMORIES BACK.
HE BROUGHT ME BACK TO THE WORLD, BUT...IT'S BEEN HARD TO ACCEPT THAT I BELONG HERE.
SOMETIMES I FORGET HE WAS TRYING TO SAVE ME...
VERY FUNNY...I HOPE THERE'S SOME CAKE UNDER ALL THOSE CANDLES, NATASHA...
YOU LOVE IT.
...TRYING TO GIVE ME A FAMILY AGAIN.
WAIT. AREN'T YOU GOING TO MAKE A WISH?
NAH...I'M GOOD.
HAPPY BIRTHDAY BUCKY
WHHHOO--

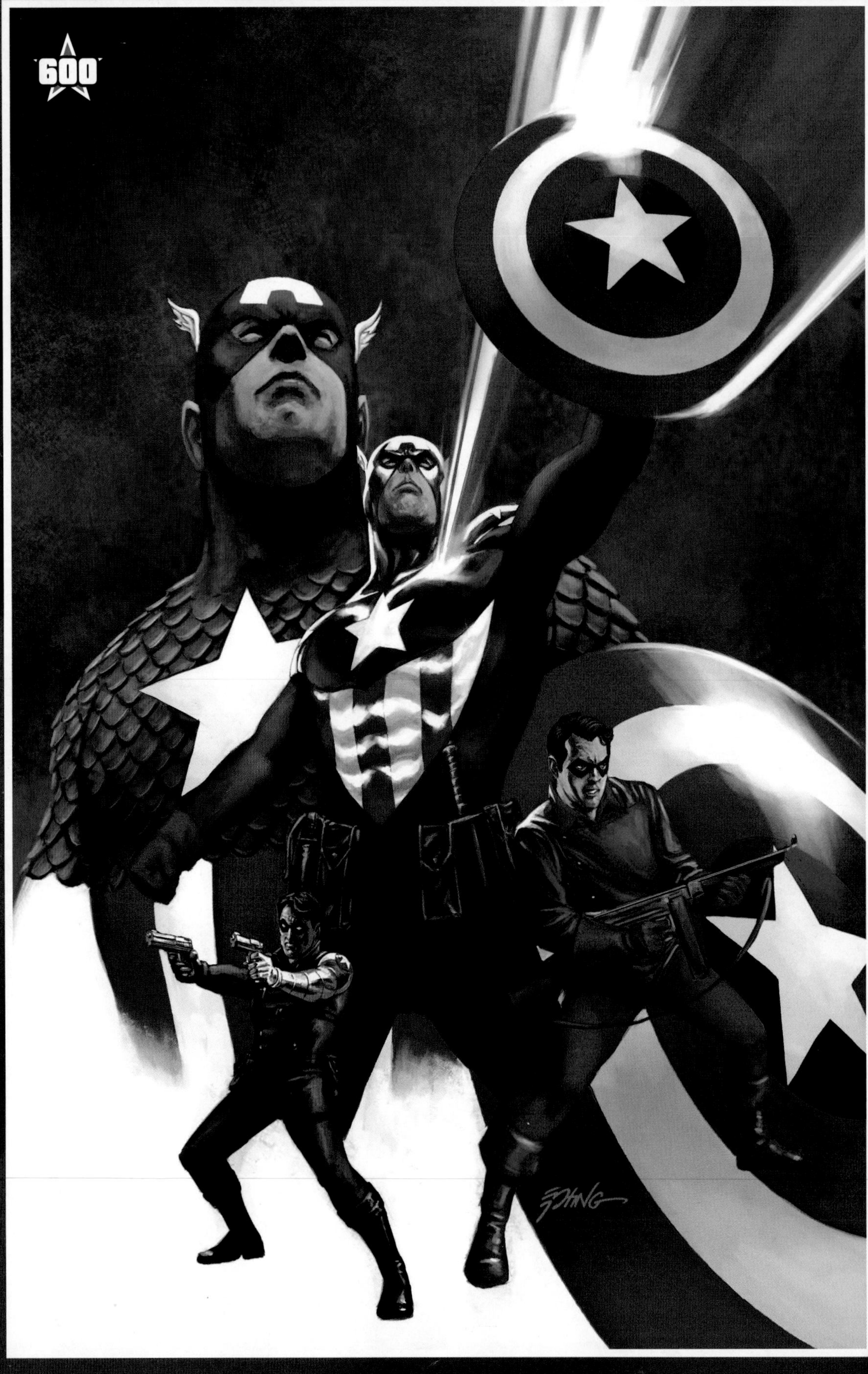
600

ONE YEAR AFTER

CAPTAIN AMERICA #600

ORIGIN
BY **ALEX ROSS, PAUL DINI** AND **TODD KLEIN,** WAS FIRST PUBLISHED IN
CAPTAIN AMERICA: RED, WHITE AND BLUE; SEPTEMBER, 2002

ONE YEAR AFTER
ED BRUBAKER: SCRIPT
BUTCH GUICE WITH **HOWARD CHAYKIN, RAFAEL ALBUQUERQUE,
DAVID AJA** AND **MITCH BREITWEISER:** ART
FRANK D'ARMATA WITH **EDGAR DELGADO,
MATT HOLLINGSWORTH** AND **MITCH BREITWEISER:** COLOR ART
VC'S JOE CARAMAGNA AND **CHRIS ELIOPOULOS:** LETTERS

IN MEMORIUM
ROGER STERN: SCRIPT
KALMAN ANDRASOFSZKY: ART
MARTE GRACIA: COLOR ART
VC'S JOE CARAMAGNA AND **CHRIS ELIOPOULOS:** LETTERS

THE PERSISTENCE OF MEMORABILIA
MARK WAID: SCRIPT
DALE EAGLESHAM: ART
PAUL MOUNTS: COLOR ART
VC'S JOE CARAMAGNA AND **CHRIS ELIOPOULOS:** LETTERS

PASSING THE TORCH
FRED HEMBECK: STORY & ART
CHRIS GIARRUSSO: COLORS

MY BULLETIN BOARD
BY **JOE SIMON**

JEANINE SCHAEFER: ASSOCIATE EDITOR
TOM BREVOORT: EDITOR
JOE QUESADA: EDITOR IN CHIEF
DAN BUCKLEY: PUBLISHER
ALAN FINE: EXECUTIVE PRODUCER

CAPTAIN AMERICA CREATED BY **JOE SIMON** AND **JACK KIRBY**

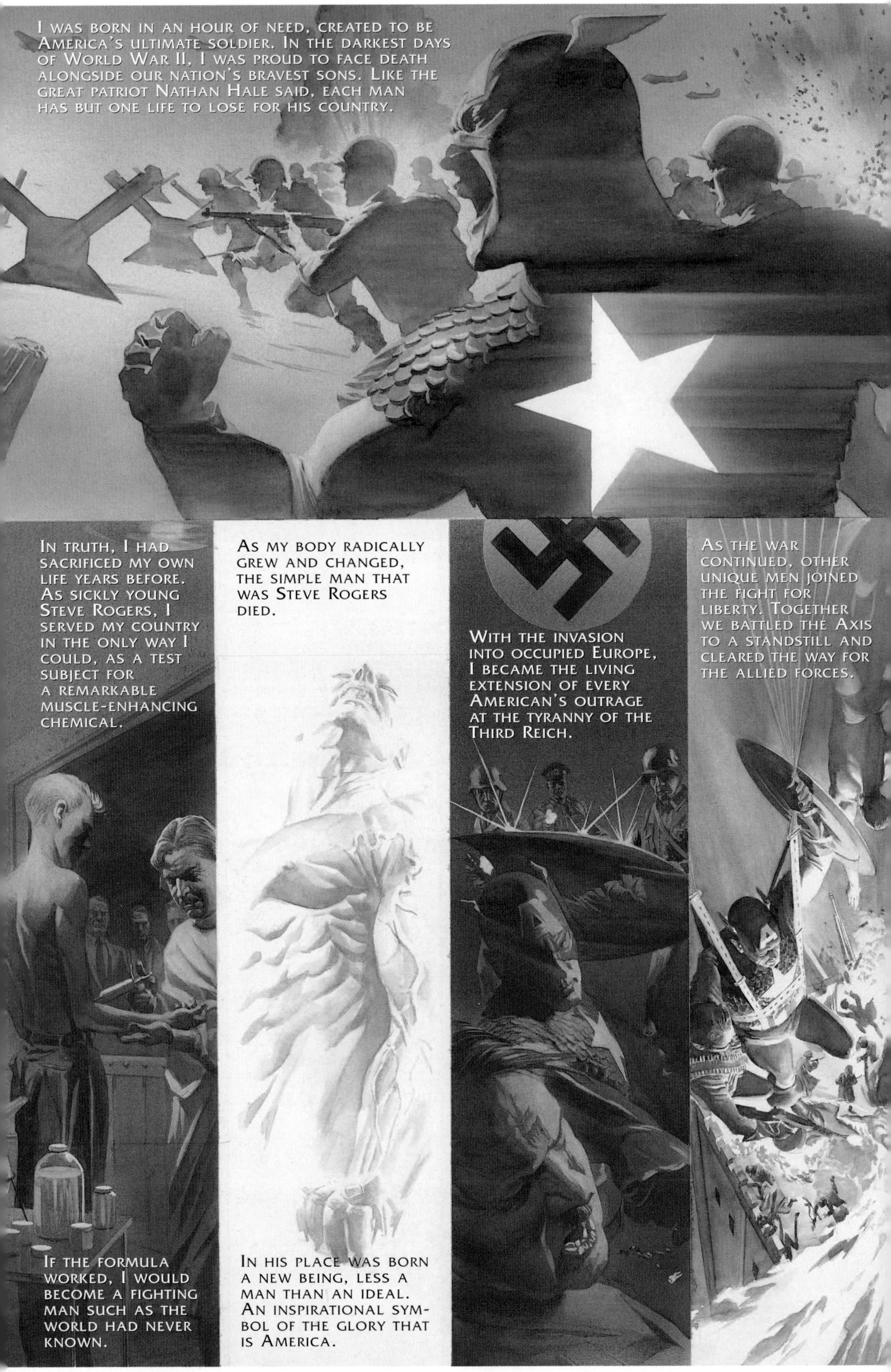
I was born in an hour of need, created to be America's ultimate soldier. In the darkest days of World War II, I was proud to face death alongside our nation's bravest sons. Like the great patriot Nathan Hale said, each man has but one life to lose for his country.
In truth, I had sacrificed my own life years before. As sickly young Steve Rogers, I served my country in the only way I could, as a test subject for a remarkable muscle-enhancing chemical.
If the formula worked, I would become a fighting man such as the world had never known.
As my body radically grew and changed, the simple man that was Steve Rogers died.
In his place was born a new being, less a man than an ideal. An inspirational symbol of the glory that is America.
With the invasion into occupied Europe, I became the living extension of every American's outrage at the tyranny of the Third Reich.
As the war continued, other unique men joined the fight for liberty. Together we battled the Axis to a standstill and cleared the way for the allied forces.

But it was a victory bought at a terrible price. In the war's final days, my young partner was killed in a Nazi trap.

And so I "died" once more.

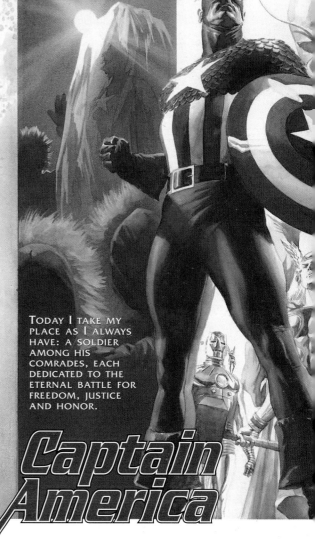

Today I take my place as I always have: a soldier among his comrades, each dedicated to the eternal battle for freedom, justice and honor.

Decades later my ice-bound body was recovered by superstitious tribesmen, and ultimately resurrected by a new generation of modern-day heroes.

Shielded by my body's advanced physiology, I was thrown into a near-death coma.

Captain America

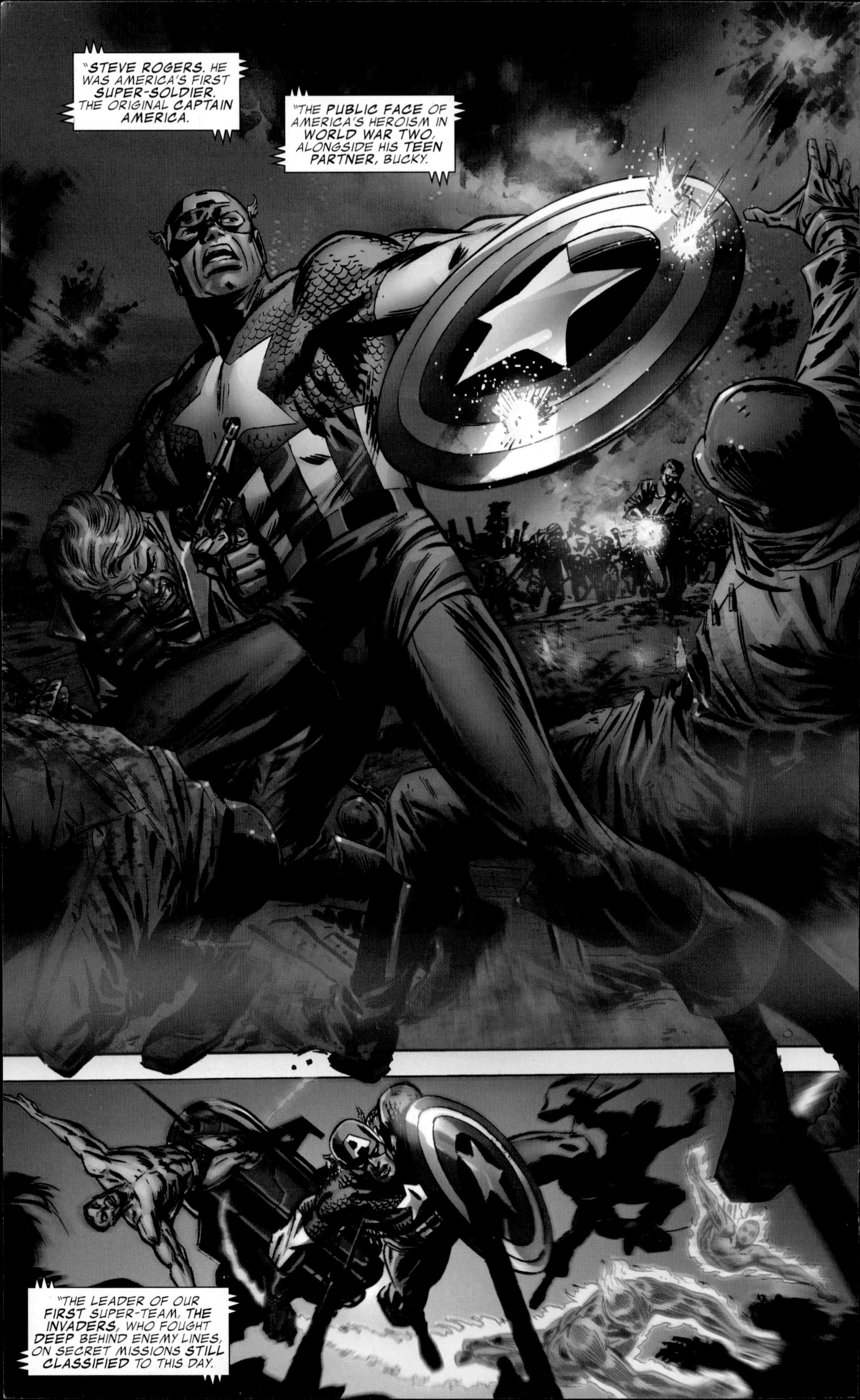
"STEVE ROGERS. HE WAS AMERICA'S FIRST SUPER-SOLDIER. THE ORIGINAL CAPTAIN AMERICA.
"THE PUBLIC FACE OF AMERICA'S HEROISM IN WORLD WAR TWO, ALONGSIDE HIS TEEN PARTNER, BUCKY.
"THE LEADER OF OUR FIRST SUPER-TEAM, THE INVADERS, WHO FOUGHT DEEP BEHIND ENEMY LINES, ON SECRET MISSIONS STILL CLASSIFIED TO THIS DAY.

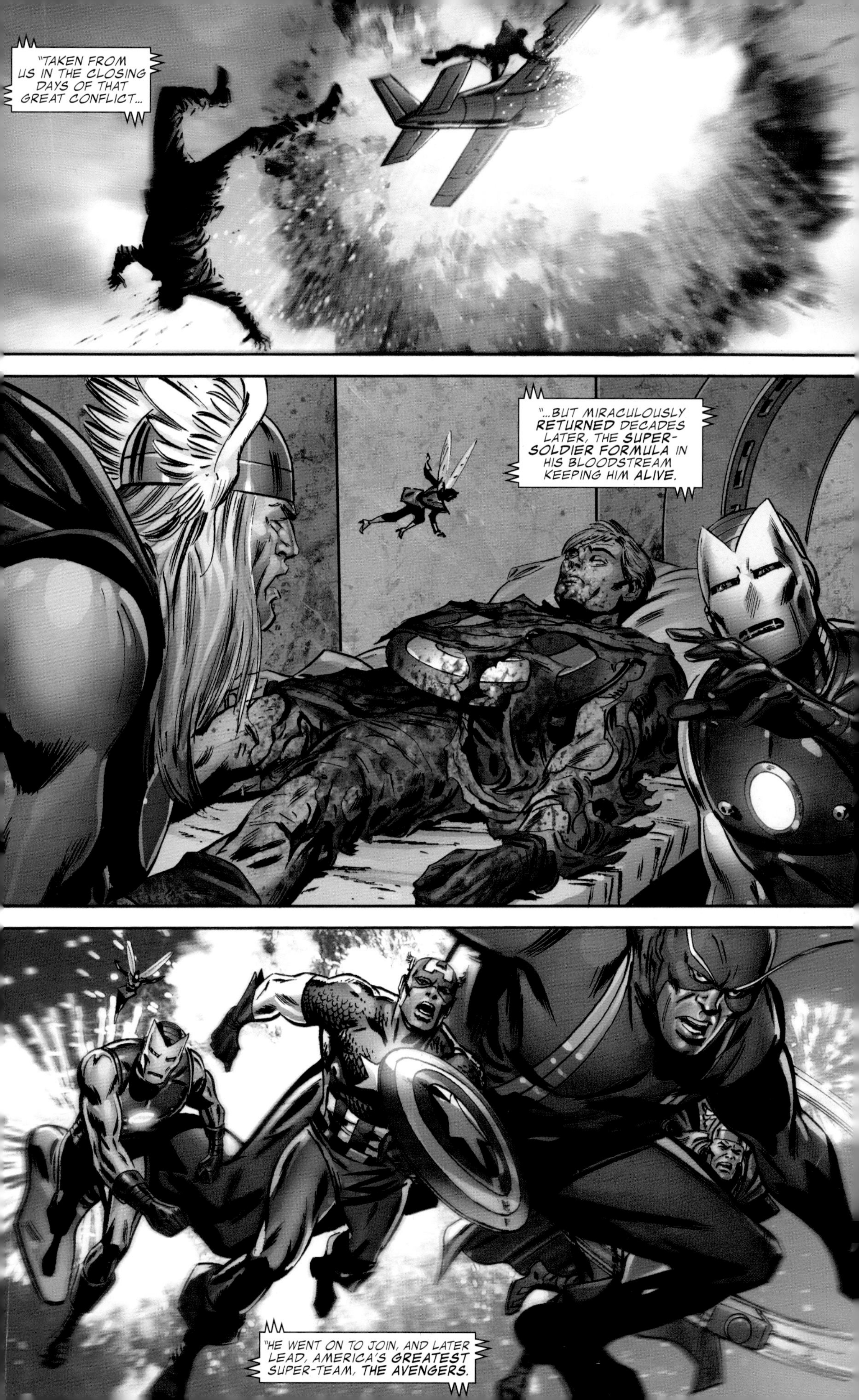
"TAKEN FROM US IN THE CLOSING DAYS OF THAT GREAT CONFLICT...
"...BUT MIRACULOUSLY RETURNED DECADES LATER, THE SUPER-SOLDIER FORMULA IN HIS BLOODSTREAM KEEPING HIM ALIVE.
"HE WENT ON TO JOIN, AND LATER LEAD, AMERICA'S GREATEST SUPER-TEAM, THE AVENGERS.

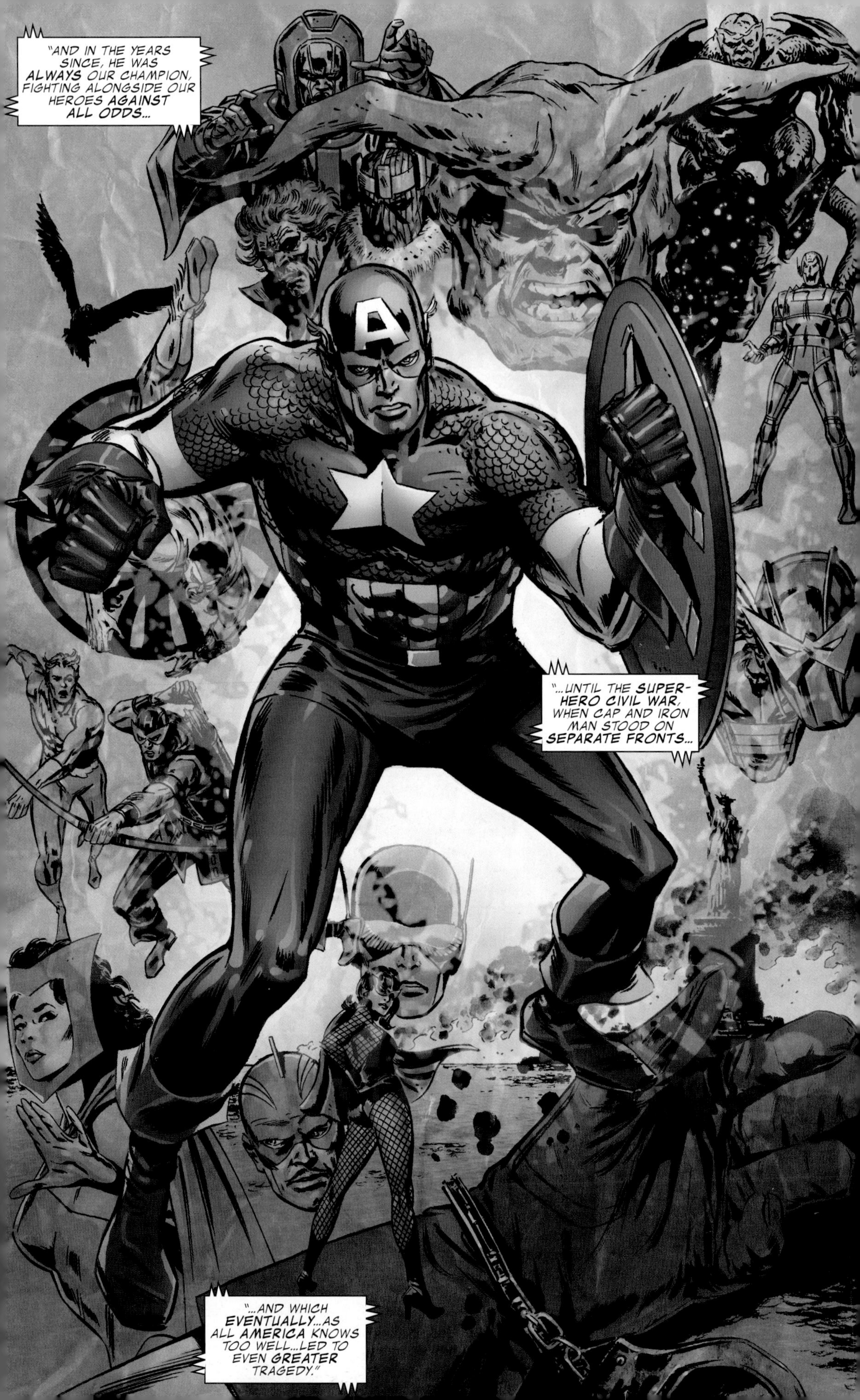
"AND IN THE YEARS SINCE, HE WAS ALWAYS OUR CHAMPION, FIGHTING ALONGSIDE OUR HEROES AGAINST ALL ODDS...
"...UNTIL THE SUPER-HERO CIVIL WAR, WHEN CAP AND IRON MAN STOOD ON SEPARATE FRONTS...
"...AND WHICH EVENTUALLY...AS ALL AMERICA KNOWS TOO WELL...LED TO EVEN GREATER TRAGEDY."

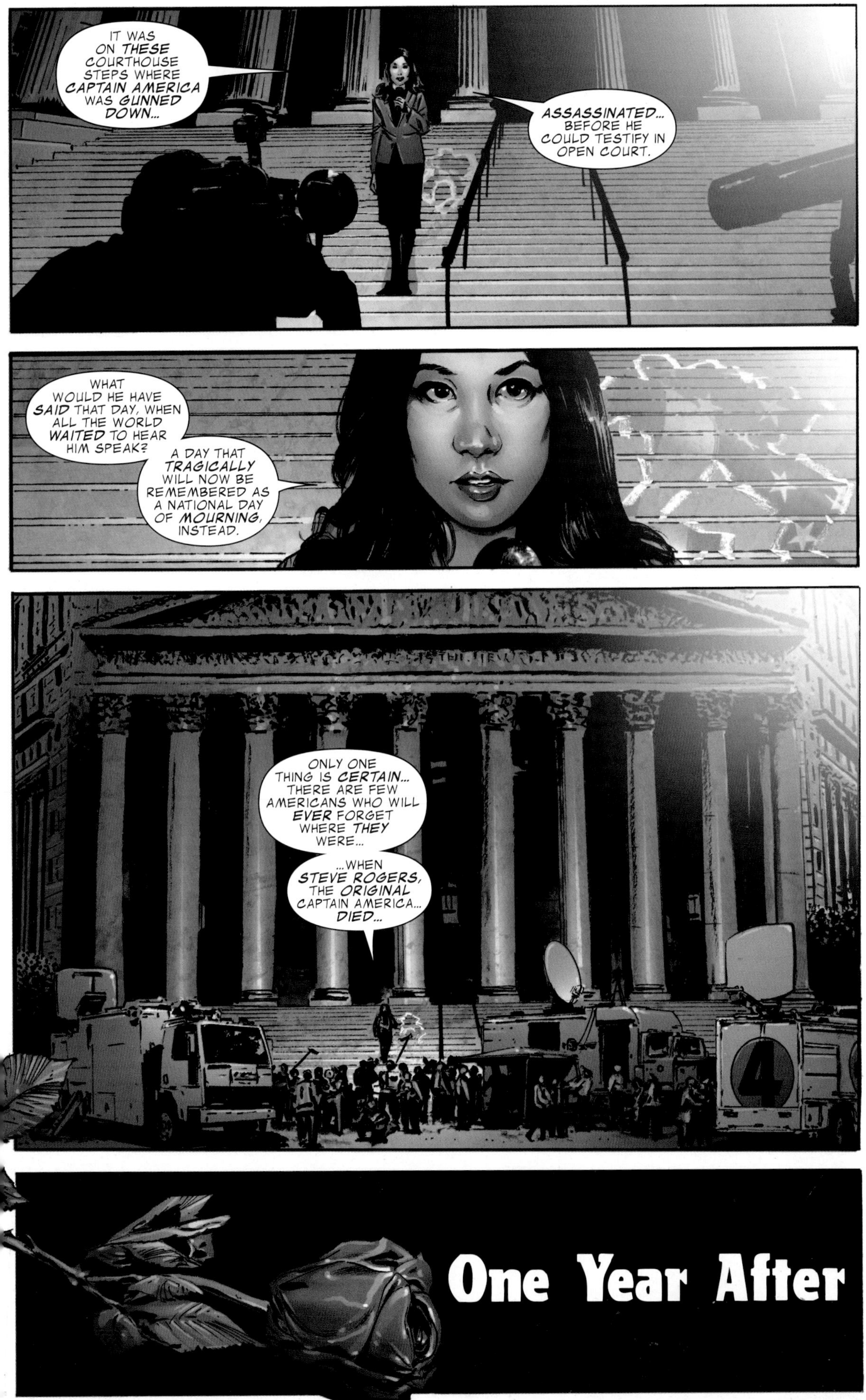
IT WAS ON THESE COURTHOUSE STEPS WHERE CAPTAIN AMERICA WAS GUNNED DOWN...
ASSASSINATED... BEFORE HE COULD TESTIFY IN OPEN COURT.
WHAT WOULD HE HAVE SAID THAT DAY, WHEN ALL THE WORLD WAITED TO HEAR HIM SPEAK?
A DAY THAT TRAGICALLY WILL NOW BE REMEMBERED AS A NATIONAL DAY OF MOURNING, INSTEAD.
ONLY ONE THING IS CERTAIN... THERE ARE FEW AMERICANS WHO WILL EVER FORGET WHERE THEY WERE...
...WHEN STEVE ROGERS, THE ORIGINAL CAPTAIN AMERICA... DIED...
4
One Year After

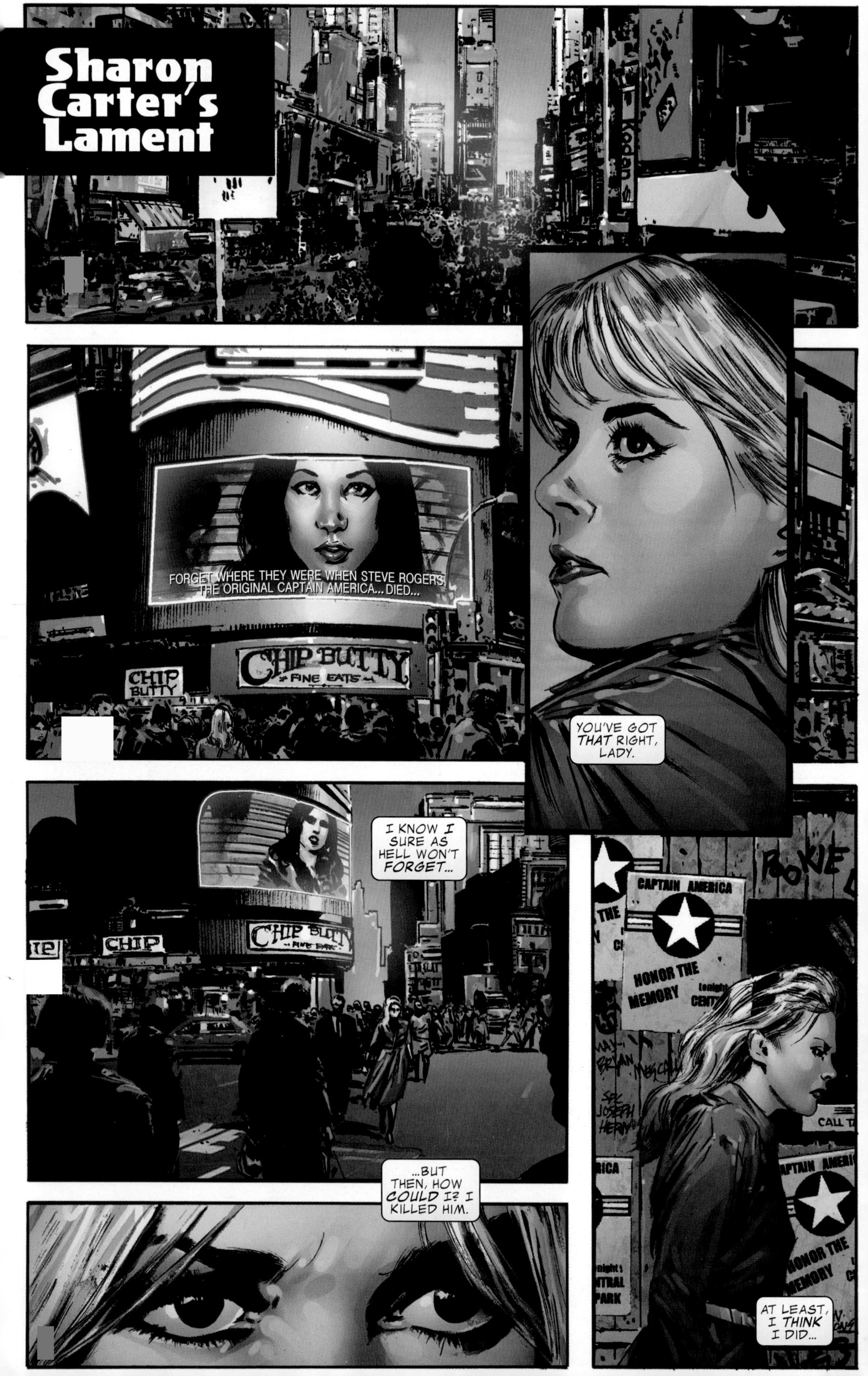
Sharon Carter's Lament
FORGET WHERE THEY WERE WHEN STEVE ROGERS, THE ORIGINAL CAPTAIN AMERICA... DIED...
CHIP BUTTY
FINE EATS
CHIP BUTTY
YOU'VE GOT THAT RIGHT, LADY.
I KNOW I SURE AS HELL WON'T FORGET...
...BUT THEN, HOW COULD I? I KILLED HIM.
CAPTAIN AMERICA
HONOR THE MEMORY
AT LEAST, I THINK I DID...

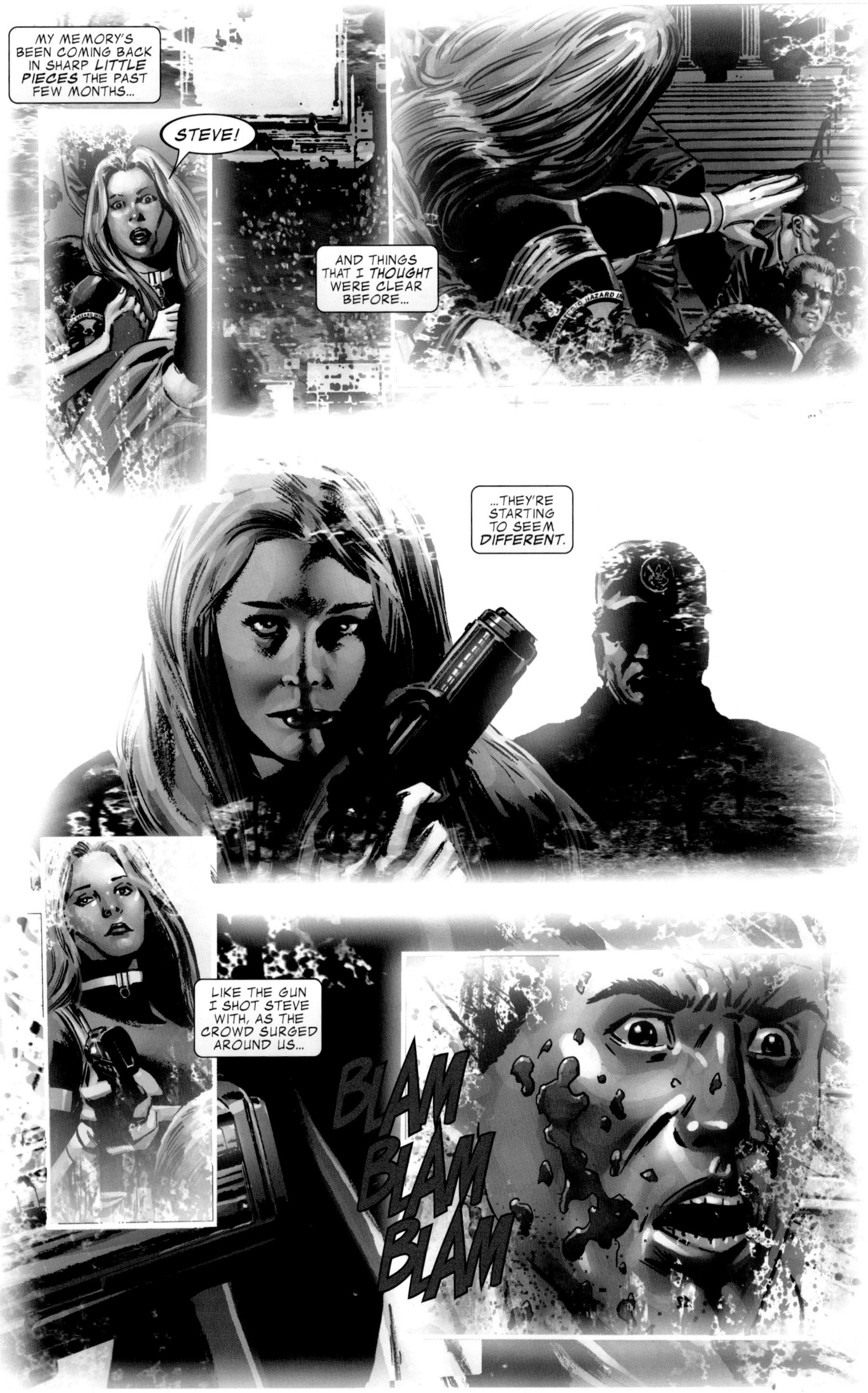

MY MEMORY'S BEEN COMING BACK IN SHARP LITTLE PIECES THE PAST FEW MONTHS...
STEVE!
AND THINGS THAT I THOUGHT WERE CLEAR BEFORE...
...THEY'RE STARTING TO SEEM DIFFERENT.
LIKE THE GUN I SHOT STEVE WITH, AS THE CROWD SURGED AROUND US...
BLAM
BLAM
BLAM

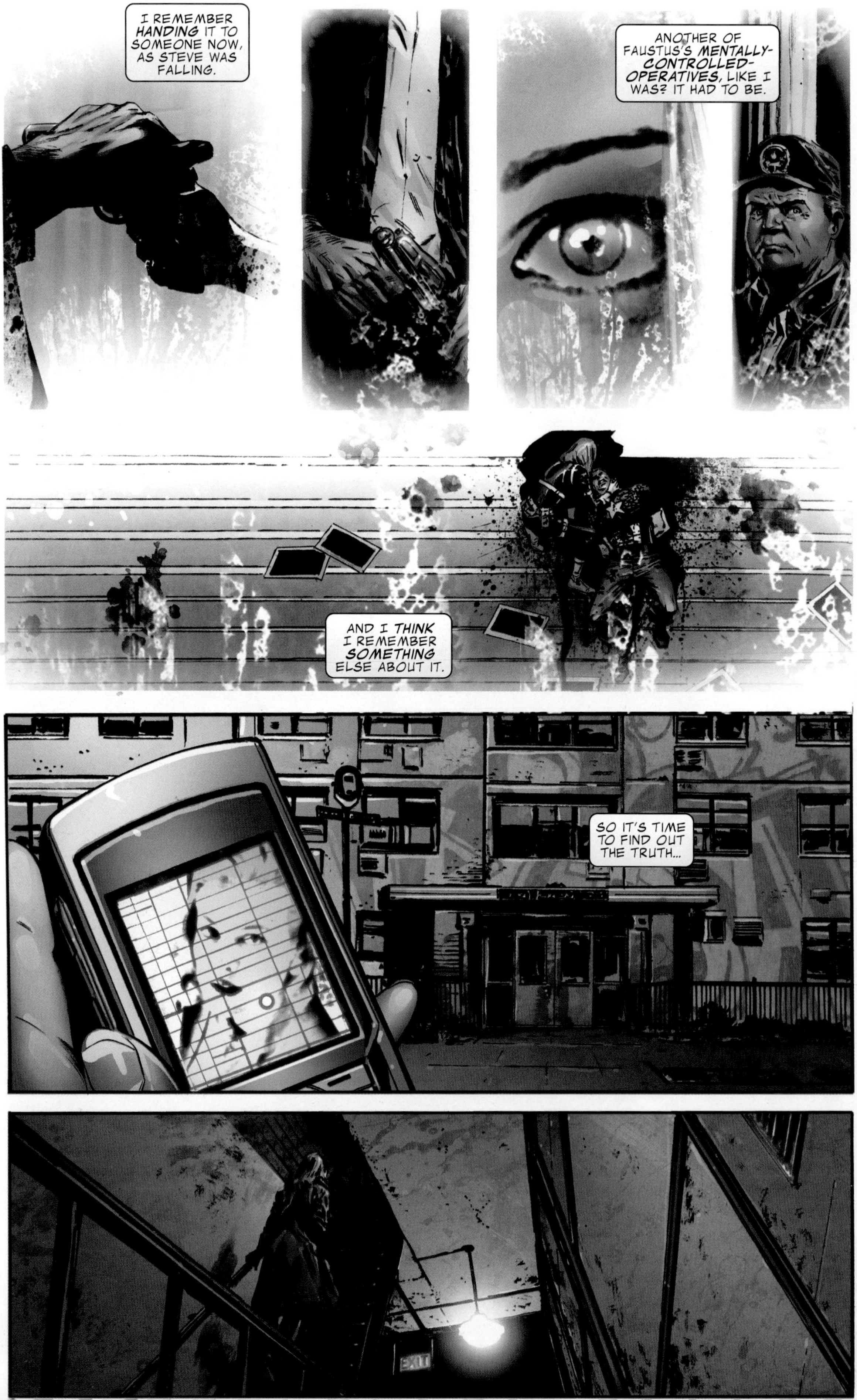
I REMEMBER HANDING IT TO SOMEONE NOW, AS STEVE WAS FALLING.
ANOTHER OF FAUSTUS'S MENTALLY-CONTROLLED-OPERATIVES, LIKE I WAS? IT HAD TO BE.
AND I THINK I REMEMBER SOMETHING ELSE ABOUT IT.
SO IT'S TIME TO FIND OUT THE TRUTH...
EXIT

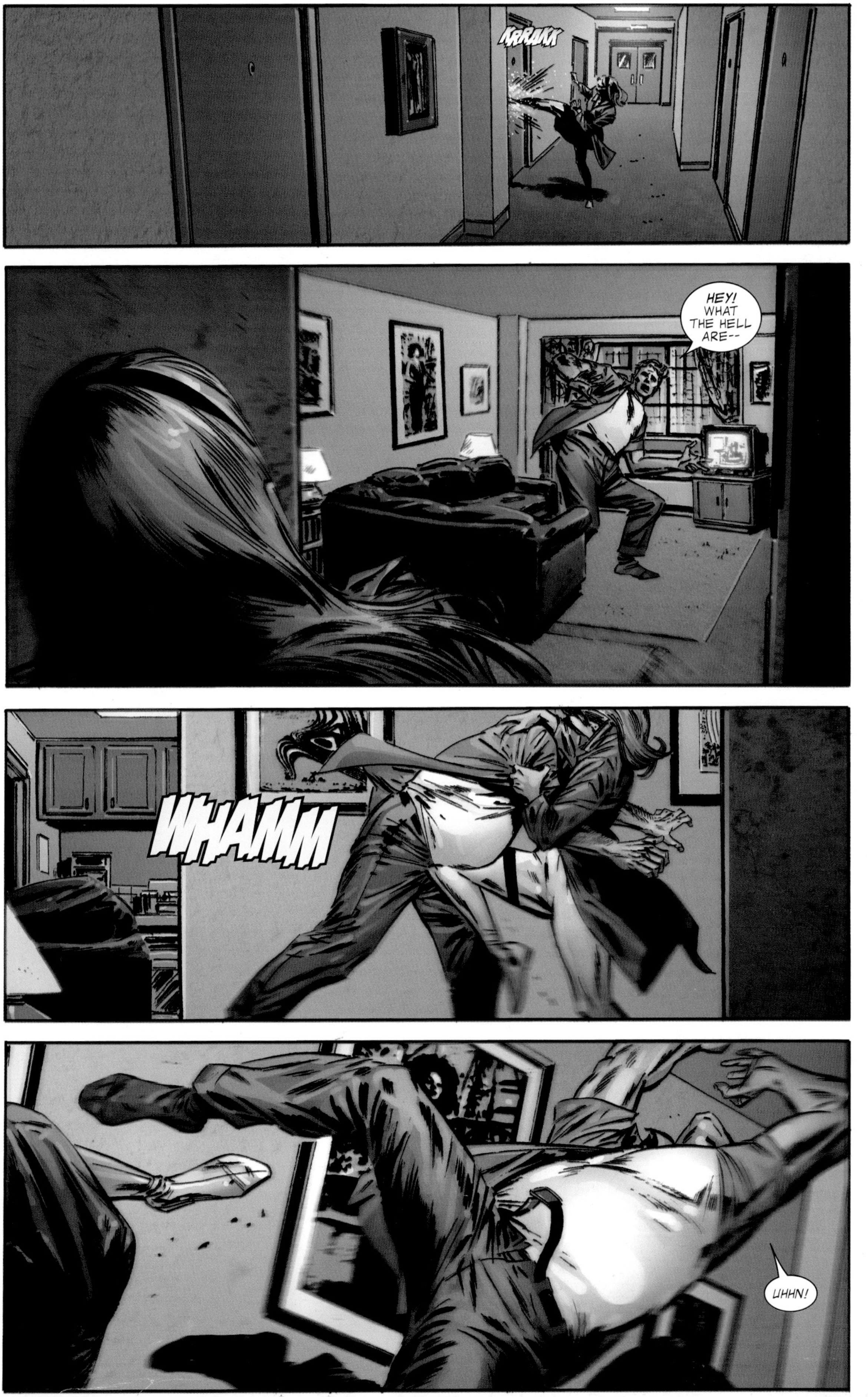
KRRAKK
HEY! WHAT THE HELL ARE--
WHAMM
UHHN!

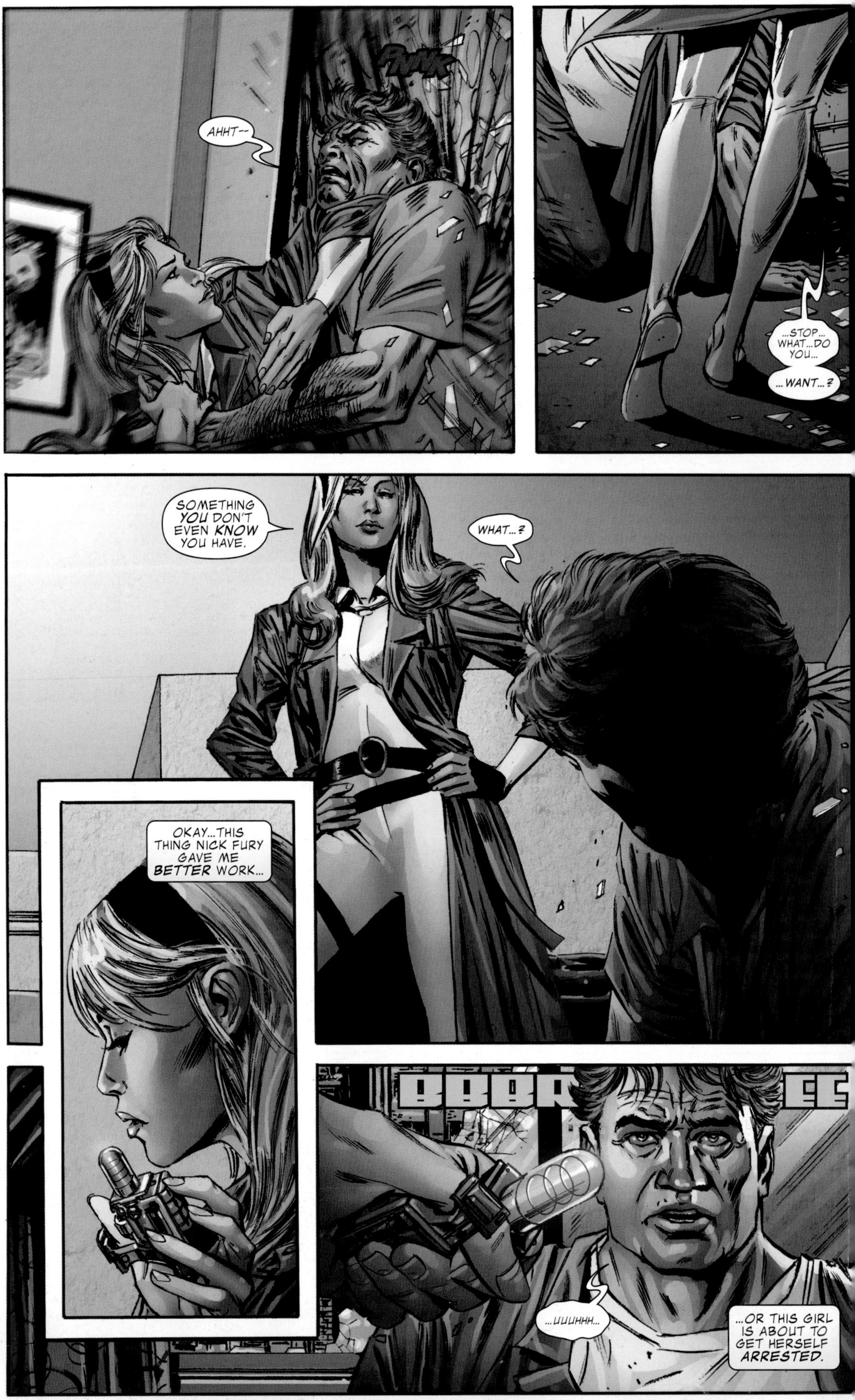
PWAK
AHHT--
...STOP... WHAT...DO YOU...
...WANT...?
SOMETHING YOU DON'T EVEN KNOW YOU HAVE.
WHAT...?
OKAY...THIS THING NICK FURY GAVE ME BETTER WORK...
BBBR
EE
...UUUHHH...
...OR THIS GIRL IS ABOUT TO GET HERSELF ARRESTED.

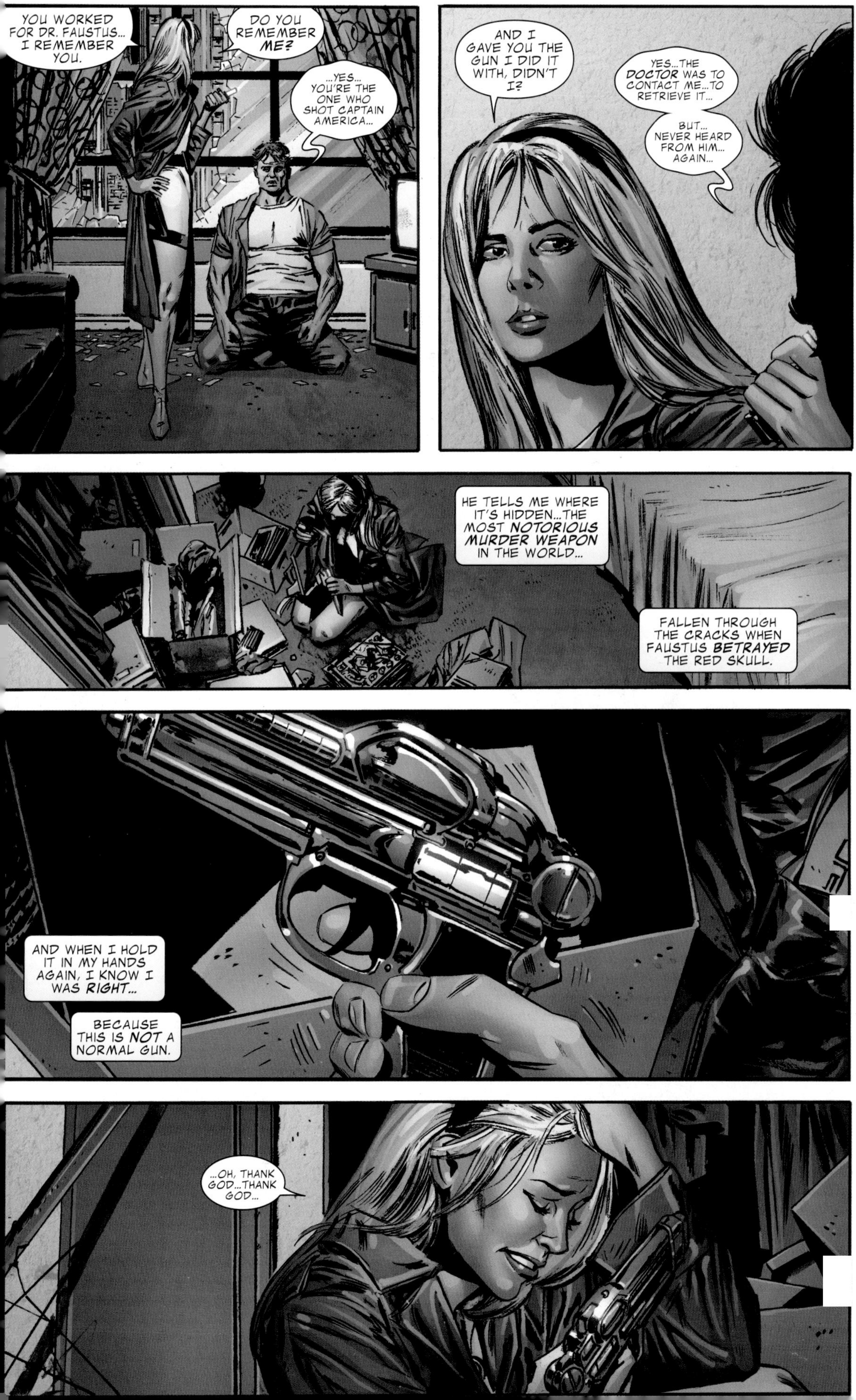
YOU WORKED FOR DR. FAUSTUS... I REMEMBER YOU.
DO YOU REMEMBER ME?
...YES... YOU'RE THE ONE WHO SHOT CAPTAIN AMERICA...
AND I GAVE YOU THE GUN I DID IT WITH, DIDN'T I?
YES...THE DOCTOR WAS TO CONTACT ME...TO RETRIEVE IT...
BUT... NEVER HEARD FROM HIM... AGAIN...
HE TELLS ME WHERE IT'S HIDDEN...THE MOST NOTORIOUS MURDER WEAPON IN THE WORLD...
FALLEN THROUGH THE CRACKS WHEN FAUSTUS BETRAYED THE RED SKULL.
AND WHEN I HOLD IT IN MY HANDS AGAIN, I KNOW I WAS RIGHT...
BECAUSE THIS IS NOT A NORMAL GUN.
...OH, THANK GOD...THANK GOD...

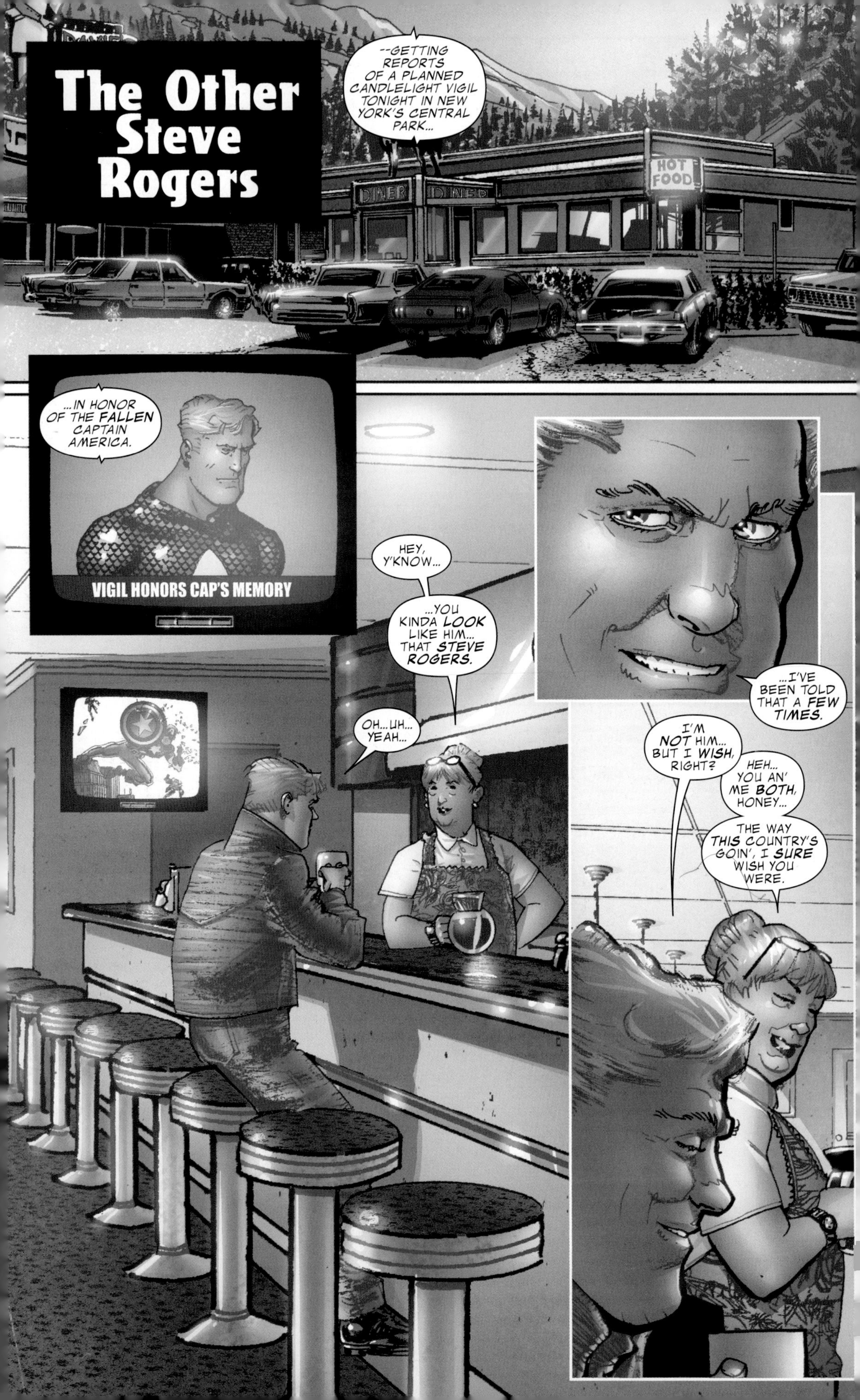
The Other Steve Rogers
--GETTING REPORTS OF A PLANNED CANDLELIGHT VIGIL TONIGHT IN NEW YORK'S CENTRAL PARK...
HOT FOOD
DINER
DINER
...IN HONOR OF THE FALLEN CAPTAIN AMERICA.
VIGIL HONORS CAP'S MEMORY
HEY, Y'KNOW...
...YOU KINDA LOOK LIKE HIM... THAT STEVE ROGERS.
OH...UH... YEAH...
...I'VE BEEN TOLD THAT A FEW TIMES.
I'M NOT HIM... BUT I WISH, RIGHT?
HEH... YOU AN' ME BOTH, HONEY...
THE WAY THIS COUNTRY'S GOIN', I SURE WISH YOU WERE.

DO I REALLY WISH THAT?

IS THAT STILL WHAT I WANT?

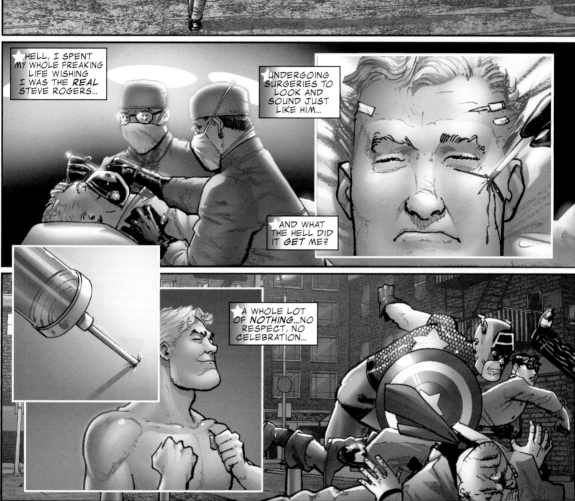

HELL, I SPENT MY WHOLE FREAKING LIFE WISHING I WAS THE *REAL* STEVE ROGERS...

UNDERGOING SURGERIES TO LOOK AND SOUND JUST LIKE HIM...

AND WHAT THE HELL DID IT *GET* ME?

A WHOLE LOT OF *NOTHING*...NO RESPECT, NO CELEBRATION...

JUST BEING LOCKED AWAY AND FORGOTTEN WHEN THEY DIDN'T WANT ME ANYMORE.

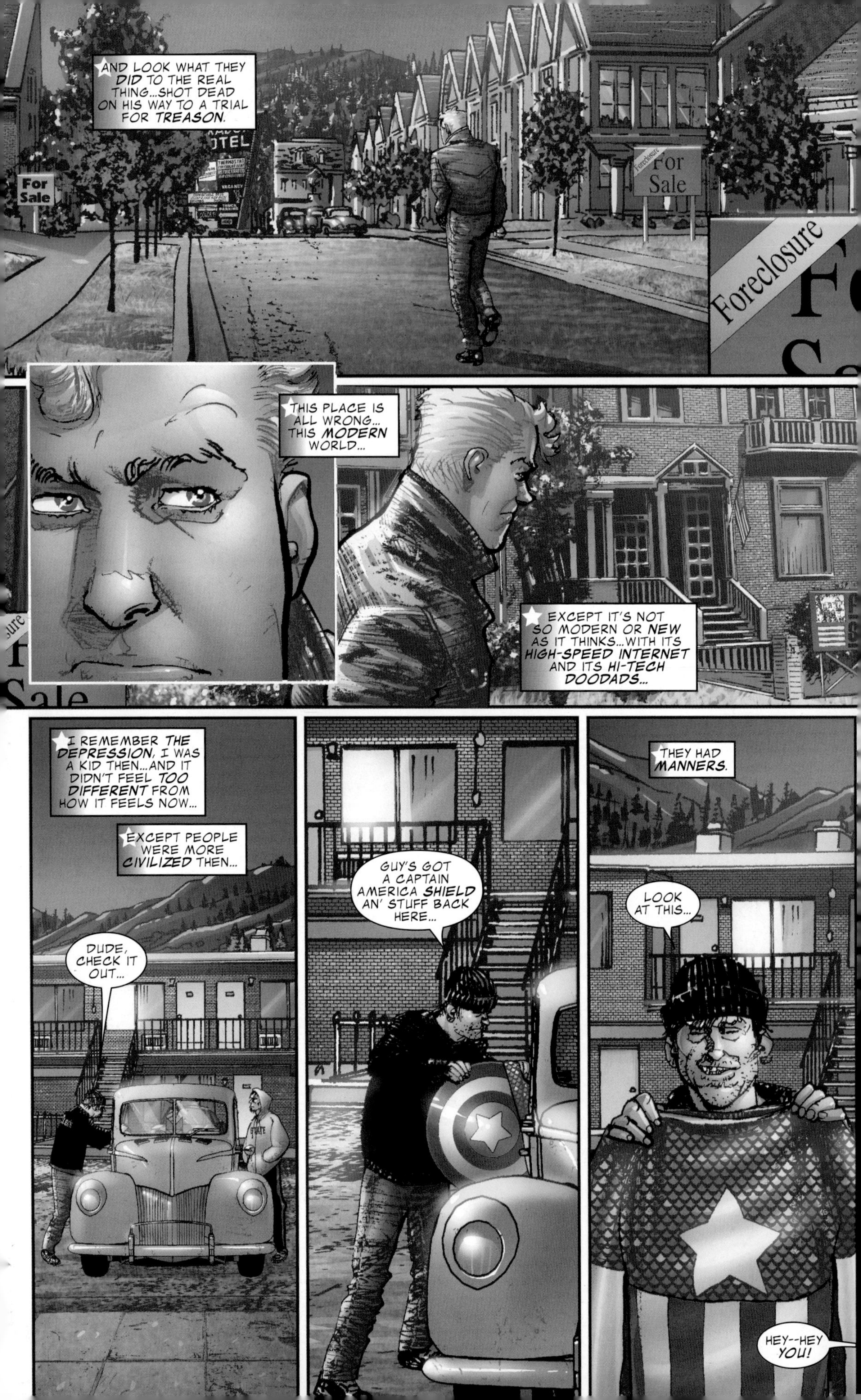
AND LOOK WHAT THEY DID TO THE REAL THING...SHOT DEAD ON HIS WAY TO A TRIAL FOR TREASON.
For Sale
Foreclosure
For Sale
Foreclosure
THIS PLACE IS ALL WRONG... THIS MODERN WORLD...
EXCEPT IT'S NOT SO MODERN OR NEW AS IT THINKS...WITH ITS HIGH-SPEED INTERNET AND ITS HI-TECH DOODADS...
I REMEMBER THE DEPRESSION, I WAS A KID THEN...AND IT DIDN'T FEEL TOO DIFFERENT FROM HOW IT FEELS NOW...
EXCEPT PEOPLE WERE MORE CIVILIZED THEN...
DUDE, CHECK IT OUT...
GUY'S GOT A CAPTAIN AMERICA SHIELD AN' STUFF BACK HERE...
THEY HAD MANNERS.
LOOK AT THIS...
HEY--HEY YOU!

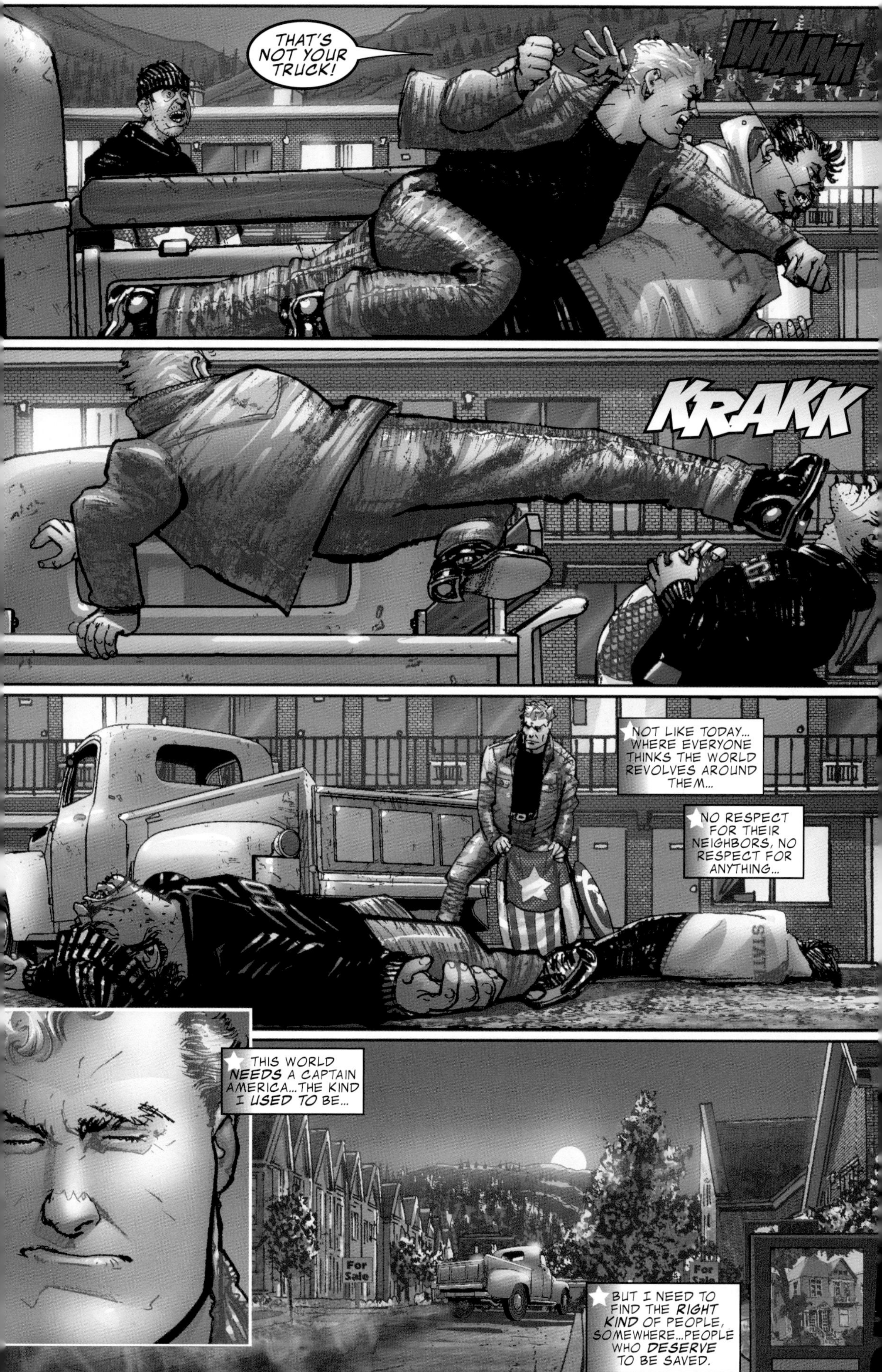

THAT'S NOT YOUR TRUCK!
WHAMM
KRAKK
NOT LIKE TODAY... WHERE EVERYONE THINKS THE WORLD REVOLVES AROUND THEM...
NO RESPECT FOR THEIR NEIGHBORS, NO RESPECT FOR ANYTHING...
THIS WORLD NEEDS A CAPTAIN AMERICA...THE KIND I USED TO BE...
For Sale
BUT I NEED TO FIND THE RIGHT KIND OF PEOPLE, SOMEWHERE...PEOPLE WHO DESERVE TO BE SAVED.

The Youth Of Today

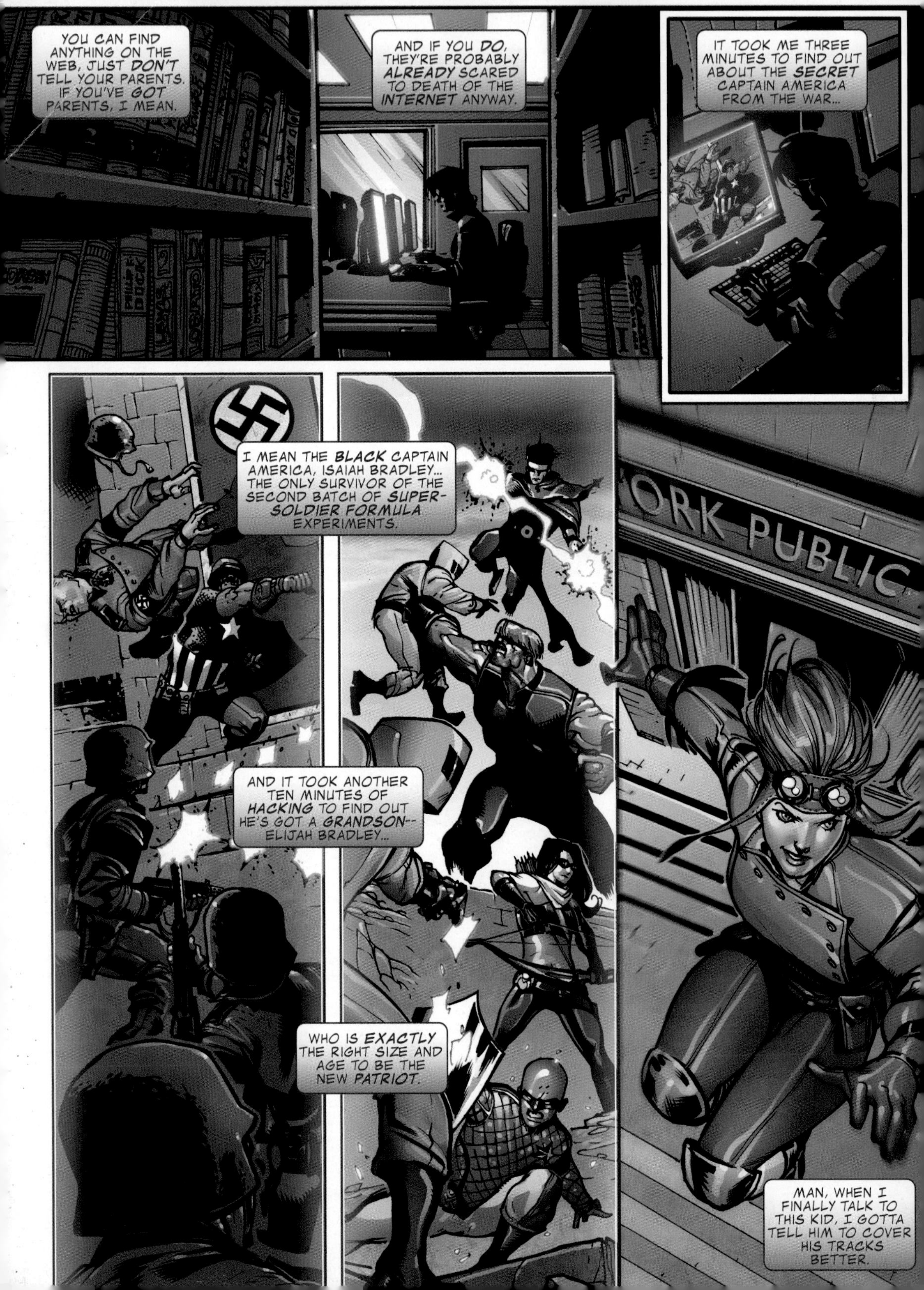

YOU CAN FIND ANYTHING ON THE WEB, JUST DON'T TELL YOUR PARENTS. IF YOU'VE GOT PARENTS, I MEAN.
AND IF YOU DO, THEY'RE PROBABLY ALREADY SCARED TO DEATH OF THE INTERNET ANYWAY.
IT TOOK ME THREE MINUTES TO FIND OUT ABOUT THE SECRET CAPTAIN AMERICA FROM THE WAR...
I MEAN THE BLACK CAPTAIN AMERICA, ISAIAH BRADLEY... THE ONLY SURVIVOR OF THE SECOND BATCH OF SUPER-SOLDIER FORMULA EXPERIMENTS.
AND IT TOOK ANOTHER TEN MINUTES OF HACKING TO FIND OUT HE'S GOT A GRANDSON-- ELIJAH BRADLEY...
WHO IS EXACTLY THE RIGHT SIZE AND AGE TO BE THE NEW PATRIOT.
ORK PUBLIC
MAN, WHEN I FINALLY TALK TO THIS KID, I GOTTA TELL HIM TO COVER HIS TRACKS BETTER.

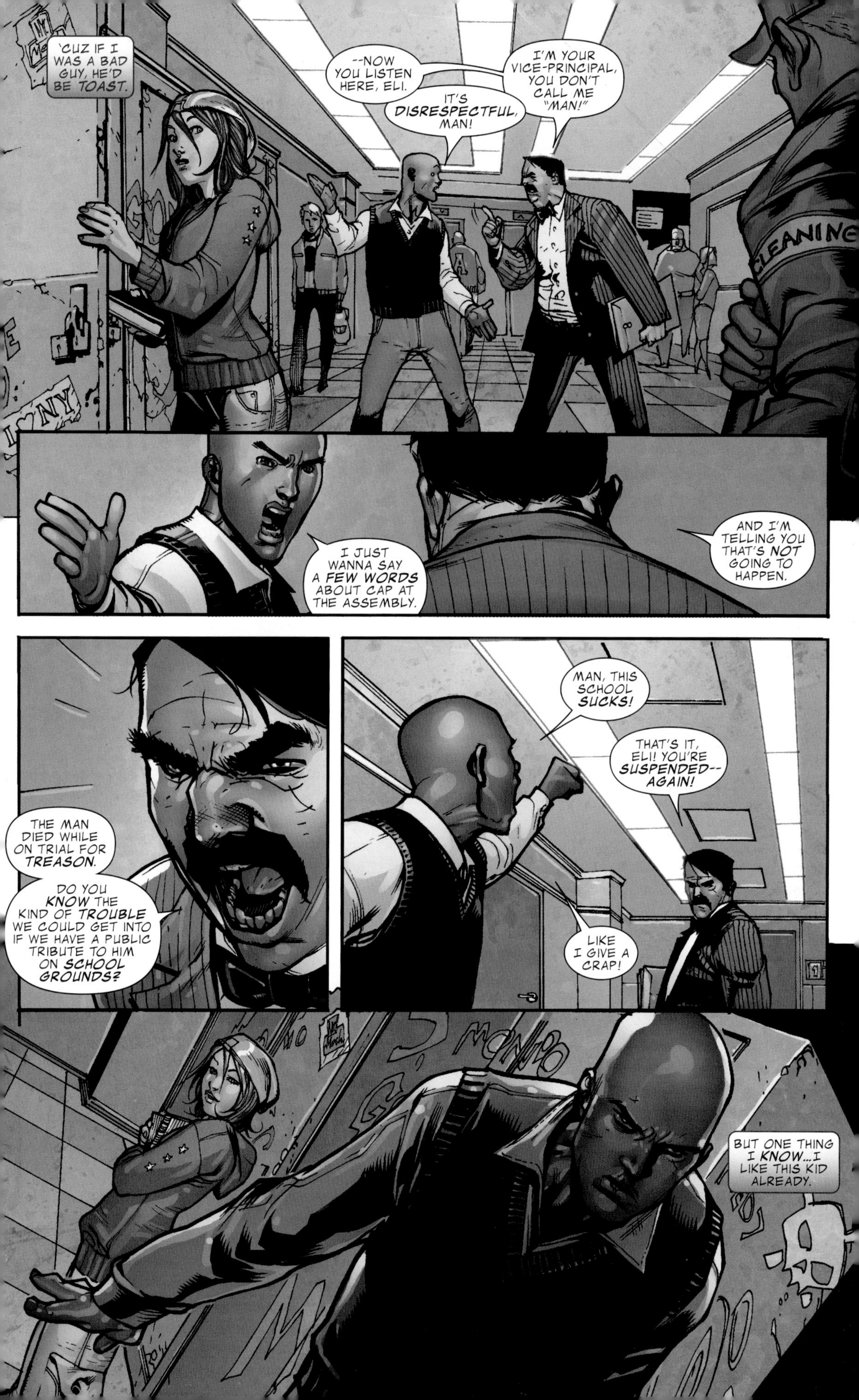

'CUZ IF I WAS A BAD GUY, HE'D BE *TOAST*.
--NOW YOU LISTEN HERE, ELI.
I'M YOUR VICE-PRINCIPAL, YOU DON'T CALL ME "MAN!"
IT'S **DISRESPECTFUL**, MAN!
I JUST WANNA SAY A **FEW WORDS** ABOUT CAP AT THE ASSEMBLY.
AND I'M TELLING YOU THAT'S **NOT** GOING TO HAPPEN.
THE MAN DIED WHILE ON TRIAL FOR **TREASON**.
DO YOU **KNOW** THE KIND OF **TROUBLE** WE COULD GET INTO IF WE HAVE A PUBLIC TRIBUTE TO HIM ON **SCHOOL GROUNDS**?
MAN, THIS SCHOOL **SUCKS!**
THAT'S IT, ELI! YOU'RE **SUSPENDED--** AGAIN!
LIKE I GIVE A CRAP!
BUT ONE THING I *KNOW*...I LIKE THIS KID ALREADY.
CLEANING
I ♥ NY

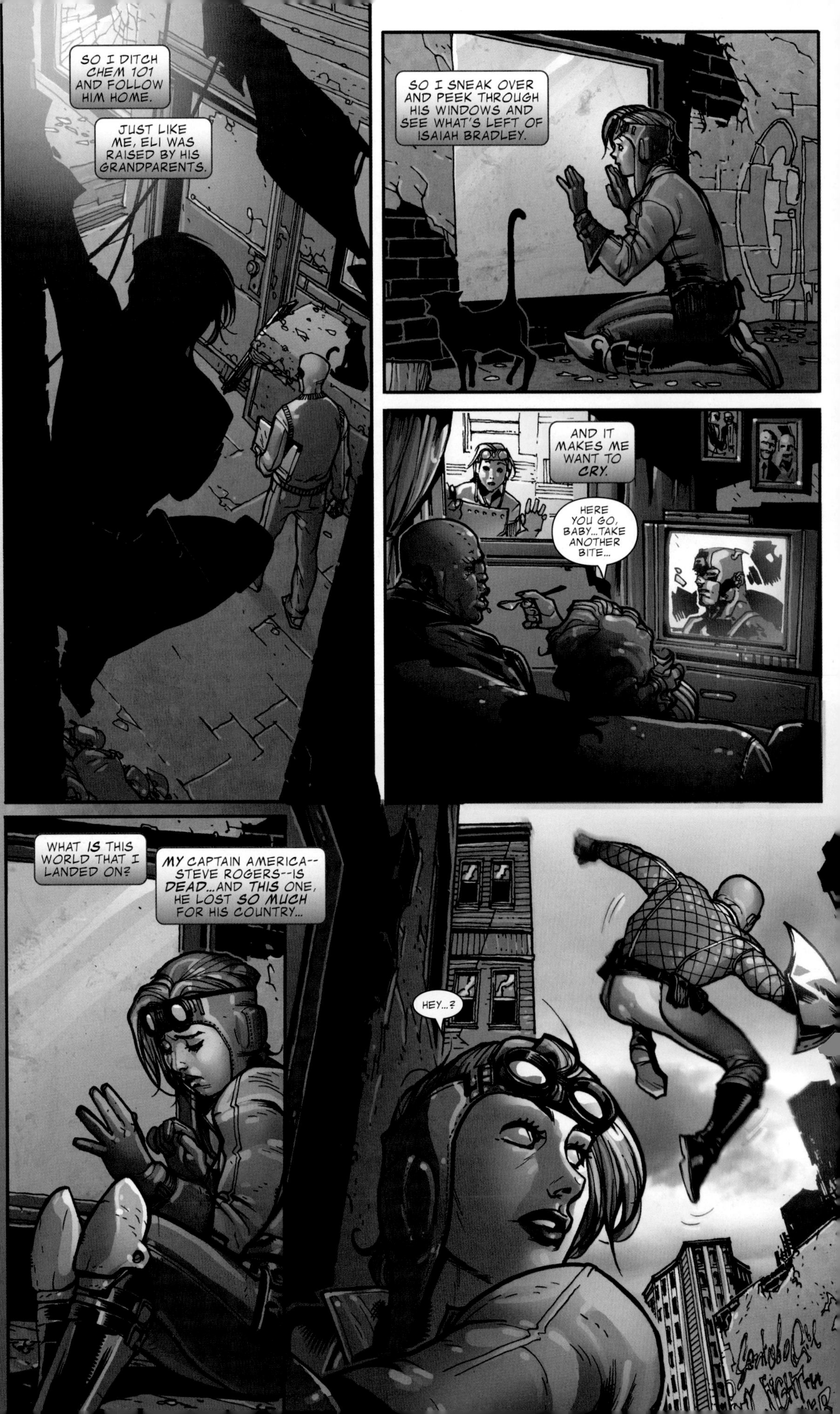
SO I DITCH CHEM 101 AND FOLLOW HIM HOME.
JUST LIKE ME, ELI WAS RAISED BY HIS GRANDPARENTS.
SO I SNEAK OVER AND PEEK THROUGH HIS WINDOWS AND SEE WHAT'S LEFT OF ISAIAH BRADLEY.
AND IT MAKES ME WANT TO CRY.
HERE YOU GO, BABY...TAKE ANOTHER BITE...
WHAT IS THIS WORLD THAT I LANDED ON?
MY CAPTAIN AMERICA--STEVE ROGERS--IS DEAD...AND THIS ONE, HE LOST SO MUCH FOR HIS COUNTRY...
HEY...?

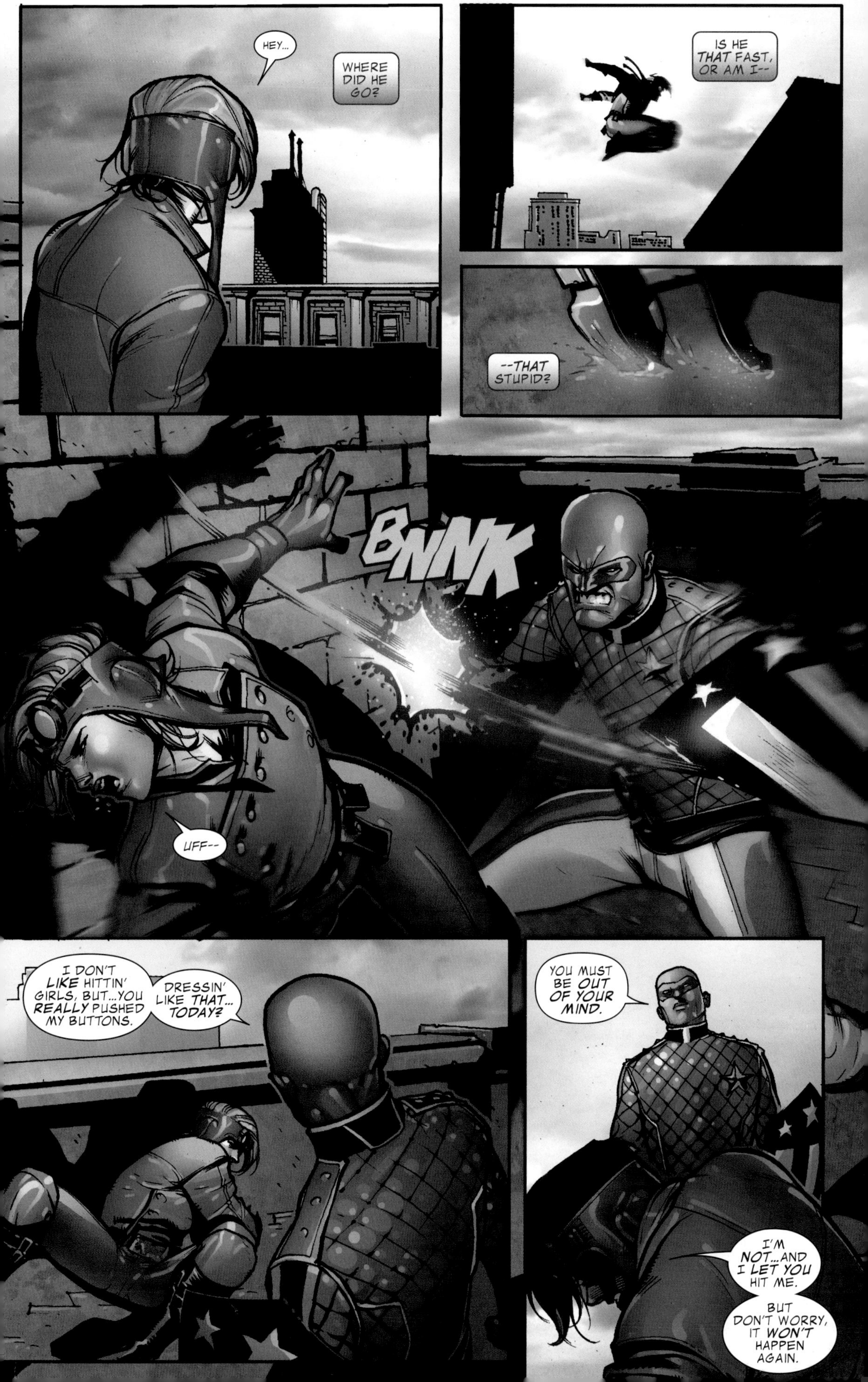
HEY...
WHERE DID HE GO?
IS HE THAT FAST, OR AM I--
--THAT STUPID?
BNNK
UFF--
I DON'T LIKE HITTIN' GIRLS, BUT...YOU REALLY PUSHED MY BUTTONS.
DRESSIN' LIKE THAT... TODAY?
YOU MUST BE OUT OF YOUR MIND.
I'M NOT...AND I LET YOU HIT ME.
BUT DON'T WORRY, IT WON'T HAPPEN AGAIN.

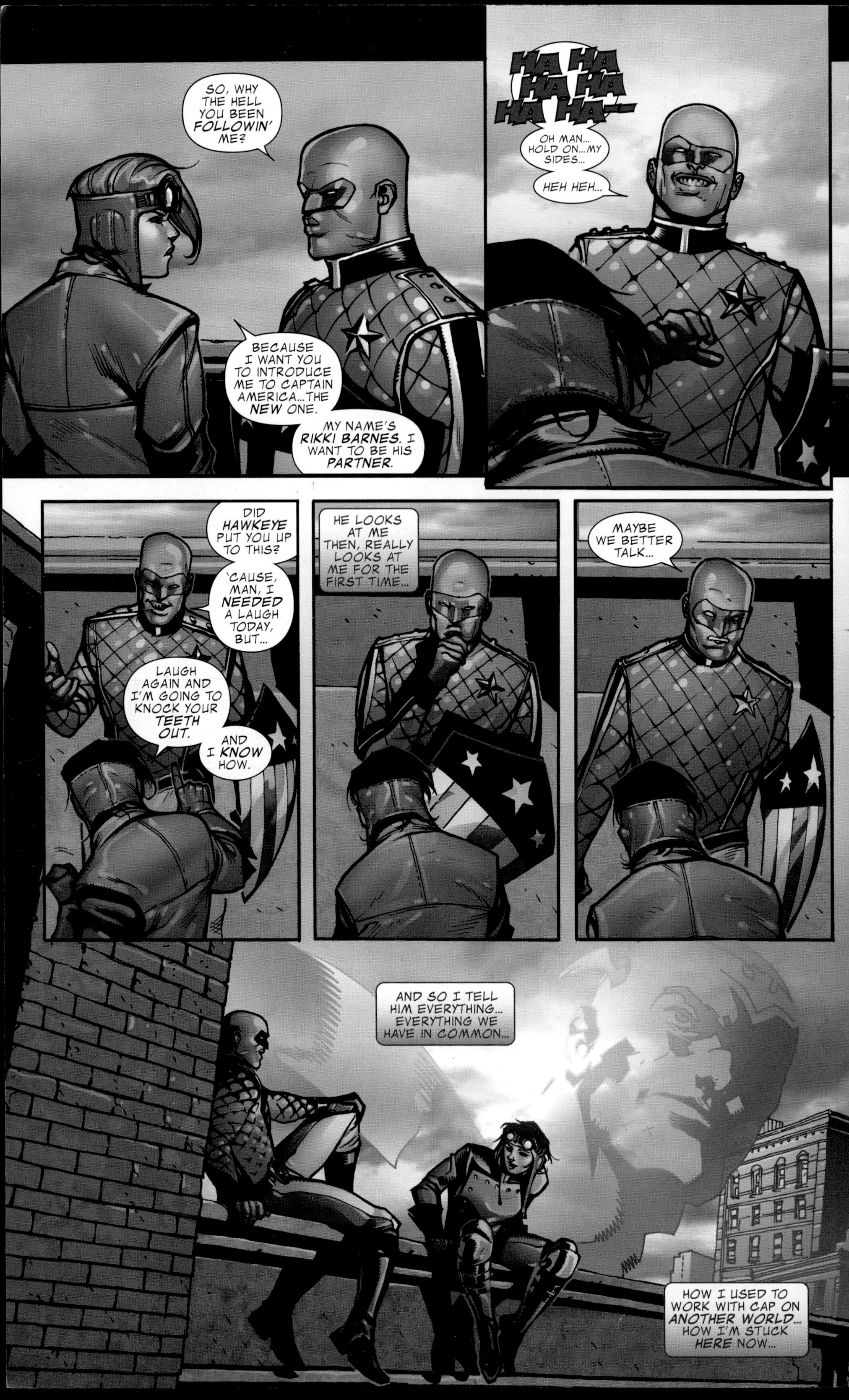
SO, WHY THE HELL YOU BEEN FOLLOWIN' ME?
BECAUSE I WANT YOU TO INTRODUCE ME TO CAPTAIN AMERICA...THE NEW ONE.
MY NAME'S RIKKI BARNES. I WANT TO BE HIS PARTNER.
HA HA HA HA HA HA--
OH MAN... HOLD ON...MY SIDES...
HEH HEH...
DID HAWKEYE PUT YOU UP TO THIS?
'CAUSE, MAN, I NEEDED A LAUGH TODAY, BUT...
LAUGH AGAIN AND I'M GOING TO KNOCK YOUR TEETH OUT.
AND I KNOW HOW.
HE LOOKS AT ME THEN, REALLY LOOKS AT ME FOR THE FIRST TIME...
MAYBE WE BETTER TALK...
AND SO I TELL HIM EVERYTHING... EVERYTHING WE HAVE IN COMMON...
HOW I USED TO WORK WITH CAP ON ANOTHER WORLD... HOW I'M STUCK HERE NOW...

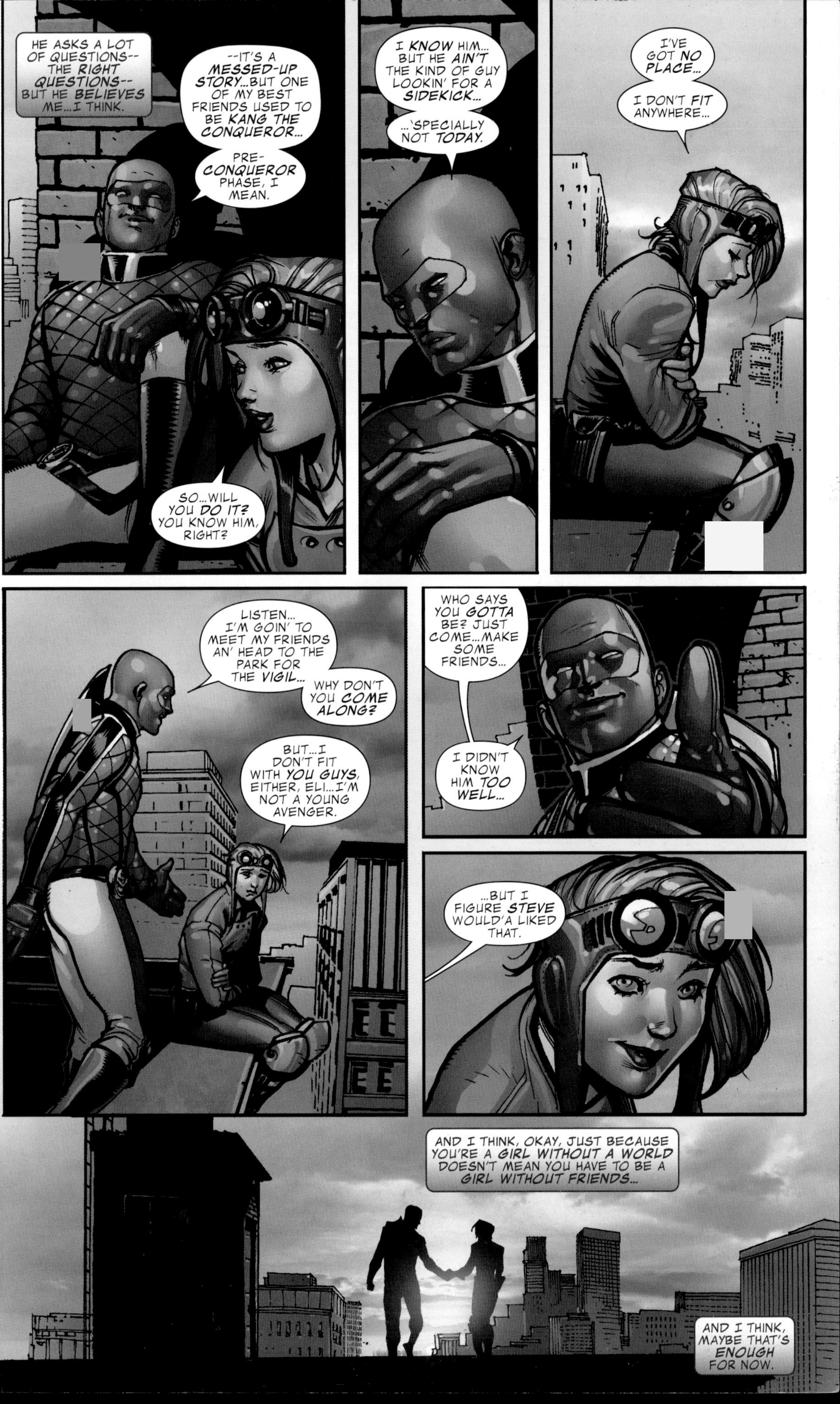

HE ASKS A LOT OF QUESTIONS-- THE RIGHT QUESTIONS-- BUT HE BELIEVES ME...I THINK.
--IT'S A MESSED-UP STORY...BUT ONE OF MY BEST FRIENDS USED TO BE KANG THE CONQUEROR...
PRE-CONQUEROR PHASE, I MEAN.
SO...WILL YOU DO IT? YOU KNOW HIM, RIGHT?
I KNOW HIM... BUT HE AIN'T THE KIND OF GUY LOOKIN' FOR A SIDEKICK...
...'SPECIALLY NOT TODAY.
I'VE GOT NO PLACE...
I DON'T FIT ANYWHERE...
LISTEN... I'M GOIN' TO MEET MY FRIENDS AN' HEAD TO THE PARK FOR THE VIGIL...
WHY DON'T YOU COME ALONG?
BUT...I DON'T FIT WITH YOU GUYS, EITHER, ELI...I'M NOT A YOUNG AVENGER.
WHO SAYS YOU GOTTA BE? JUST COME...MAKE SOME FRIENDS...
I DIDN'T KNOW HIM TOO WELL...
...BUT I FIGURE STEVE WOULD'A LIKED THAT.
AND I THINK, OKAY, JUST BECAUSE YOU'RE A GIRL WITHOUT A WORLD DOESN'T MEAN YOU HAVE TO BE A GIRL WITHOUT FRIENDS...
AND I THINK, MAYBE THAT'S ENOUGH FOR NOW.

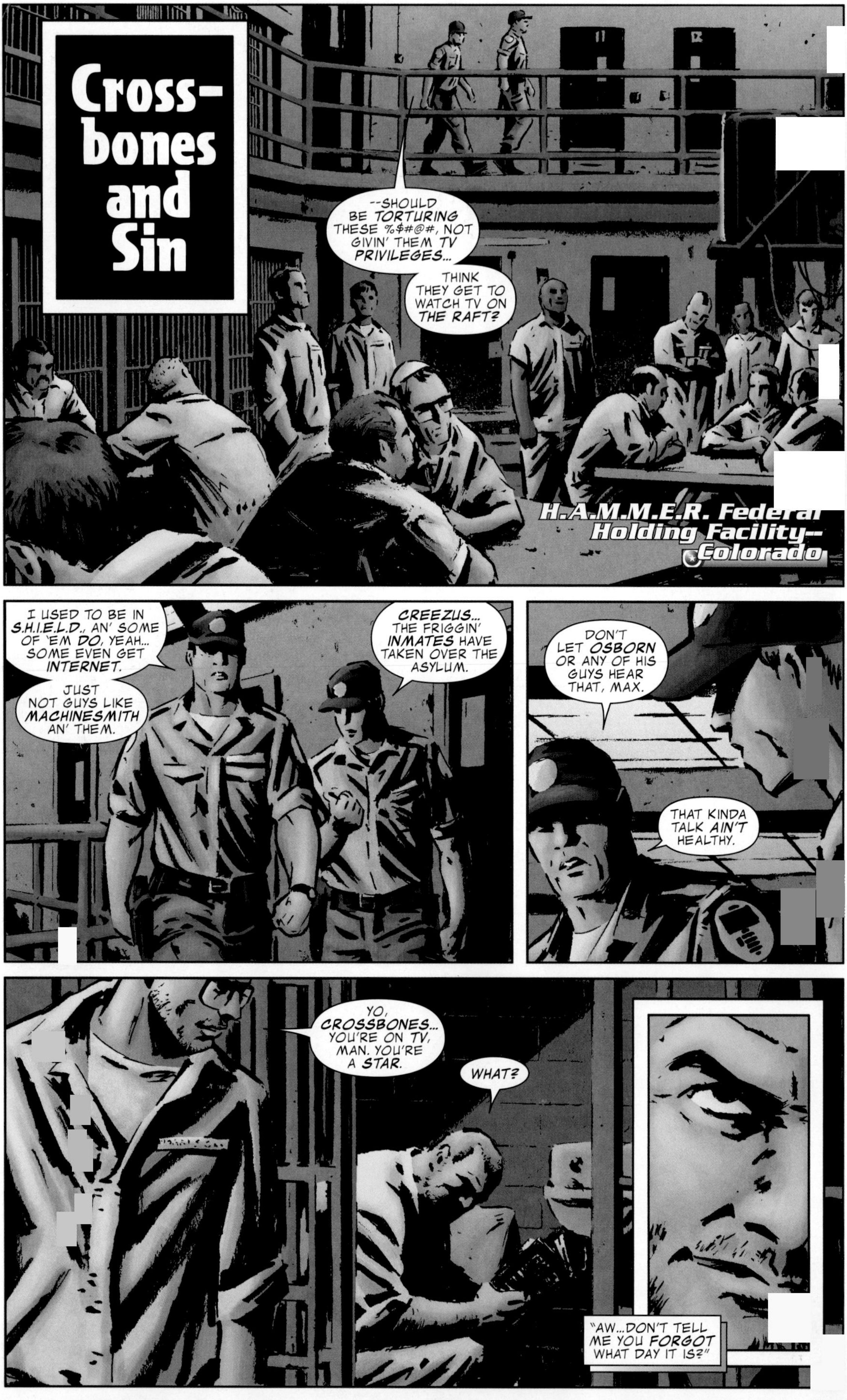
Cross-bones and Sin
--SHOULD BE TORTURING THESE %$#@#, NOT GIVIN' THEM TV PRIVILEGES...
THINK THEY GET TO WATCH TV ON THE RAFT?
H.A.M.M.E.R. Federal Holding Facility-- Colorado
I USED TO BE IN S.H.I.E.L.D., AN' SOME OF 'EM DO, YEAH... SOME EVEN GET INTERNET.
JUST NOT GUYS LIKE MACHINESMITH AN' THEM.
CREEZUS... THE FRIGGIN' INMATES HAVE TAKEN OVER THE ASYLUM.
DON'T LET OSBORN OR ANY OF HIS GUYS HEAR THAT, MAX.
THAT KINDA TALK AIN'T HEALTHY.
YO, CROSSBONES... YOU'RE ON TV, MAN. YOU'RE A STAR.
WHAT?
"AW...DON'T TELL ME YOU FORGOT WHAT DAY IT IS?"

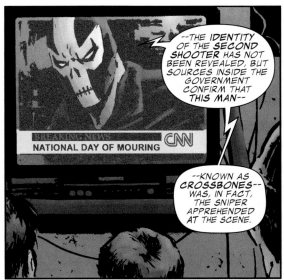

--THE IDENTITY OF THE *SECOND SHOOTER* HAS NOT BEEN REVEALED, BUT SOURCES INSIDE THE GOVERNMENT CONFIRM THAT *THIS MAN*--

BREAKING NEWS CNN
NATIONAL DAY OF MOURING

--KNOWN AS *CROSSBONES*-- WAS, IN FACT, THE SNIPER APPREHENDED AT THE SCENE.

YOU *FAMOUS*, DOG!

RIGHT ON, BROCK!

NATIONAL DAY OF MOURING CNN

PFFT...NATIONAL DAY OF MOURNING FOR *THAT LOSER...*

THEY DON'T EVEN *KNOW* WHAT HAPPENED... A FRIGGIN' *JOKE...*

BROCK

HEH HEH HEH...

OH, THAT IS IT...

YOU'RE GONNA *LAUGH* ABOUT IT?!

BZZZZ

YOU'RE GONNA *LAUGH* ABOUT *KILLIN'* CAP?!

GYAAH--

BZZZAATT

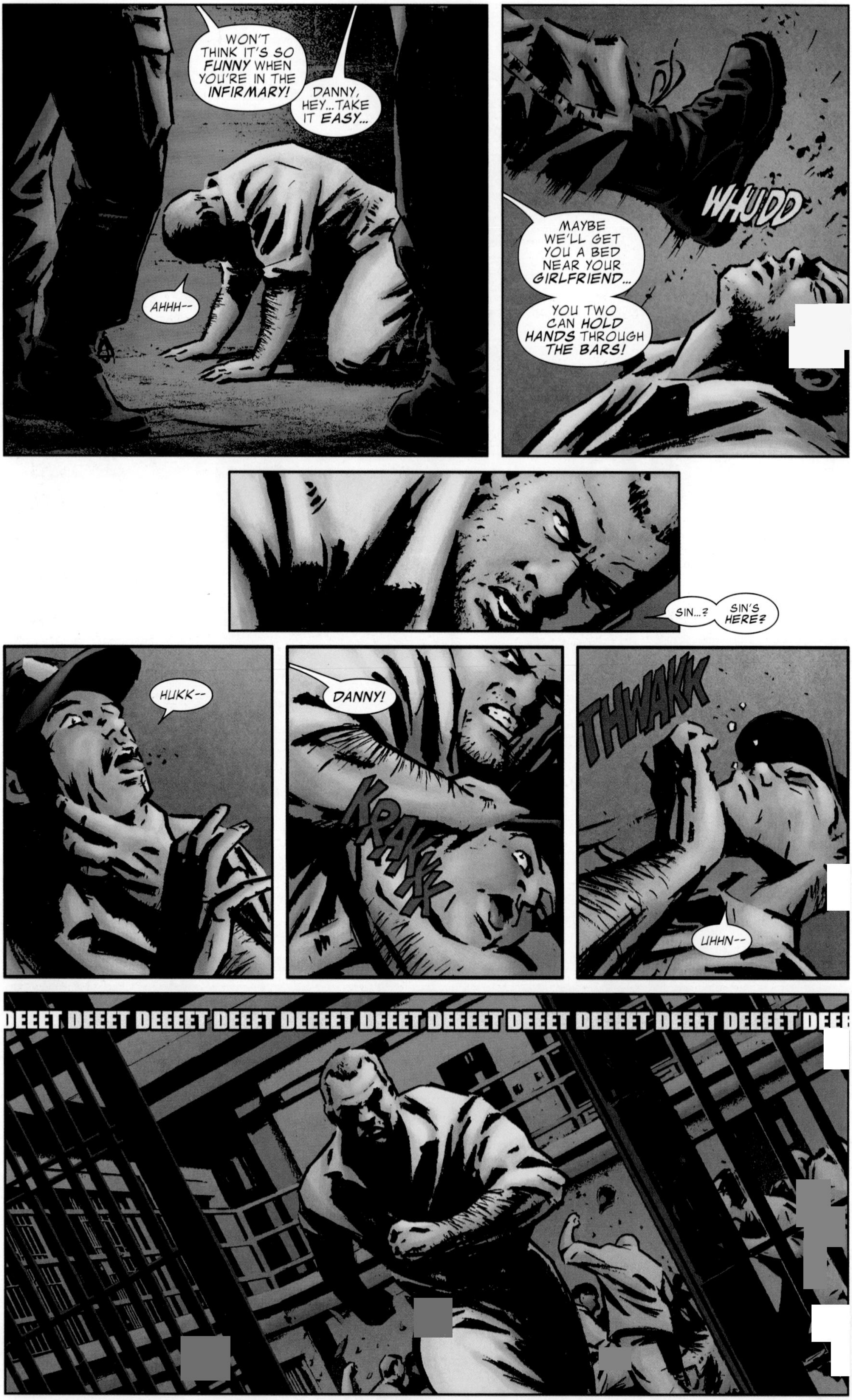

WON'T THINK IT'S SO FUNNY WHEN YOU'RE IN THE INFIRMARY!
DANNY, HEY...TAKE IT EASY...
AHHH--
WHUDD
MAYBE WE'LL GET YOU A BED NEAR YOUR GIRLFRIEND...
YOU TWO CAN HOLD HANDS THROUGH THE BARS!
SIN...?
SIN'S HERE?
HUKK--
DANNY!
KRAKKK
THWAKK
UHHN--
DEEET DEEET DEEEET DEEET DEEEET DEEET DEEEET DEEET DEEEET DEEET DEEEET

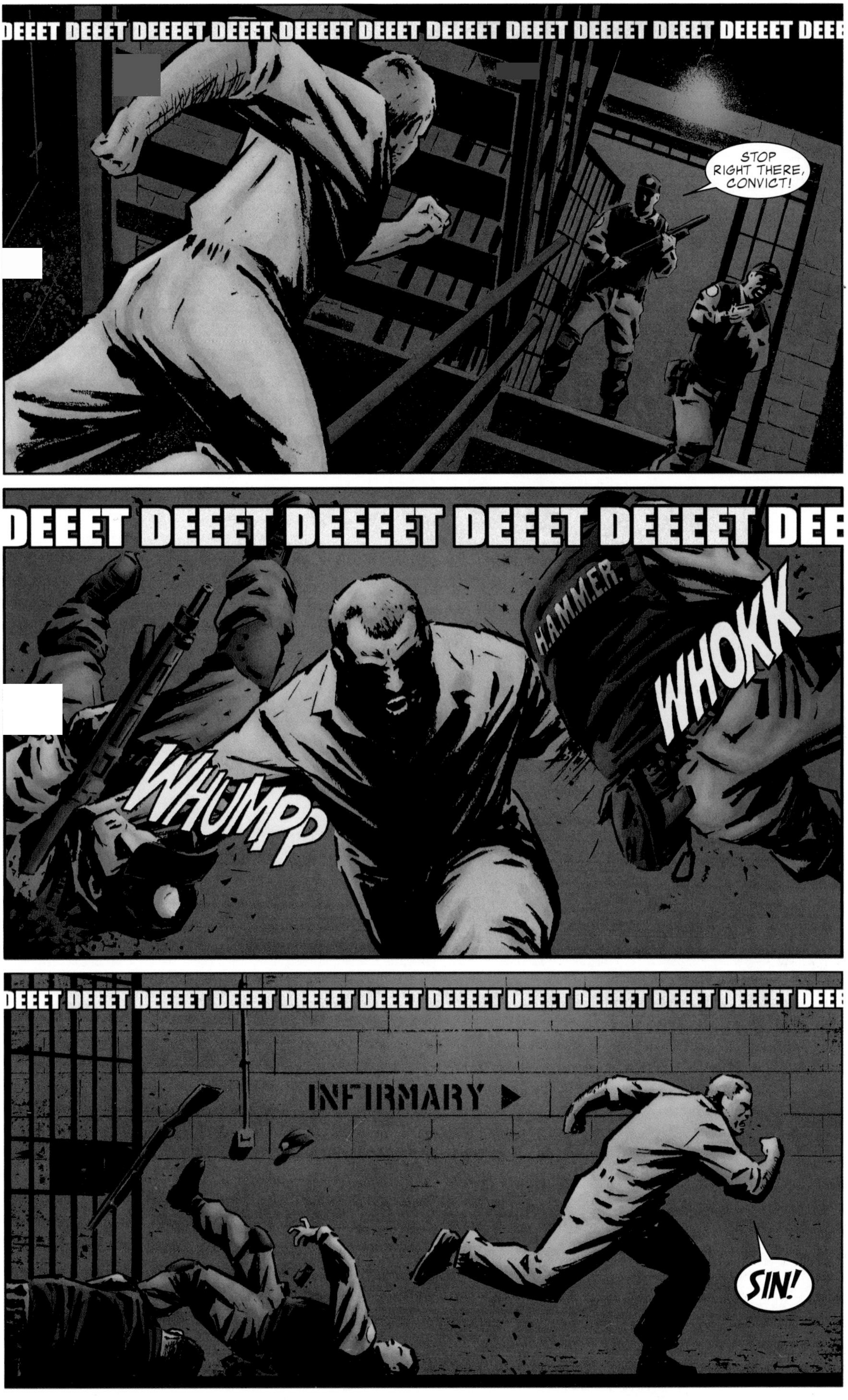
DEEET DEEET DEEEET DEEET DEEEET DEEET DEEEET DEEET DEEEET DEEET DEEEET DEE
STOP RIGHT THERE, CONVICT!
DEEET DEEET DEEEET DEEET DEEEET DEE
H.A.M.M.E.R.
WHUMPP
WHOKK
DEEET DEEET DEEEET DEEET DEEEET DEEET DEEEET DEEET DEEEET DEEET DEEEET DEE
INFIRMARY ▶
SIN!

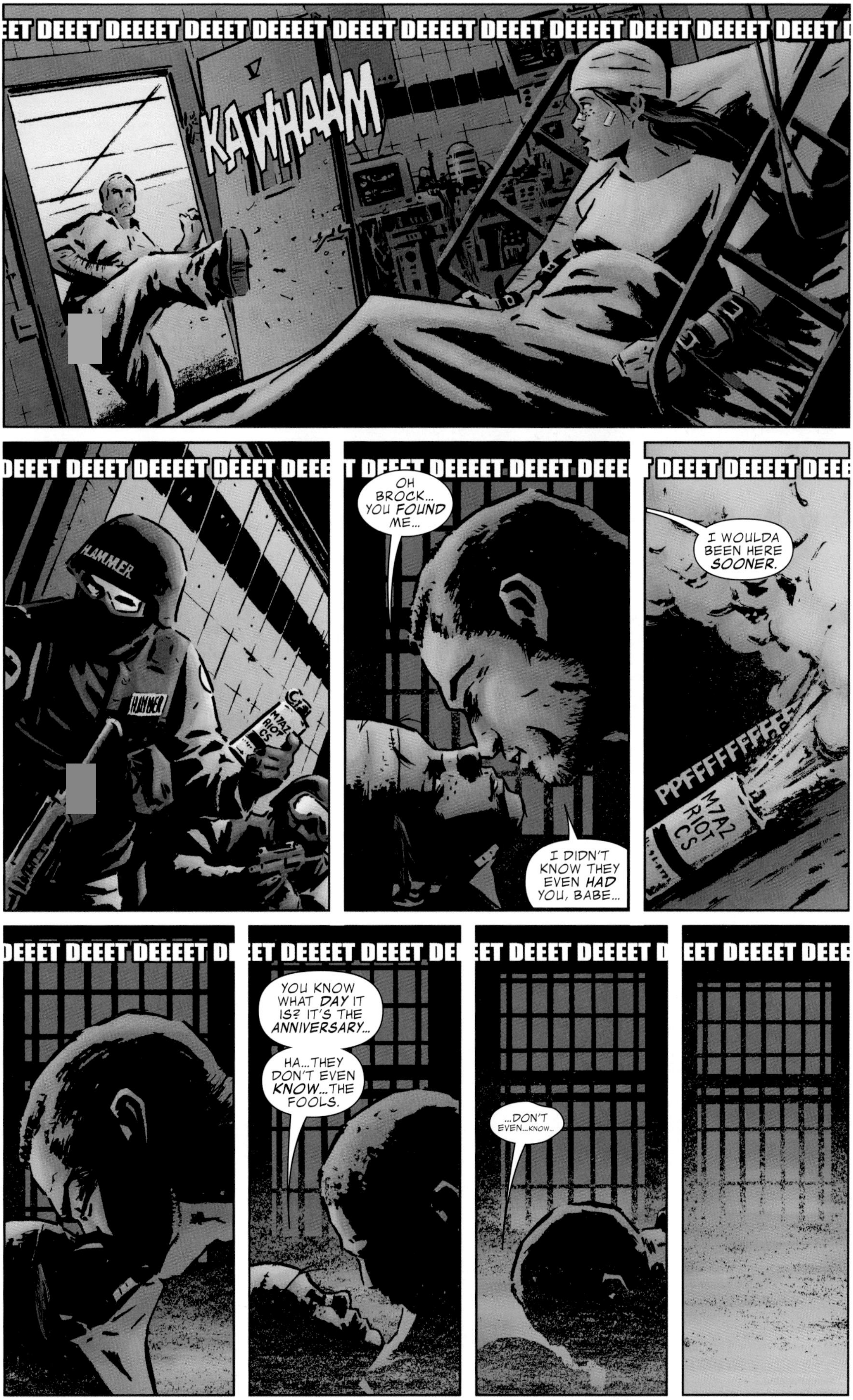
DEEET DEEEET DEEET DEEEET DEEET DEEEET DEEET DEEEET DEEEET DEEET
KAWHAAM
DEEET DEEET DEEEET DEEET
HAMMER
M7A2 RIOT CS
OH BROCK... YOU FOUND ME...
I DIDN'T KNOW THEY EVEN HAD YOU, BABE...
I WOULDA BEEN HERE SOONER.
PPFFFFFFFFF
M7A2 RIOT CS
DEEET DEEET DEEEET
YOU KNOW WHAT DAY IT IS? IT'S THE ANNIVERSARY...
HA...THEY DON'T EVEN KNOW...THE FOOLS.
...DON'T EVEN...KNOW...

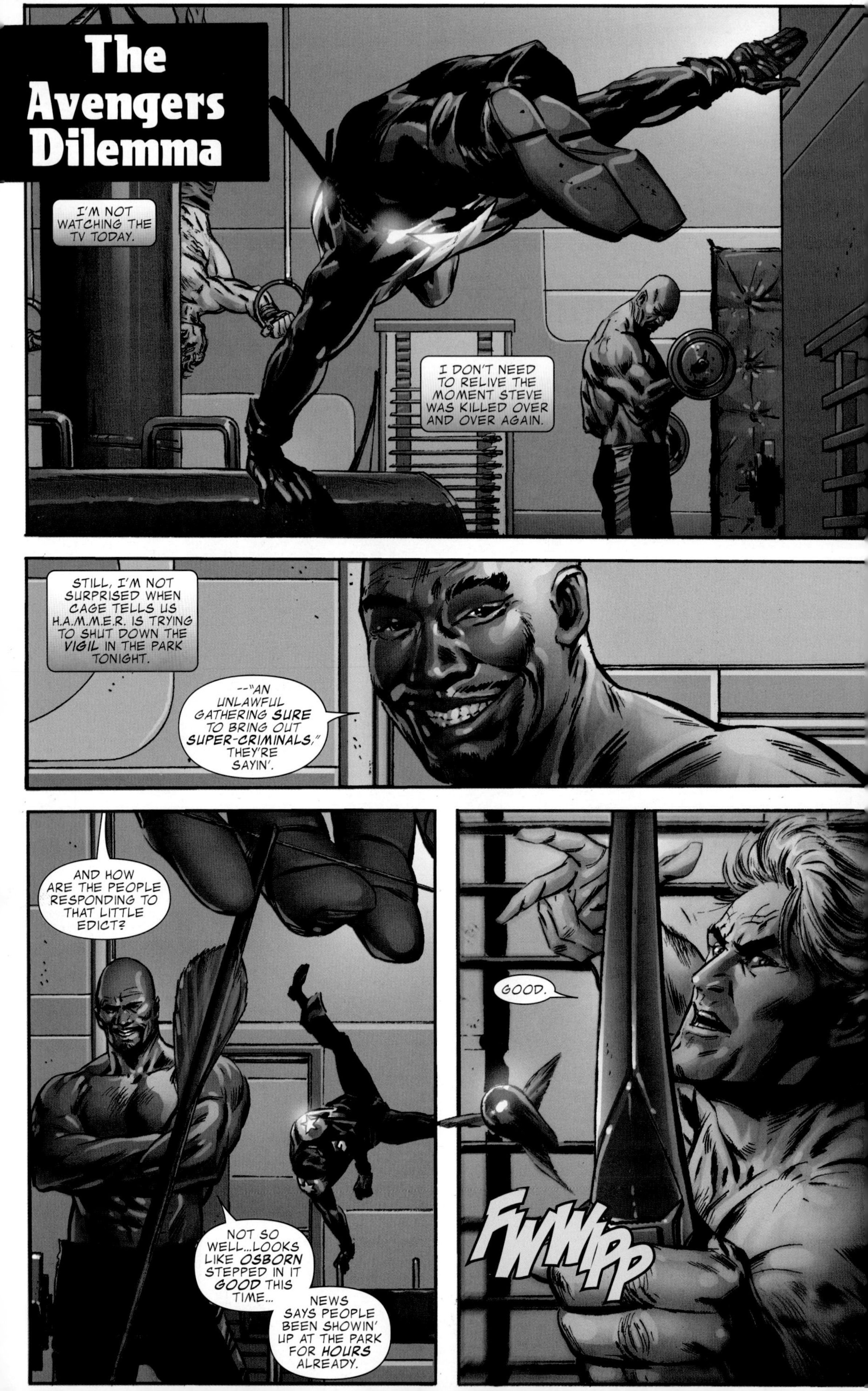

The Avengers Dilemma
I'M NOT WATCHING THE TV TODAY.
I DON'T NEED TO RELIVE THE MOMENT STEVE WAS KILLED OVER AND OVER AGAIN.
STILL, I'M NOT SURPRISED WHEN CAGE TELLS US H.A.M.M.E.R. IS TRYING TO SHUT DOWN THE VIGIL IN THE PARK TONIGHT.
--"AN UNLAWFUL GATHERING SURE TO BRING OUT SUPER-CRIMINALS," THEY'RE SAYIN'.
AND HOW ARE THE PEOPLE RESPONDING TO THAT LITTLE EDICT?
GOOD.
NOT SO WELL...LOOKS LIKE OSBORN STEPPED IN IT GOOD THIS TIME...
NEWS SAYS PEOPLE BEEN SHOWIN' UP AT THE PARK FOR HOURS ALREADY.
FWWIPP

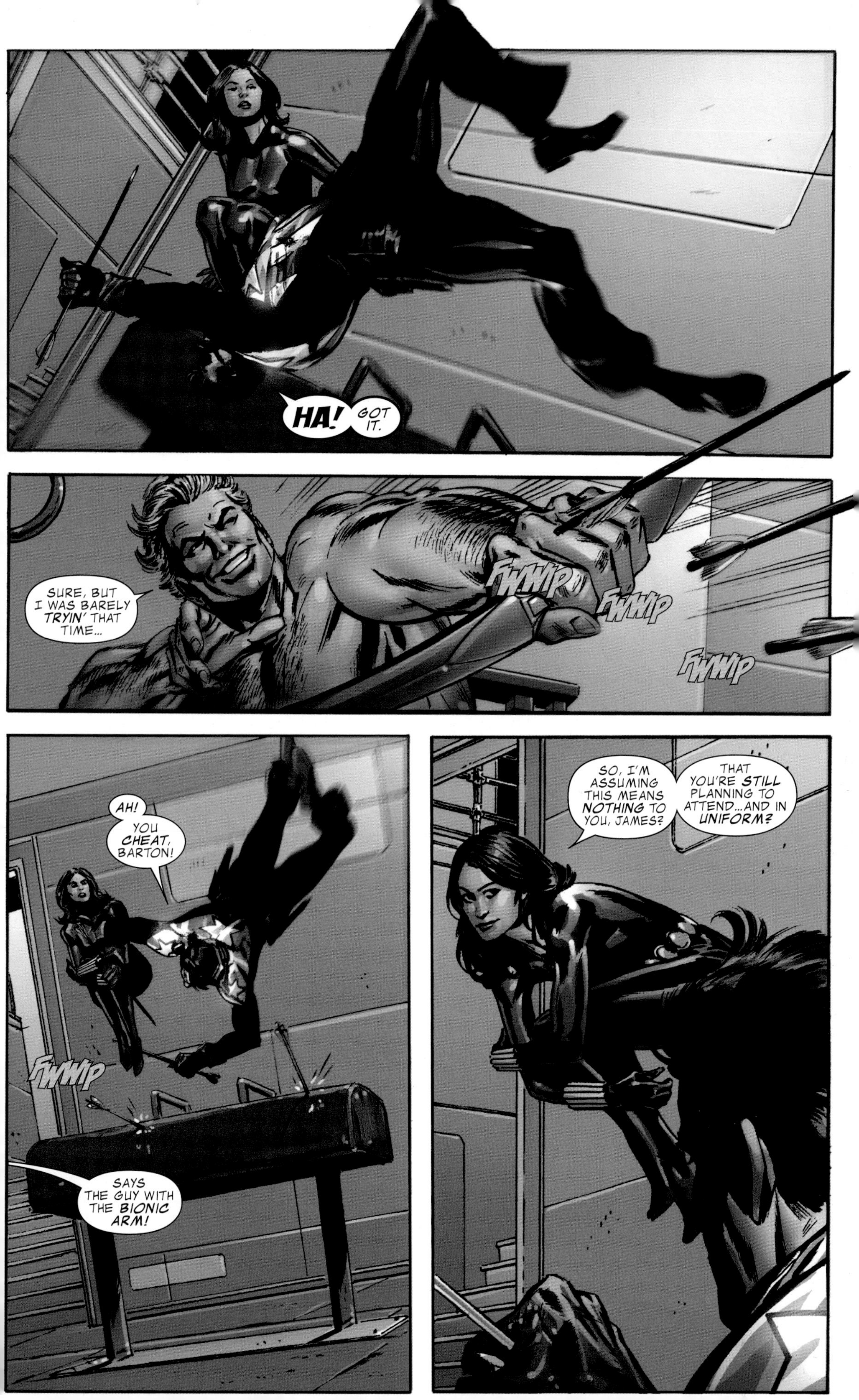
HA!
GOT IT.
SURE, BUT I WAS BARELY TRYIN' THAT TIME...
FWWIP
FWWIP
FWWIP
AH! YOU CHEAT, BARTON!
FWWIP
SAYS THE GUY WITH THE BIONIC ARM!
SO, I'M ASSUMING THIS MEANS NOTHING TO YOU, JAMES?
THAT YOU'RE STILL PLANNING TO ATTEND...AND IN UNIFORM?

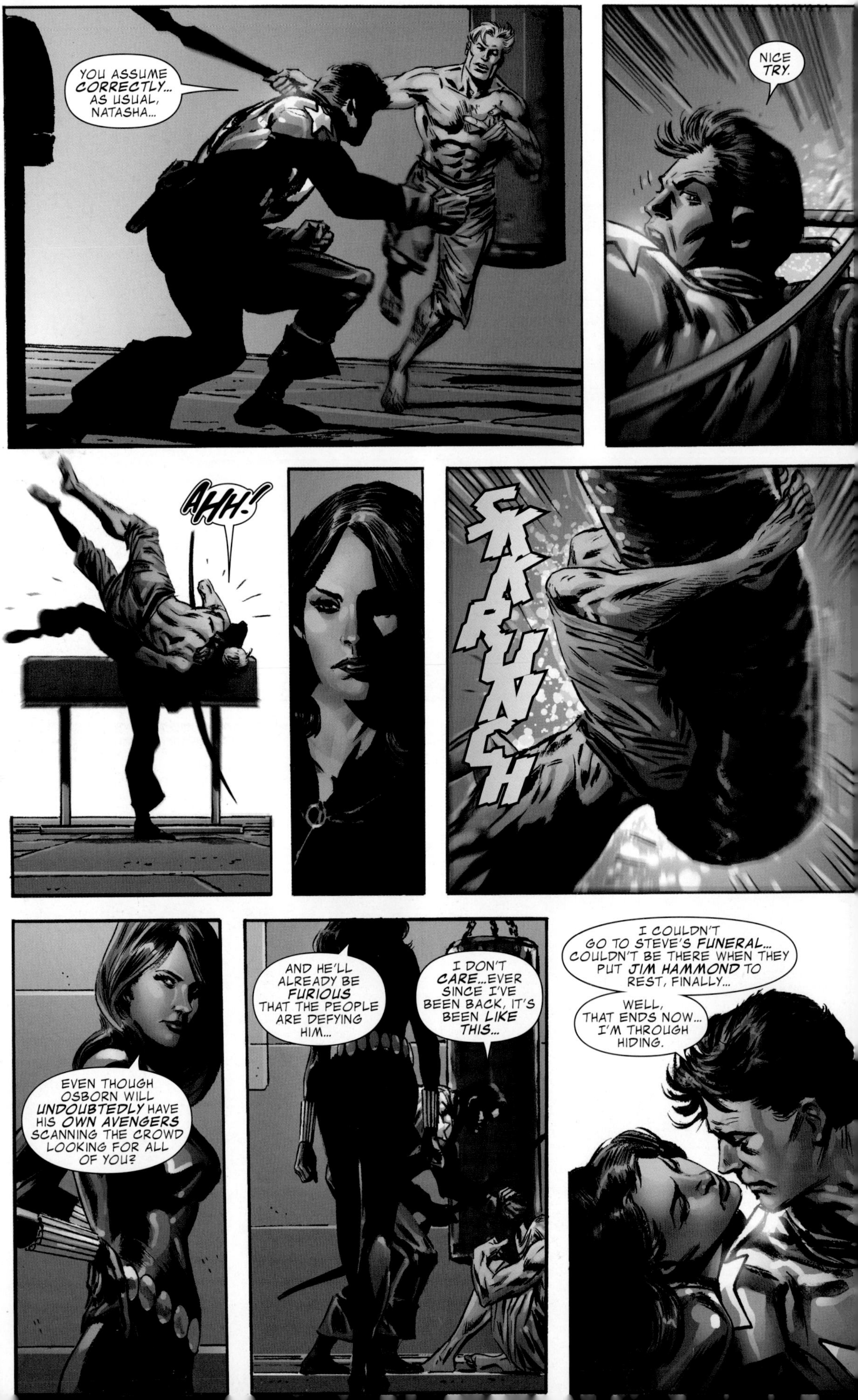
YOU ASSUME CORRECTLY... AS USUAL, NATASHA...
NICE TRY.
AHH!
SKRUNCH
EVEN THOUGH OSBORN WILL UNDOUBTEDLY HAVE HIS OWN AVENGERS SCANNING THE CROWD LOOKING FOR ALL OF YOU?
AND HE'LL ALREADY BE FURIOUS THAT THE PEOPLE ARE DEFYING HIM...
I DON'T CARE...EVER SINCE I'VE BEEN BACK, IT'S BEEN LIKE THIS...
I COULDN'T GO TO STEVE'S FUNERAL... COULDN'T BE THERE WHEN THEY PUT JIM HAMMOND TO REST, FINALLY...
WELL, THAT ENDS NOW... I'M THROUGH HIDING.

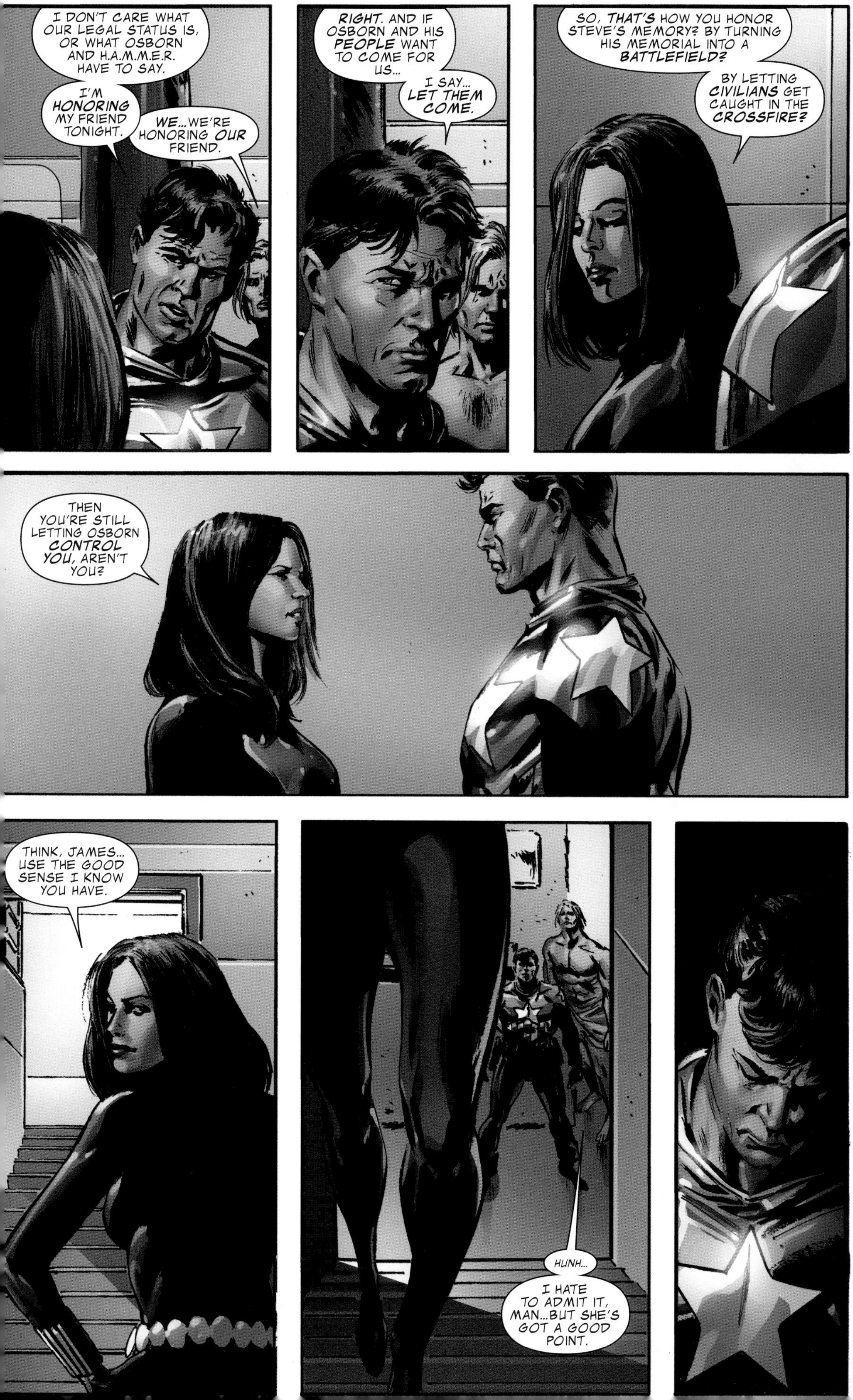
I DON'T CARE WHAT OUR LEGAL STATUS IS, OR WHAT OSBORN AND H.A.M.M.E.R. HAVE TO SAY.
I'M HONORING MY FRIEND TONIGHT.
WE...WE'RE HONORING OUR FRIEND.
RIGHT. AND IF OSBORN AND HIS PEOPLE WANT TO COME FOR US...
I SAY... LET THEM COME.
SO, THAT'S HOW YOU HONOR STEVE'S MEMORY? BY TURNING HIS MEMORIAL INTO A BATTLEFIELD?
BY LETTING CIVILIANS GET CAUGHT IN THE CROSSFIRE?
THEN YOU'RE STILL LETTING OSBORN CONTROL YOU, AREN'T YOU?
THINK, JAMES... USE THE GOOD SENSE I KNOW YOU HAVE.
HUNH...
I HATE TO ADMIT IT, MAN...BUT SHE'S GOT A GOOD POINT.

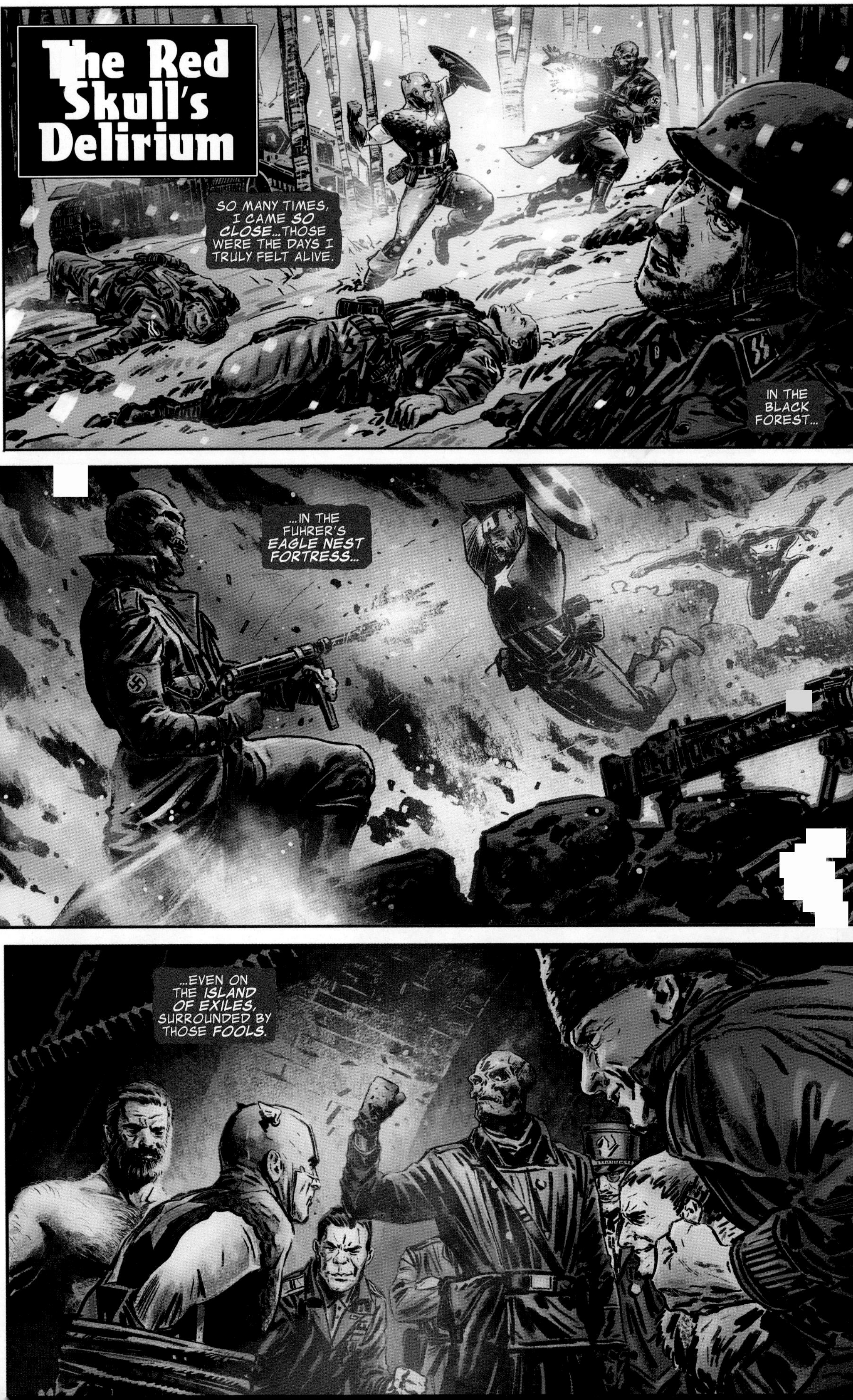

The Red Skull's Delirium
SO MANY TIMES, I CAME SO CLOSE...THOSE WERE THE DAYS I TRULY FELT ALIVE.
IN THE BLACK FOREST...
...IN THE FUHRER'S EAGLE NEST FORTRESS...
...EVEN ON THE ISLAND OF EXILES, SURROUNDED BY THOSE FOOLS.

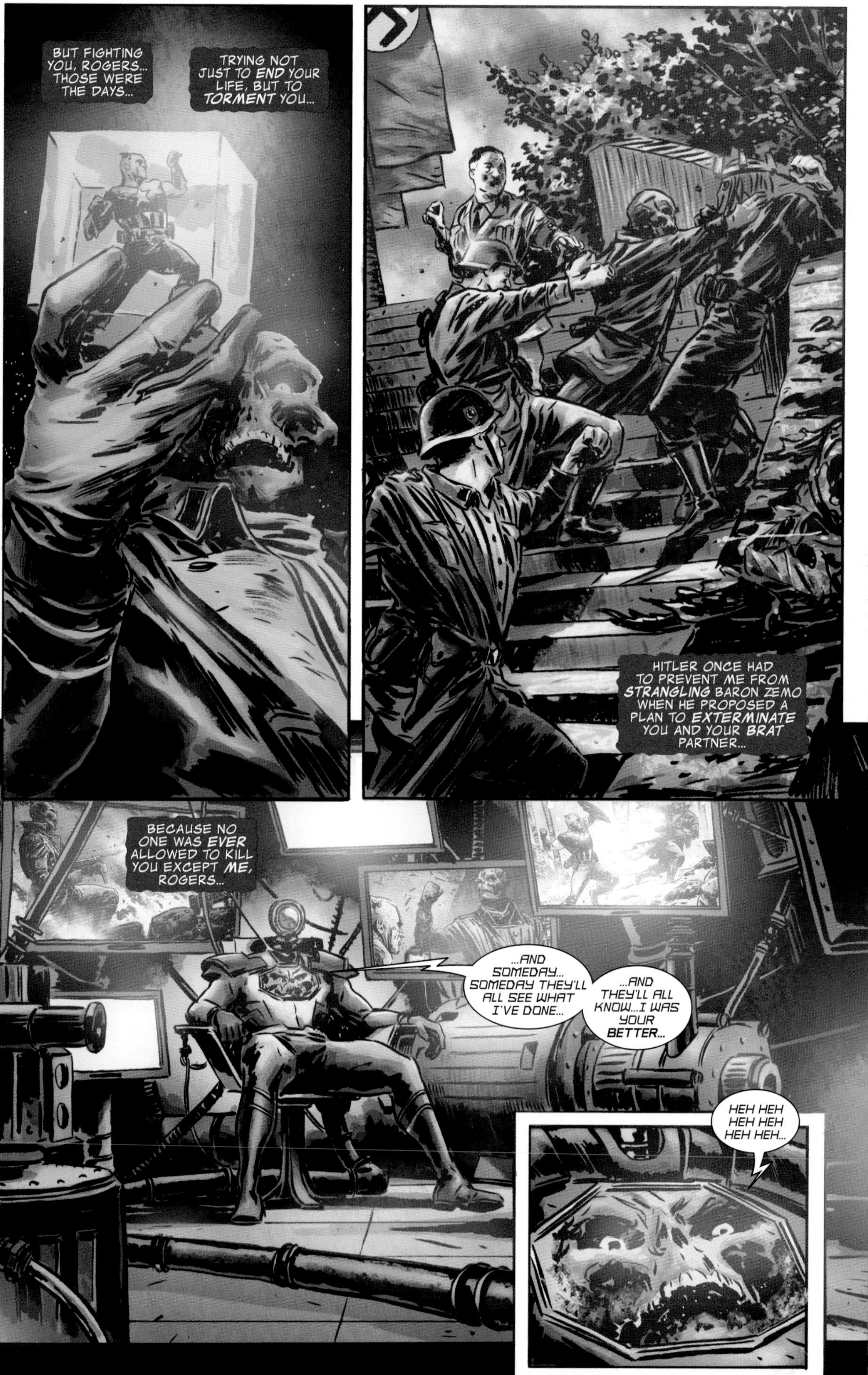
BUT FIGHTING YOU, ROGERS... THOSE WERE THE DAYS...
TRYING NOT JUST TO END YOUR LIFE, BUT TO TORMENT YOU...
HITLER ONCE HAD TO PREVENT ME FROM STRANGLING BARON ZEMO WHEN HE PROPOSED A PLAN TO EXTERMINATE YOU AND YOUR BRAT PARTNER...
BECAUSE NO ONE WAS EVER ALLOWED TO KILL YOU EXCEPT ME, ROGERS...
...AND SOMEDAY... SOMEDAY THEY'LL ALL SEE WHAT I'VE DONE...
...AND THEY'LL ALL KNOW...I WAS YOUR BETTER...
HEH HEH HEH HEH HEH HEH...

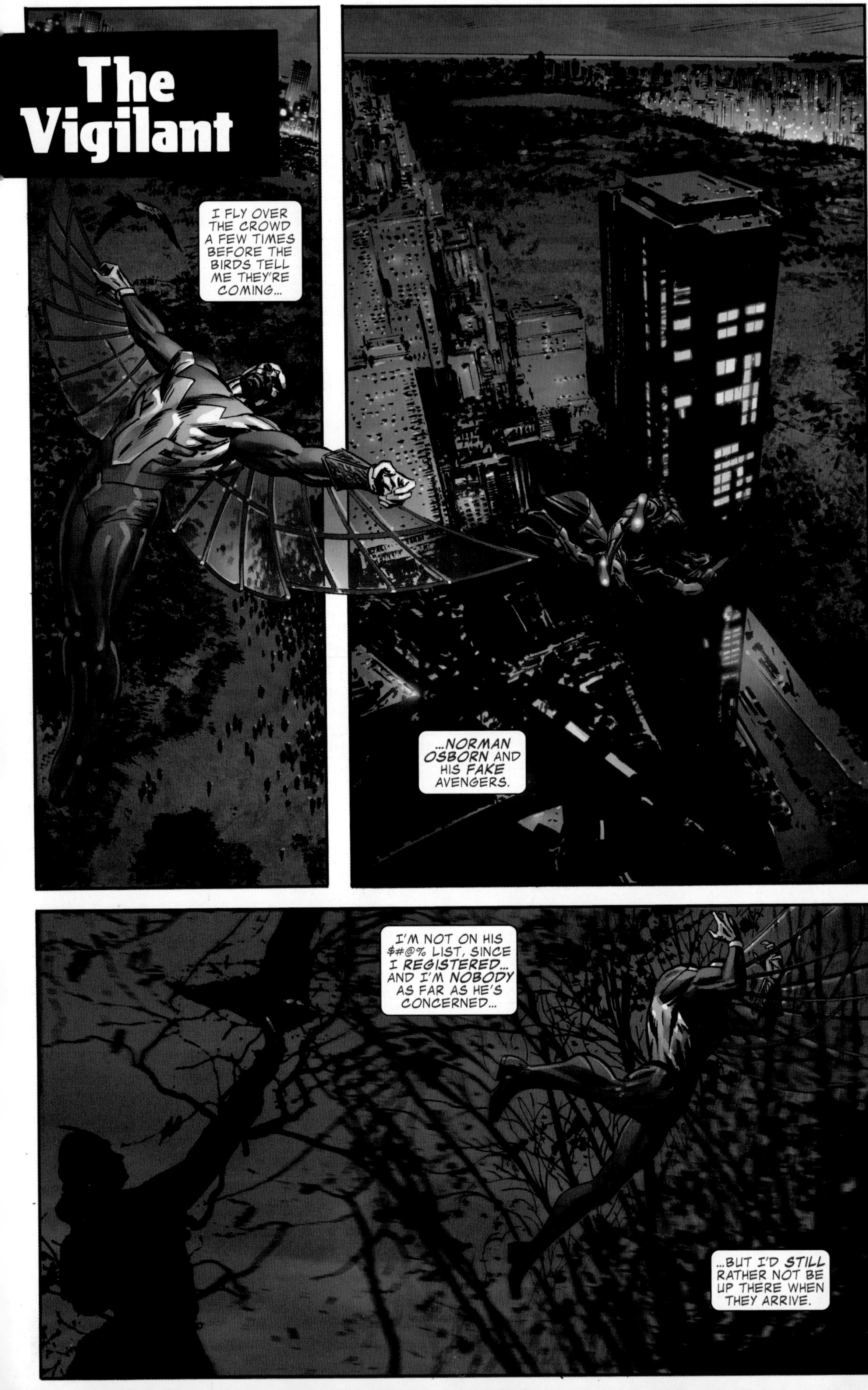
The Vigilant
I FLY OVER THE CROWD A FEW TIMES BEFORE THE BIRDS TELL ME THEY'RE COMING...
...NORMAN OSBORN AND HIS FAKE AVENGERS.
I'M NOT ON HIS $#@% LIST, SINCE I REGISTERED... AND I'M NOBODY AS FAR AS HE'S CONCERNED...
...BUT I'D STILL RATHER NOT BE UP THERE WHEN THEY ARRIVE.

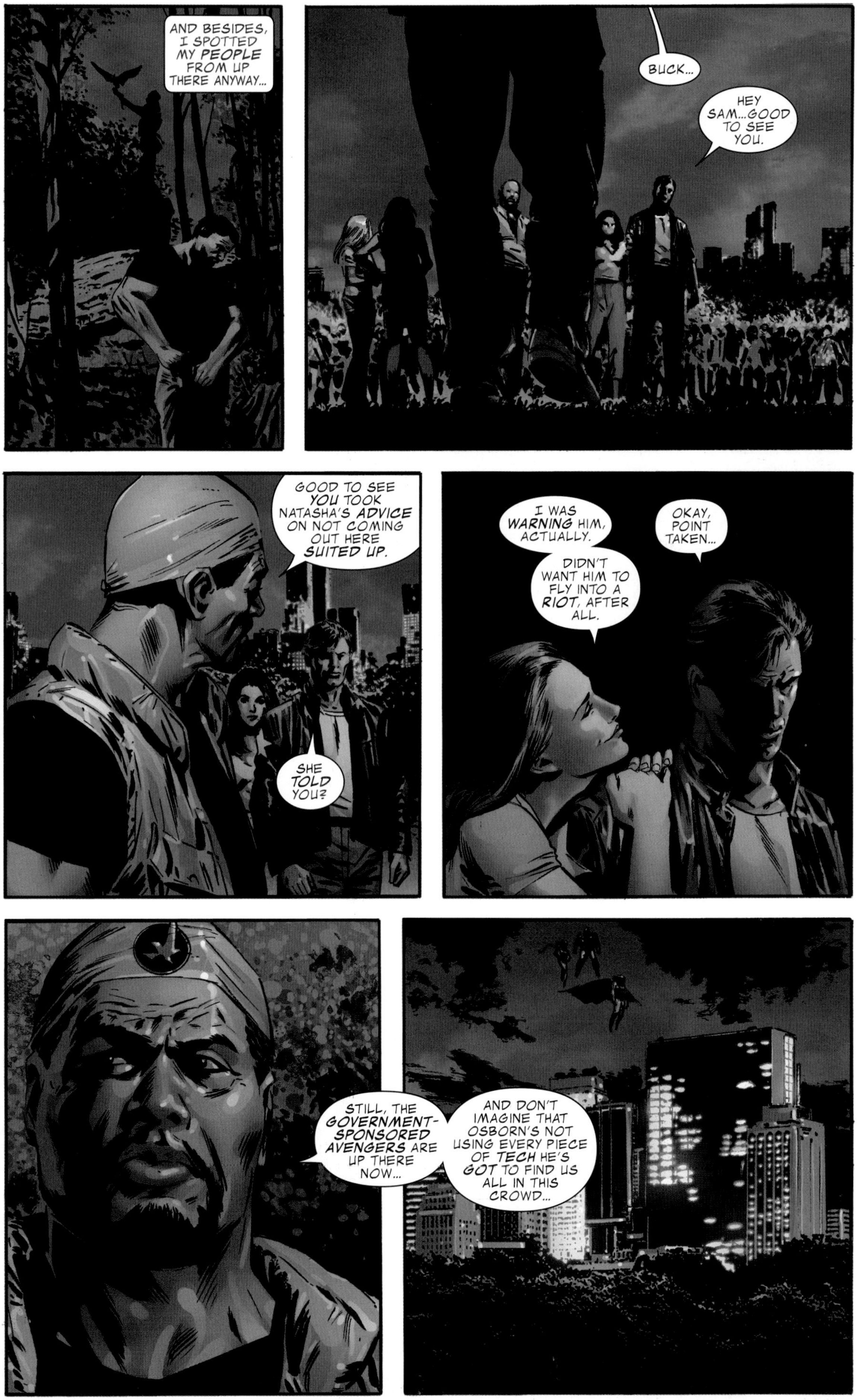
AND BESIDES, I SPOTTED MY PEOPLE FROM UP THERE ANYWAY...
BUCK...
HEY SAM...GOOD TO SEE YOU.
GOOD TO SEE YOU TOOK NATASHA'S ADVICE ON NOT COMING OUT HERE SUITED UP.
SHE TOLD YOU?
I WAS WARNING HIM, ACTUALLY.
DIDN'T WANT HIM TO FLY INTO A RIOT, AFTER ALL.
OKAY, POINT TAKEN...
STILL, THE GOVERNMENT-SPONSORED AVENGERS ARE UP THERE NOW...
AND DON'T IMAGINE THAT OSBORN'S NOT USING EVERY PIECE OF TECH HE'S GOT TO FIND US ALL IN THIS CROWD...

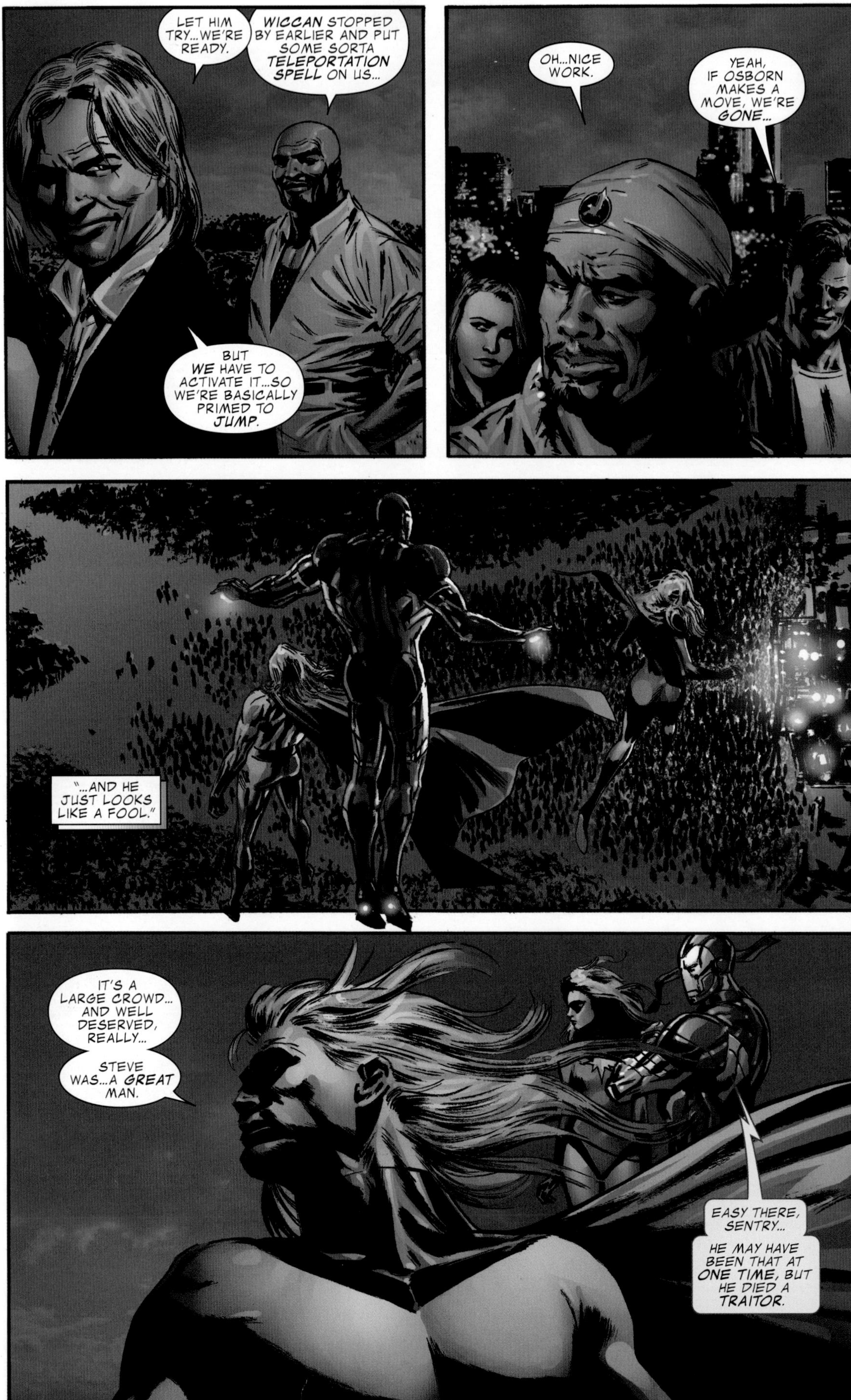
LET HIM TRY...WE'RE READY.
WICCAN STOPPED BY EARLIER AND PUT SOME SORTA TELEPORTATION SPELL ON US...
BUT WE HAVE TO ACTIVATE IT...SO WE'RE BASICALLY PRIMED TO JUMP.
OH...NICE WORK.
YEAH, IF OSBORN MAKES A MOVE, WE'RE GONE...
"...AND HE JUST LOOKS LIKE A FOOL."
IT'S A LARGE CROWD... AND WELL DESERVED, REALLY...
STEVE WAS...A GREAT MAN.
EASY THERE, SENTRY...
HE MAY HAVE BEEN THAT AT ONE TIME, BUT HE DIED A TRAITOR.

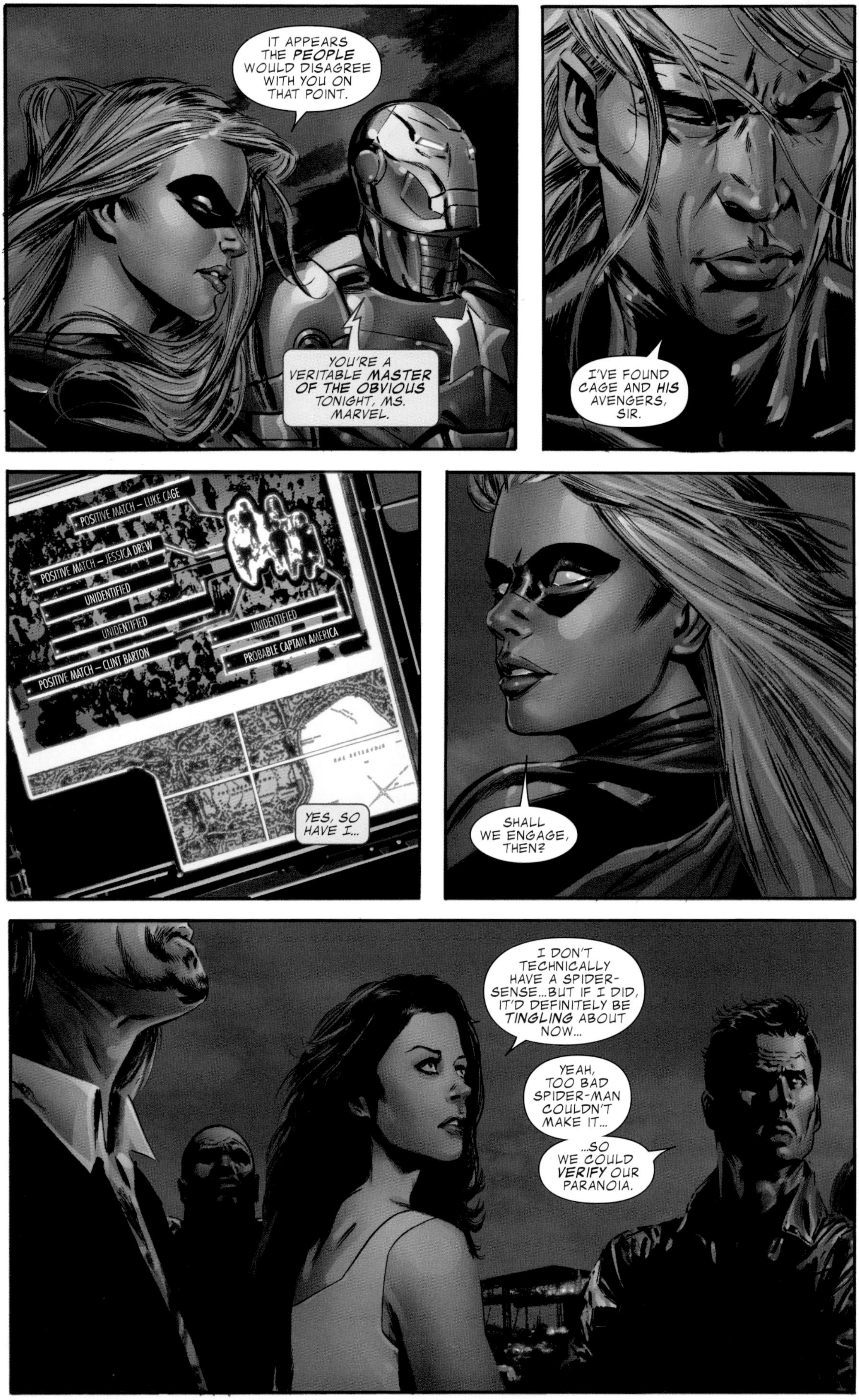
IT APPEARS THE PEOPLE WOULD DISAGREE WITH YOU ON THAT POINT.
YOU'RE A VERITABLE MASTER OF THE OBVIOUS TONIGHT, MS. MARVEL.
I'VE FOUND CAGE AND HIS AVENGERS, SIR.
POSITIVE MATCH – LUKE CAGE
POSITIVE MATCH – JESSICA DREW
UNIDENTIFIED
UNIDENTIFIED
UNIDENTIFIED
PROBABLE CAPTAIN AMERICA
POSITIVE MATCH – CLINT BARTON
YES, SO HAVE I...
SHALL WE ENGAGE, THEN?
I DON'T TECHNICALLY HAVE A SPIDER-SENSE...BUT IF I DID, IT'D DEFINITELY BE TINGLING ABOUT NOW...
YEAH, TOO BAD SPIDER-MAN COULDN'T MAKE IT...
...SO WE COULD VERIFY OUR PARANOIA.

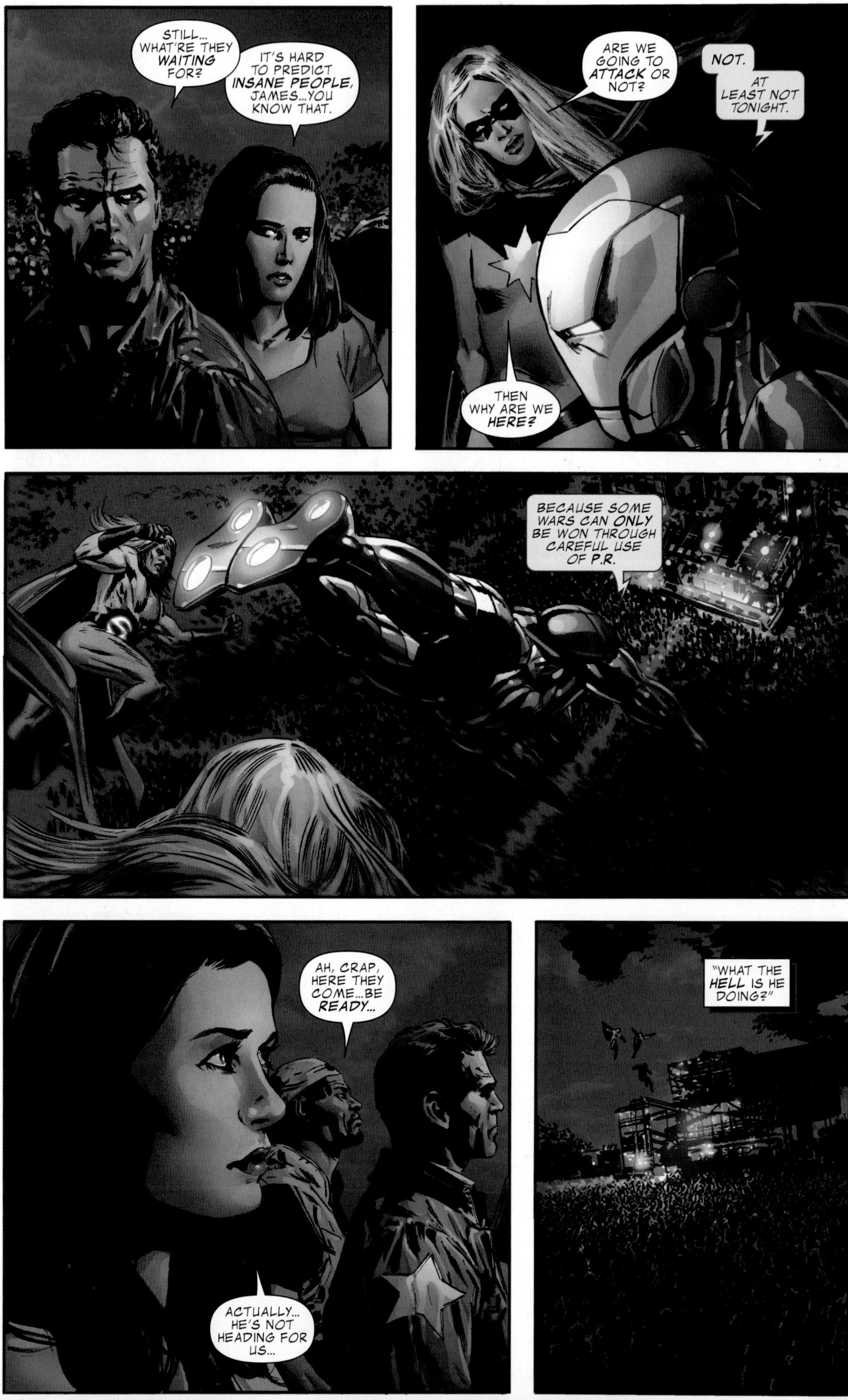
STILL... WHAT'RE THEY WAITING FOR?
IT'S HARD TO PREDICT INSANE PEOPLE, JAMES...YOU KNOW THAT.
ARE WE GOING TO ATTACK OR NOT?
NOT.
AT LEAST NOT TONIGHT.
THEN WHY ARE WE HERE?
BECAUSE SOME WARS CAN ONLY BE WON THROUGH CAREFUL USE OF P.R.
AH, CRAP, HERE THEY COME...BE READY...
ACTUALLY... HE'S NOT HEADING FOR US...
"WHAT THE HELL IS HE DOING?"

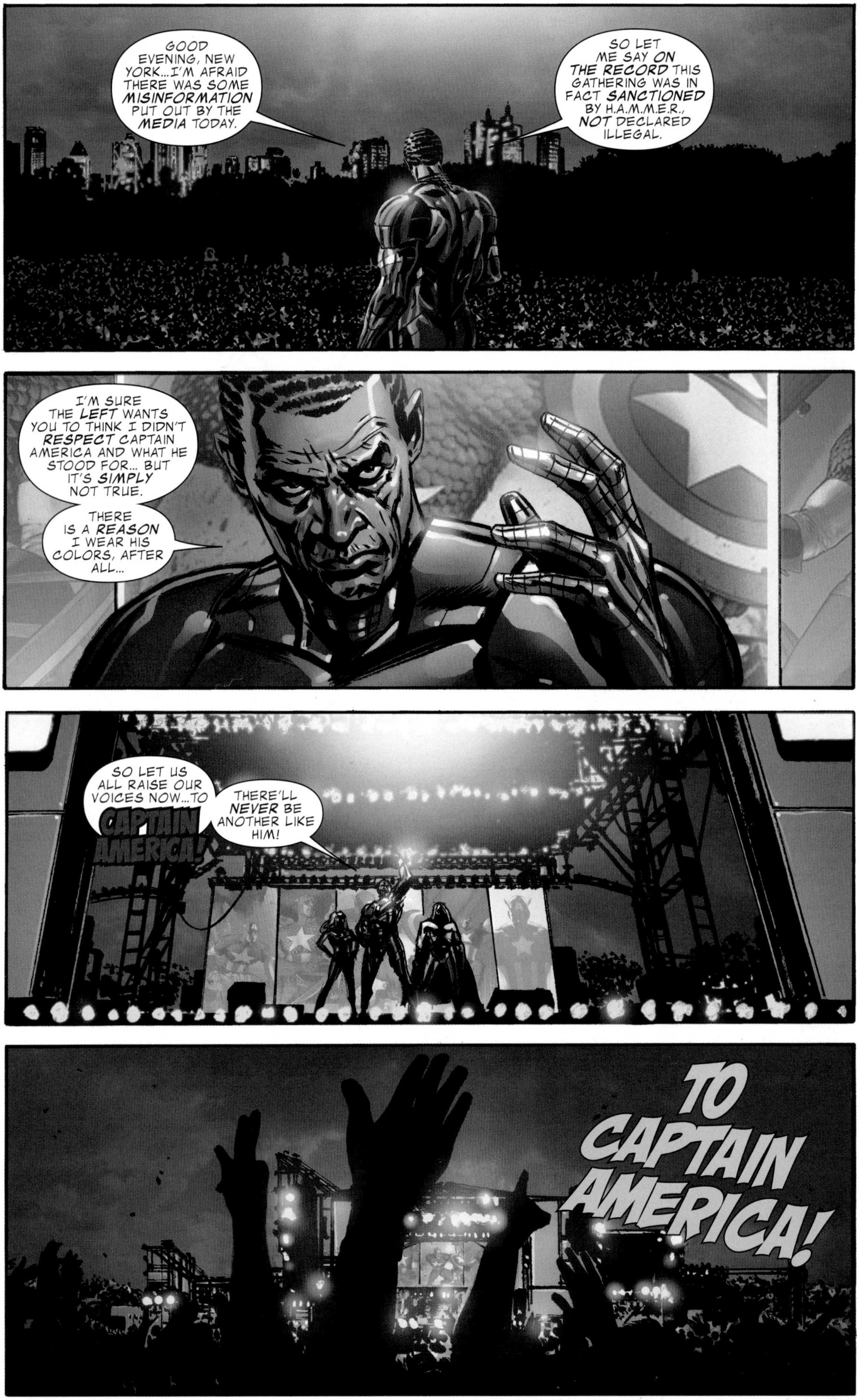
GOOD EVENING, NEW YORK...I'M AFRAID THERE WAS SOME MISINFORMATION PUT OUT BY THE MEDIA TODAY.
SO LET ME SAY ON THE RECORD THIS GATHERING WAS IN FACT SANCTIONED BY H.A.M.M.E.R., NOT DECLARED ILLEGAL.
I'M SURE THE LEFT WANTS YOU TO THINK I DIDN'T RESPECT CAPTAIN AMERICA AND WHAT HE STOOD FOR... BUT IT'S SIMPLY NOT TRUE.
THERE IS A REASON I WEAR HIS COLORS, AFTER ALL...
SO LET US ALL RAISE OUR VOICES NOW...TO CAPTAIN AMERICA!
THERE'LL NEVER BE ANOTHER LIKE HIM!
TO CAPTAIN AMERICA!

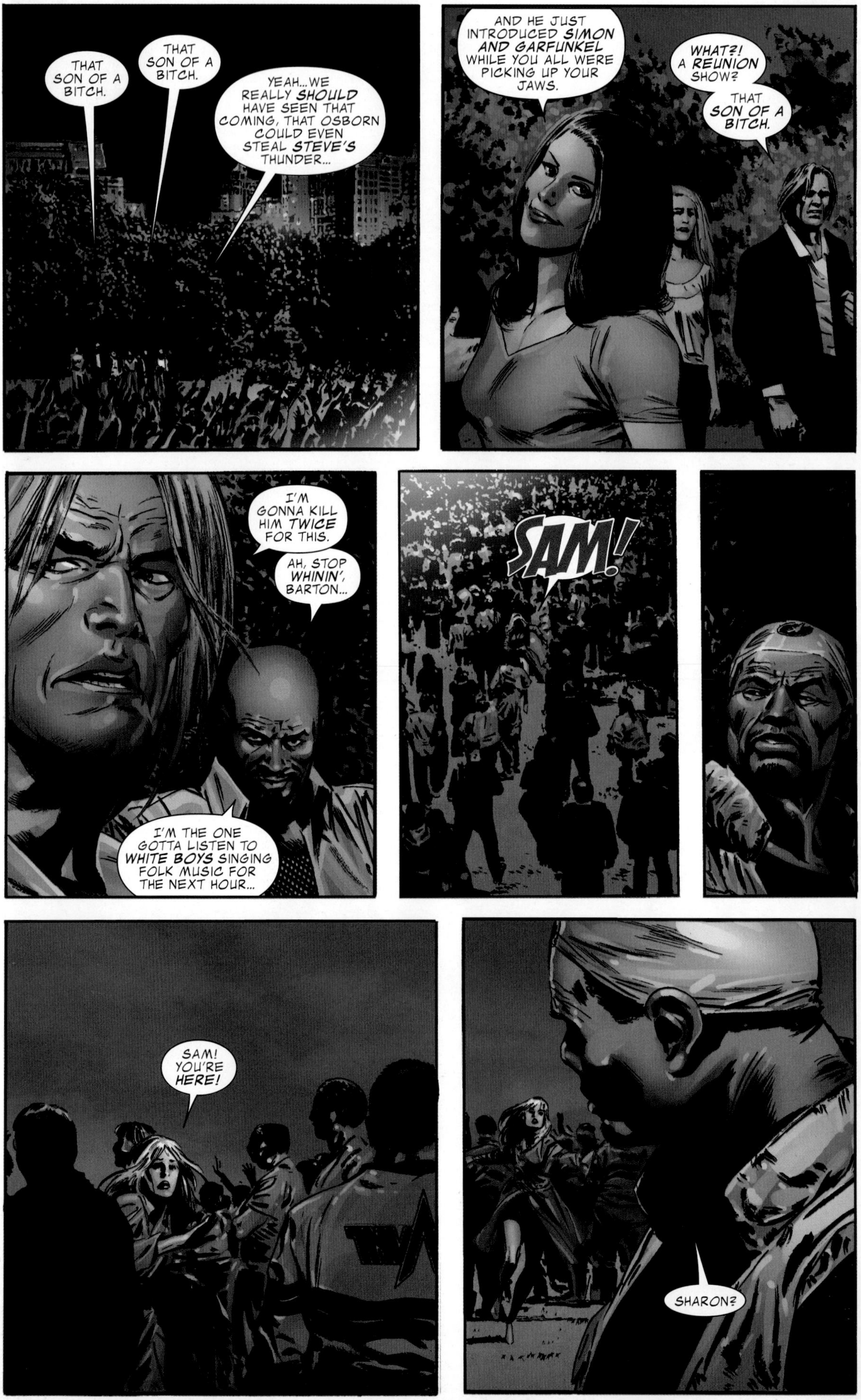
THAT SON OF A BITCH.
THAT SON OF A BITCH.
YEAH...WE REALLY SHOULD HAVE SEEN THAT COMING, THAT OSBORN COULD EVEN STEAL STEVE'S THUNDER...
AND HE JUST INTRODUCED SIMON AND GARFUNKEL WHILE YOU ALL WERE PICKING UP YOUR JAWS.
WHAT?! A REUNION SHOW?
THAT SON OF A BITCH.
I'M GONNA KILL HIM TWICE FOR THIS.
AH, STOP WHININ', BARTON...
I'M THE ONE GOTTA LISTEN TO WHITE BOYS SINGING FOLK MUSIC FOR THE NEXT HOUR...
SAM!
SAM! YOU'RE HERE!
SHARON?

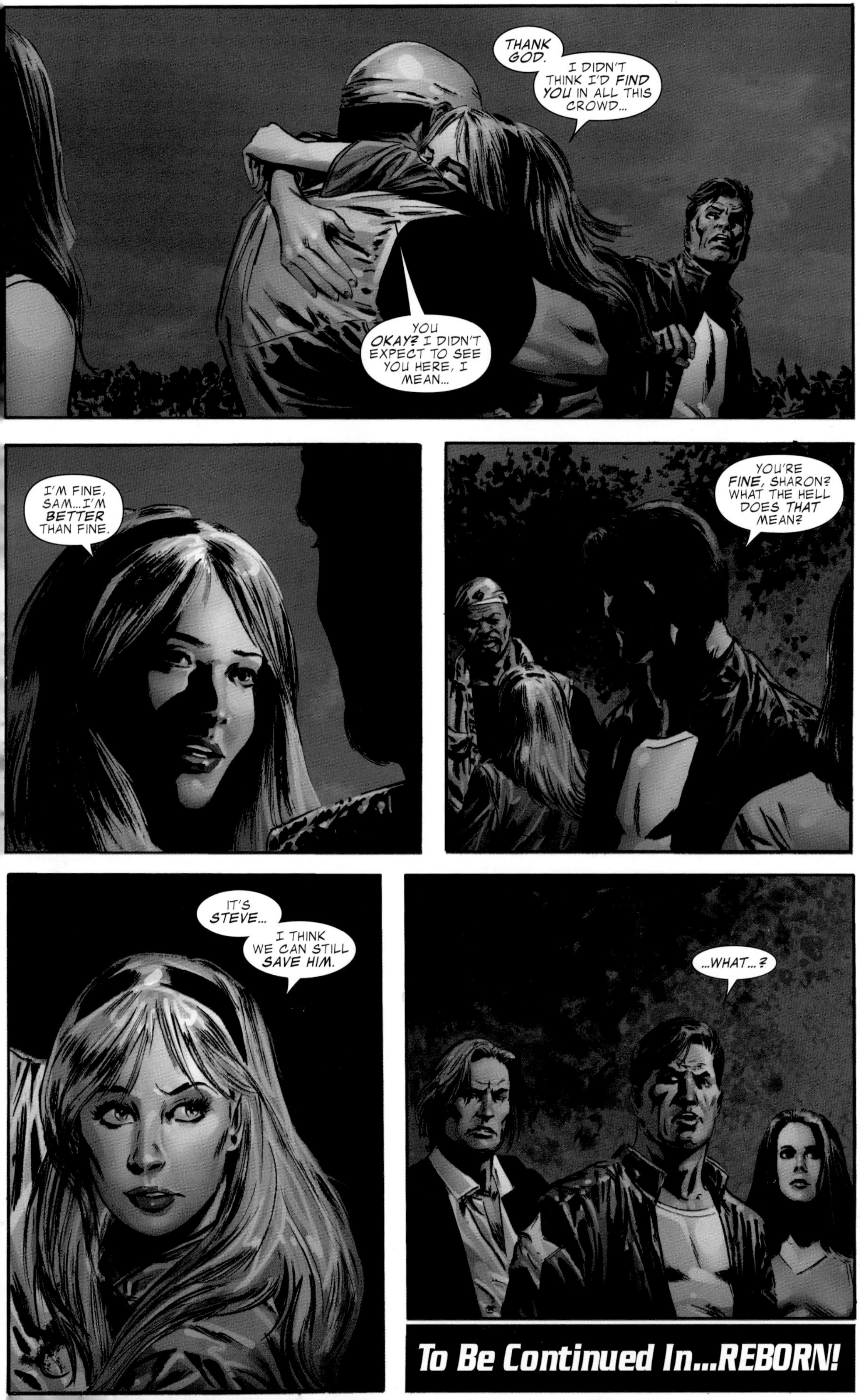
THANK GOD.
I DIDN'T THINK I'D FIND YOU IN ALL THIS CROWD...
YOU OKAY? I DIDN'T EXPECT TO SEE YOU HERE, I MEAN...
I'M FINE, SAM...I'M BETTER THAN FINE.
YOU'RE FINE, SHARON? WHAT THE HELL DOES THAT MEAN?
IT'S STEVE...
I THINK WE CAN STILL SAVE HIM.
...WHAT...?
To Be Continued In...REBORN!

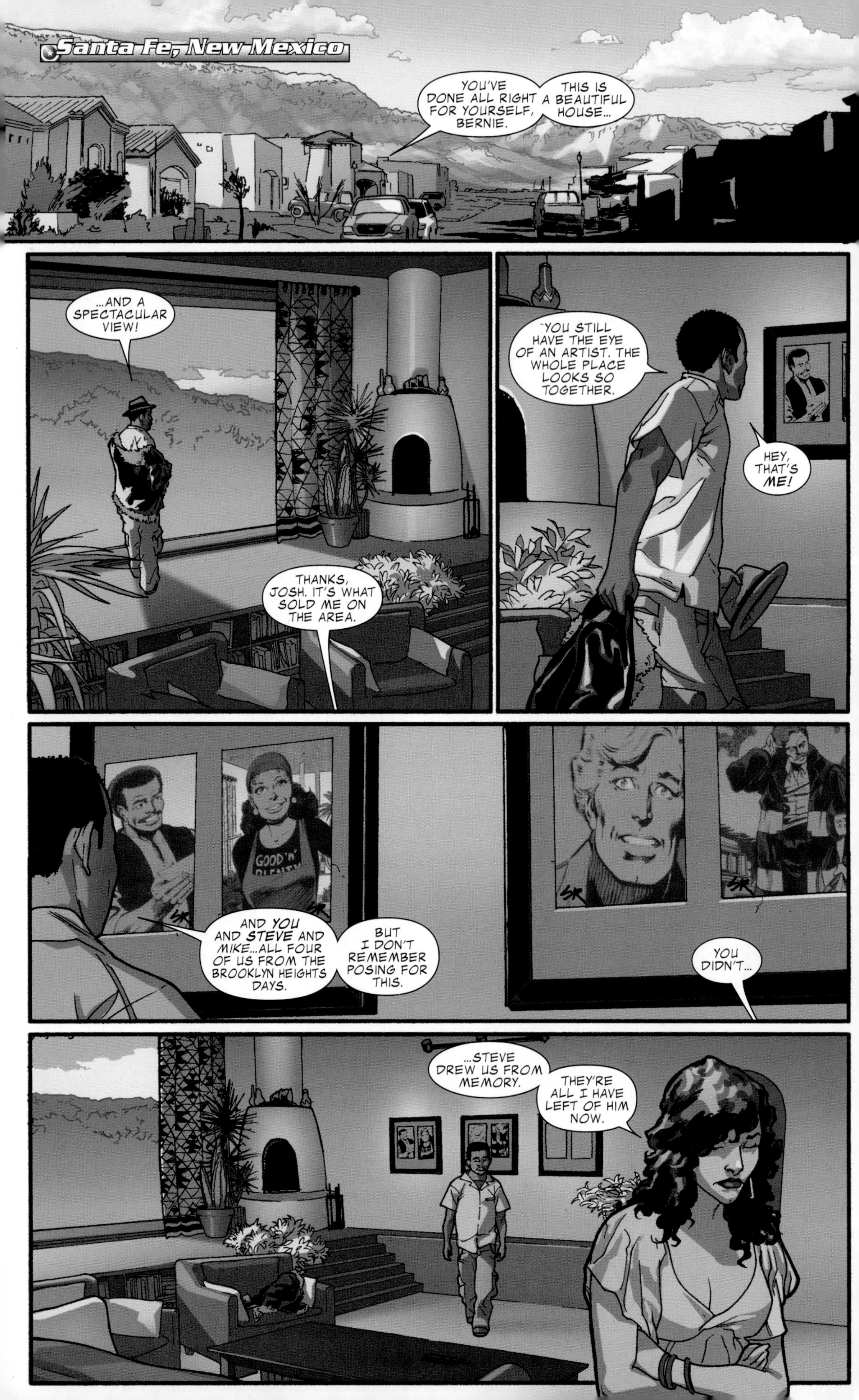
Santa Fe, New Mexico
YOU'VE DONE ALL RIGHT FOR YOURSELF, BERNIE.
THIS IS A BEAUTIFUL HOUSE...
...AND A SPECTACULAR VIEW!
THANKS, JOSH. IT'S WHAT SOLD ME ON THE AREA.
YOU STILL HAVE THE EYE OF AN ARTIST. THE WHOLE PLACE LOOKS SO TOGETHER.
HEY, THAT'S ME!
GOOD 'n' PLENTY
AND YOU AND STEVE AND MIKE...ALL FOUR OF US FROM THE BROOKLYN HEIGHTS DAYS.
BUT I DON'T REMEMBER POSING FOR THIS.
YOU DIDN'T...
...STEVE DREW US FROM MEMORY.
THEY'RE ALL I HAVE LEFT OF HIM NOW.

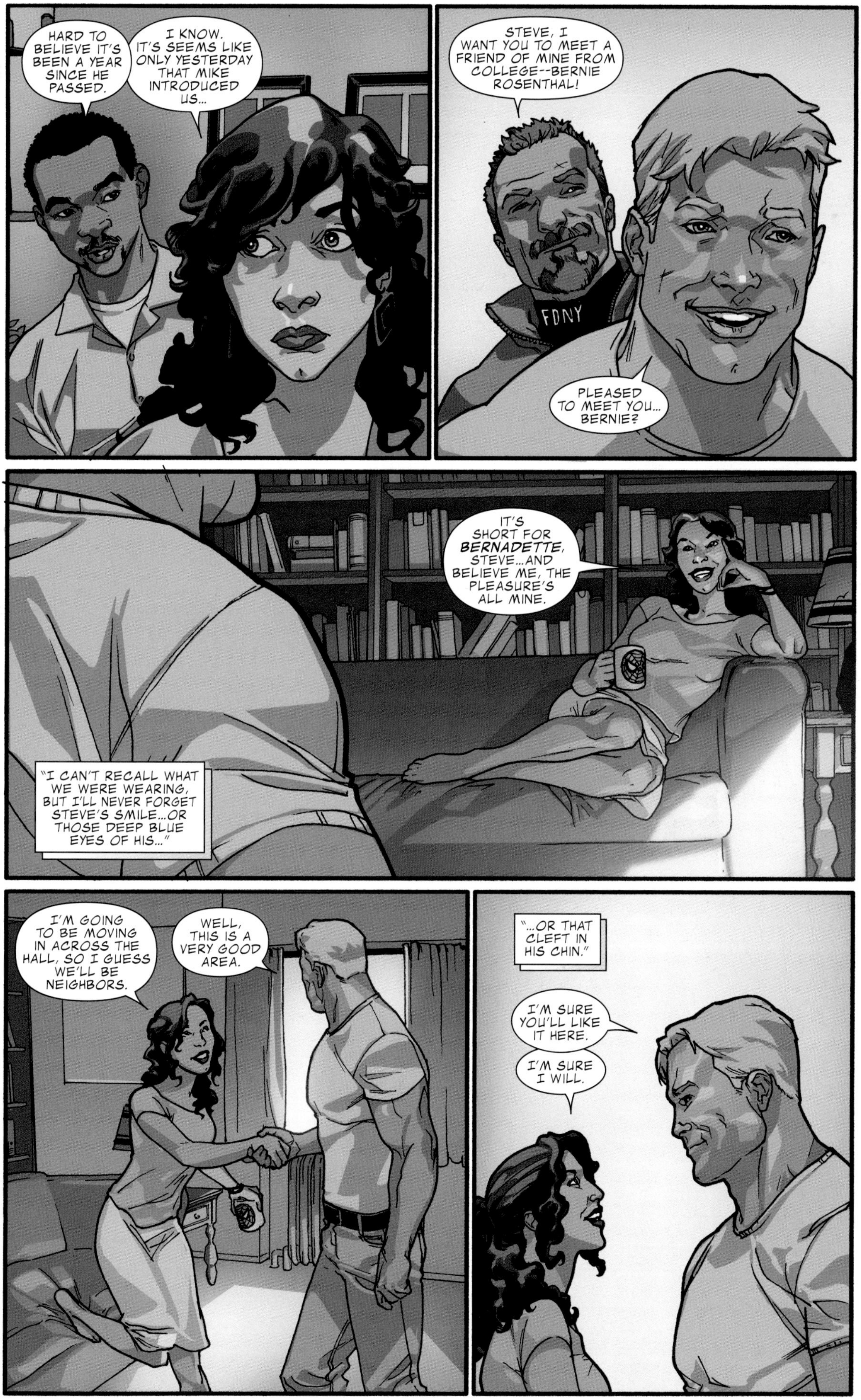
HARD TO BELIEVE IT'S BEEN A YEAR SINCE HE PASSED.
I KNOW. IT'S SEEMS LIKE ONLY YESTERDAY THAT MIKE INTRODUCED US...
STEVE, I WANT YOU TO MEET A FRIEND OF MINE FROM COLLEGE--BERNIE ROSENTHAL!
FDNY
PLEASED TO MEET YOU... BERNIE?
IT'S SHORT FOR BERNADETTE, STEVE...AND BELIEVE ME, THE PLEASURE'S ALL MINE.
"I CAN'T RECALL WHAT WE WERE WEARING, BUT I'LL NEVER FORGET STEVE'S SMILE...OR THOSE DEEP BLUE EYES OF HIS..."
I'M GOING TO BE MOVING IN ACROSS THE HALL, SO I GUESS WE'LL BE NEIGHBORS.
WELL, THIS IS A VERY GOOD AREA.
"...OR THAT CLEFT IN HIS CHIN."
I'M SURE YOU'LL LIKE IT HERE.
I'M SURE I WILL.

THE MAN WAS DEFINITELY ONE OF A KIND. WHEN I FINALLY FOUND OUT THAT STEVE WAS CAPTAIN AMERICA...A WHOLE LOT OF THINGS SUDDENLY MADE SENSE.

I CAN'T BEGIN TO IMAGINE HOW HARD THIS HAS BEEN ON YOU.

I NEVER STOP THINKING OF HIM, JOSH...

...THE GOOD, AS WELL AS THE BAD. REMEMBER WHEN YOU BOTH HELPED ME MOVE...?

OH, YEAH...

"...I'D NEVER FELT SO BEAT. BUT STEVE WASN'T EVEN WINDED."

THIS IS THE LAST OF THE BOXES, BERNIE. WHERE DO YOU WANT IT?

JUST SET IT DOWN ANYWHERE, STEVE. I'LL UNPACK EVERYTHING LATER.

"MIKE SHOWED UP TOO LATE TO HELP. CLAIMED HE'D GOTTEN INVOLVED TALKING POLITICS DOWN AT THE FIREHOUSE--

"--AND YOU GAVE HIM A HARD TIME ABOUT IT..."

I DON'T BELIEVE IT. MIKE FARREL, YOU ARE THE MOST APOLITICAL MAN I KNOW.

NOT WHEN THERE'S NEWS LIKE THIS!

The Daily Globe
CAP FOR PRESIDENT!

CAPTAIN AMERICA? FOR PRESIDENT?

The Daily G
CAP FOR PRESI

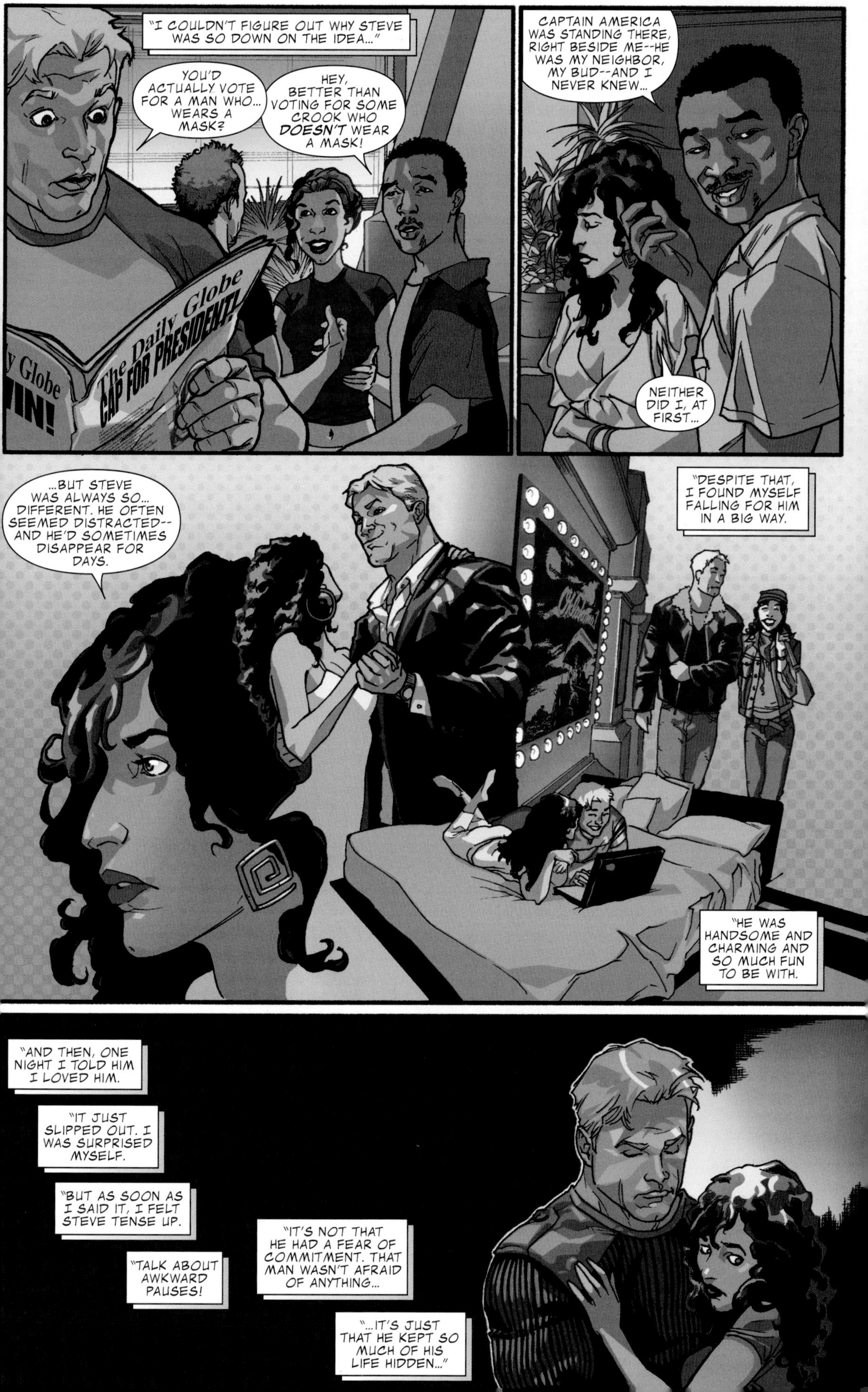
"I COULDN'T FIGURE OUT WHY STEVE WAS SO DOWN ON THE IDEA..."
YOU'D ACTUALLY VOTE FOR A MAN WHO... WEARS A MASK?
HEY, BETTER THAN VOTING FOR SOME CROOK WHO DOESN'T WEAR A MASK!
The Daily Globe
CAP FOR PRESIDENT!
y Globe
VIN!
CAPTAIN AMERICA WAS STANDING THERE, RIGHT BESIDE ME--HE WAS MY NEIGHBOR, MY BUD--AND I NEVER KNEW...
NEITHER DID I, AT FIRST...
...BUT STEVE WAS ALWAYS SO... DIFFERENT. HE OFTEN SEEMED DISTRACTED-- AND HE'D SOMETIMES DISAPPEAR FOR DAYS.
"DESPITE THAT, I FOUND MYSELF FALLING FOR HIM IN A BIG WAY.
"HE WAS HANDSOME AND CHARMING AND SO MUCH FUN TO BE WITH.
"AND THEN, ONE NIGHT I TOLD HIM I LOVED HIM.
"IT JUST SLIPPED OUT. I WAS SURPRISED MYSELF.
"BUT AS SOON AS I SAID IT, I FELT STEVE TENSE UP.
"TALK ABOUT AWKWARD PAUSES!
"IT'S NOT THAT HE HAD A FEAR OF COMMITMENT. THAT MAN WASN'T AFRAID OF ANYTHING...
"...IT'S JUST THAT HE KEPT SO MUCH OF HIS LIFE HIDDEN..."

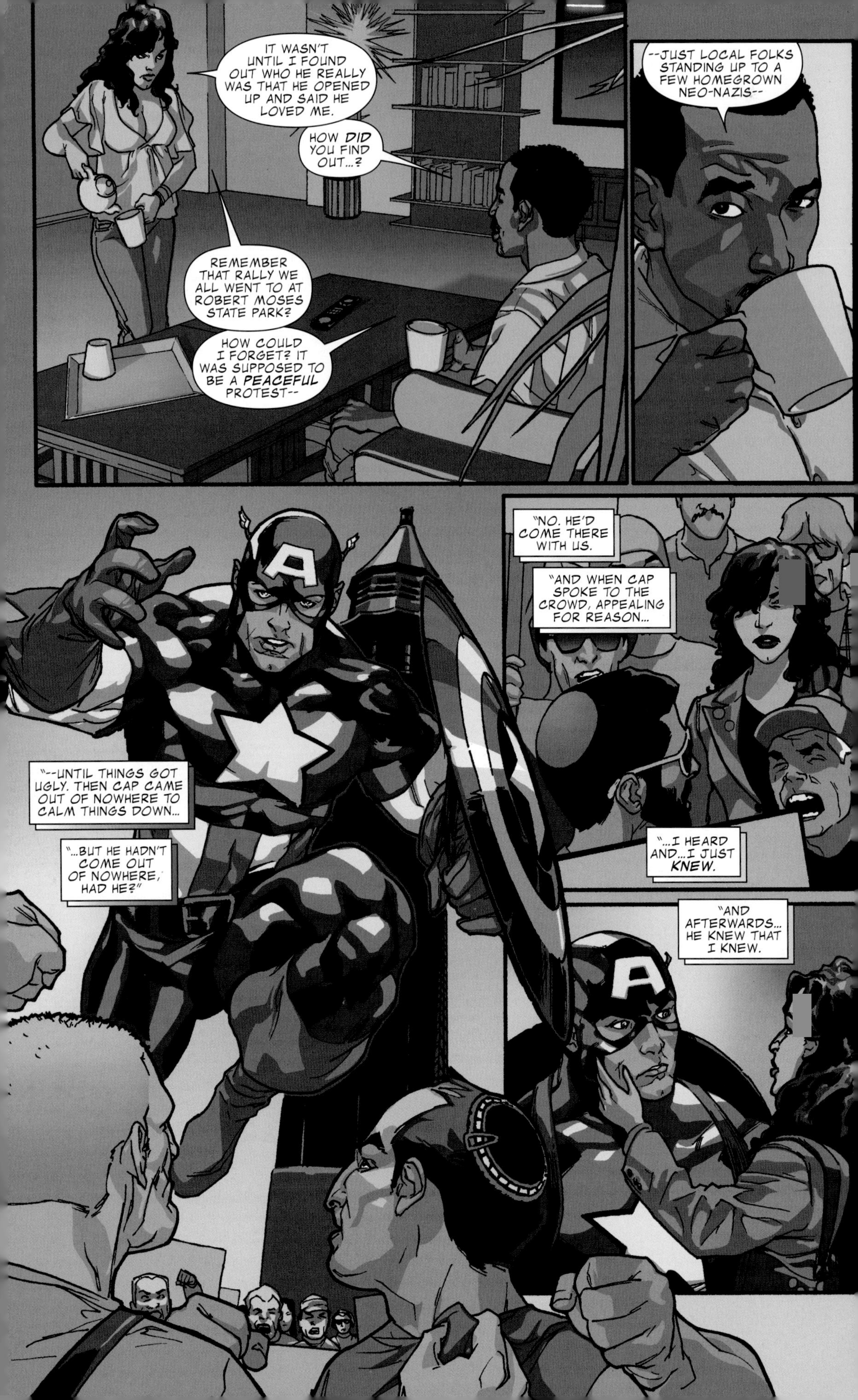
IT WASN'T UNTIL I FOUND OUT WHO HE REALLY WAS THAT HE OPENED UP AND SAID HE LOVED ME.
HOW DID YOU FIND OUT...?
REMEMBER THAT RALLY WE ALL WENT TO AT ROBERT MOSES STATE PARK?
HOW COULD I FORGET? IT WAS SUPPOSED TO BE A PEACEFUL PROTEST--
--JUST LOCAL FOLKS STANDING UP TO A FEW HOMEGROWN NEO-NAZIS--
"--UNTIL THINGS GOT UGLY. THEN CAP CAME OUT OF NOWHERE TO CALM THINGS DOWN...
"...BUT HE HADN'T COME OUT OF NOWHERE, HAD HE?"
"NO. HE'D COME THERE WITH US.
"AND WHEN CAP SPOKE TO THE CROWD, APPEALING FOR REASON...
"...I HEARD AND...I JUST KNEW.
"AND AFTERWARDS... HE KNEW THAT I KNEW.

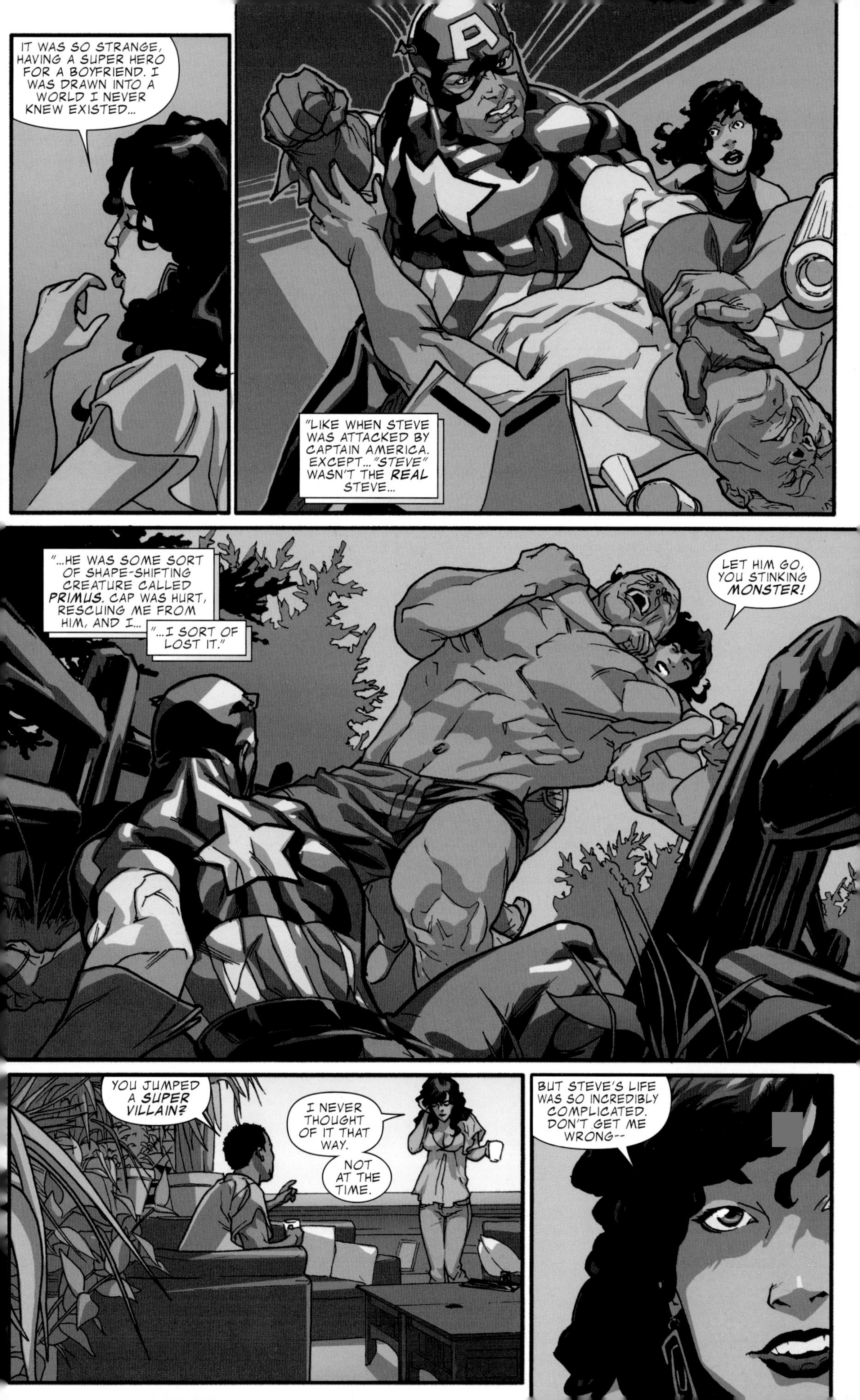
IT WAS SO STRANGE, HAVING A SUPER HERO FOR A BOYFRIEND. I WAS DRAWN INTO A WORLD I NEVER KNEW EXISTED...
"LIKE WHEN STEVE WAS ATTACKED BY CAPTAIN AMERICA. EXCEPT... "STEVE" WASN'T THE REAL STEVE...
"...HE WAS SOME SORT OF SHAPE-SHIFTING CREATURE CALLED PRIMUS. CAP WAS HURT, RESCUING ME FROM HIM, AND I...
"...I SORT OF LOST IT."
LET HIM GO, YOU STINKING MONSTER!
YOU JUMPED A SUPER VILLAIN?
I NEVER THOUGHT OF IT THAT WAY.
NOT AT THE TIME.
BUT STEVE'S LIFE WAS SO INCREDIBLY COMPLICATED. DON'T GET ME WRONG--

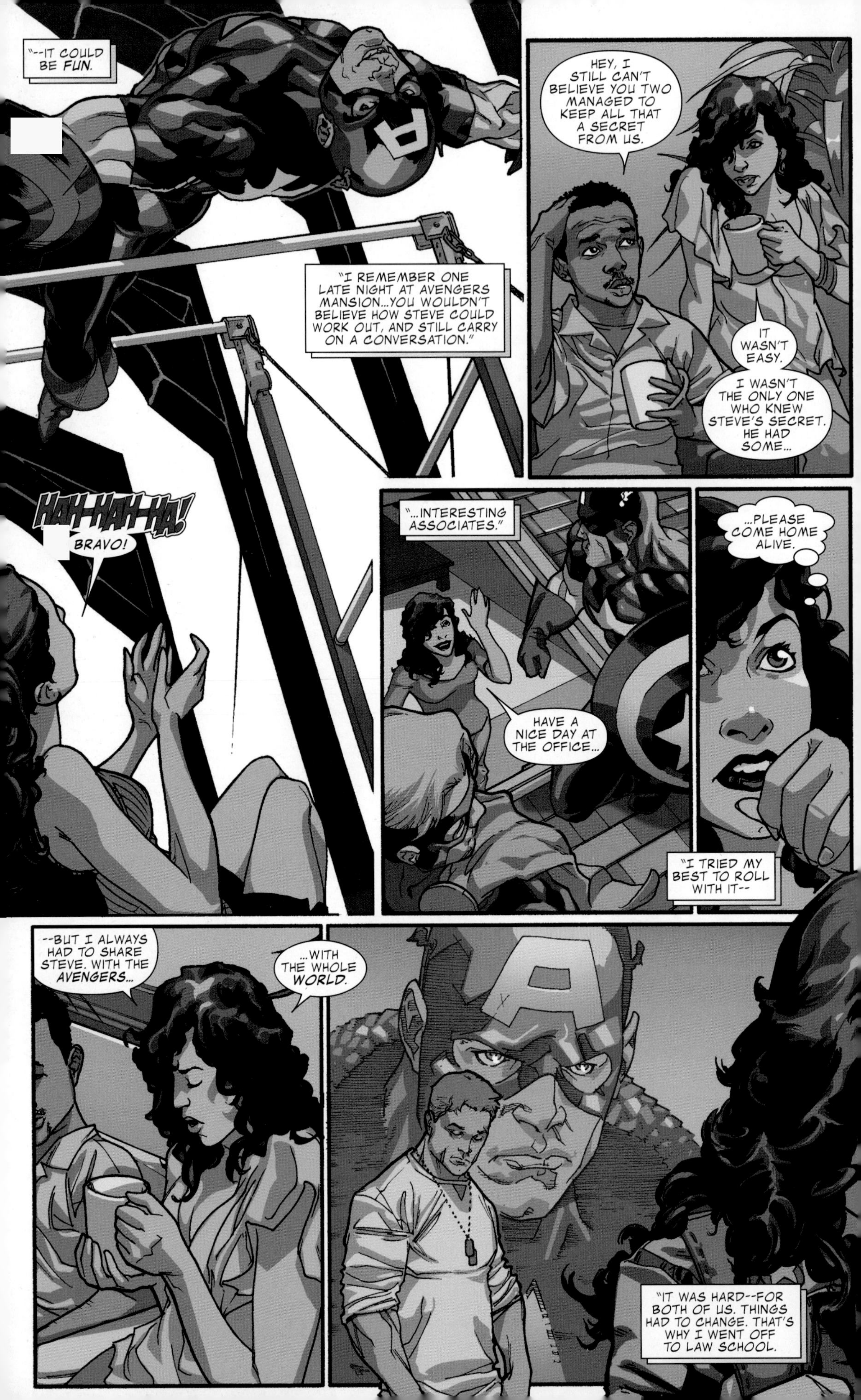
"--IT COULD BE FUN.
"I REMEMBER ONE LATE NIGHT AT AVENGERS MANSION...YOU WOULDN'T BELIEVE HOW STEVE COULD WORK OUT, AND STILL CARRY ON A CONVERSATION."
HEY, I STILL CAN'T BELIEVE YOU TWO MANAGED TO KEEP ALL THAT A SECRET FROM US.
IT WASN'T EASY.
I WASN'T THE ONLY ONE WHO KNEW STEVE'S SECRET. HE HAD SOME...
HAH-HAH-HA!
BRAVO!
"...INTERESTING ASSOCIATES."
HAVE A NICE DAY AT THE OFFICE...
...PLEASE COME HOME ALIVE.
"I TRIED MY BEST TO ROLL WITH IT--
--BUT I ALWAYS HAD TO SHARE STEVE. WITH THE AVENGERS...
...WITH THE WHOLE WORLD.
"IT WAS HARD--FOR BOTH OF US. THINGS HAD TO CHANGE. THAT'S WHY I WENT OFF TO LAW SCHOOL.

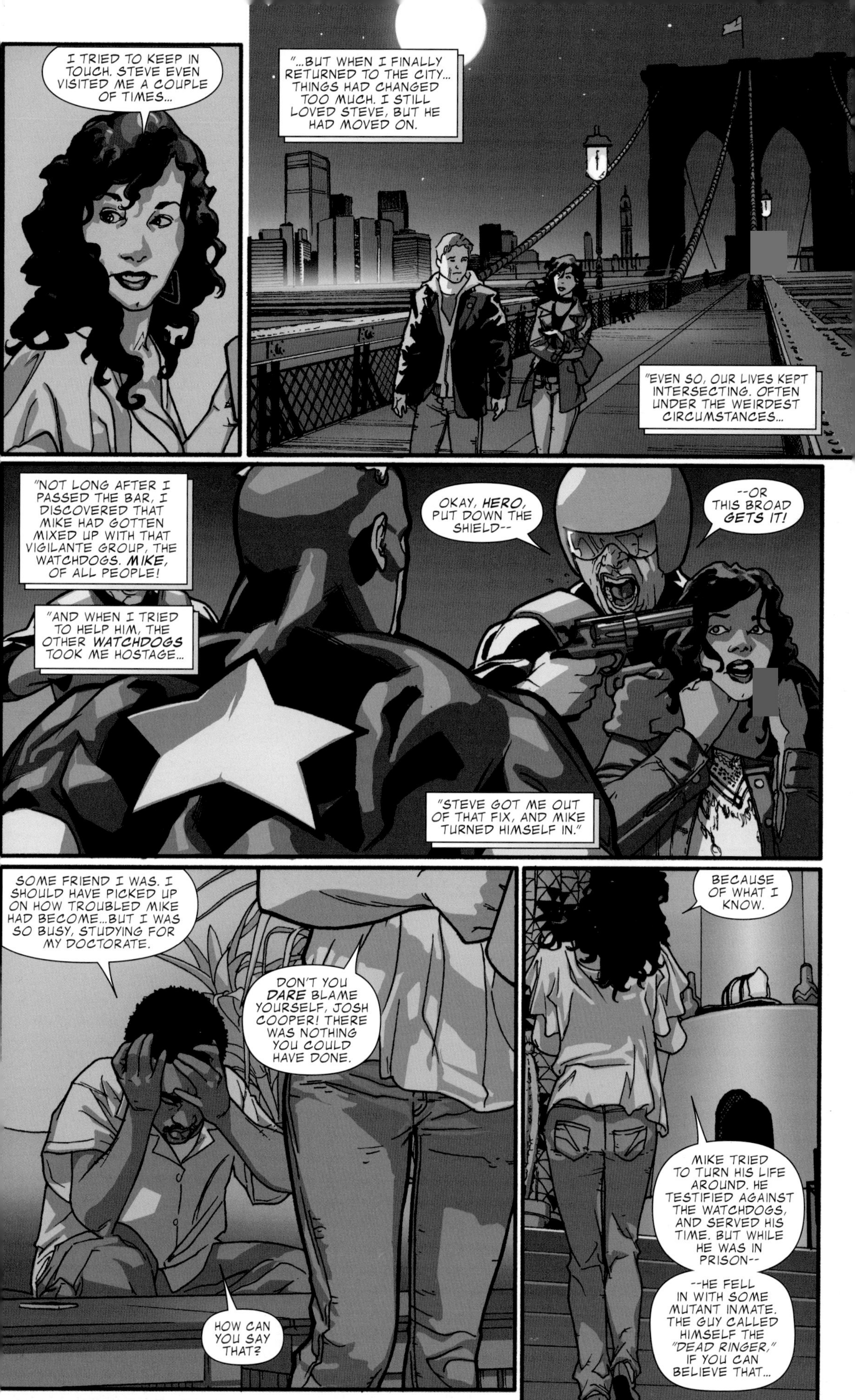
I TRIED TO KEEP IN TOUCH. STEVE EVEN VISITED ME A COUPLE OF TIMES...
"...BUT WHEN I FINALLY RETURNED TO THE CITY... THINGS HAD CHANGED TOO MUCH. I STILL LOVED STEVE, BUT HE HAD MOVED ON.
"EVEN SO, OUR LIVES KEPT INTERSECTING. OFTEN UNDER THE WEIRDEST CIRCUMSTANCES...
"NOT LONG AFTER I PASSED THE BAR, I DISCOVERED THAT MIKE HAD GOTTEN MIXED UP WITH THAT VIGILANTE GROUP, THE WATCHDOGS. **MIKE,** OF ALL PEOPLE!
"AND WHEN I TRIED TO HELP HIM, THE OTHER ***WATCHDOGS*** TOOK ME HOSTAGE...
OKAY, **HERO,** PUT DOWN THE SHIELD--
--OR THIS BROAD ***GETS IT!***
"STEVE GOT ME OUT OF THAT FIX, AND MIKE TURNED HIMSELF IN."
SOME FRIEND I WAS. I SHOULD HAVE PICKED UP ON HOW TROUBLED MIKE HAD BECOME...BUT I WAS SO BUSY, STUDYING FOR MY DOCTORATE.
DON'T YOU **DARE** BLAME YOURSELF, JOSH COOPER! THERE WAS NOTHING YOU COULD HAVE DONE.
HOW CAN YOU SAY THAT?
BECAUSE OF WHAT I KNOW.
MIKE TRIED TO TURN HIS LIFE AROUND. HE TESTIFIED AGAINST THE WATCHDOGS, AND SERVED HIS TIME. BUT WHILE HE WAS IN PRISON--
--HE FELL IN WITH SOME MUTANT INMATE. THE GUY CALLED HIMSELF THE "DEAD RINGER," IF YOU CAN BELIEVE THAT...

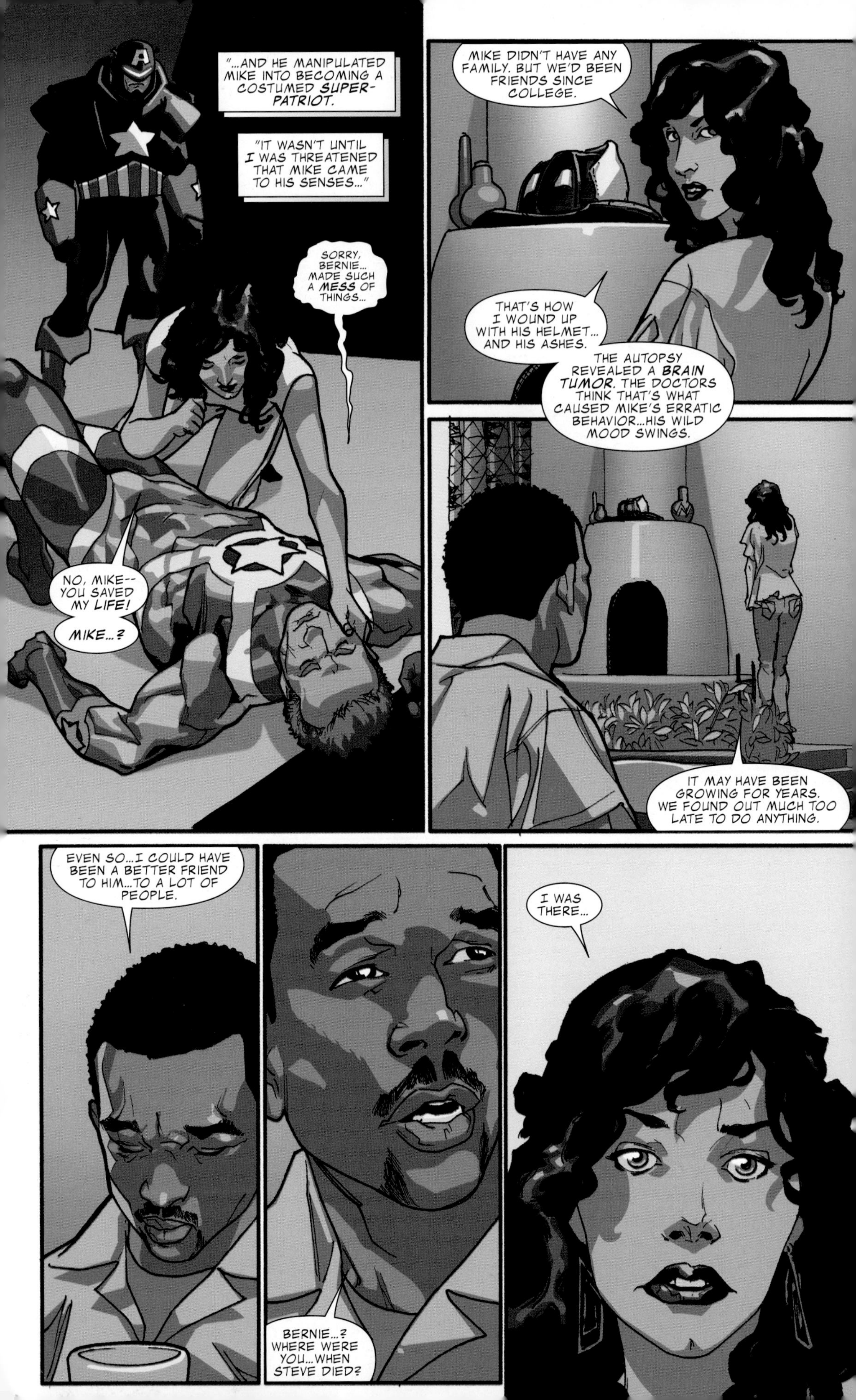
"...AND HE MANIPULATED MIKE INTO BECOMING A COSTUMED SUPER-PATRIOT.
"IT WASN'T UNTIL I WAS THREATENED THAT MIKE CAME TO HIS SENSES..."
SORRY, BERNIE... MADE SUCH A MESS OF THINGS...
NO, MIKE-- YOU SAVED MY LIFE!
MIKE...?
MIKE DIDN'T HAVE ANY FAMILY. BUT WE'D BEEN FRIENDS SINCE COLLEGE.
THAT'S HOW I WOUND UP WITH HIS HELMET... AND HIS ASHES.
THE AUTOPSY REVEALED A BRAIN TUMOR. THE DOCTORS THINK THAT'S WHAT CAUSED MIKE'S ERRATIC BEHAVIOR...HIS WILD MOOD SWINGS.
IT MAY HAVE BEEN GROWING FOR YEARS. WE FOUND OUT MUCH TOO LATE TO DO ANYTHING.
EVEN SO...I COULD HAVE BEEN A BETTER FRIEND TO HIM...TO A LOT OF PEOPLE.
BERNIE...? WHERE WERE YOU...WHEN STEVE DIED?
I WAS THERE...

"I'D BEEN MONITORING THE CONTROVERSY OVER THE *SUPERHUMAN REGISTRATION ACT*, FIGURING IT WAS JUST A MATTER OF TIME BEFORE THE COURTS GOT INVOLVED."

TRAITOR

"WHEN THE NEWS CAME DOWN THAT CAP HAD BEEN ARRESTED AND WAS GOING TO BE ARRAIGNED, I HEADED STRAIGHT FOR THE FEDERAL COURTHOUSE."

"I WANTED HIM TO SEE AT LEAST ONE FRIENDLY FACE IN THE CROWD. AS IT TURNED OUT, THERE WERE *THOUSANDS*."

FREE CAPTAIN AMERICA

FREE CAPT AM

FI E CAP AI AMERIC

"IT WAS *SHAMEFUL*, THE WAY THEY TREATED HIM."

"I'D NEVER SEEN STEVE LOOK SO GRIM."

POLICE
S. MARSHA

"I CALLED OUT TO HIM...BUT SO DID A LOT OF PEOPLE. I DON'T THINK HE HEARD ME OVER THE CROWD."

"AND THEN..."

BLAM

NO!

AND THERE WAS NOTHING I COULD DO.

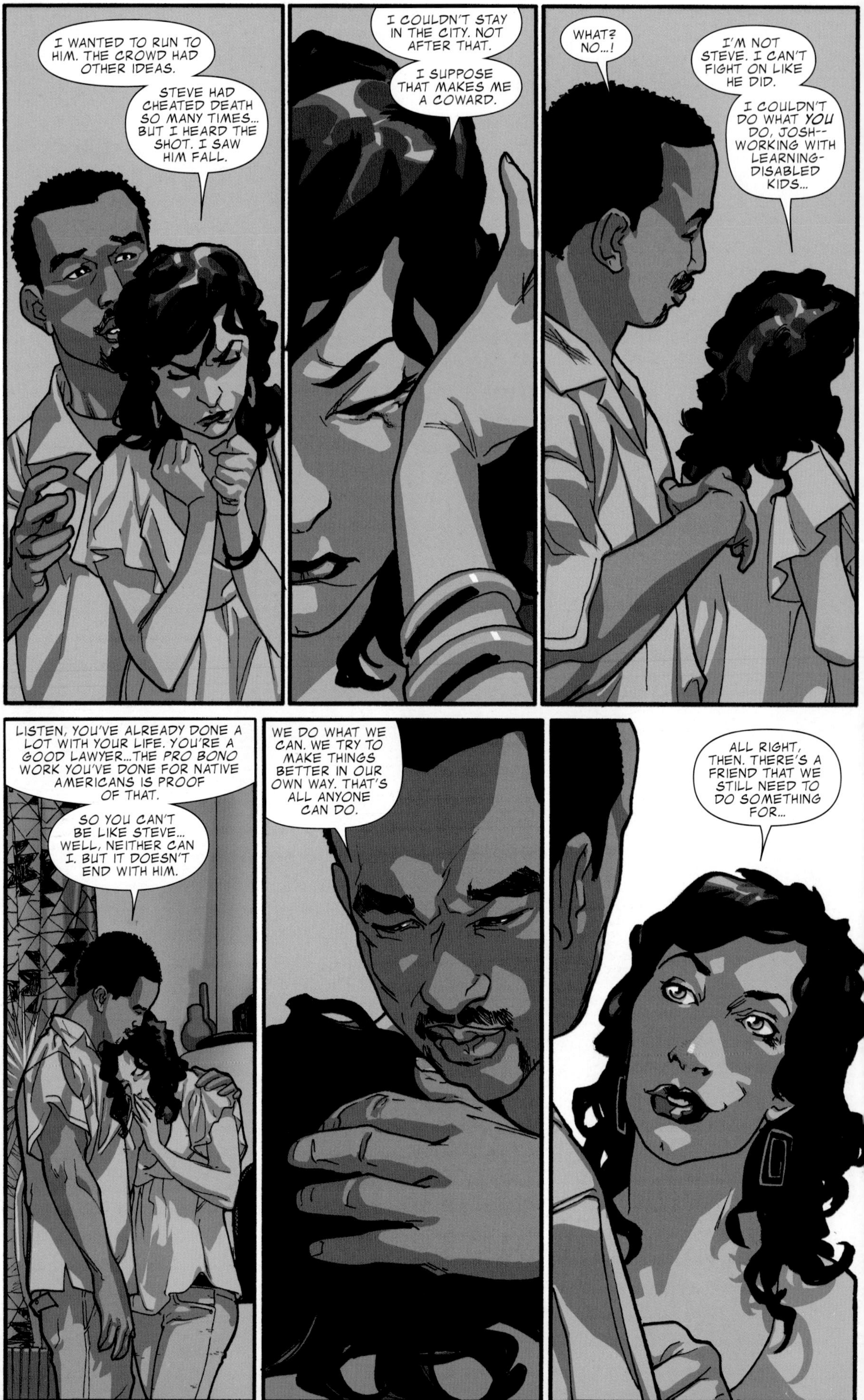
I WANTED TO RUN TO HIM. THE CROWD HAD OTHER IDEAS.
STEVE HAD CHEATED DEATH SO MANY TIMES... BUT I HEARD THE SHOT. I SAW HIM FALL.
I COULDN'T STAY IN THE CITY. NOT AFTER THAT.
I SUPPOSE THAT MAKES ME A COWARD.
WHAT? NO...!
I'M NOT STEVE. I CAN'T FIGHT ON LIKE HE DID.
I COULDN'T DO WHAT YOU DO, JOSH-- WORKING WITH LEARNING-DISABLED KIDS...
LISTEN, YOU'VE ALREADY DONE A LOT WITH YOUR LIFE. YOU'RE A GOOD LAWYER...THE PRO BONO WORK YOU'VE DONE FOR NATIVE AMERICANS IS PROOF OF THAT.
SO YOU CAN'T BE LIKE STEVE... WELL, NEITHER CAN I. BUT IT DOESN'T END WITH HIM.
WE DO WHAT WE CAN. WE TRY TO MAKE THINGS BETTER IN OUR OWN WAY. THAT'S ALL ANYONE CAN DO.
ALL RIGHT, THEN. THERE'S A FRIEND THAT WE STILL NEED TO DO SOMETHING FOR...

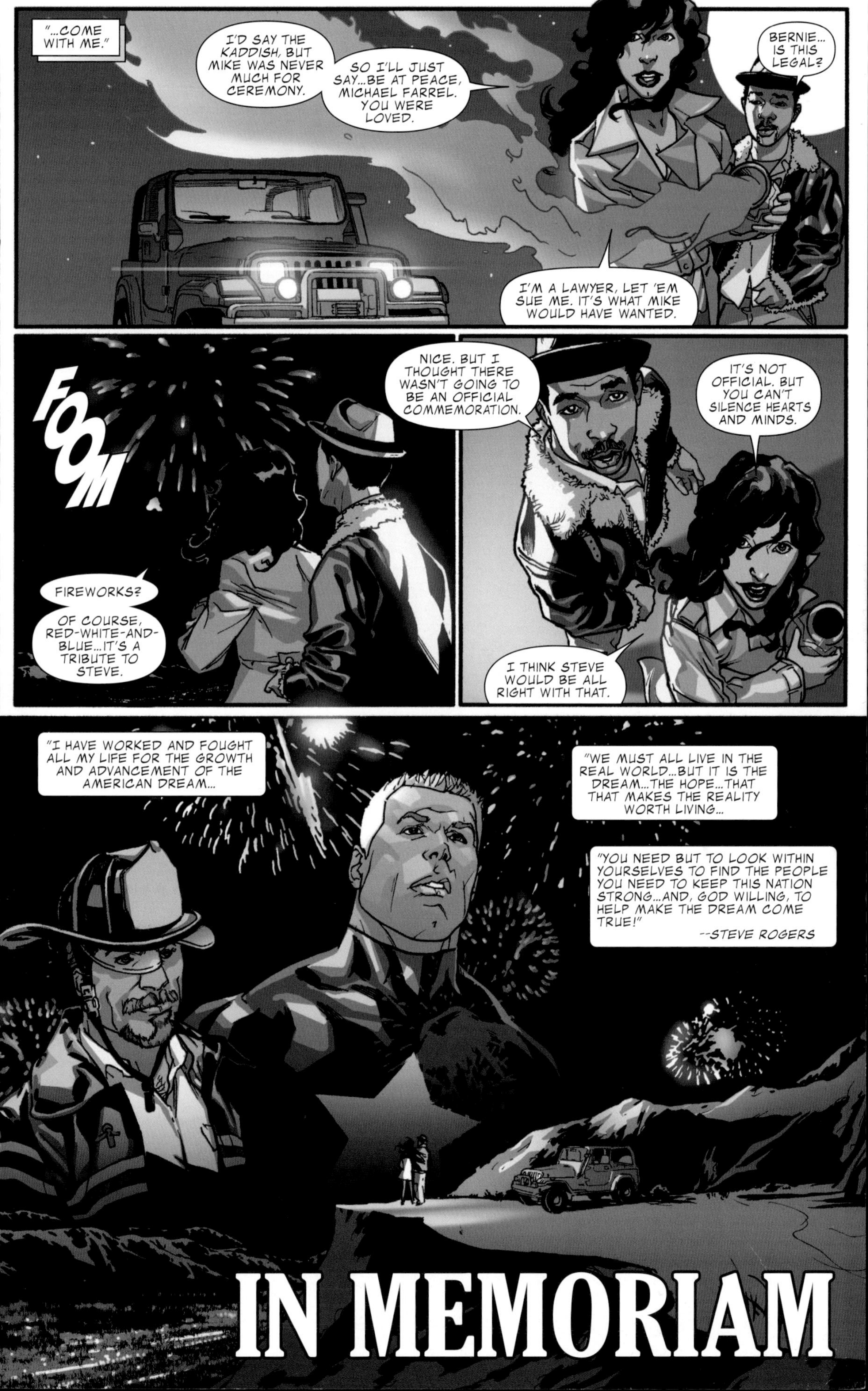
"...COME WITH ME."
I'D SAY THE KADDISH, BUT MIKE WAS NEVER MUCH FOR CEREMONY.
SO I'LL JUST SAY...BE AT PEACE, MICHAEL FARREL. YOU WERE LOVED.
BERNIE... IS THIS LEGAL?
I'M A LAWYER, LET 'EM SUE ME. IT'S WHAT MIKE WOULD HAVE WANTED.
FOOM
FIREWORKS?
OF COURSE, RED-WHITE-AND-BLUE...IT'S A TRIBUTE TO STEVE.
NICE. BUT I THOUGHT THERE WASN'T GOING TO BE AN OFFICIAL COMMEMORATION.
IT'S NOT OFFICIAL. BUT YOU CAN'T SILENCE HEARTS AND MINDS.
I THINK STEVE WOULD BE ALL RIGHT WITH THAT.
"I HAVE WORKED AND FOUGHT ALL MY LIFE FOR THE GROWTH AND ADVANCEMENT OF THE AMERICAN DREAM...
"WE MUST ALL LIVE IN THE REAL WORLD...BUT IT IS THE DREAM...THE HOPE...THAT THAT MAKES THE REALITY WORTH LIVING...
"YOU NEED BUT TO LOOK WITHIN YOURSELVES TO FIND THE PEOPLE YOU NEED TO KEEP THIS NATION STRONG...AND, GOD WILLING, TO HELP MAKE THE DREAM COME TRUE!"
--STEVE ROGERS
IN MEMORIAM

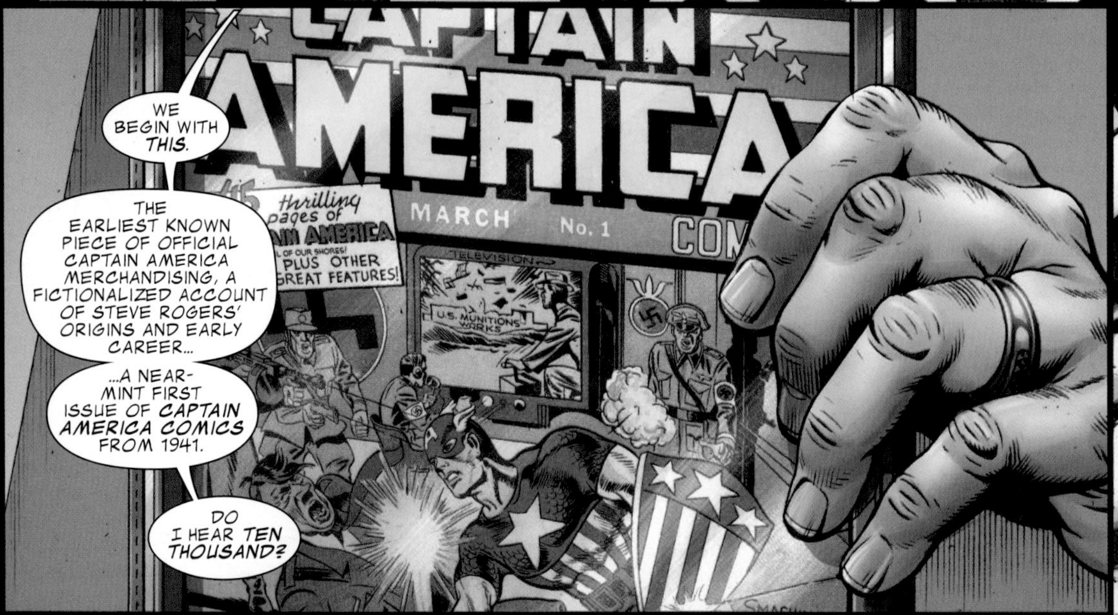
WE BEGIN WITH THIS.
THE EARLIEST KNOWN PIECE OF OFFICIAL CAPTAIN AMERICA MERCHANDISING, A FICTIONALIZED ACCOUNT OF STEVE ROGERS' ORIGINS AND EARLY CAREER...
...A NEAR-MINT FIRST ISSUE OF CAPTAIN AMERICA COMICS FROM 1941.
DO I HEAR TEN THOUSAND?

THE PERSISTENCE OF MEMORABILIA

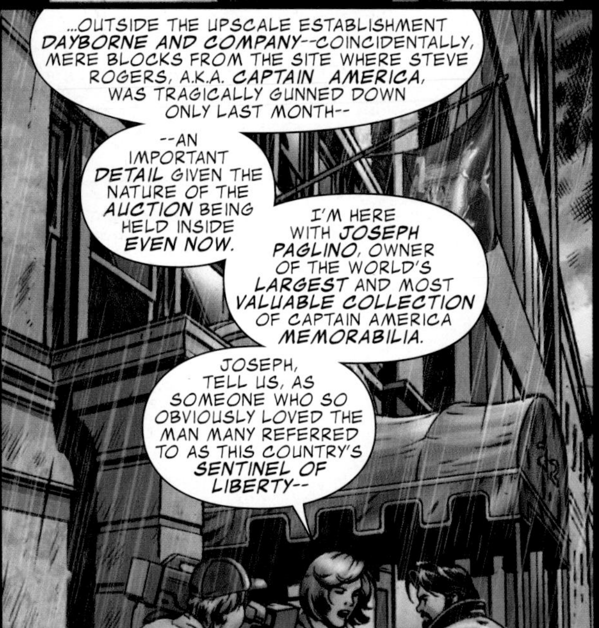
...OUTSIDE THE UPSCALE ESTABLISHMENT DAYBORNE AND COMPANY--COINCIDENTALLY, MERE BLOCKS FROM THE SITE WHERE STEVE ROGERS, A.K.A. CAPTAIN AMERICA, WAS TRAGICALLY GUNNED DOWN ONLY LAST MONTH--
--AN IMPORTANT DETAIL GIVEN THE NATURE OF THE AUCTION BEING HELD INSIDE EVEN NOW.
I'M HERE WITH JOSEPH PAGLINO, OWNER OF THE WORLD'S LARGEST AND MOST VALUABLE COLLECTION OF CAPTAIN AMERICA MEMORABILIA.
JOSEPH, TELL US, AS SOMEONE WHO SO OBVIOUSLY LOVED THE MAN MANY REFERRED TO AS THIS COUNTRY'S SENTINEL OF LIBERTY--

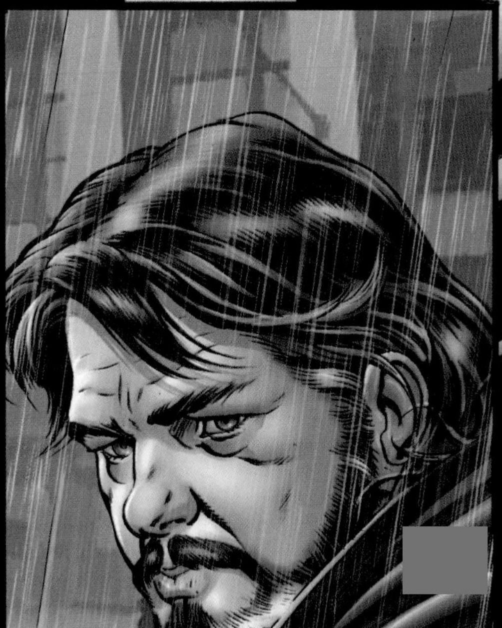
--WHY HAVE YOU SUDDENLY PUT THAT COLLECTION UP FOR SALE?

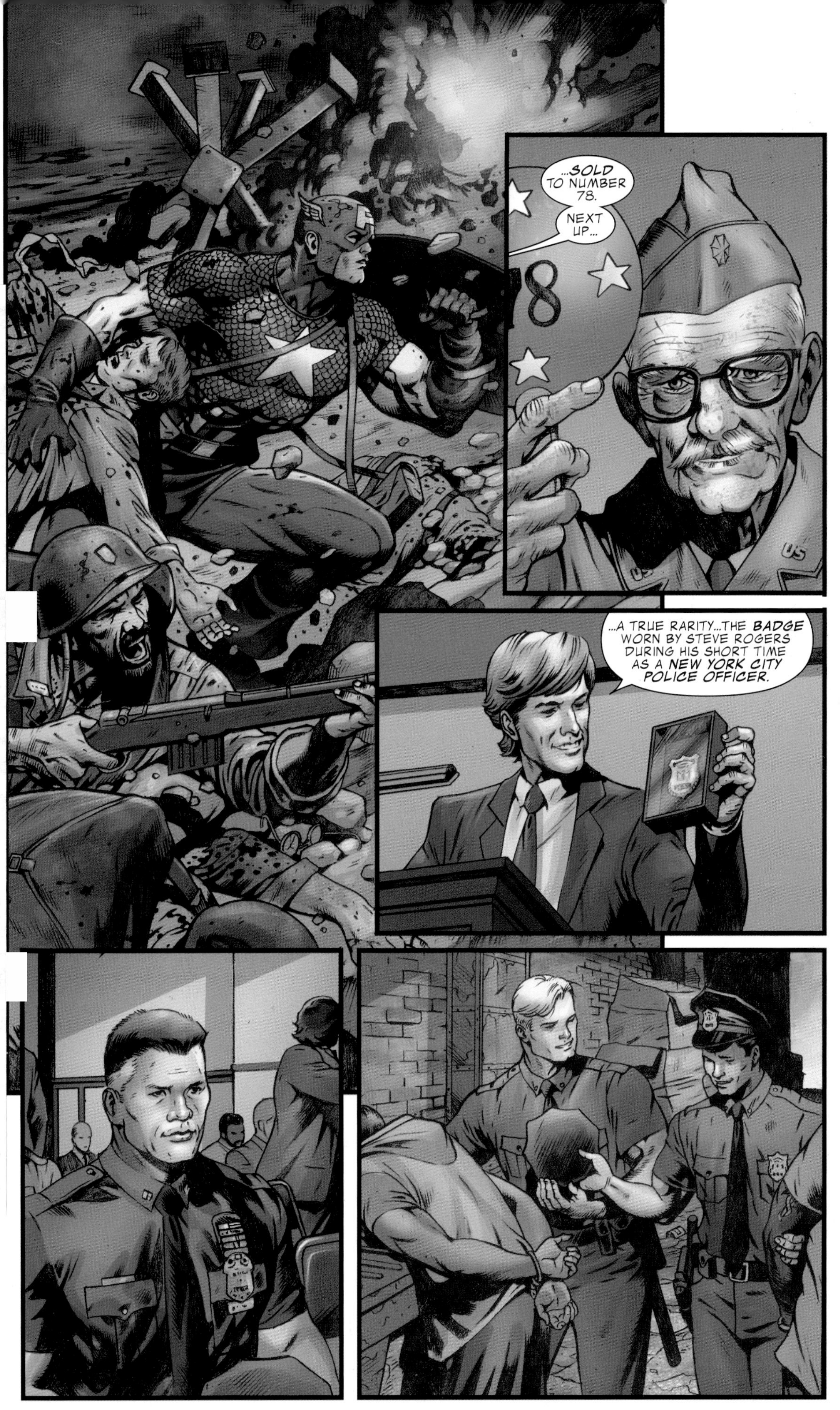
...SOLD TO NUMBER 78.
NEXT UP...
...A TRUE RARITY...THE BADGE WORN BY STEVE ROGERS DURING HIS SHORT TIME AS A NEW YORK CITY POLICE OFFICER.

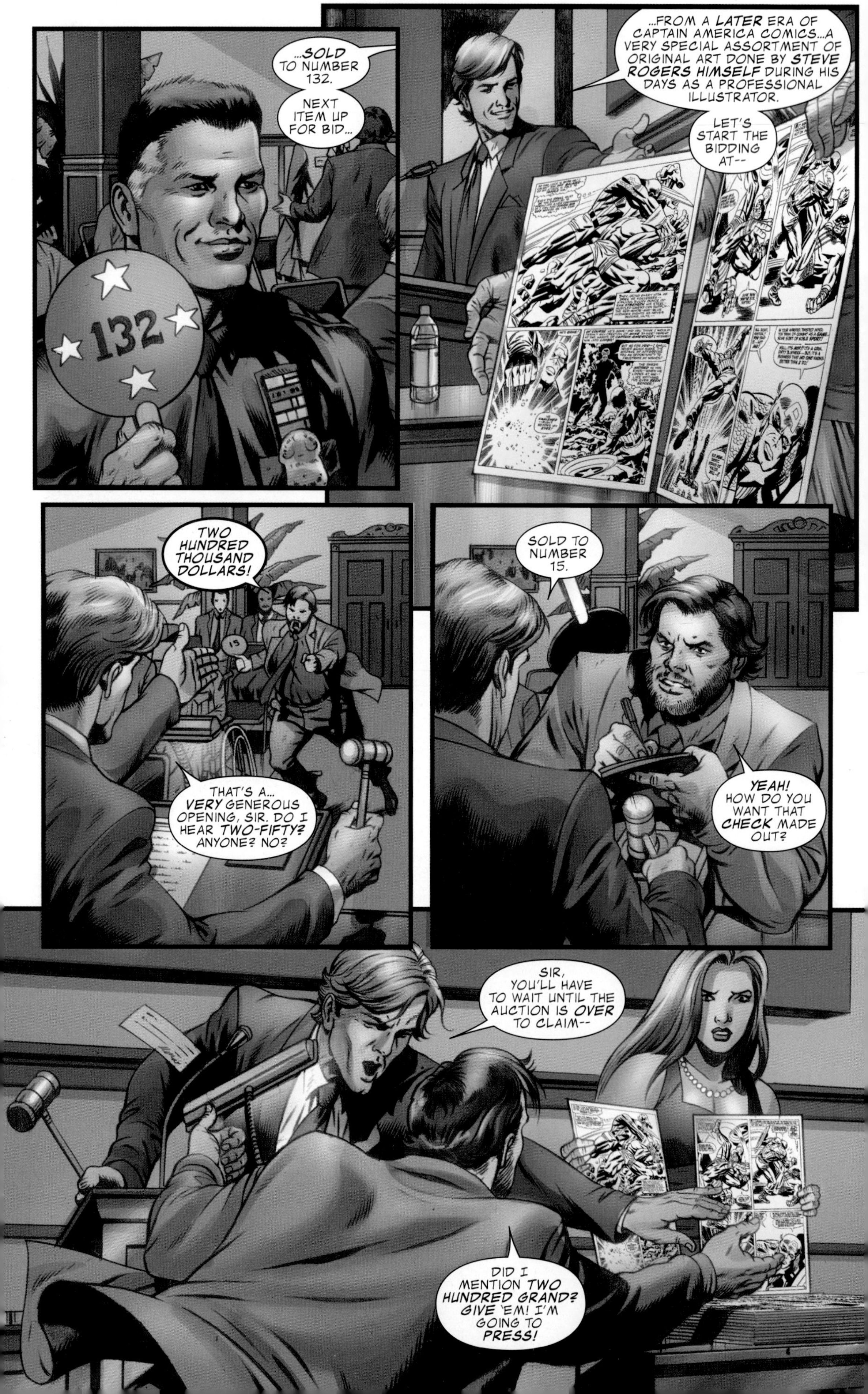

...SOLD TO NUMBER 132.
NEXT ITEM UP FOR BID...
132
...FROM A LATER ERA OF CAPTAIN AMERICA COMICS...A VERY SPECIAL ASSORTMENT OF ORIGINAL ART DONE BY STEVE ROGERS HIMSELF DURING HIS DAYS AS A PROFESSIONAL ILLUSTRATOR.
LET'S START THE BIDDING AT--
TWO HUNDRED THOUSAND DOLLARS!
15
THAT'S A... VERY GENEROUS OPENING, SIR. DO I HEAR TWO-FIFTY? ANYONE? NO?
SOLD TO NUMBER 15.
YEAH! HOW DO YOU WANT THAT CHECK MADE OUT?
SIR, YOU'LL HAVE TO WAIT UNTIL THE AUCTION IS OVER TO CLAIM--
DID I MENTION TWO HUNDRED GRAND? GIVE 'EM! I'M GOING TO PRESS!

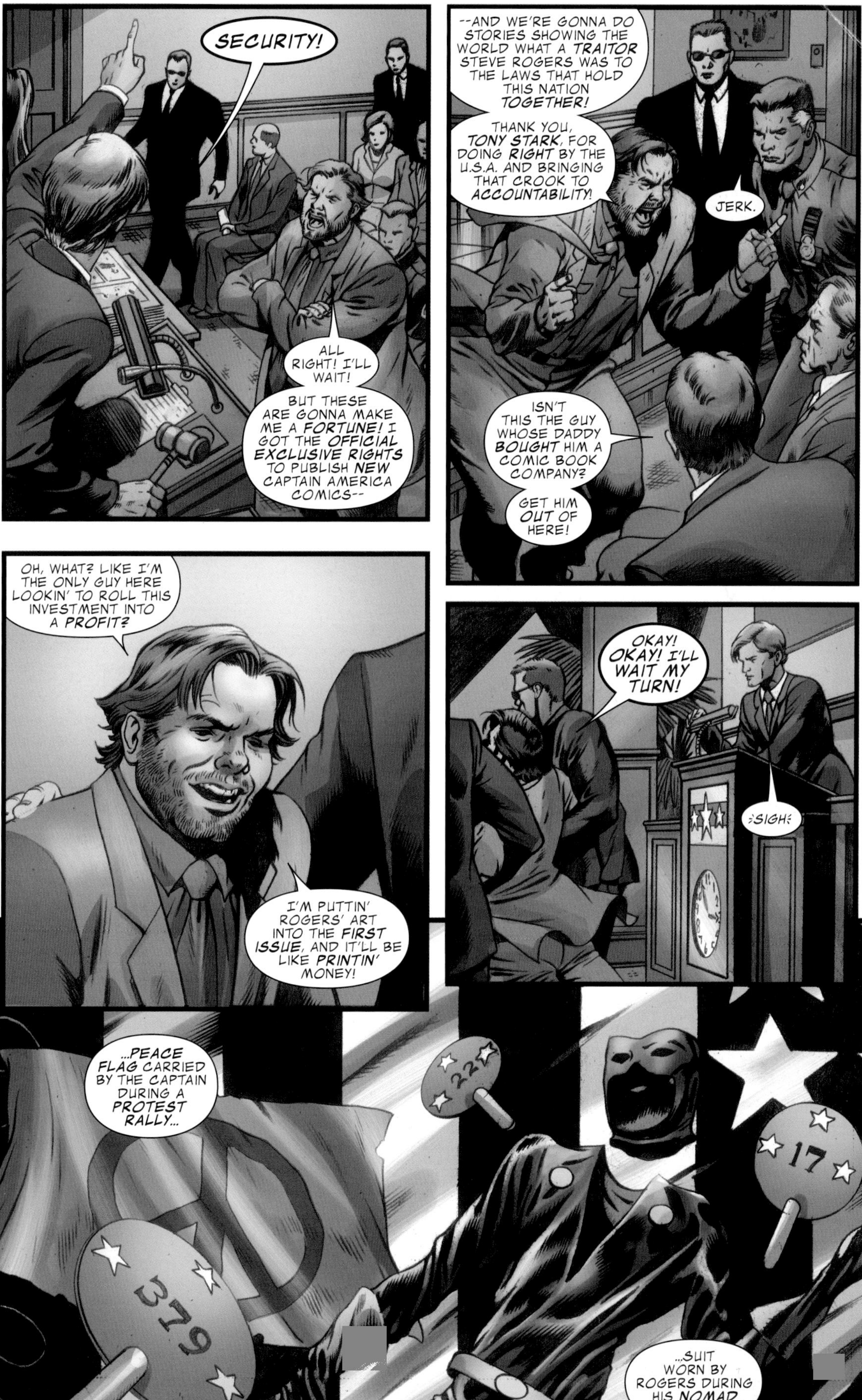
SECURITY!
ALL RIGHT! I'LL WAIT!
BUT THESE ARE GONNA MAKE ME A FORTUNE! I GOT THE OFFICIAL EXCLUSIVE RIGHTS TO PUBLISH NEW CAPTAIN AMERICA COMICS--
--AND WE'RE GONNA DO STORIES SHOWING THE WORLD WHAT A TRAITOR STEVE ROGERS WAS TO THE LAWS THAT HOLD THIS NATION TOGETHER!
THANK YOU, TONY STARK, FOR DOING RIGHT BY THE U.S.A. AND BRINGING THAT CROOK TO ACCOUNTABILITY!
JERK.
ISN'T THIS THE GUY WHOSE DADDY BOUGHT HIM A COMIC BOOK COMPANY?
GET HIM OUT OF HERE!
OH, WHAT? LIKE I'M THE ONLY GUY HERE LOOKIN' TO ROLL THIS INVESTMENT INTO A PROFIT?
I'M PUTTIN' ROGERS' ART INTO THE FIRST ISSUE, AND IT'LL BE LIKE PRINTIN' MONEY!
OKAY! OKAY! I'LL WAIT MY TURN!
SIGH
...PEACE FLAG CARRIED BY THE CAPTAIN DURING A PROTEST RALLY...
22
17
379
...SUIT WORN BY ROGERS DURING HIS NOMAD PHASE...

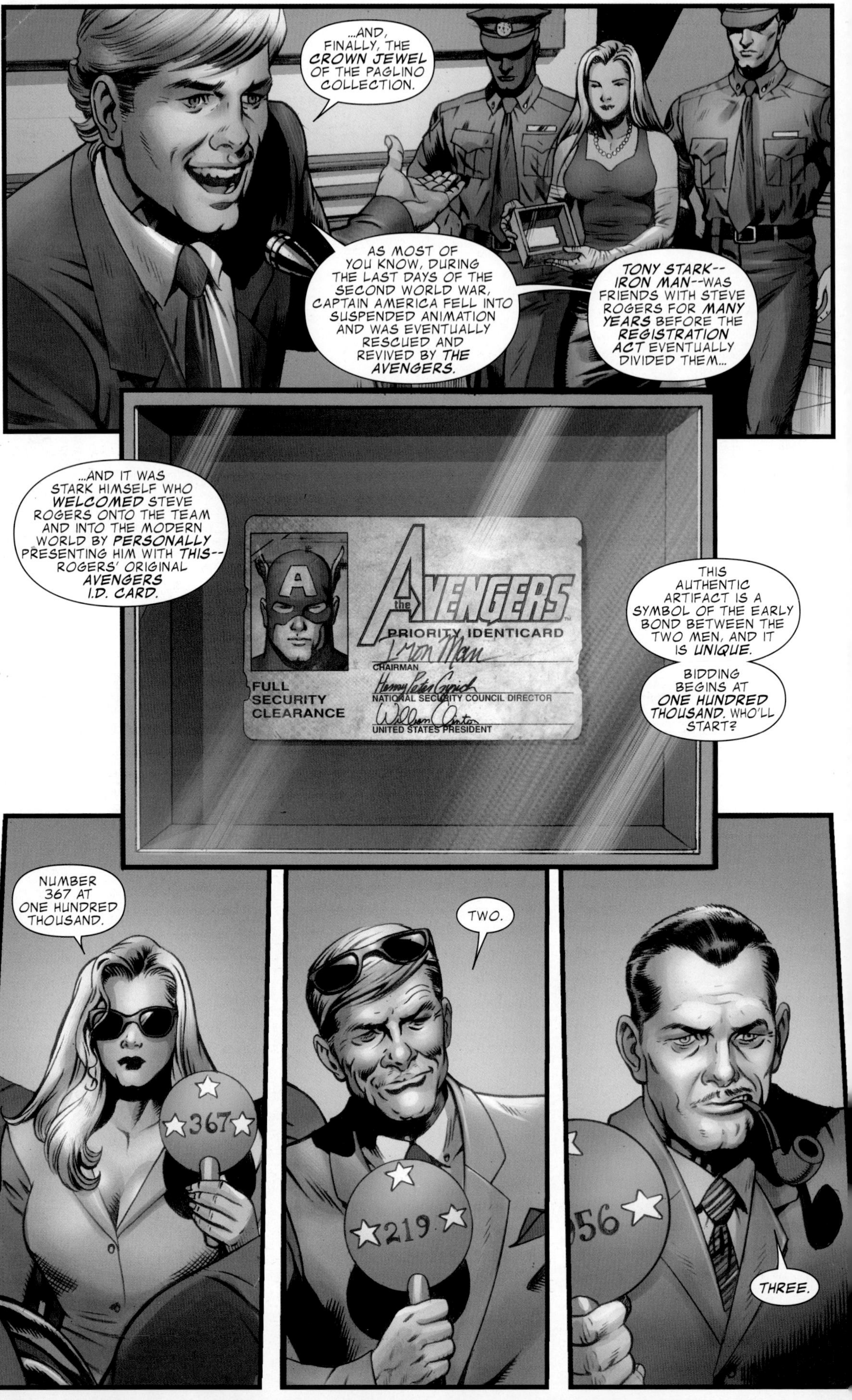
...AND, FINALLY, THE CROWN JEWEL OF THE PAGLINO COLLECTION.
AS MOST OF YOU KNOW, DURING THE LAST DAYS OF THE SECOND WORLD WAR, CAPTAIN AMERICA FELL INTO SUSPENDED ANIMATION AND WAS EVENTUALLY RESCUED AND REVIVED BY THE AVENGERS.
TONY STARK--IRON MAN--WAS FRIENDS WITH STEVE ROGERS FOR MANY YEARS BEFORE THE REGISTRATION ACT EVENTUALLY DIVIDED THEM...
...AND IT WAS STARK HIMSELF WHO WELCOMED STEVE ROGERS ONTO THE TEAM AND INTO THE MODERN WORLD BY PERSONALLY PRESENTING HIM WITH THIS--ROGERS' ORIGINAL AVENGERS I.D. CARD.
A
the AVENGERS
PRIORITY IDENTICARD
CHAIRMAN
FULL SECURITY CLEARANCE
NATIONAL SECURITY COUNCIL DIRECTOR
UNITED STATES PRESIDENT
THIS AUTHENTIC ARTIFACT IS A SYMBOL OF THE EARLY BOND BETWEEN THE TWO MEN, AND IT IS UNIQUE.
BIDDING BEGINS AT ONE HUNDRED THOUSAND. WHO'LL START?
NUMBER 367 AT ONE HUNDRED THOUSAND.
367
TWO.
219
THREE.

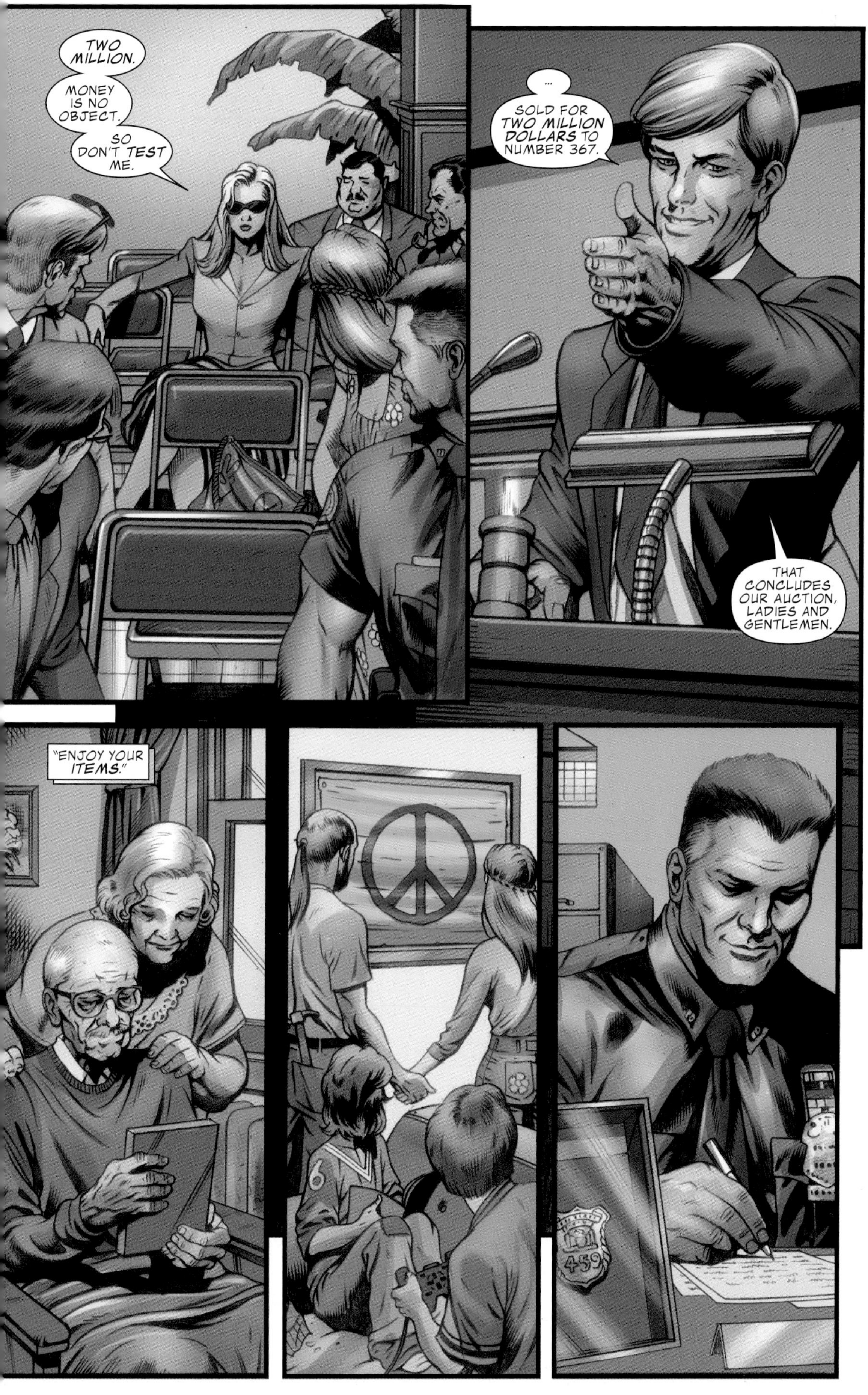

TWO MILLION.
MONEY IS NO OBJECT.
SO DON'T TEST ME.
...
SOLD FOR TWO MILLION DOLLARS TO NUMBER 367.
THAT CONCLUDES OUR AUCTION, LADIES AND GENTLEMEN.
"ENJOY YOUR ITEMS."

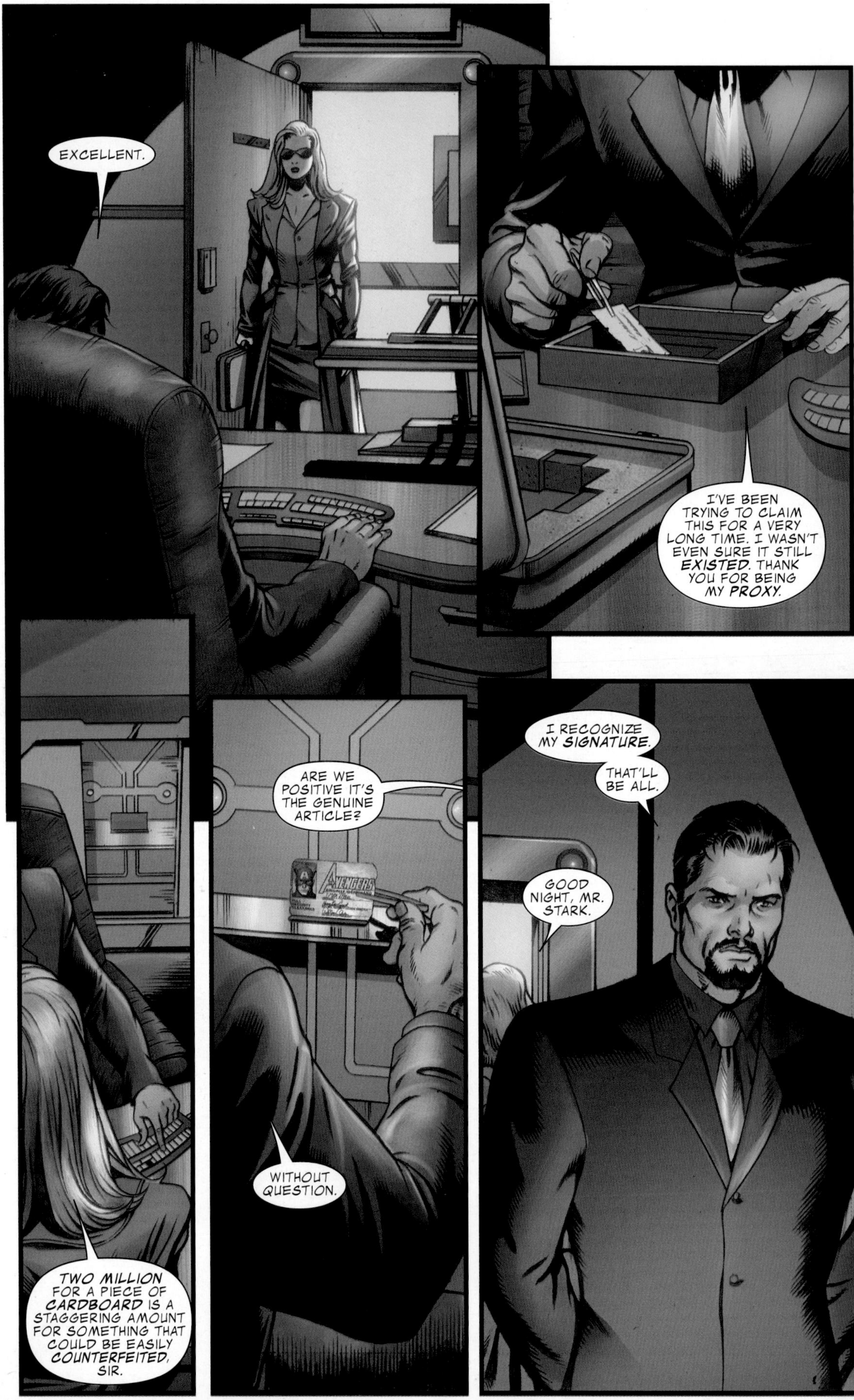
EXCELLENT.
I'VE BEEN TRYING TO CLAIM THIS FOR A VERY LONG TIME. I WASN'T EVEN SURE IT STILL EXISTED. THANK YOU FOR BEING MY PROXY.
TWO MILLION FOR A PIECE OF CARDBOARD IS A STAGGERING AMOUNT FOR SOMETHING THAT COULD BE EASILY COUNTERFEITED, SIR.
ARE WE POSITIVE IT'S THE GENUINE ARTICLE?
WITHOUT QUESTION.
I RECOGNIZE MY SIGNATURE.
THAT'LL BE ALL.
GOOD NIGHT, MR. STARK.

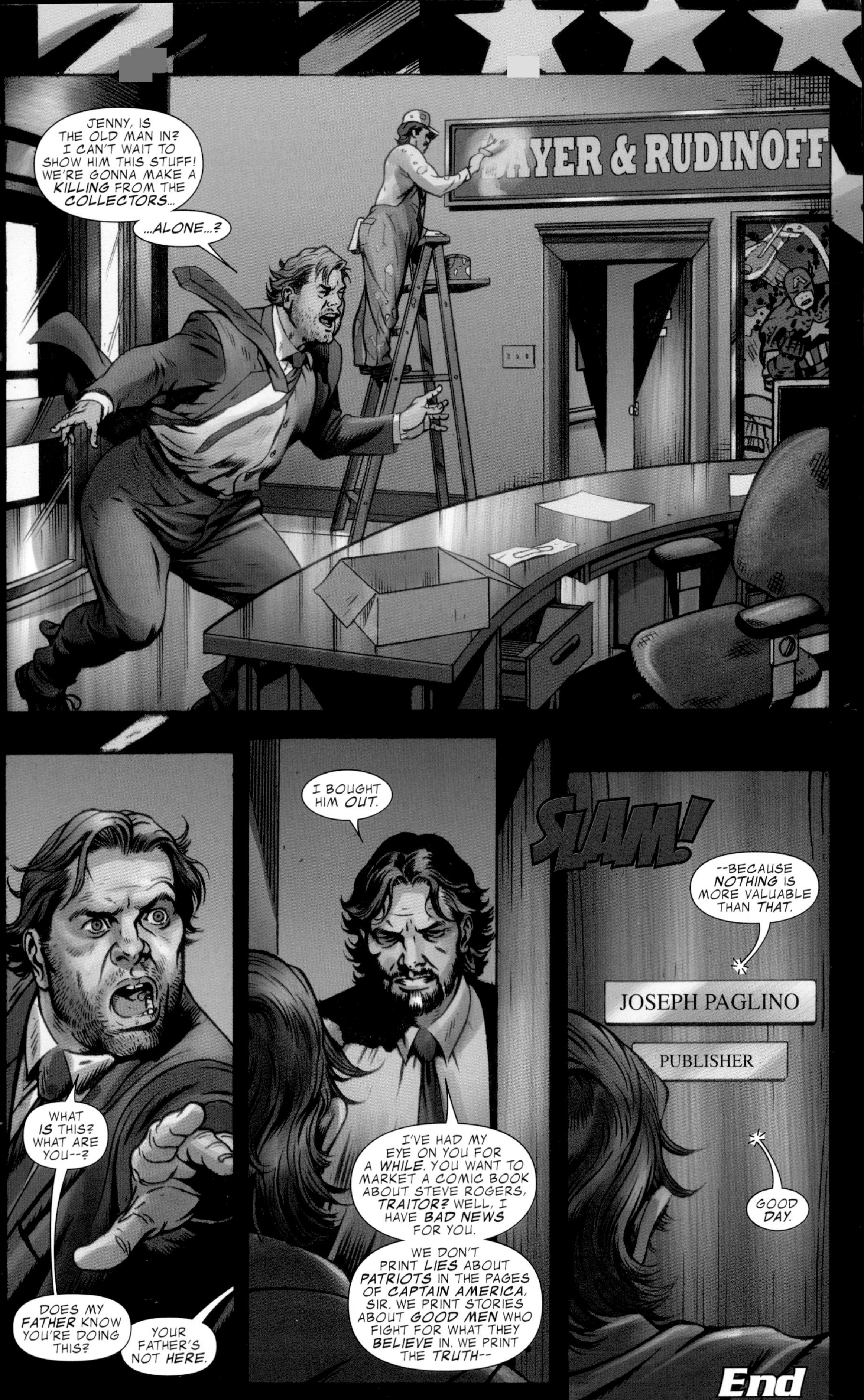
AYER & RUDINOFF
JENNY, IS THE OLD MAN IN? I CAN'T WAIT TO SHOW HIM THIS STUFF! WE'RE GONNA MAKE A KILLING FROM THE COLLECTORS...
...ALONE...?
WHAT IS THIS? WHAT ARE YOU--?
DOES MY FATHER KNOW YOU'RE DOING THIS?
YOUR FATHER'S NOT HERE.
I BOUGHT HIM OUT.
I'VE HAD MY EYE ON YOU FOR A WHILE. YOU WANT TO MARKET A COMIC BOOK ABOUT STEVE ROGERS, TRAITOR? WELL, I HAVE BAD NEWS FOR YOU.
WE DON'T PRINT LIES ABOUT PATRIOTS IN THE PAGES OF CAPTAIN AMERICA, SIR. WE PRINT STORIES ABOUT GOOD MEN WHO FIGHT FOR WHAT THEY BELIEVE IN. WE PRINT THE TRUTH--
SLAM!
--BECAUSE NOTHING IS MORE VALUABLE THAN THAT.
JOSEPH PAGLINO
PUBLISHER
GOOD DAY.
End

JOE SIMON

CAPTAIN AMERICA

was the first of our patriotic guts-and-glory super heroes, born in the midst of a Great Depression, with the world on the brink of war.

The first issue was a huge hit, and when the industry became aware of the sensational sales, John Goldwater wasn't happy. Mr. Goldwater was an owner of MLJ Comics, publishers of the Archie line. One of MLJ's characters was The Shield, a modest-selling patriotic character with a red-white-and- blue rectangular shield design on his costume, running from his chest area to his crotch. Mr. Goldwater summoned us to his office to threaten, demand, and do whatever they do in legal circles—perhaps even issue a "cease-and-desist," which seemed to be a favorite.

There were Martin Goodman, Jack Kirby and myself, facing off with Goldwater. He probably had lawyers on hand, although I don't recall that part clearly, most likely due to my aversion for the profession. I suggested that we change the shape of Captain America's shield to round, like the covers of garbage cans we had used as kids to ward off offensive snowballs. An agreement was reached, albeit gingerly.

Mr. Goodman was very quiet—even meek—during the proceedings. I had a suspicion that there was something deeper going on between the two publishers. Later I was to learn that they had been in business together for a short period of time, having met when they were both employees in the circulation department of Hugo Gernsback, a major publisher of pulp-fiction. On our way out, Mr. Goldwater took me aside to offer Simon and Kirby a better deal, although he had no knowledge of what our deal was with Timely. Martin Goodman seethed as we departed, mumbling inaudibly while Goldwater chuckled.

As it turned out, Captain America with his new round shield had a better weapon to hurl and twirl through space and what-have-you. All was zooming and booming in Capland.

We still had a problem, however: the talented Jack Kirby was plagued by memory lapses, some so severe that he would often drop his nickel fare into the turnstile when both entering and exiting from his daily subway commute. (For those readers outside of New York City, it's only required that a rider pay to enter the subway.)

Another result of Kirby's confusion was that Cap's shield would magically change, sometimes on the same page, from rectangular to round, back and forth, causing a lot of erasing and loss of time. At times even the inker got lost in the process, causing more whiting-out, pasting-over confusion. Kirby became extremely upset when this was brought to his attention but it was clear that he needed more than a verbal reminder.

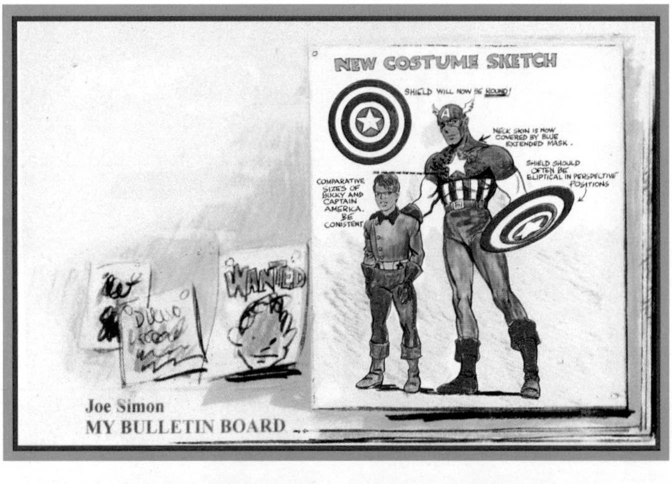

NEW COSTUME SKETCH
SHIELD WILL NOW BE ROUND!
NECK SKIN IS NOW COVERED BY BLUE EXTENDED MASK.
SHIELD SHOULD OFTEN BE ELIPTICAL IN PERSPECTIVE POSITIONS
COMPARATIVE SIZES OF BUCKY AND CAPTAIN AMERICA. BE CONISTENT
WANTED

Joe Simon
MY BULLETIN BOARD

MY BULLETIN BOARD

LOOK! I'M ELLIPTICAL!
WHOO-OOSHHHH!
THROW IT!
OUCH!
PUSH IT!
STARTING NOW! THE SHIELD IS ... ROUND!
TOSS IT! BUTT IT! FLIP IT! ELLIPT IT!
SHOVE IT!!!
WATCH FOR JOE'S TIMELY BULL-ETINS!

As first editor of the Timely-Marvel line, and with the proposed expansion of Captain America to appear in various titles, I assigned other artists to help out in the steps of production which included penciling, inking, patching and erasing the pages—as we called the individual art boards. That's when I set up my bulletin board, where staff and free-lancers would have a forum to view new policies, projects, developments and notices relating to our characters and titles.

These postings established color themes and noted the relative sizes of Cap and his boy sidekick, Bucky. They described weapons, and yes, Captain America's shield—how to draw it round, elliptical, in perspective, how to zip it, bounce it, carry it, react to it. My bulletin board proved to be the official office memo. It progressed to announce, in colorful fashion, schedules, holidays, birthdays, and milestones.

Eventually, some of the graphics on my bulletin board were defaced by rascally vandals. Most notices were discarded after their usefulness expired. A couple of them survived to this day in surprisingly good condition, considering the sixty-plus years that had elapsed.

Jack Kirby continued to have occasional lapses in remembering the shape of the shield. Sometimes he would draw a star on Cap's mask instead of an "A," and put an "A" on Cap's chest instead of a star. These were small problems, and he was worth it. Nobody could match the thunder and lightning Jack Kirby brought to the new American art form known as comic books.

That's my story. You could have posted it on **MY BULLETIN BOARD.**

JOE SIMON

***Joe Simon** was the first editor for Timely Comics, joining the staff in 1940. Late that year* Captain America Comics *#1 hit the newsstands. He and Jack Kirby produced hit comics in every genre and for every major publisher. Their finest work is collected in* The Best of Simon and Kirby, *the first book in the new Official Simon and Kirby Library.*

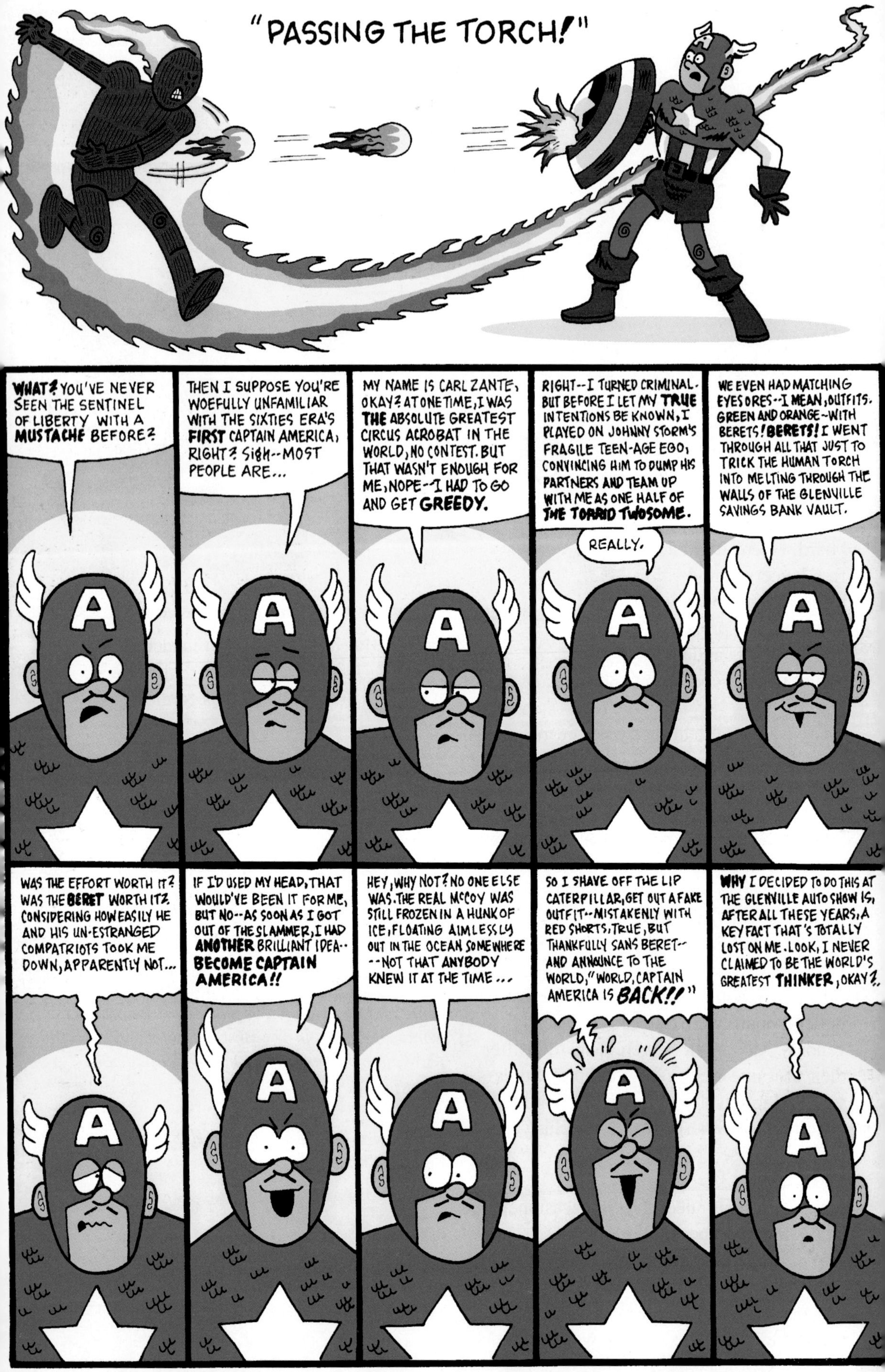
"PASSING THE TORCH!"
WHAT? YOU'VE NEVER SEEN THE SENTINEL OF LIBERTY WITH A MUSTACHE BEFORE?
THEN I SUPPOSE YOU'RE WOEFULLY UNFAMILIAR WITH THE SIXTIES ERA'S FIRST CAPTAIN AMERICA, RIGHT? SIGH--MOST PEOPLE ARE...
MY NAME IS CARL ZANTE, OKAY? AT ONE TIME, I WAS THE ABSOLUTE GREATEST CIRCUS ACROBAT IN THE WORLD, NO CONTEST. BUT THAT WASN'T ENOUGH FOR ME, NOPE--I HAD TO GO AND GET GREEDY.
RIGHT--I TURNED CRIMINAL. BUT BEFORE I LET MY TRUE INTENTIONS BE KNOWN, I PLAYED ON JOHNNY STORM'S FRAGILE TEEN-AGE EGO, CONVINCING HIM TO DUMP HIS PARTNERS AND TEAM UP WITH ME AS ONE HALF OF THE TORRID TWOSOME.
REALLY.
WE EVEN HAD MATCHING EYESORES--I MEAN, OUTFITS. GREEN AND ORANGE--WITH BERETS! BERETS! I WENT THROUGH ALL THAT JUST TO TRICK THE HUMAN TORCH INTO MELTING THROUGH THE WALLS OF THE GLENVILLE SAVINGS BANK VAULT.
WAS THE EFFORT WORTH IT? WAS THE BERET WORTH IT? CONSIDERING HOW EASILY HE AND HIS UN-ESTRANGED COMPATRIOTS TOOK ME DOWN, APPARENTLY NOT...
IF I'D USED MY HEAD, THAT WOULD'VE BEEN IT FOR ME, BUT NO--AS SOON AS I GOT OUT OF THE SLAMMER, I HAD ANOTHER BRILLIANT IDEA-- BECOME CAPTAIN AMERICA!!
HEY, WHY NOT? NO ONE ELSE WAS. THE REAL McCOY WAS STILL FROZEN IN A HUNK OF ICE, FLOATING AIMLESSLY OUT IN THE OCEAN SOMEWHERE --NOT THAT ANYBODY KNEW IT AT THE TIME...
SO I SHAVE OFF THE LIP CATERPILLAR, GET OUT A FAKE OUTFIT--MISTAKENLY WITH RED SHORTS, TRUE, BUT THANKFULLY SANS BERET-- AND ANNOUNCE TO THE WORLD, "WORLD, CAPTAIN AMERICA IS BACK!!"
WHY I DECIDED TO DO THIS AT THE GLENVILLE AUTO SHOW IS, AFTER ALL THESE YEARS, A KEY FACT THAT'S TOTALLY LOST ON ME. LOOK, I NEVER CLAIMED TO BE THE WORLD'S GREATEST THINKER, OKAY?

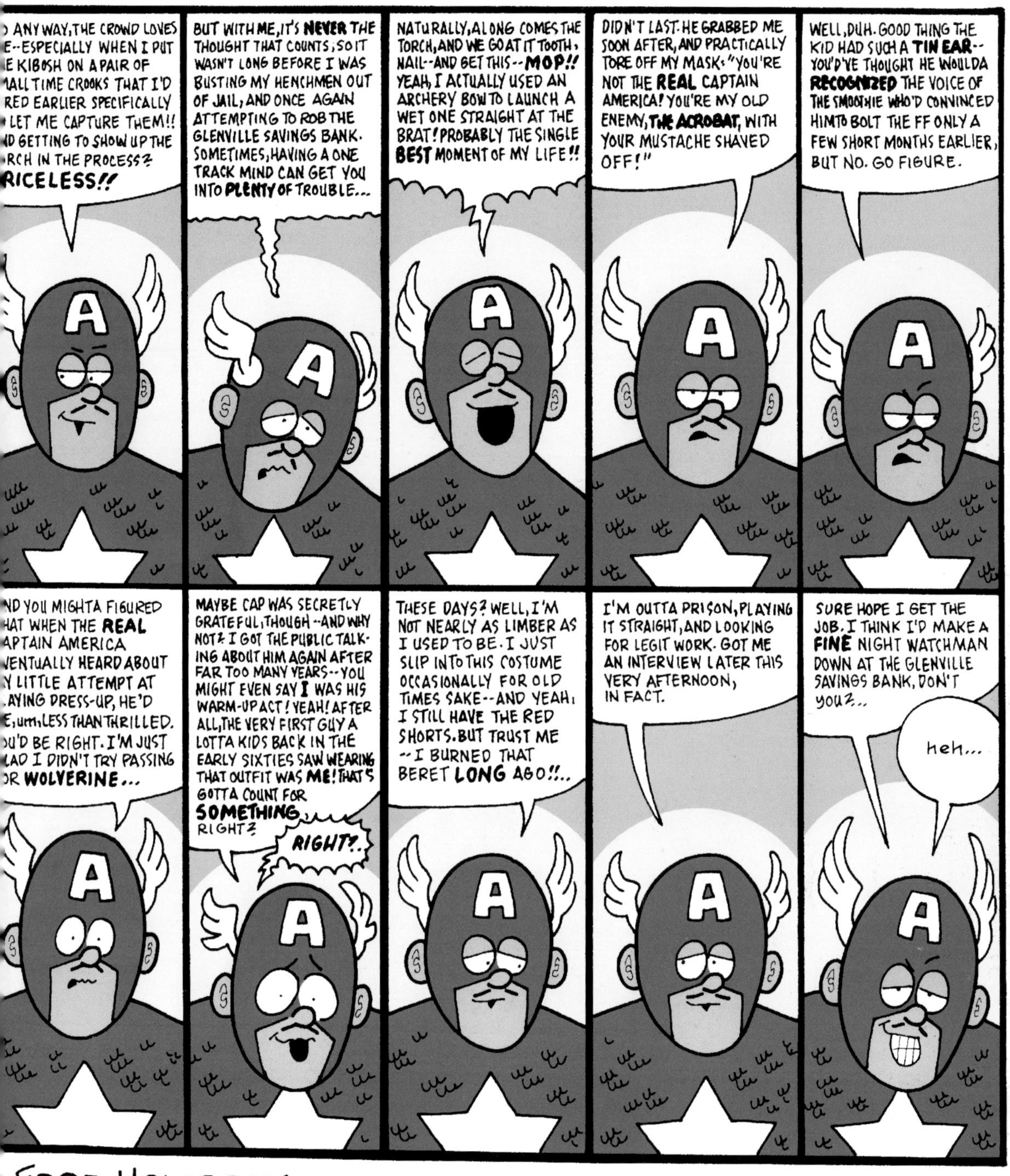

ANYWAY, THE CROWD LOVES E--ESPECIALLY WHEN I PUT E KIBOSH ON A PAIR OF MALL TIME CROOKS THAT I'D RED EARLIER SPECIFICALLY LET ME CAPTURE THEM!! ID GETTING TO SHOW UP THE RCH IN THE PROCESS? RICELESS!!
BUT WITH ME, IT'S NEVER THE THOUGHT THAT COUNTS, SO IT WASN'T LONG BEFORE I WAS BUSTING MY HENCHMEN OUT OF JAIL, AND ONCE AGAIN ATTEMPTING TO ROB THE GLENVILLE SAVINGS BANK. SOMETIMES, HAVING A ONE TRACK MIND CAN GET YOU INTO PLENTY OF TROUBLE...
NATURALLY, ALONG COMES THE TORCH, AND WE GO AT IT TOOTH, NAIL--AND GET THIS--MOP!! YEAH, I ACTUALLY USED AN ARCHERY BOW TO LAUNCH A WET ONE STRAIGHT AT THE BRAT! PROBABLY THE SINGLE BEST MOMENT OF MY LIFE!!
DIDN'T LAST. HE GRABBED ME SOON AFTER, AND PRACTICALLY TORE OFF MY MASK: "YOU'RE NOT THE REAL CAPTAIN AMERICA! YOU'RE MY OLD ENEMY, THE ACROBAT, WITH YOUR MUSTACHE SHAVED OFF!"
WELL, DUH. GOOD THING THE KID HAD SUCH A TIN EAR-- YOU'D'VE THOUGHT HE WOULDA RECOGNIZED THE VOICE OF THE SMOOTHIE WHO'D CONVINCED HIM TO BOLT THE FF ONLY A FEW SHORT MONTHS EARLIER, BUT NO. GO FIGURE.
ND YOU MIGHTA FIGURED HAT WHEN THE REAL APTAIN AMERICA VENTUALLY HEARD ABOUT Y LITTLE ATTEMPT AT LAYING DRESS-UP, HE'D E, um, LESS THAN THRILLED. OU'D BE RIGHT. I'M JUST LAD I DIDN'T TRY PASSING OR WOLVERINE...
MAYBE CAP WAS SECRETLY GRATEFUL, THOUGH--AND WHY NOT? I GOT THE PUBLIC TALKING ABOUT HIM AGAIN AFTER FAR TOO MANY YEARS--YOU MIGHT EVEN SAY I WAS HIS WARM-UP ACT! YEAH! AFTER ALL, THE VERY FIRST GUY A LOTTA KIDS BACK IN THE EARLY SIXTIES SAW WEARING THAT OUTFIT WAS ME! THAT'S GOTTA COUNT FOR SOMETHING, RIGHT?
RIGHT?..
THESE DAYS? WELL, I'M NOT NEARLY AS LIMBER AS I USED TO BE. I JUST SLIP INTO THIS COSTUME OCCASIONALLY FOR OLD TIMES SAKE--AND YEAH, I STILL HAVE THE RED SHORTS. BUT TRUST ME --I BURNED THAT BERET LONG AGO!!..
I'M OUTTA PRISON, PLAYING IT STRAIGHT, AND LOOKING FOR LEGIT WORK. GOT ME AN INTERVIEW LATER THIS VERY AFTERNOON, IN FACT.
SURE HOPE I GET THE JOB. I THINK I'D MAKE A FINE NIGHT WATCHMAN DOWN AT THE GLENVILLE SAVINGS BANK, DON'T YOU?..
heh...

FRED HEMBECK 2009
LORS by CHRIS GIARRUSSO
SED ON MATERIAL by
an Lee, JACK KIRBY,
CK AYERS, and LARRY LIEBER:
RANGE TALES #106 and 114, 1963!

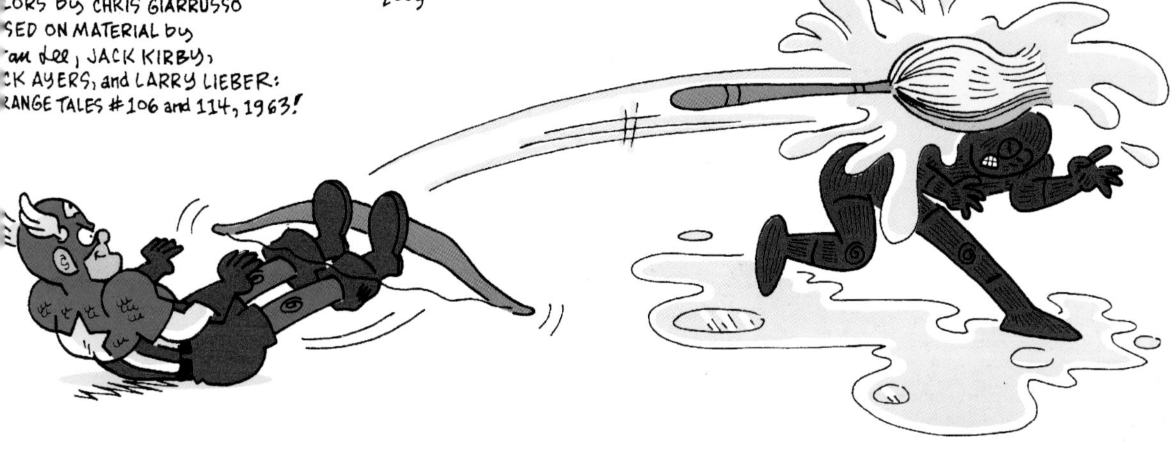

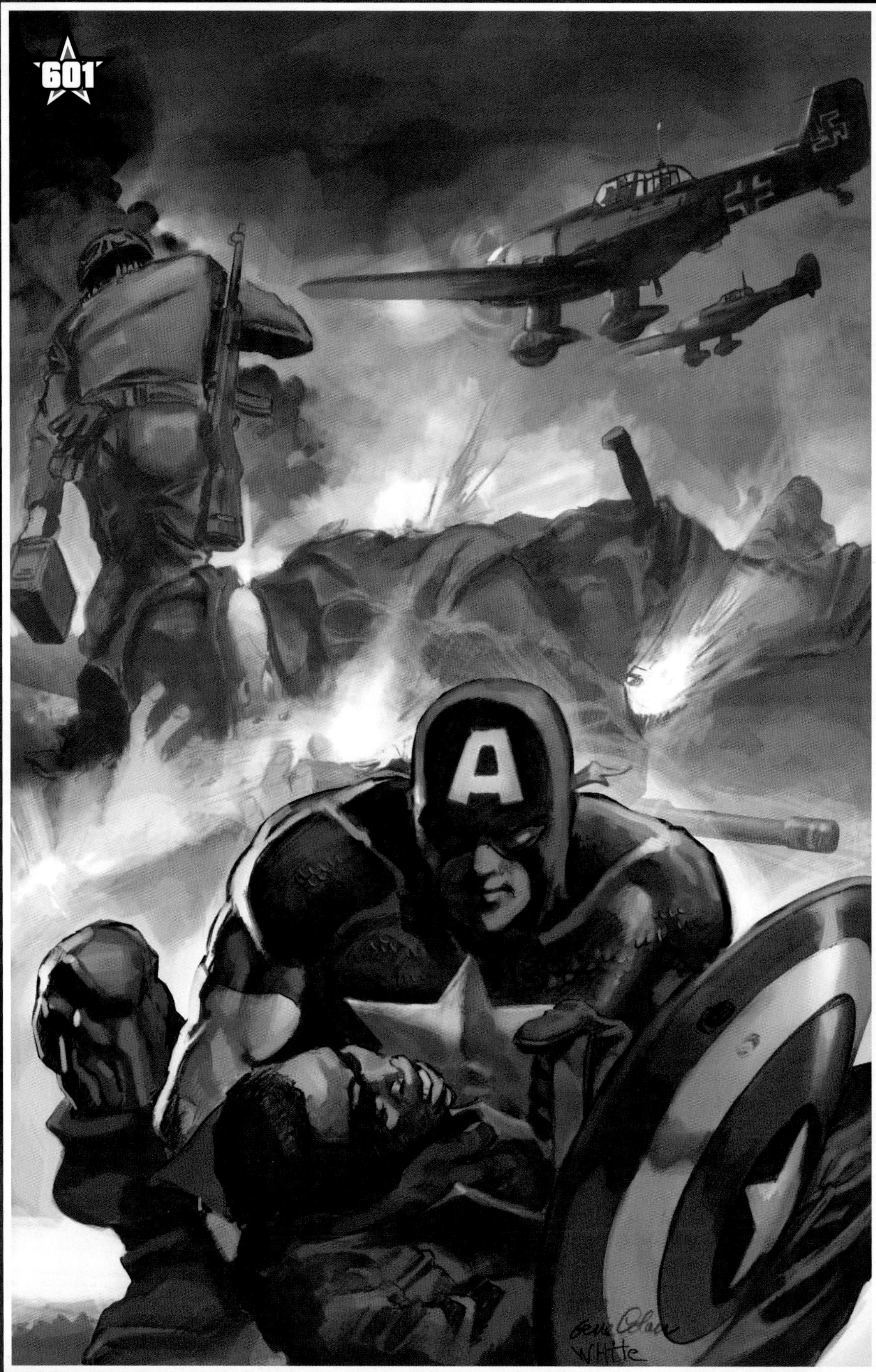
601

RED, WHITE & BLUE-BLOOD

In the dark days of the early 1940s,

STEVE ROGERS,

a struggling young artist from the
LOWER EAST SIDE OF MANHATTAN,
found himself horrified by the war raging overseas.
Desperate to help, he was rejected by the

U.S. ARMY

as unfit for service when he tried to enlist.

Undeterred, convinced this was where he needed to be, he was
selected to participate in a covert military project called

OPERATION: REBIRTH.

There, he was chosen by scientist
ABRAHAM ERSKINE
as the first human test subject, and overnight was transformed into

AMERICA'S FIRST SUPER-SOLDIER,

CAPTAIN AMERICA.

Now he and his former partner from World War II, James "Bucky" Barnes, aka the Winter Soldier,
fight to protect the people and the country they love from the forces that would destroy them!

This story takes place during Civil War and before Captain America #25
Captain America created by Joe Simon and Jack Kirby

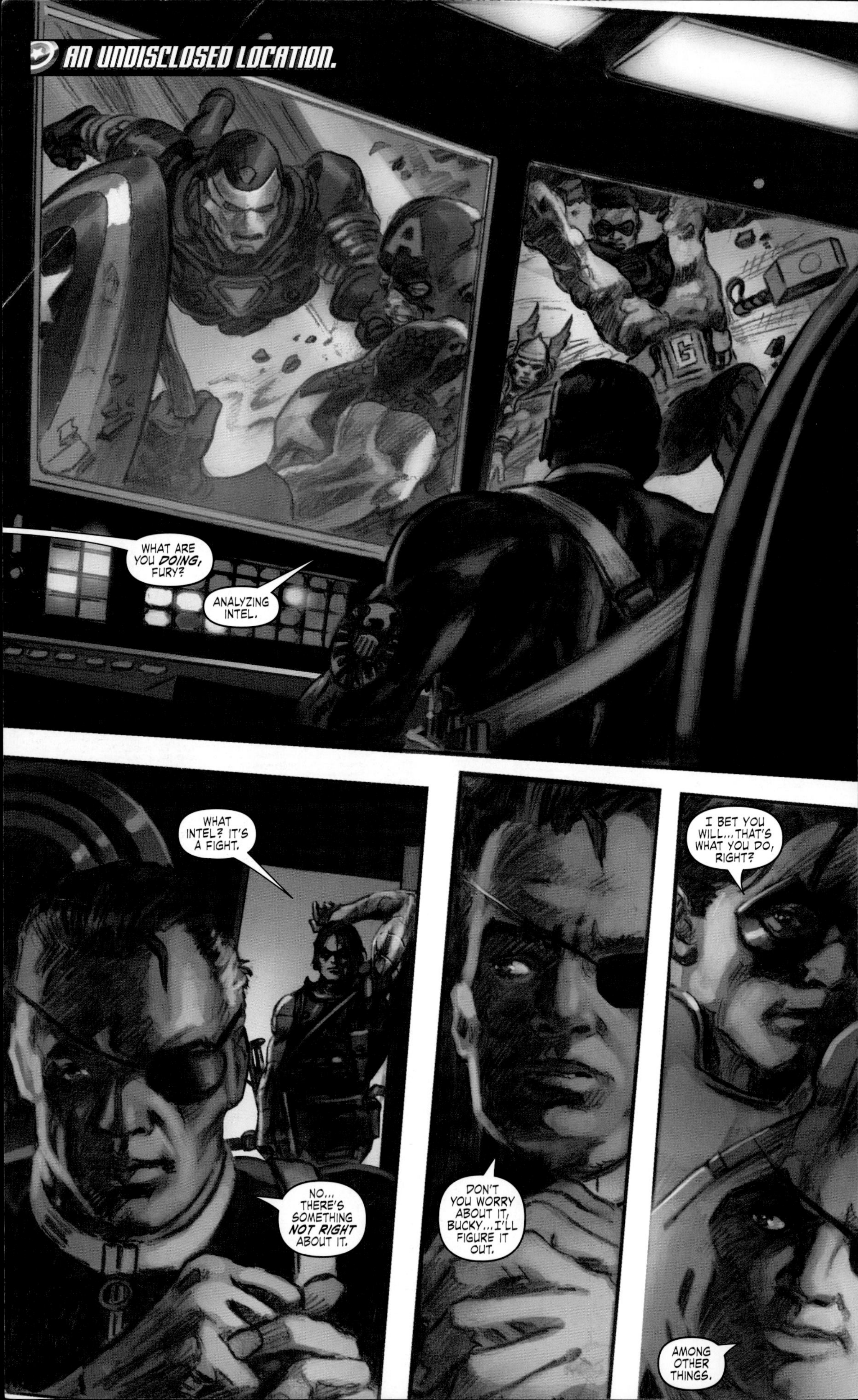
AN UNDISCLOSED LOCATION.
WHAT ARE YOU *DOING*, FURY?
ANALYZING INTEL.
WHAT INTEL? IT'S A FIGHT.
NO... THERE'S SOMETHING ***NOT RIGHT*** ABOUT IT.
DON'T YOU WORRY ABOUT IT, BUCKY... I'LL FIGURE IT OUT.
I BET YOU WILL... THAT'S WHAT YOU DO, RIGHT?
AMONG OTHER THINGS.

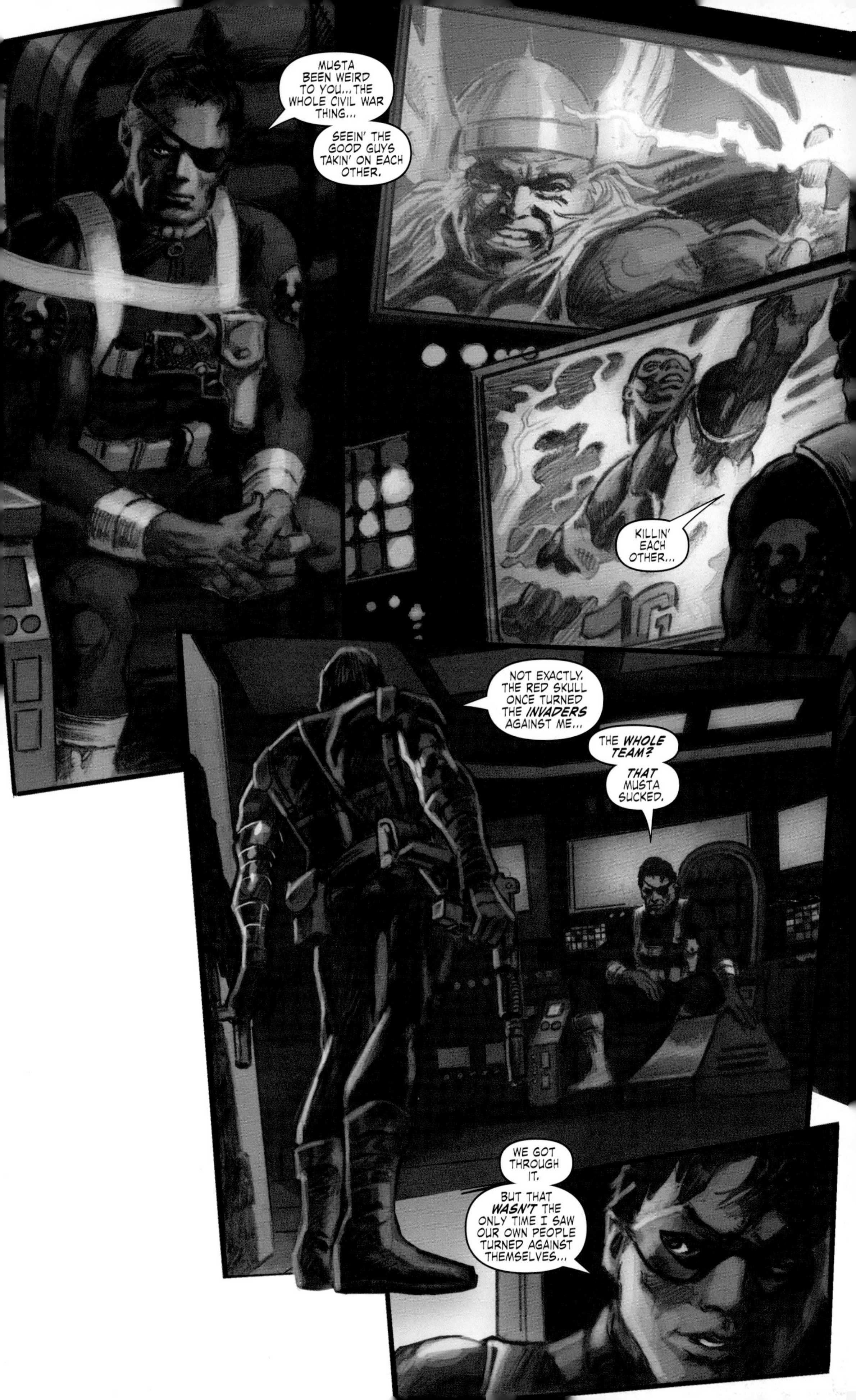
MUSTA BEEN WEIRD TO YOU...THE WHOLE CIVIL WAR THING...
SEEIN' THE GOOD GUYS TAKIN' ON EACH OTHER.
KILLIN' EACH OTHER...
NOT EXACTLY. THE RED SKULL ONCE TURNED THE *INVADERS* AGAINST ME...
THE *WHOLE TEAM?*
THAT MUSTA SUCKED.
WE GOT THROUGH IT.
BUT THAT *WASN'T* THE ONLY TIME I SAW OUR OWN PEOPLE TURNED AGAINST THEMSELVES...

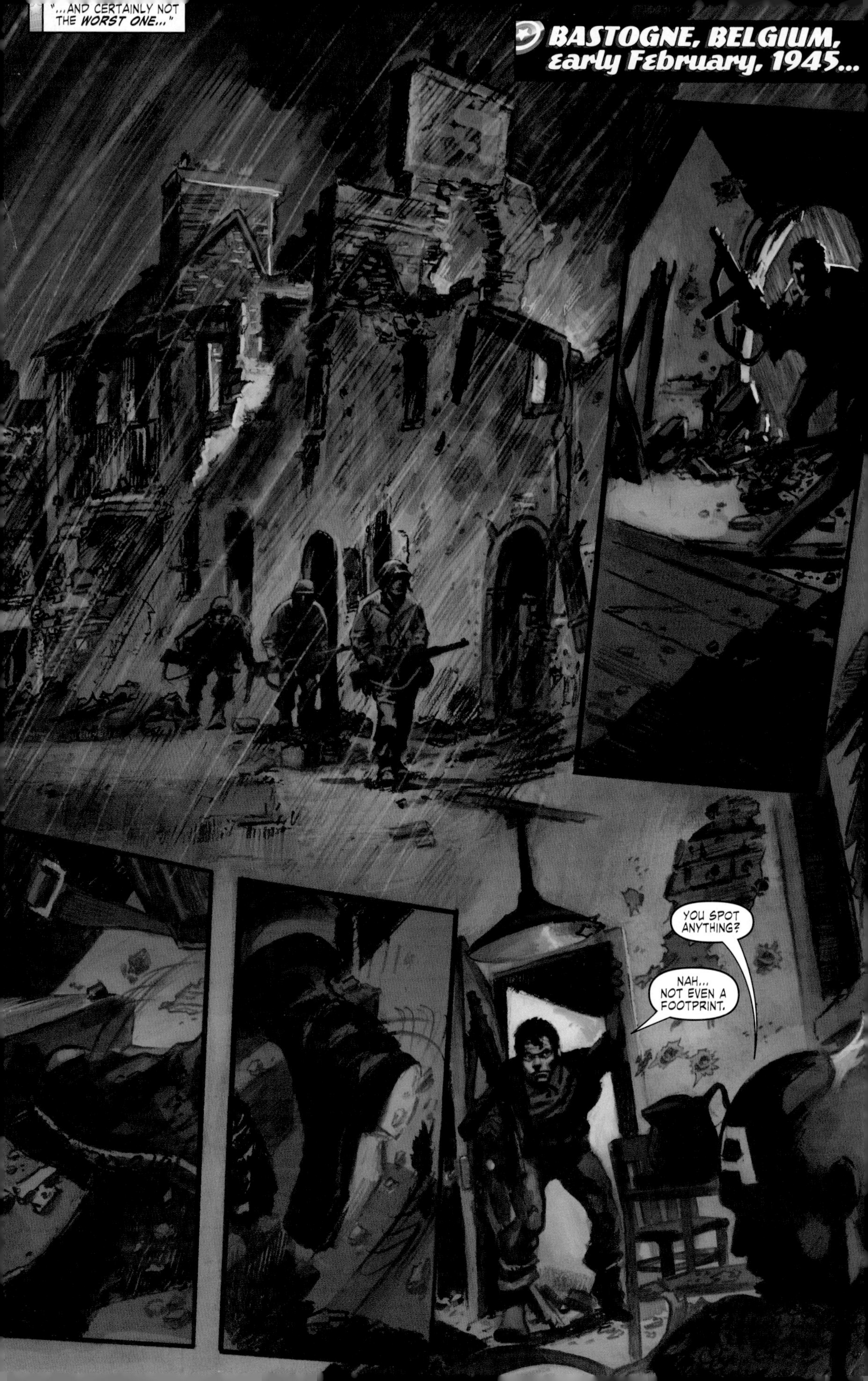
"...AND CERTAINLY NOT THE WORST ONE..."
BASTOGNE, BELGIUM, early February, 1945...
YOU SPOT ANYTHING?
NAH... NOT EVEN A FOOTPRINT.

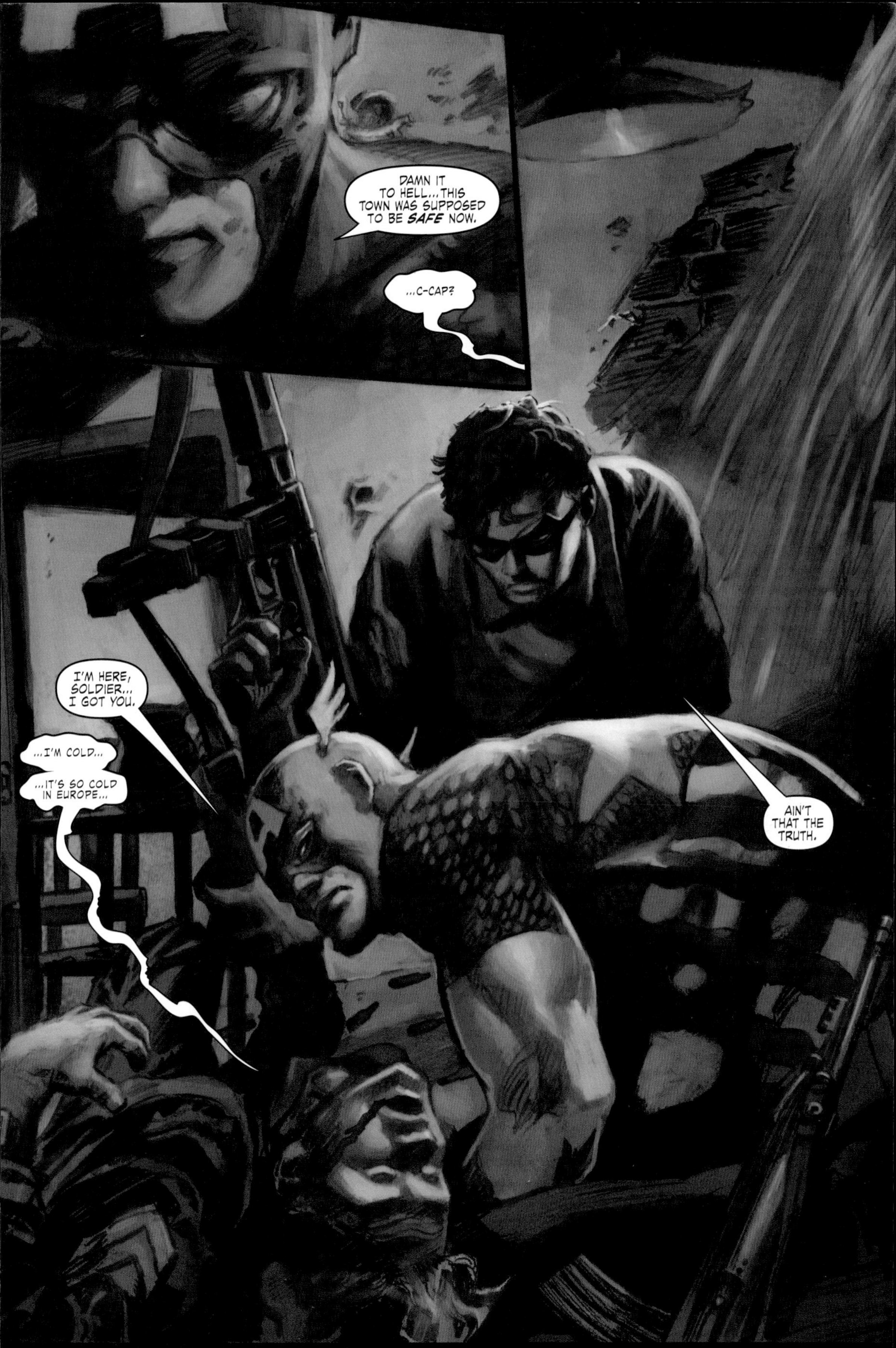
DAMN IT TO HELL... THIS TOWN WAS SUPPOSED TO BE SAFE NOW.
...C-CAP?
I'M HERE, SOLDIER... I GOT YOU.
...I'M COLD...
...IT'S SO COLD IN EUROPE...
AIN'T THAT THE TRUTH.

Red, White & Blue-Blood

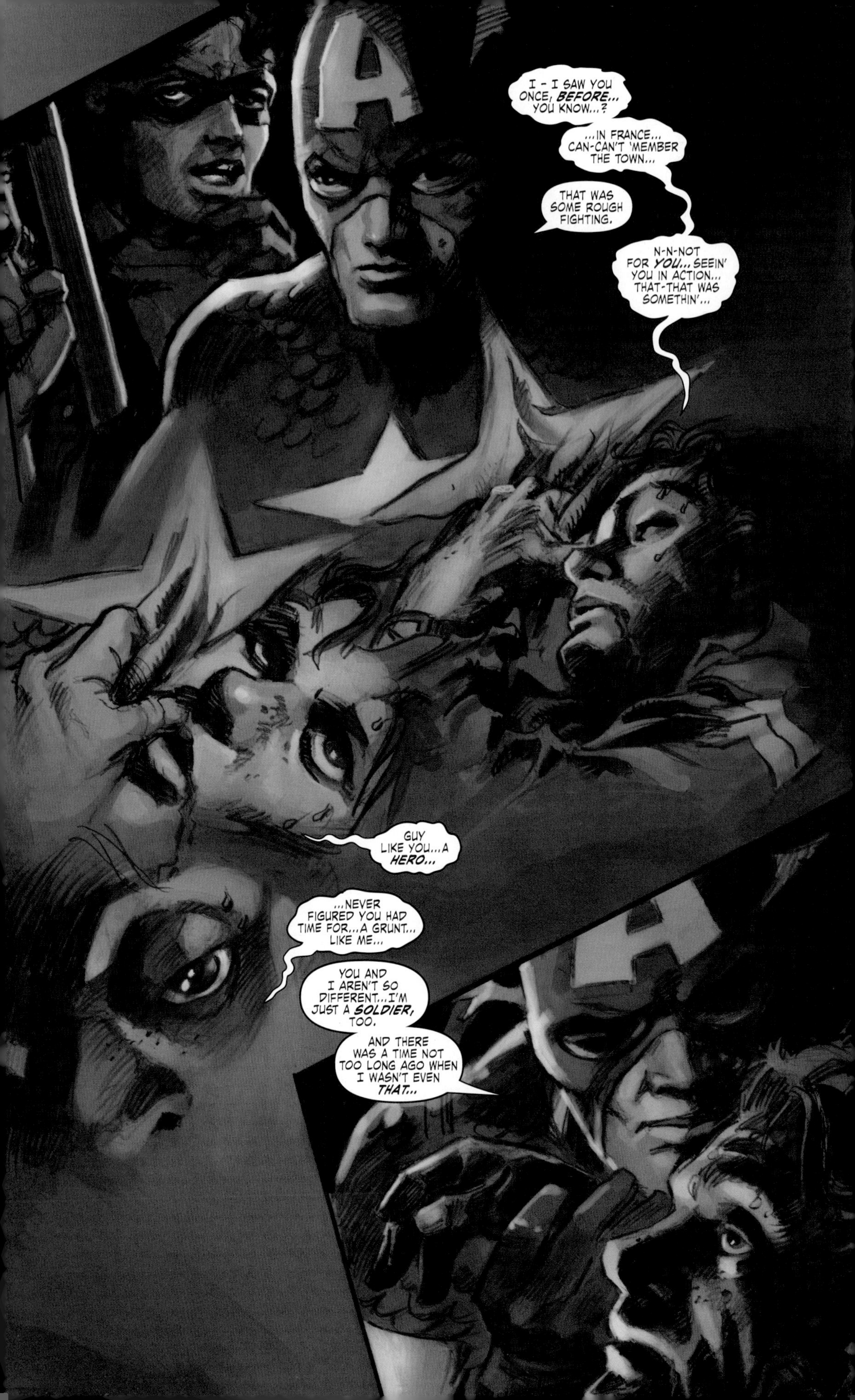
I - I SAW YOU ONCE, BEFORE... YOU KNOW...?
...IN FRANCE... CAN-CAN'T 'MEMBER THE TOWN...
THAT WAS SOME ROUGH FIGHTING.
N-N-NOT FOR YOU... SEEIN' YOU IN ACTION... THAT-THAT WAS SOMETHIN'...
GUY LIKE YOU...A HERO...
...NEVER FIGURED YOU HAD TIME FOR...A GRUNT... LIKE ME...
YOU AND I AREN'T SO DIFFERENT...I'M JUST A SOLDIER, TOO.
AND THERE WAS A TIME NOT TOO LONG AGO WHEN I WASN'T EVEN THAT...

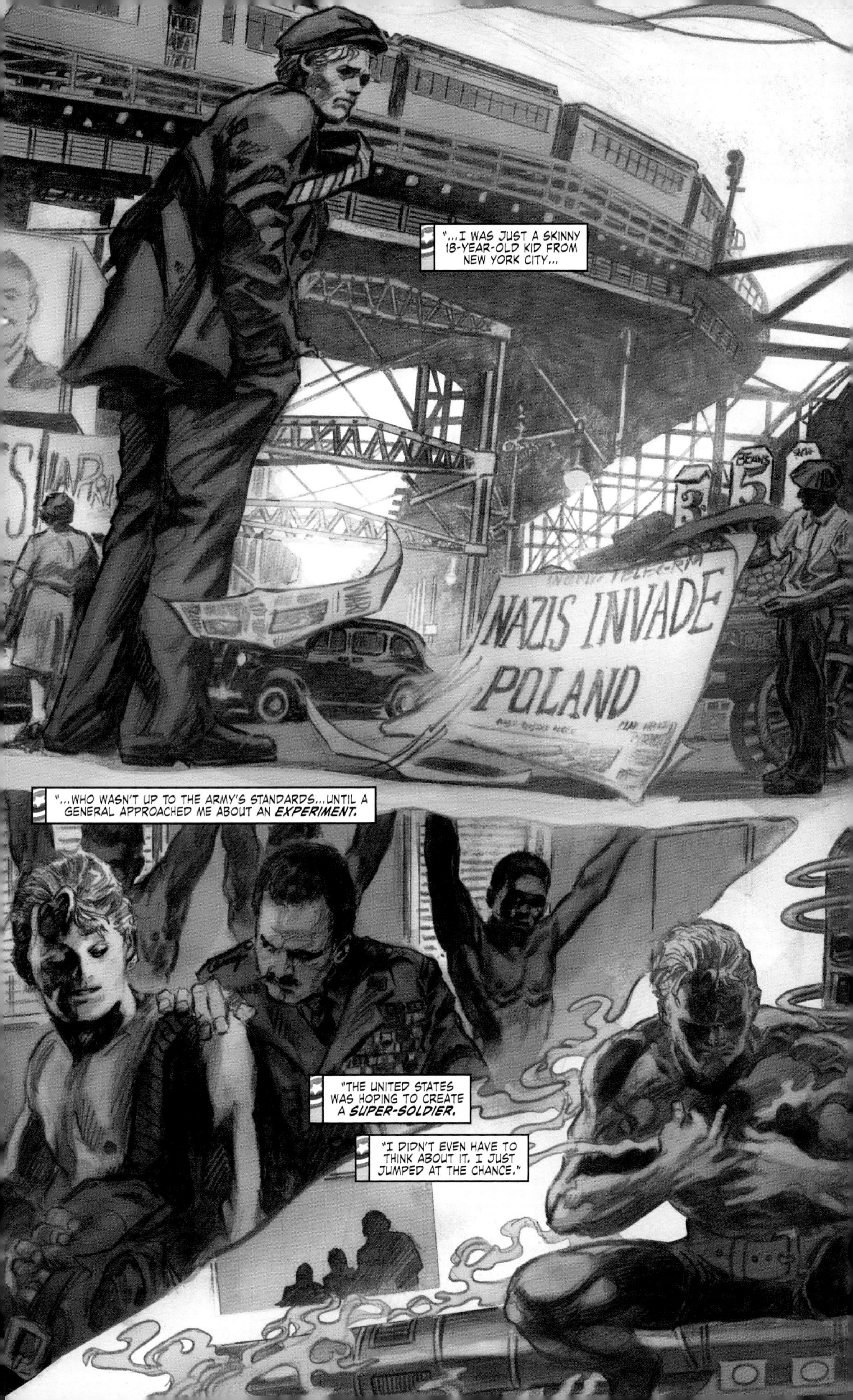
"...I WAS JUST A SKINNY 18-YEAR-OLD KID FROM NEW YORK CITY...
NAZIS INVADE POLAND
"...WHO WASN'T UP TO THE ARMY'S STANDARDS...UNTIL A GENERAL APPROACHED ME ABOUT AN EXPERIMENT.
"THE UNITED STATES WAS HOPING TO CREATE A SUPER-SOLDIER.
"I DIDN'T EVEN HAVE TO THINK ABOUT IT. I JUST JUMPED AT THE CHANCE."

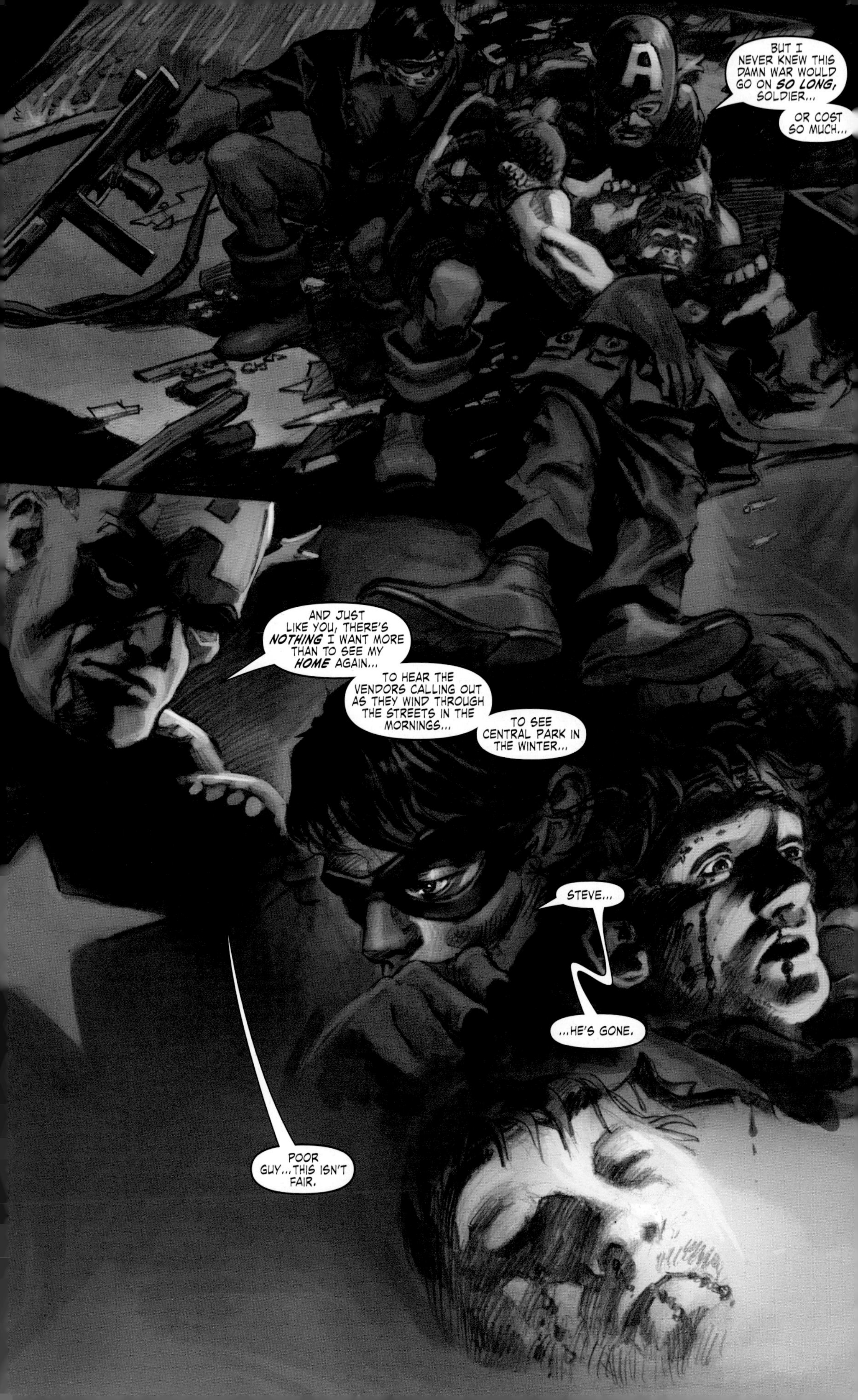
BUT I NEVER KNEW THIS DAMN WAR WOULD GO ON **SO LONG,** SOLDIER...
OR COST SO MUCH...
AND JUST LIKE YOU, THERE'S **NOTHING** I WANT MORE THAN TO SEE MY **HOME** AGAIN...
TO HEAR THE VENDORS CALLING OUT AS THEY WIND THROUGH THE STREETS IN THE MORNINGS...
TO SEE CENTRAL PARK IN THE WINTER...
STEVE...
...HE'S GONE.
POOR GUY...THIS ISN'T FAIR.

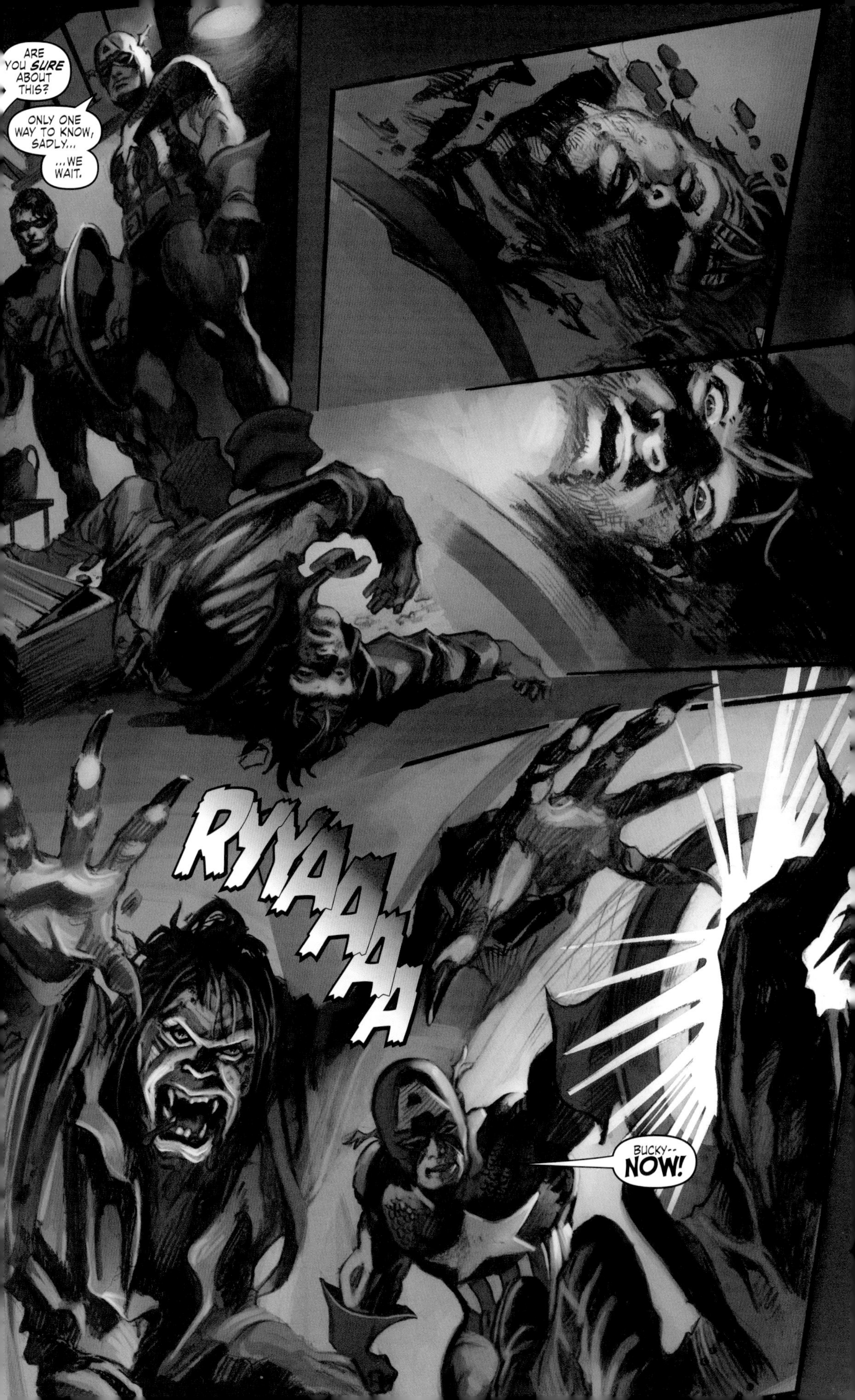
ARE YOU SURE ABOUT THIS?
ONLY ONE WAY TO KNOW, SADLY...
...WE WAIT.
RYAAAA
BUCKY-- NOW!

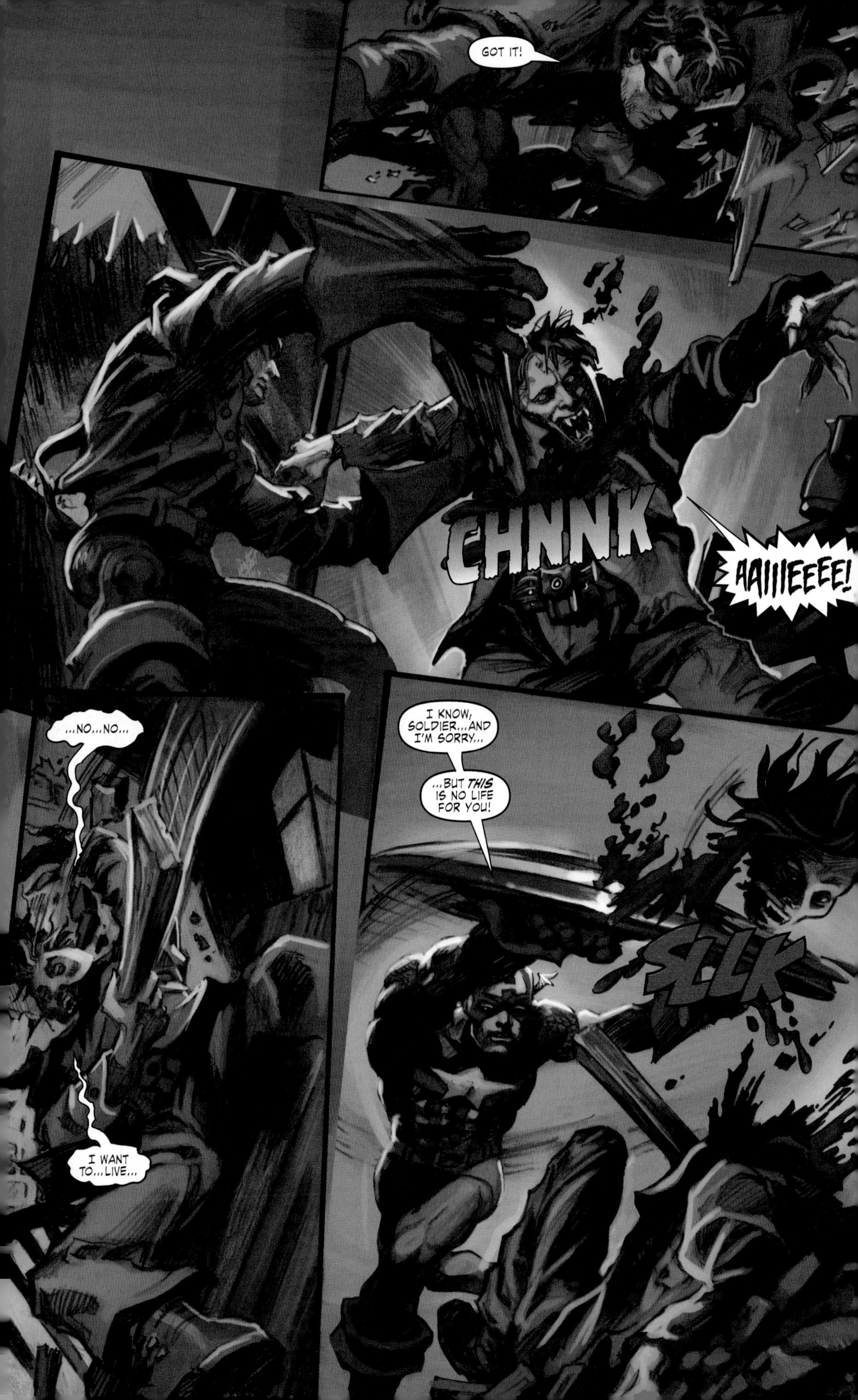
GOT IT!
CHNNK
AAIIIIEEEE!
...NO...NO...
I WANT TO...LIVE...
I KNOW, SOLDIER...AND I'M SORRY...
...BUT *THIS* IS NO LIFE FOR YOU!
SLLK

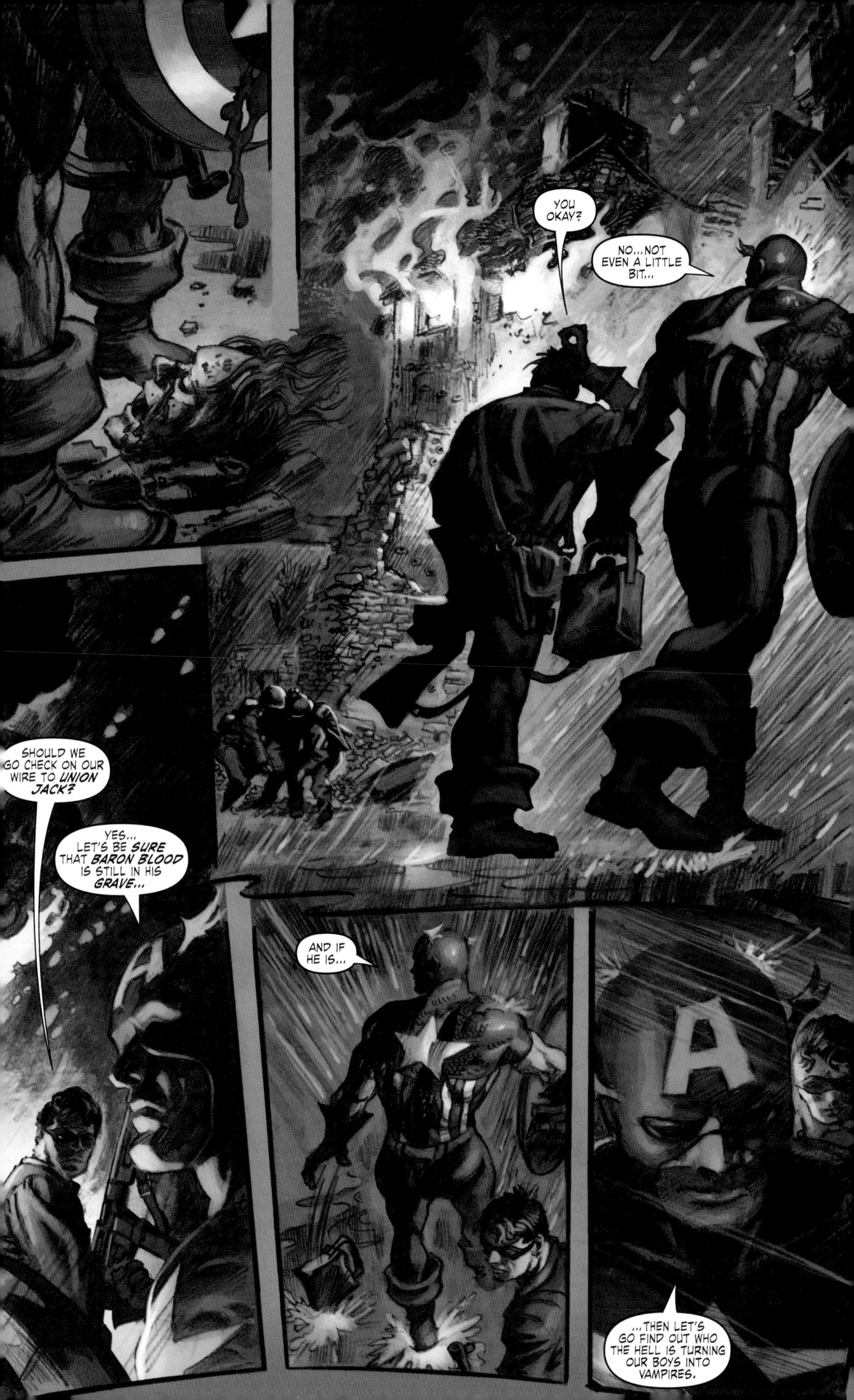
YOU OKAY?
NO...NOT EVEN A LITTLE BIT...
SHOULD WE GO CHECK ON OUR WIRE TO UNION JACK?
YES... LET'S BE SURE THAT BARON BLOOD IS STILL IN HIS GRAVE...
AND IF HE IS...
...THEN LET'S GO FIND OUT WHO THE HELL IS TURNING OUR BOYS INTO VAMPIRES.

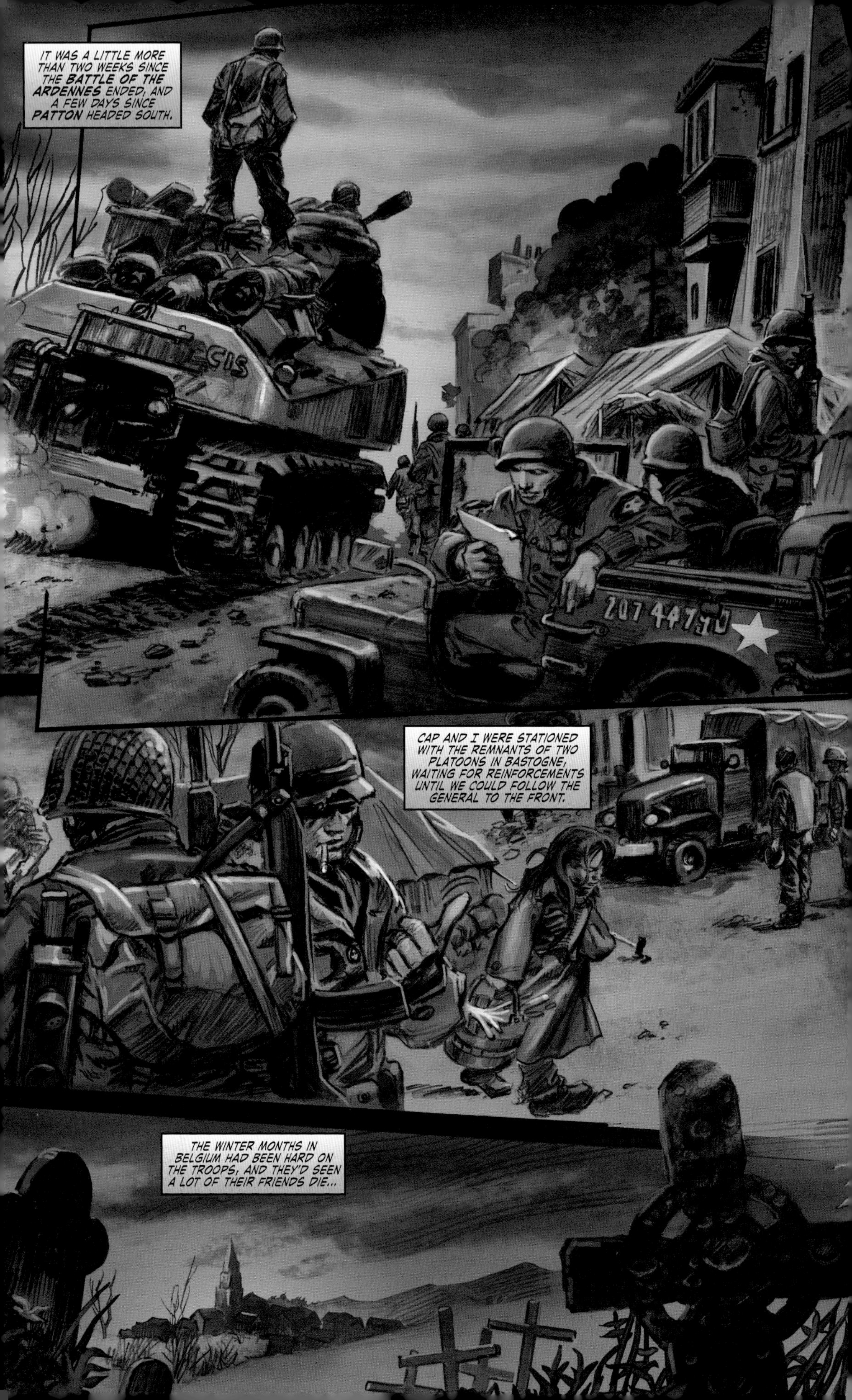
IT WAS A LITTLE MORE THAN TWO WEEKS SINCE THE BATTLE OF THE ARDENNES ENDED, AND A FEW DAYS SINCE PATTON HEADED SOUTH.
CAP AND I WERE STATIONED WITH THE REMNANTS OF TWO PLATOONS IN BASTOGNE, WAITING FOR REINFORCEMENTS UNTIL WE COULD FOLLOW THE GENERAL TO THE FRONT.
THE WINTER MONTHS IN BELGIUM HAD BEEN HARD ON THE TROOPS, AND THEY'D SEEN A LOT OF THEIR FRIENDS DIE...

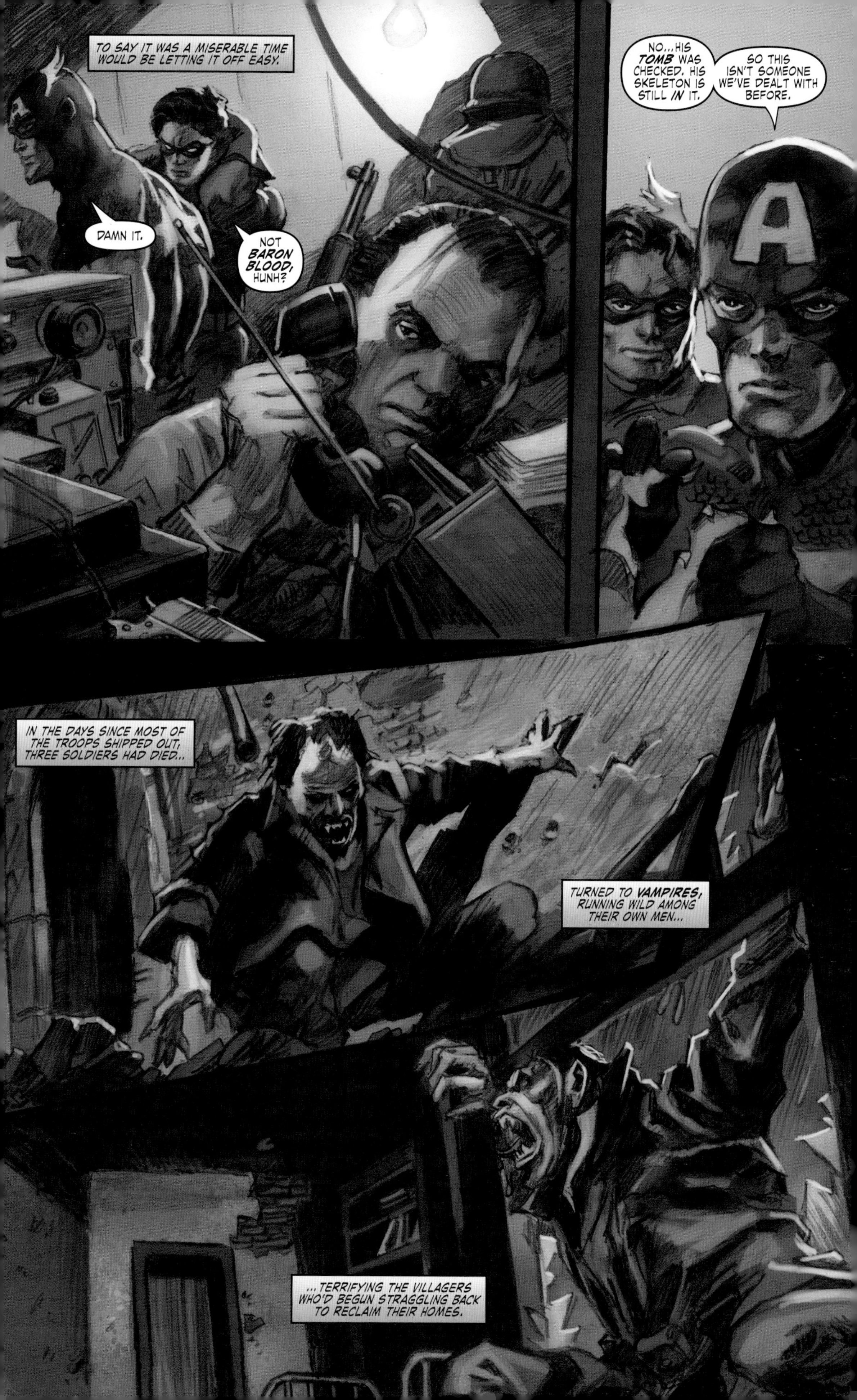
TO SAY IT WAS A MISERABLE TIME WOULD BE LETTING IT OFF EASY.
DAMN IT.
NOT BARON BLOOD, HUNH?
NO...HIS TOMB WAS CHECKED. HIS SKELETON IS STILL IN IT.
SO THIS ISN'T SOMEONE WE'VE DEALT WITH BEFORE.
IN THE DAYS SINCE MOST OF THE TROOPS SHIPPED OUT, THREE SOLDIERS HAD DIED...
TURNED TO VAMPIRES, RUNNING WILD AMONG THEIR OWN MEN...
...TERRIFYING THE VILLAGERS WHO'D BEGUN STRAGGLING BACK TO RECLAIM THEIR HOMES.

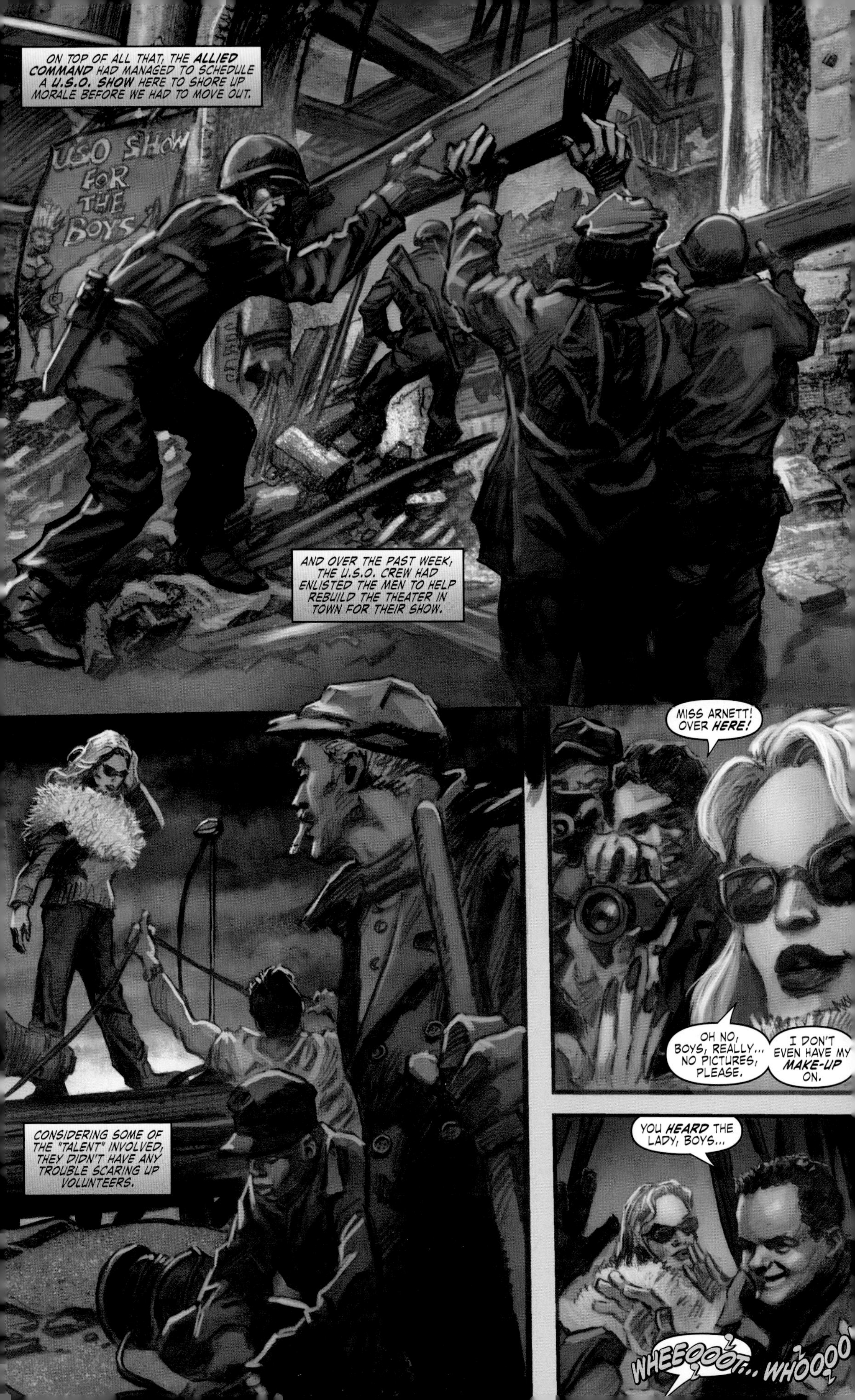
ON TOP OF ALL THAT, THE ALLIED COMMAND HAD MANAGED TO SCHEDULE A U.S.O. SHOW HERE TO SHORE UP MORALE BEFORE WE HAD TO MOVE OUT.
USO SHOW FOR THE BOYS
AND OVER THE PAST WEEK, THE U.S.O. CREW HAD ENLISTED THE MEN TO HELP REBUILD THE THEATER IN TOWN FOR THEIR SHOW.
CONSIDERING SOME OF THE "TALENT" INVOLVED, THEY DIDN'T HAVE ANY TROUBLE SCARING UP VOLUNTEERS.
MISS ARNETT! OVER HERE!
OH NO, BOYS, REALLY... NO PICTURES, PLEASE.
I DON'T EVEN HAVE MY MAKE-UP ON.
YOU HEARD THE LADY, BOYS...
WHEEOOOT... WHOOOO

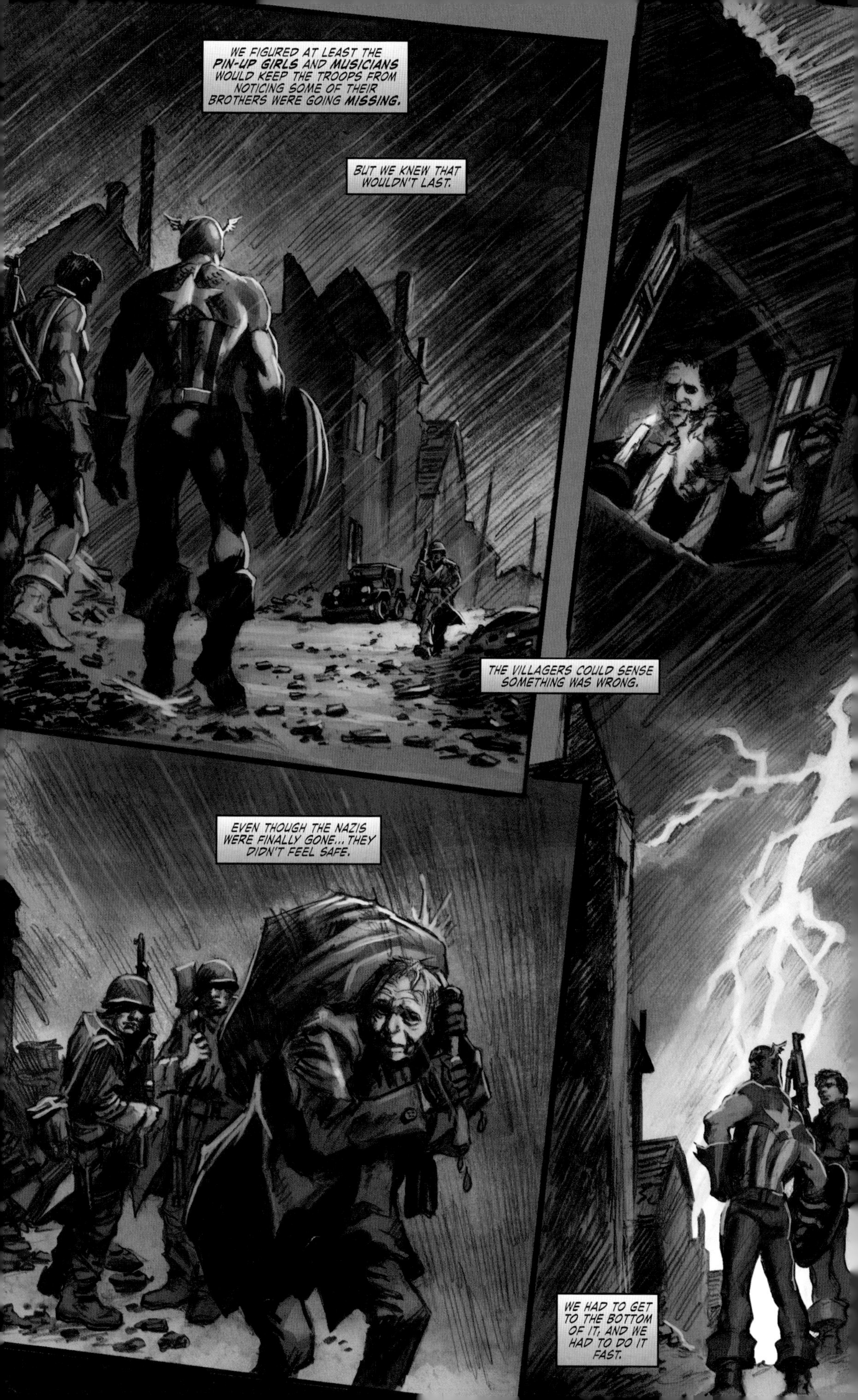
WE FIGURED AT LEAST THE PIN-UP GIRLS AND MUSICIANS WOULD KEEP THE TROOPS FROM NOTICING SOME OF THEIR BROTHERS WERE GOING MISSING.
BUT WE KNEW THAT WOULDN'T LAST.
THE VILLAGERS COULD SENSE SOMETHING WAS WRONG.
EVEN THOUGH THE NAZIS WERE FINALLY GONE... THEY DIDN'T FEEL SAFE.
WE HAD TO GET TO THE BOTTOM OF IT, AND WE HAD TO DO IT FAST.

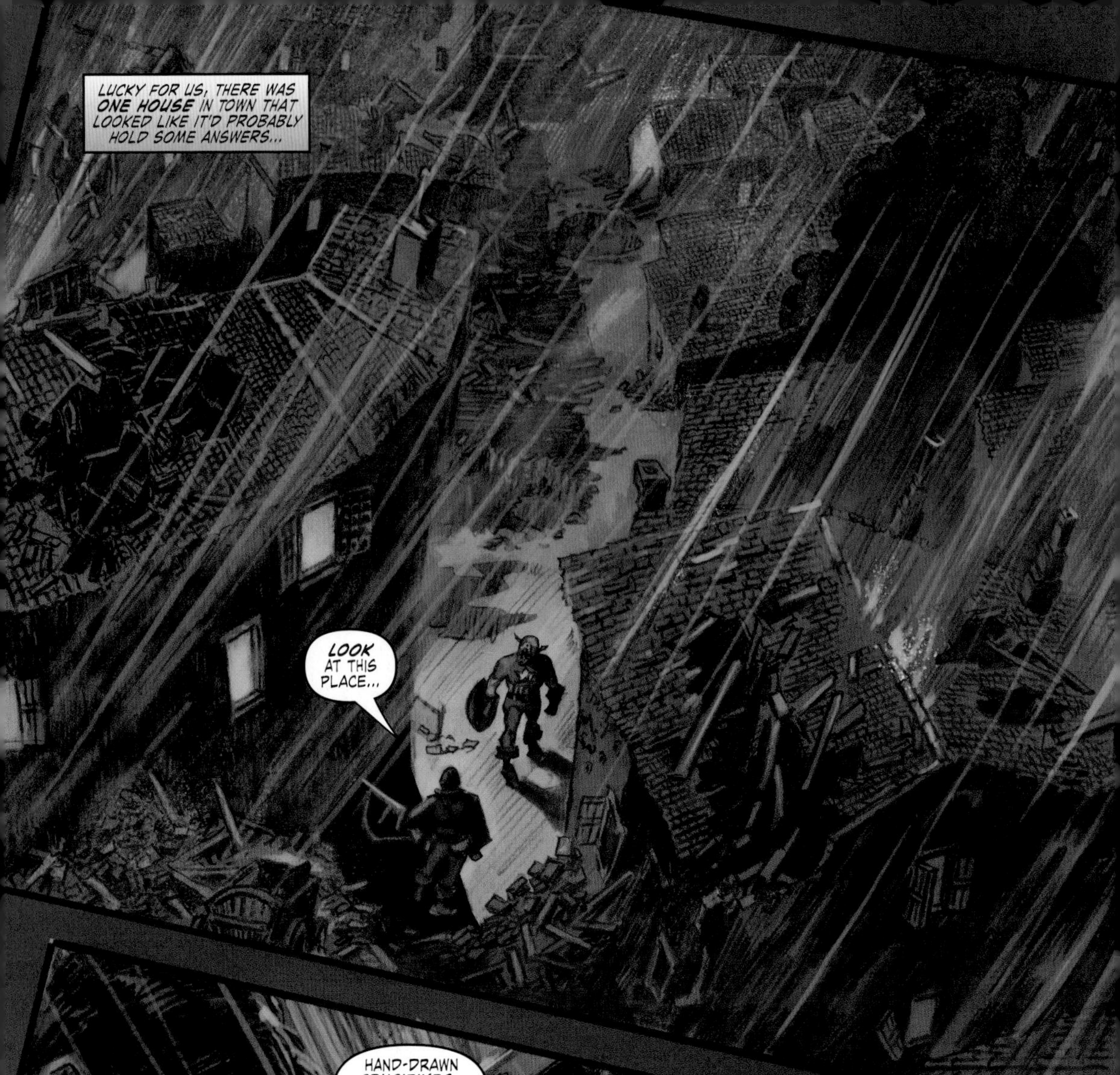
LUCKY FOR US, THERE WAS ONE HOUSE IN TOWN THAT LOOKED LIKE IT'D PROBABLY HOLD SOME ANSWERS...
LOOK AT THIS PLACE...

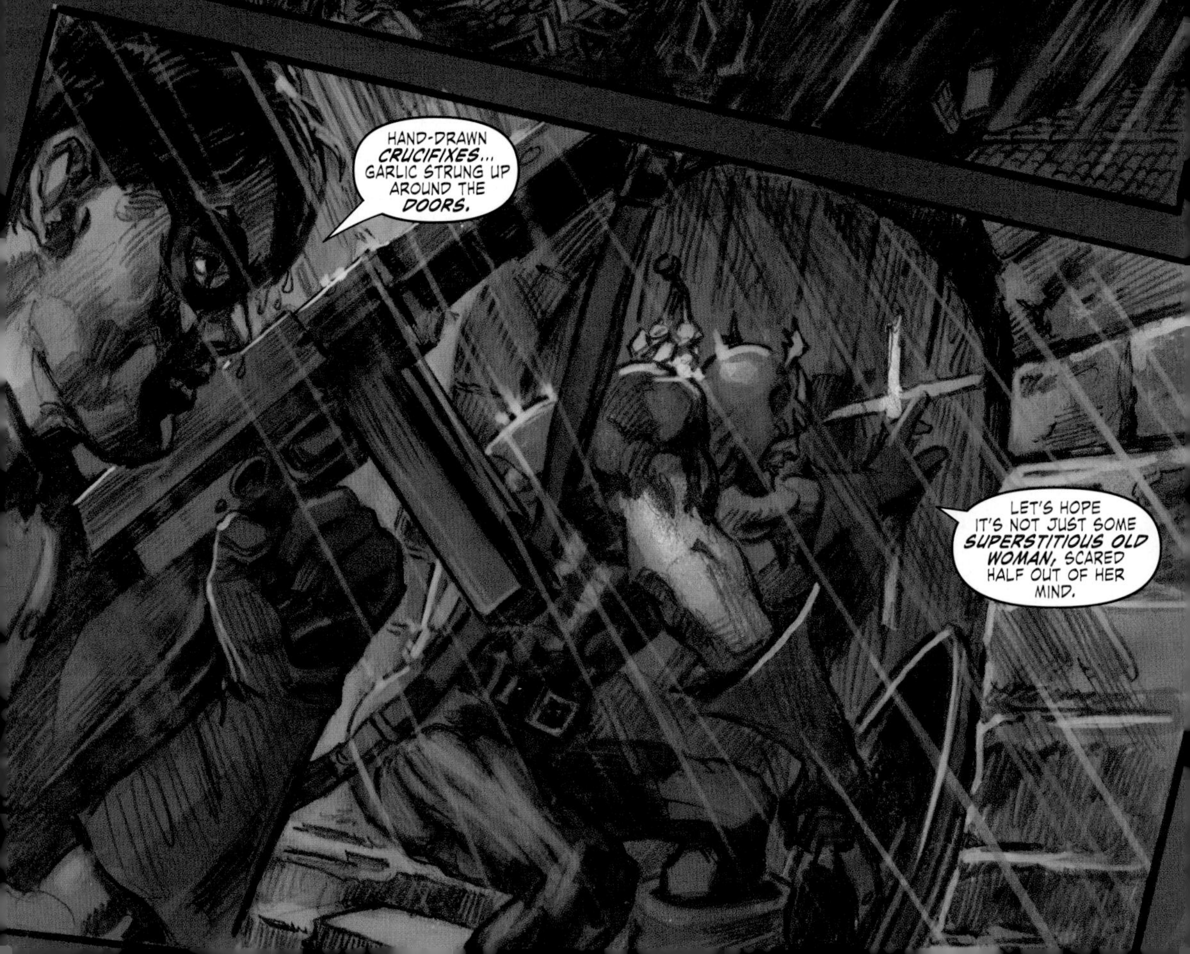
HAND-DRAWN CRUCIFIXES... GARLIC STRUNG UP AROUND THE DOORS.
LET'S HOPE IT'S NOT JUST SOME SUPERSTITIOUS OLD WOMAN, SCARED HALF OUT OF HER MIND.

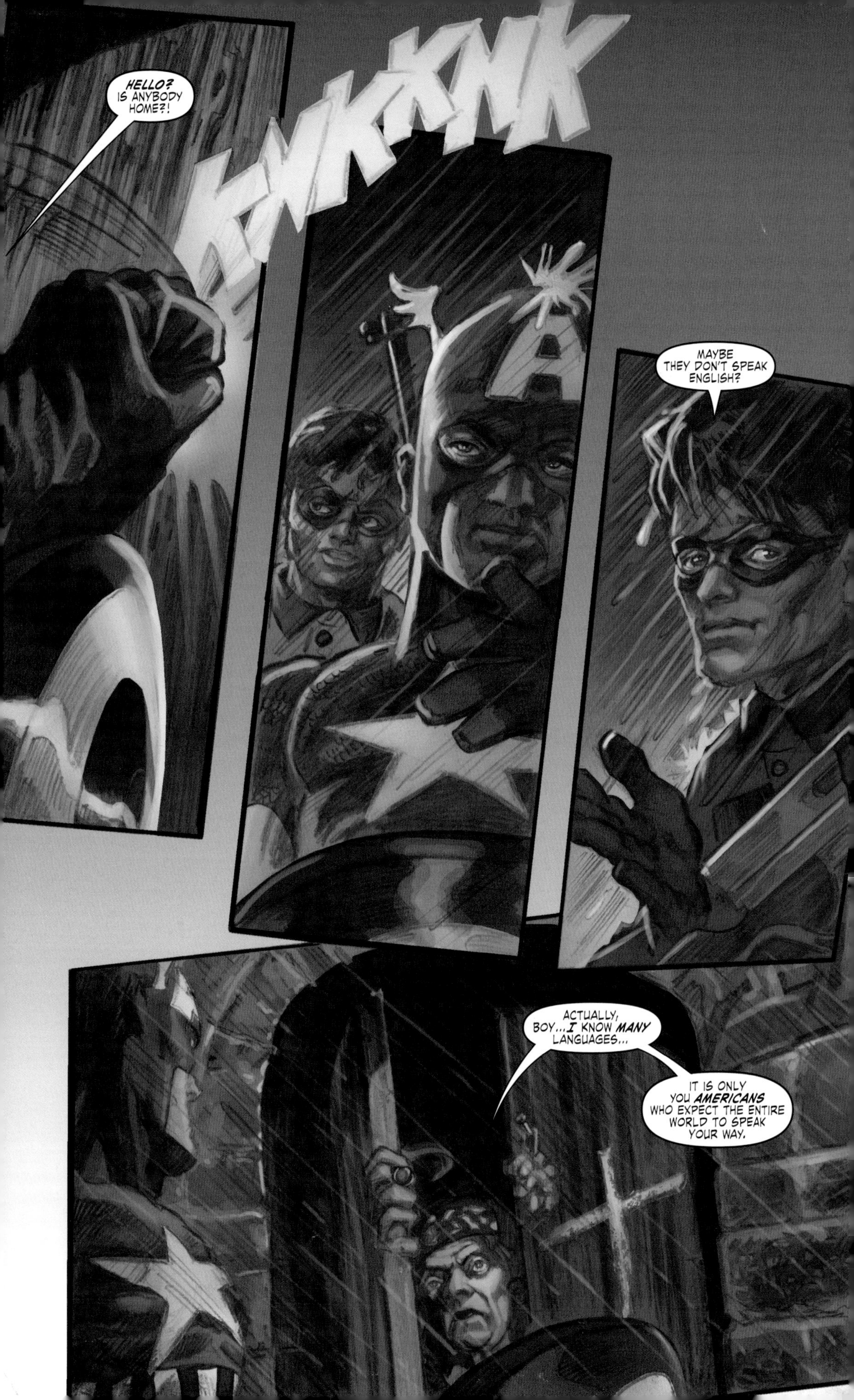
HELLO? IS ANYBODY HOME?!
K-NKKNK
MAYBE THEY DON'T SPEAK ENGLISH?
ACTUALLY, BOY...I KNOW MANY LANGUAGES...
IT IS ONLY YOU AMERICANS WHO EXPECT THE ENTIRE WORLD TO SPEAK YOUR WAY.

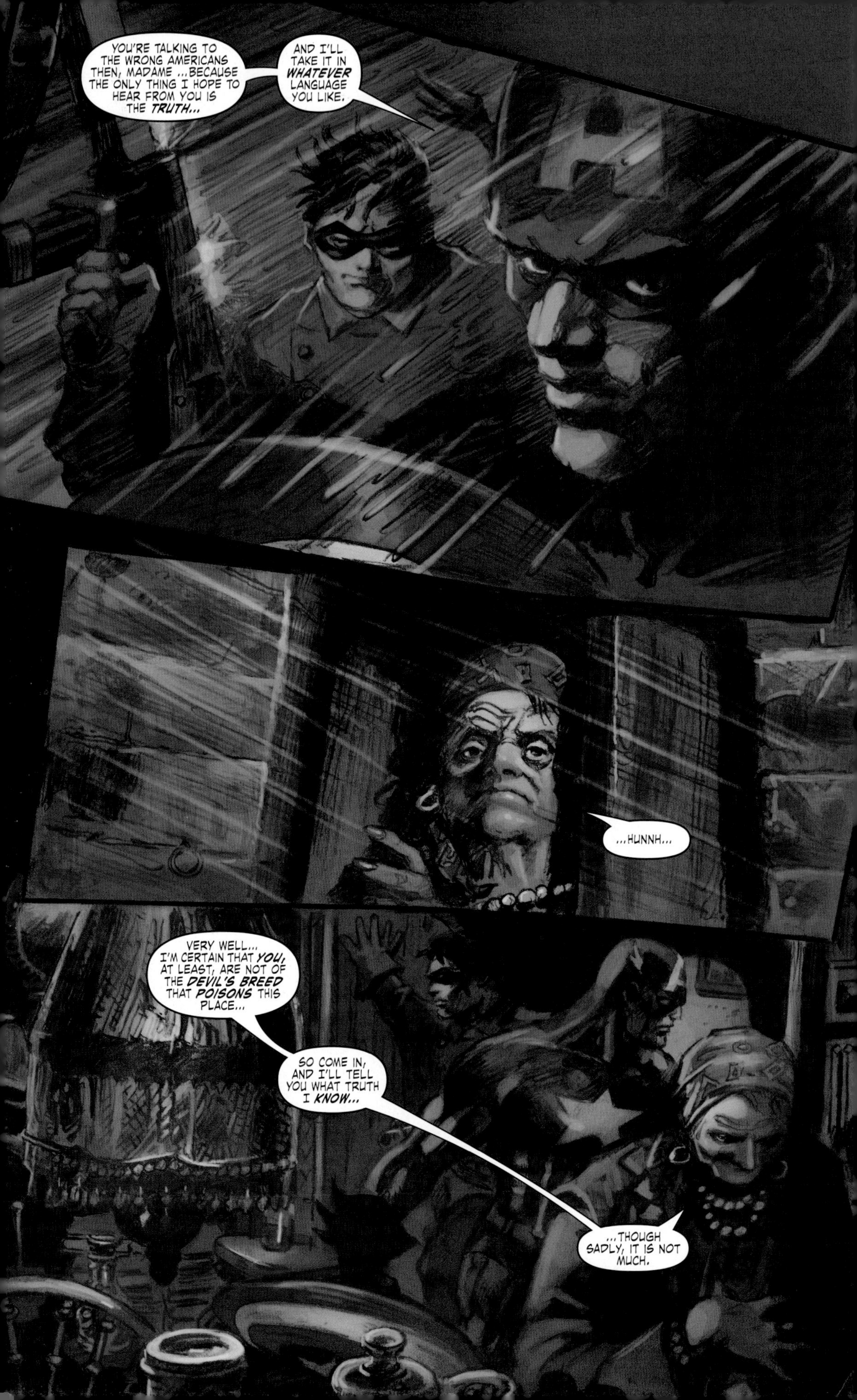
YOU'RE TALKING TO THE WRONG AMERICANS THEN, MADAME ...BECAUSE THE ONLY THING I HOPE TO HEAR FROM YOU IS THE TRUTH...
AND I'LL TAKE IT IN WHATEVER LANGUAGE YOU LIKE.
...HUNNH...
VERY WELL... I'M CERTAIN THAT YOU, AT LEAST, ARE NOT OF THE DEVIL'S BREED THAT POISONS THIS PLACE...
SO COME IN, AND I'LL TELL YOU WHAT TRUTH I KNOW...
...THOUGH SADLY, IT IS NOT MUCH.

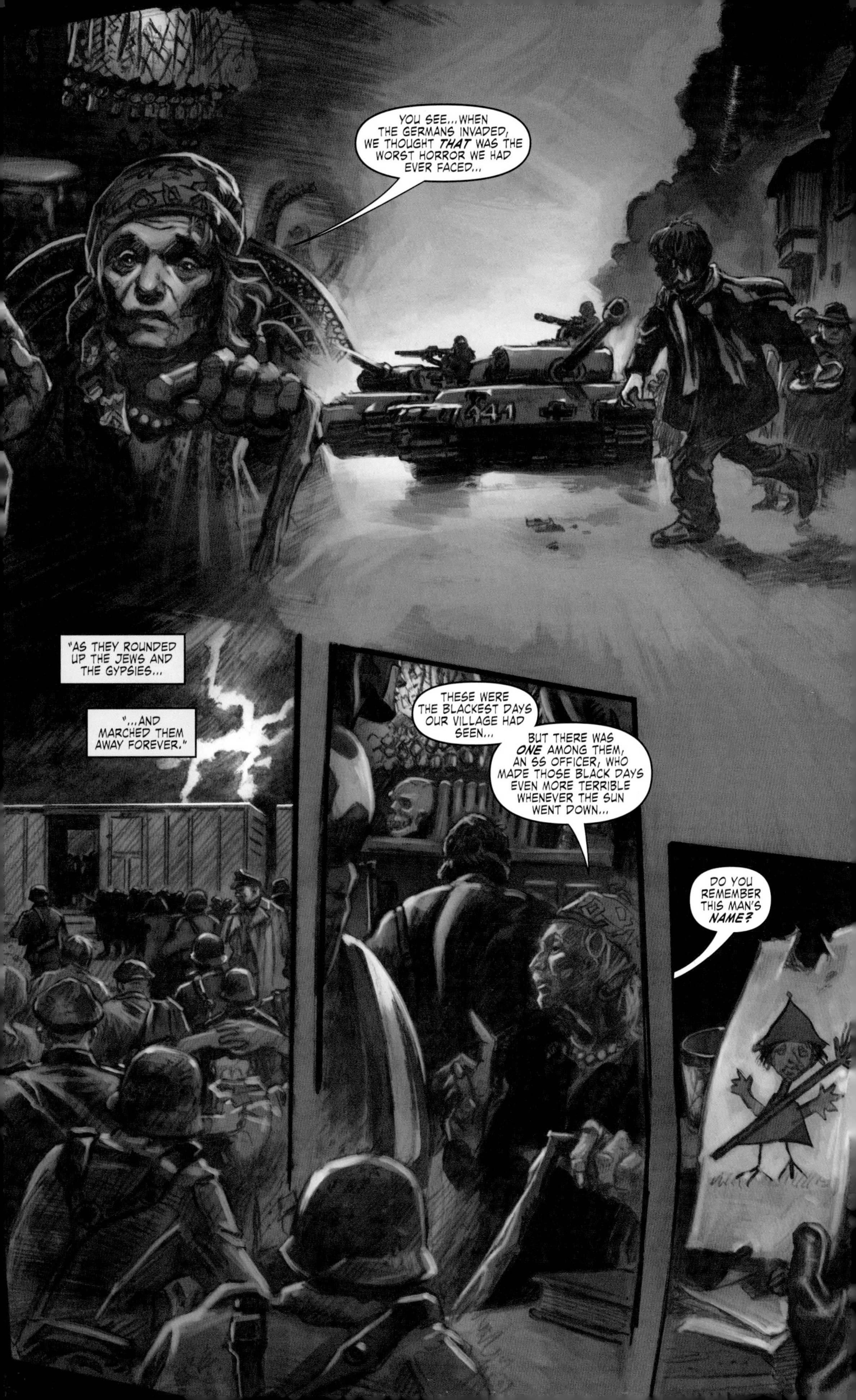

YOU SEE...WHEN THE GERMANS INVADED, WE THOUGHT *THAT* WAS THE WORST HORROR WE HAD EVER FACED...
"AS THEY ROUNDED UP THE JEWS AND THE GYPSIES...
"...AND MARCHED THEM AWAY FOREVER."
THESE WERE THE BLACKEST DAYS OUR VILLAGE HAD SEEN...
BUT THERE WAS *ONE* AMONG THEM, AN SS OFFICER, WHO MADE THOSE BLACK DAYS EVEN MORE TERRIBLE WHENEVER THE SUN WENT DOWN...
DO YOU REMEMBER THIS MAN'S *NAME?*

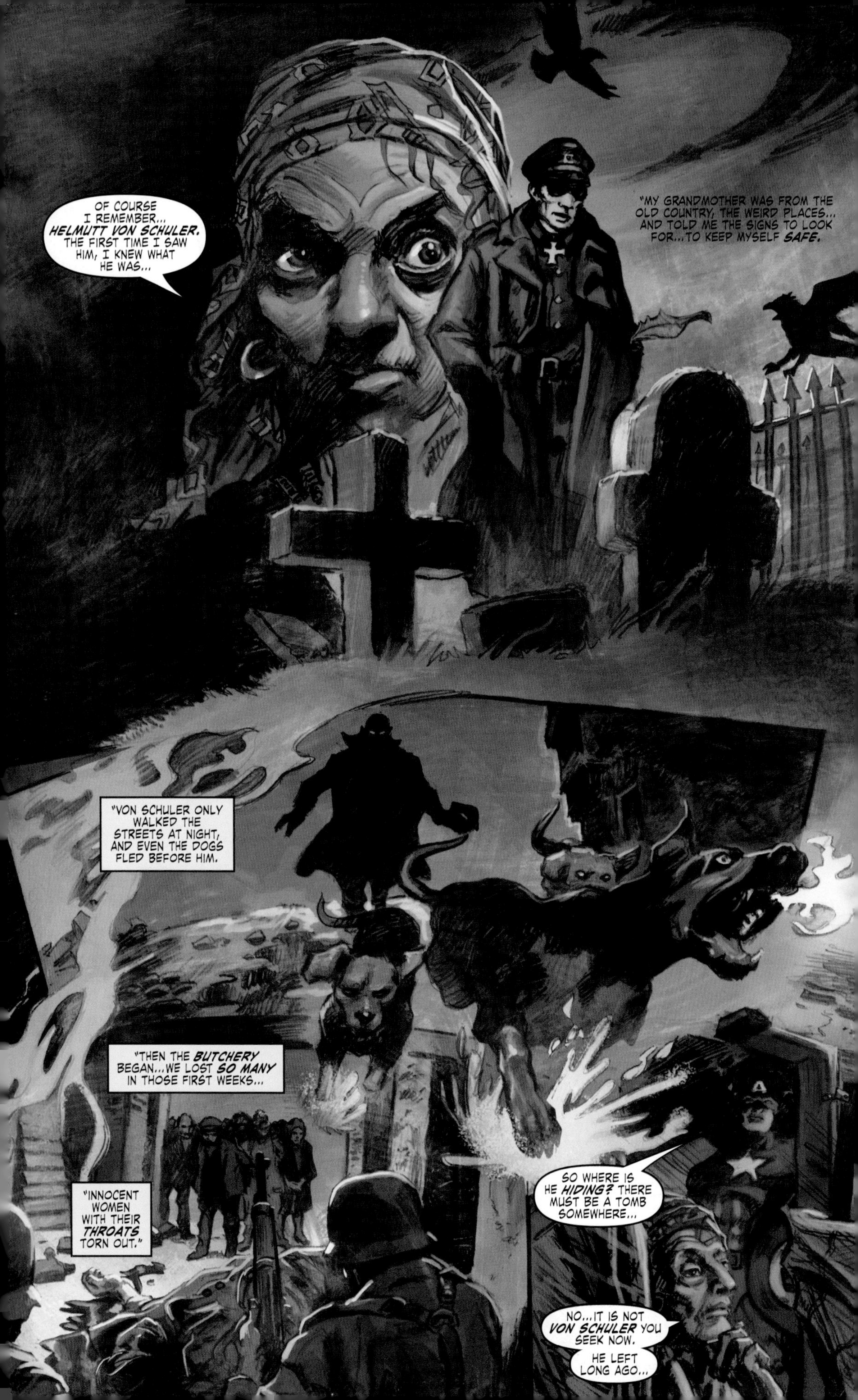
OF COURSE I REMEMBER... HELMUTT VON SCHULER. THE FIRST TIME I SAW HIM, I KNEW WHAT HE WAS...
"MY GRANDMOTHER WAS FROM THE OLD COUNTRY, THE WEIRD PLACES... AND TOLD ME THE SIGNS TO LOOK FOR...TO KEEP MYSELF SAFE.
"VON SCHULER ONLY WALKED THE STREETS AT NIGHT, AND EVEN THE DOGS FLED BEFORE HIM.
"THEN THE BUTCHERY BEGAN...WE LOST SO MANY IN THOSE FIRST WEEKS...
"INNOCENT WOMEN WITH THEIR THROATS TORN OUT."
SO WHERE IS HE HIDING? THERE MUST BE A TOMB SOMEWHERE...
NO...IT IS NOT VON SCHULER YOU SEEK NOW.
HE LEFT LONG AGO...

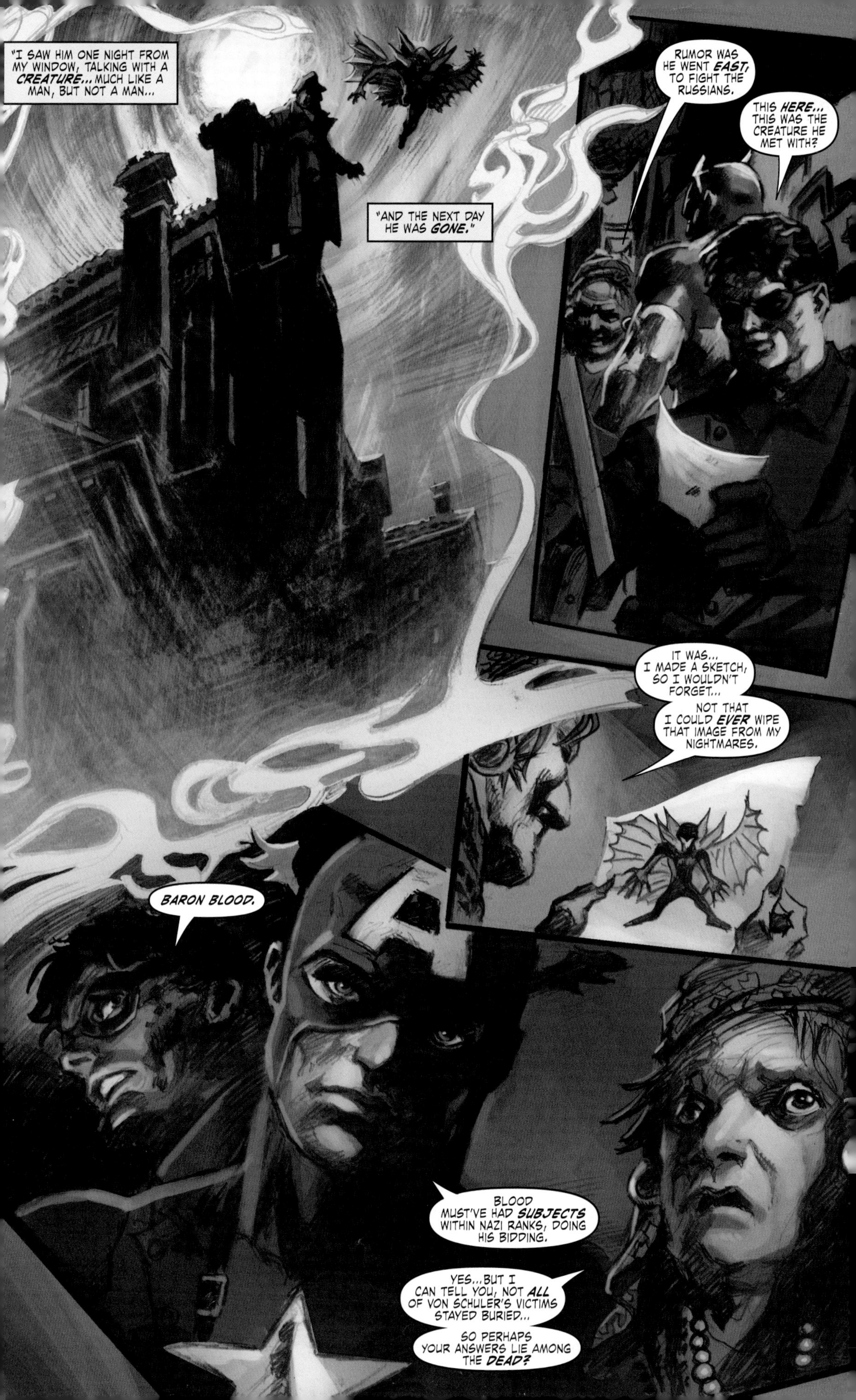
"I SAW HIM ONE NIGHT FROM MY WINDOW, TALKING WITH A CREATURE... MUCH LIKE A MAN, BUT NOT A MAN...
"AND THE NEXT DAY HE WAS GONE."
RUMOR WAS HE WENT EAST, TO FIGHT THE RUSSIANS.
THIS HERE... THIS WAS THE CREATURE HE MET WITH?
IT WAS... I MADE A SKETCH, SO I WOULDN'T FORGET...
NOT THAT I COULD EVER WIPE THAT IMAGE FROM MY NIGHTMARES.
BARON BLOOD.
BLOOD MUST'VE HAD SUBJECTS WITHIN NAZI RANKS, DOING HIS BIDDING.
YES... BUT I CAN TELL YOU, NOT ALL OF VON SCHULER'S VICTIMS STAYED BURIED...
SO PERHAPS YOUR ANSWERS LIE AMONG THE DEAD?

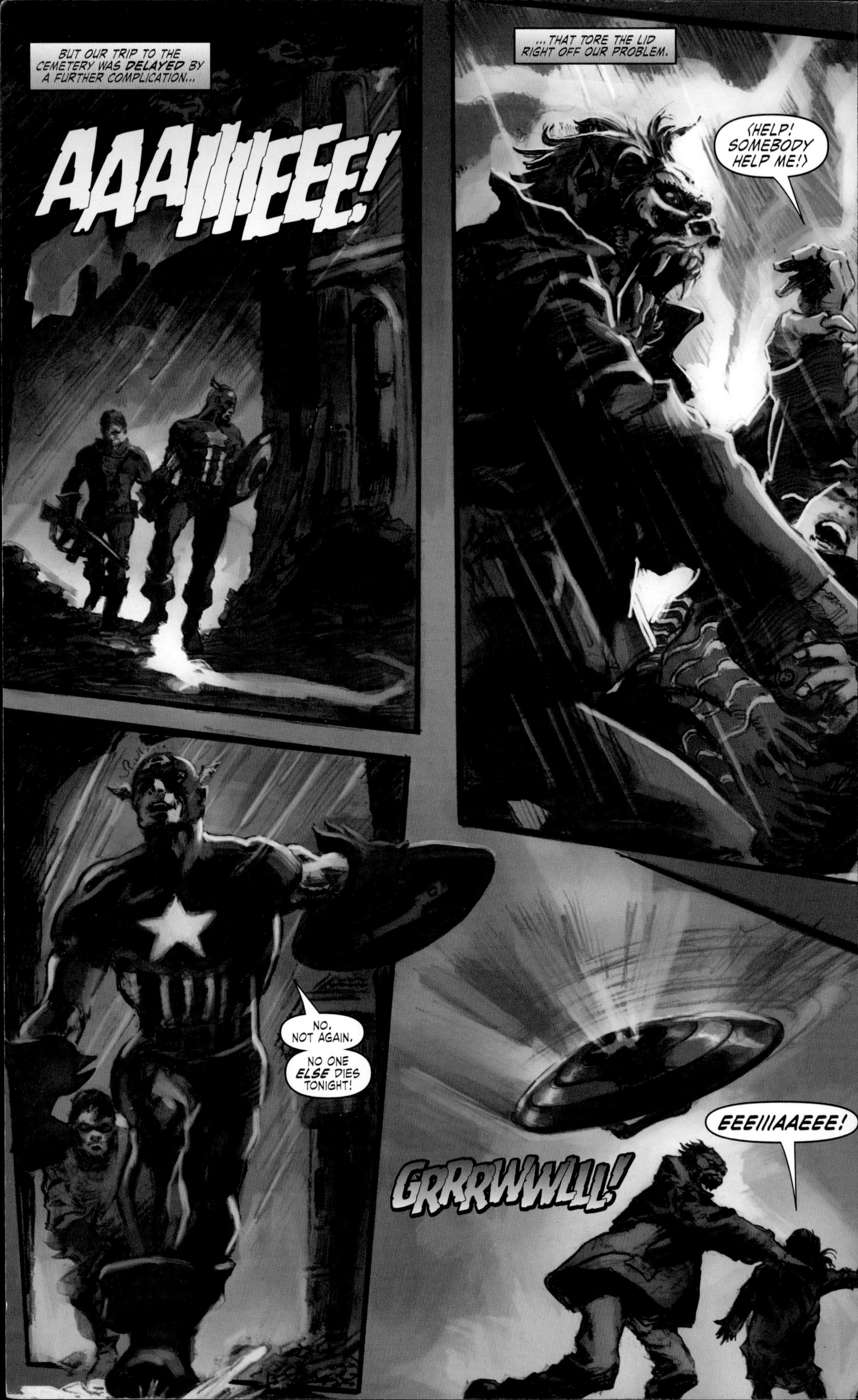
BUT OUR TRIP TO THE CEMETERY WAS DELAYED BY A FURTHER COMPLICATION...
AAAIIIIEEE!
...THAT TORE THE LID RIGHT OFF OUR PROBLEM.
‹HELP! SOMEBODY HELP ME!›
NO, NOT AGAIN.
NO ONE ELSE DIES TONIGHT!
EEEIIIAAEEE!
GRRRWWLLL!

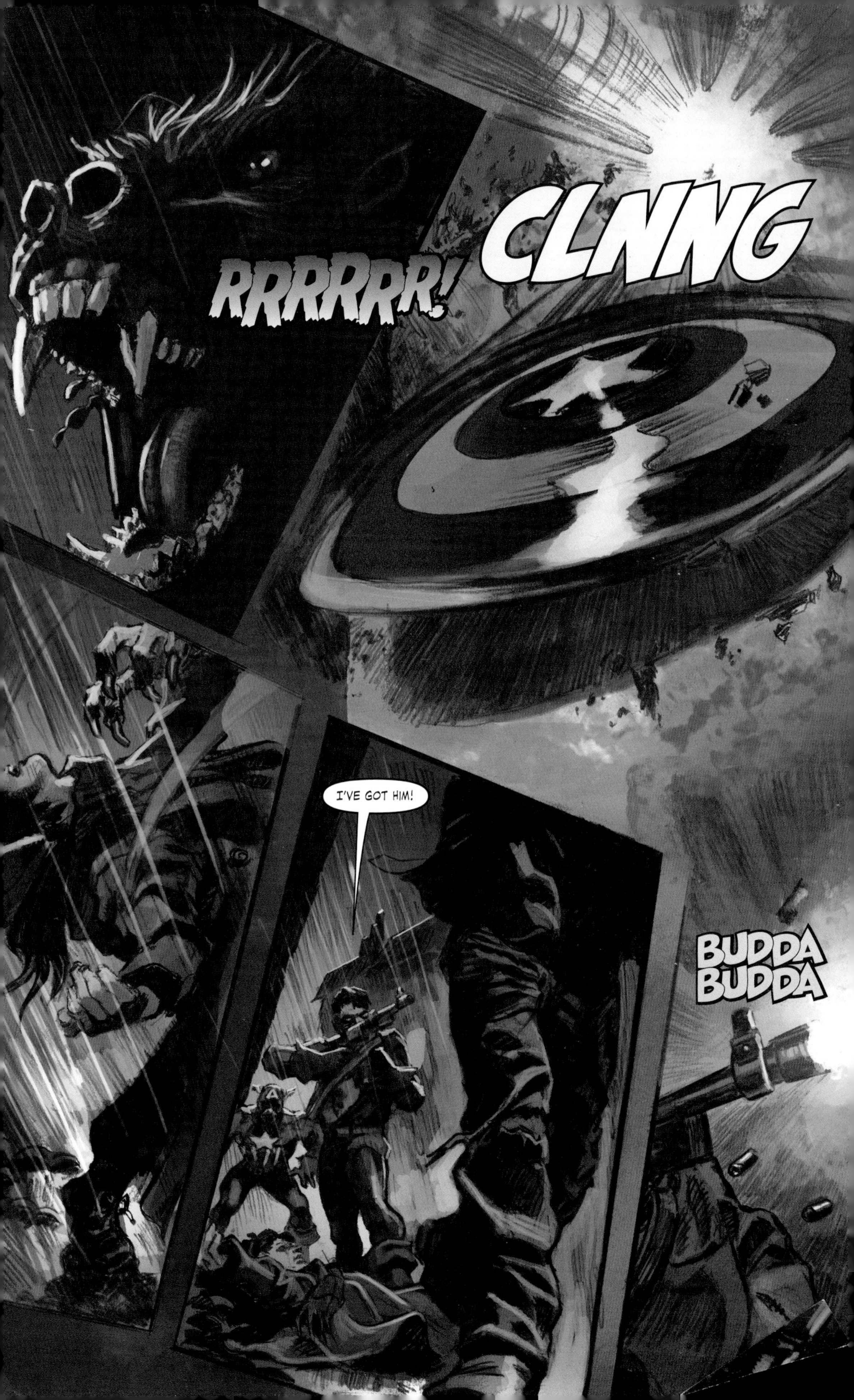
RRRRRR!
CLNNG
I'VE GOT HIM!
BUDDA
BUDDA

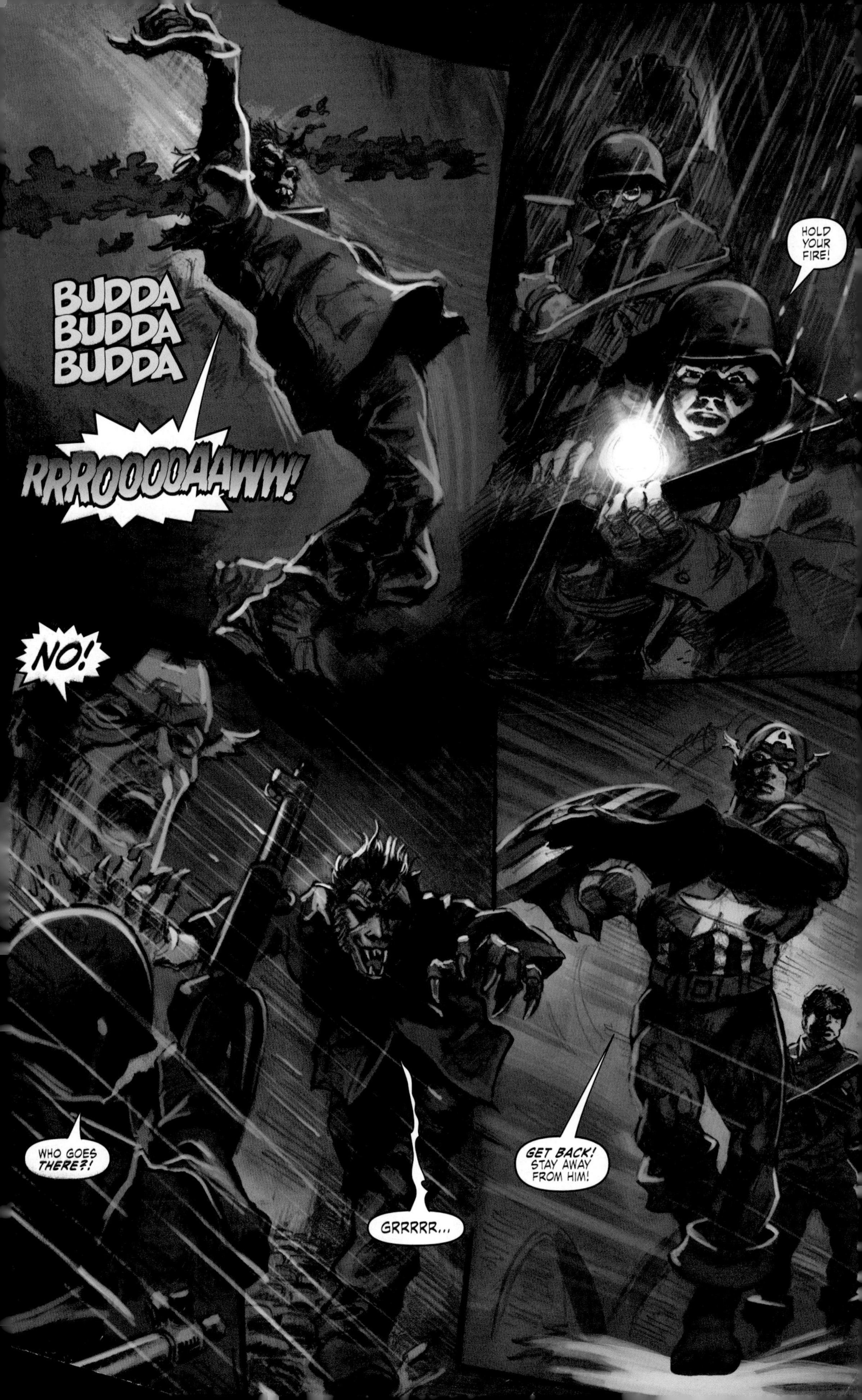
BUDDA
BUDDA
BUDDA
RRROOOOAAWW!
HOLD YOUR FIRE!
NO!
WHO GOES THERE?!
GRRRRR...
GET BACK! STAY AWAY FROM HIM!

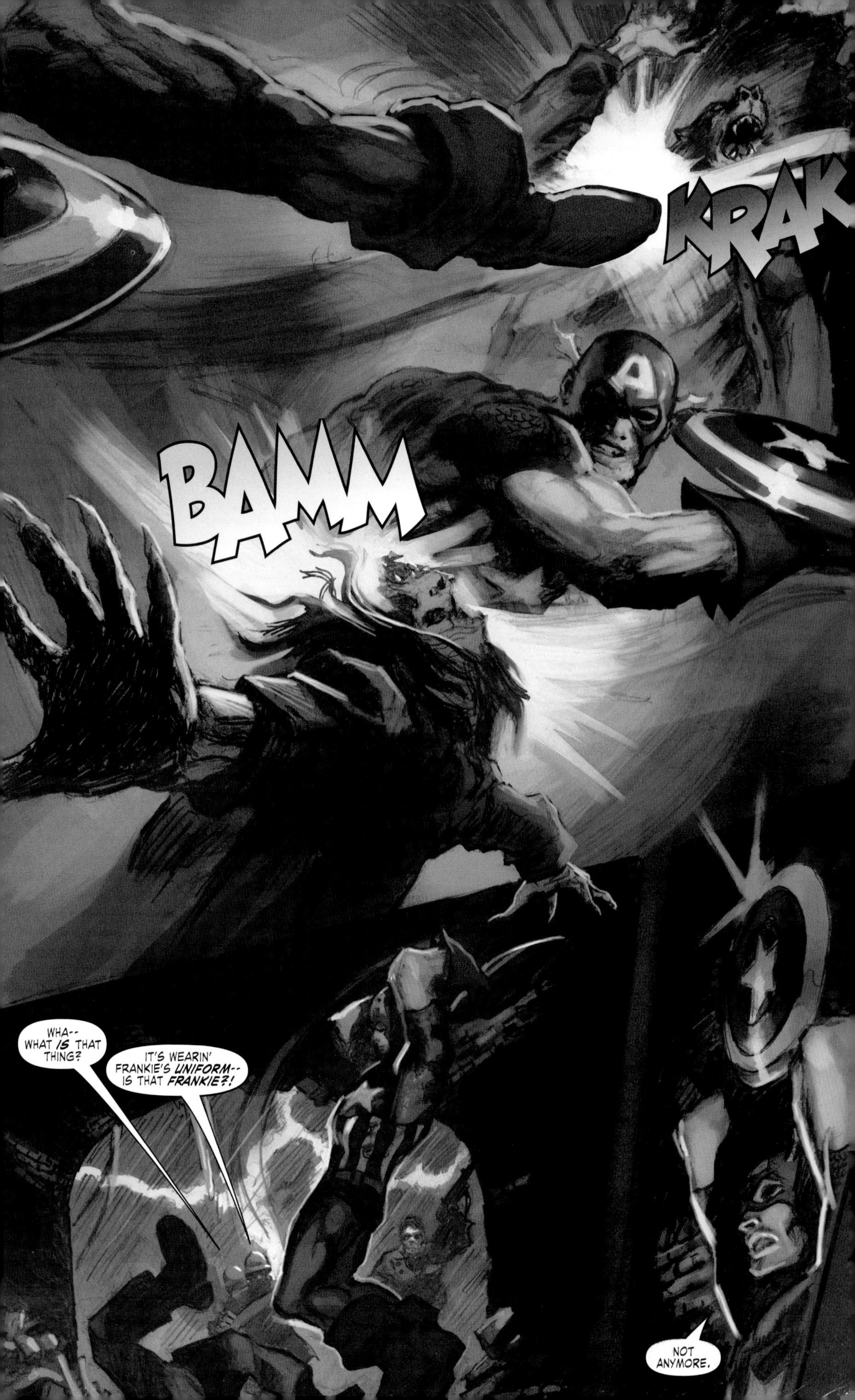
KRAK
BAMM
WHA-- WHAT IS THAT THING?
IT'S WEARIN' FRANKIE'S UNIFORM-- IS THAT FRANKIE?!
NOT ANYMORE.

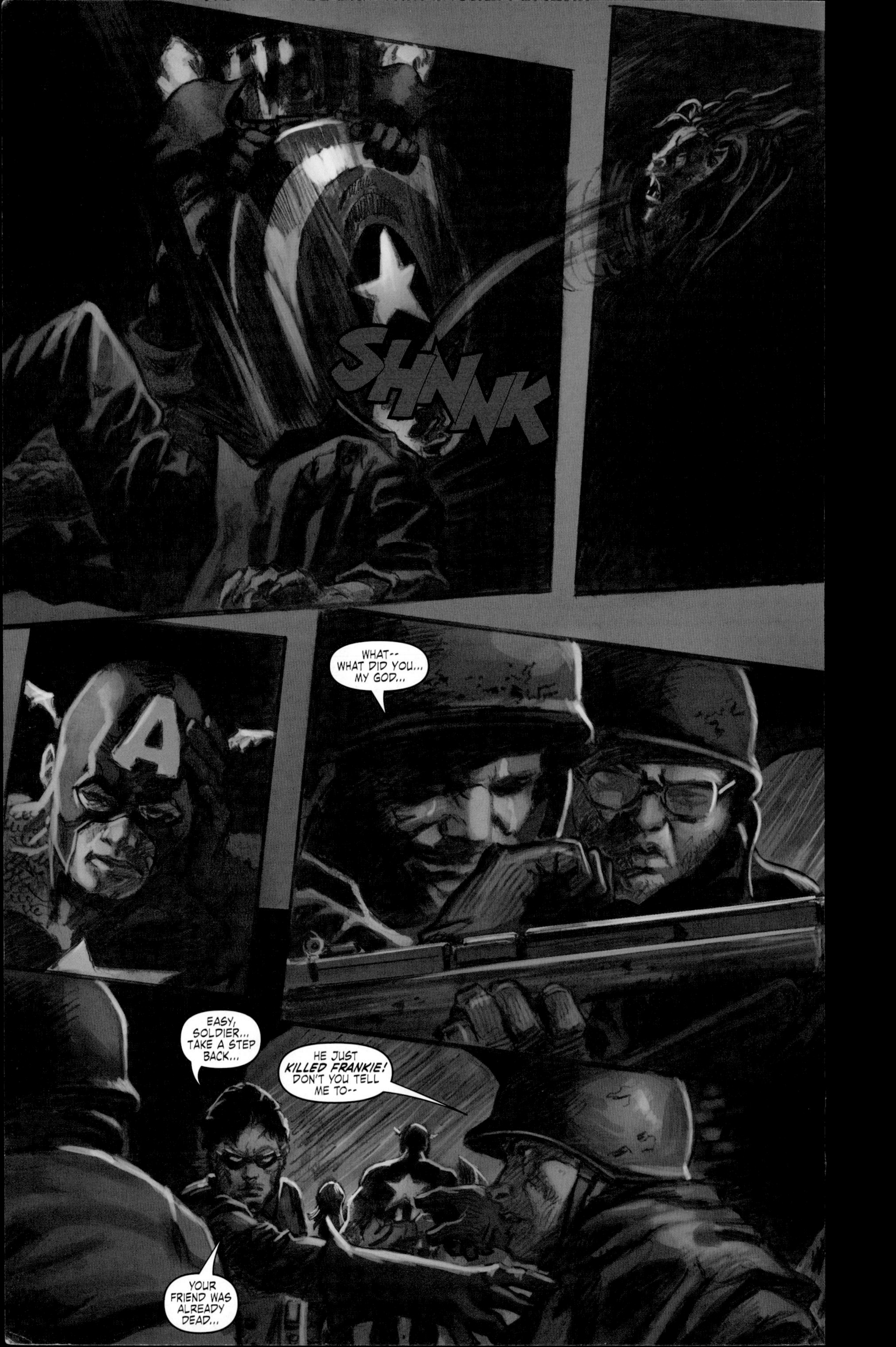
SHNNK
WHAT-- WHAT DID YOU... MY GOD...
EASY, SOLDIER... TAKE A STEP BACK...
HE JUST KILLED FRANKIE! DON'T YOU TELL ME TO--
YOUR FRIEND WAS ALREADY DEAD...

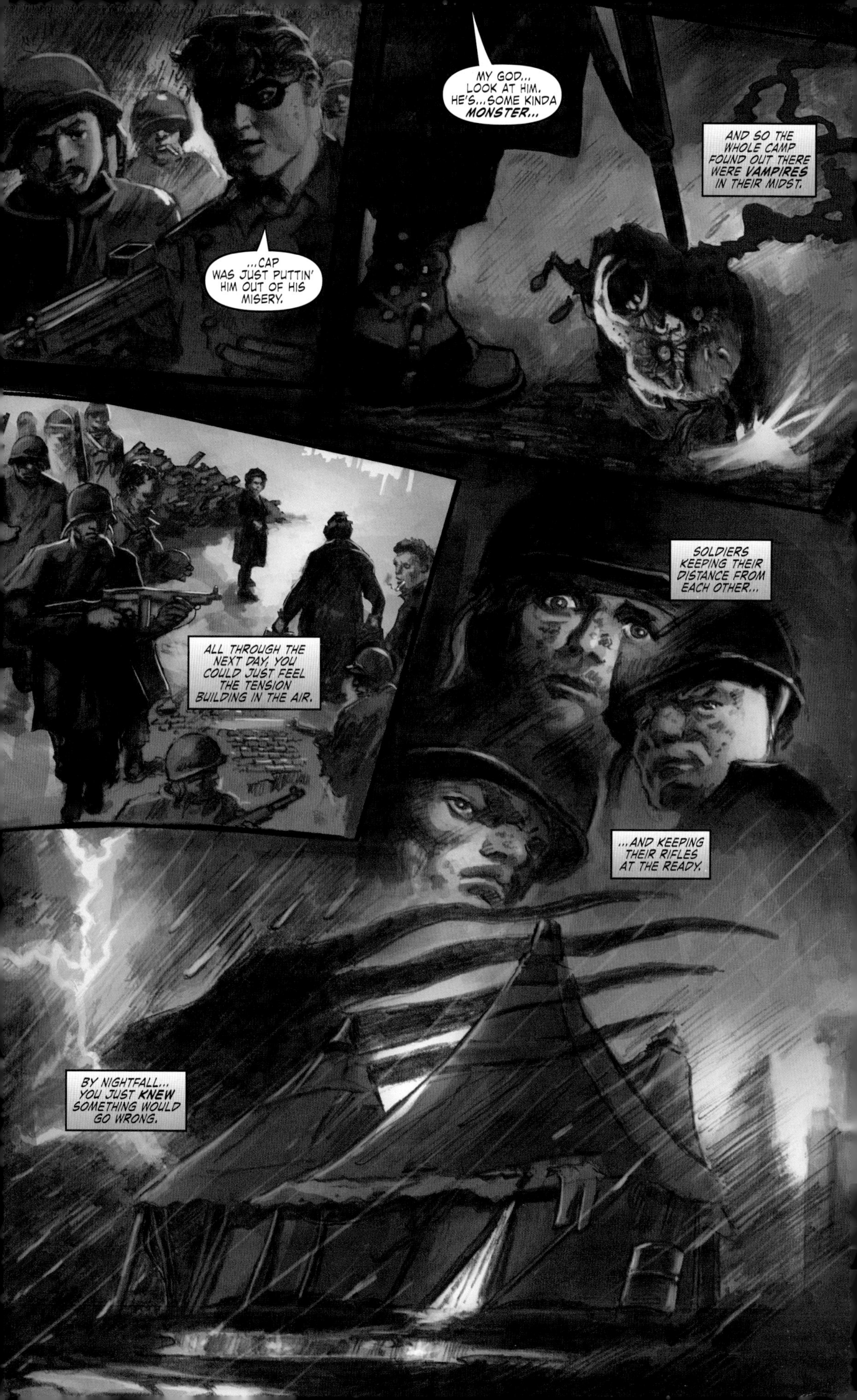

...CAP WAS JUST PUTTIN' HIM OUT OF HIS MISERY.
MY GOD... LOOK AT HIM. HE'S...SOME KINDA MONSTER...
AND SO THE WHOLE CAMP FOUND OUT THERE WERE VAMPIRES IN THEIR MIDST.
ALL THROUGH THE NEXT DAY, YOU COULD JUST FEEL THE TENSION BUILDING IN THE AIR.
SOLDIERS KEEPING THEIR DISTANCE FROM EACH OTHER...
...AND KEEPING THEIR RIFLES AT THE READY.
BY NIGHTFALL... YOU JUST KNEW SOMETHING WOULD GO WRONG.

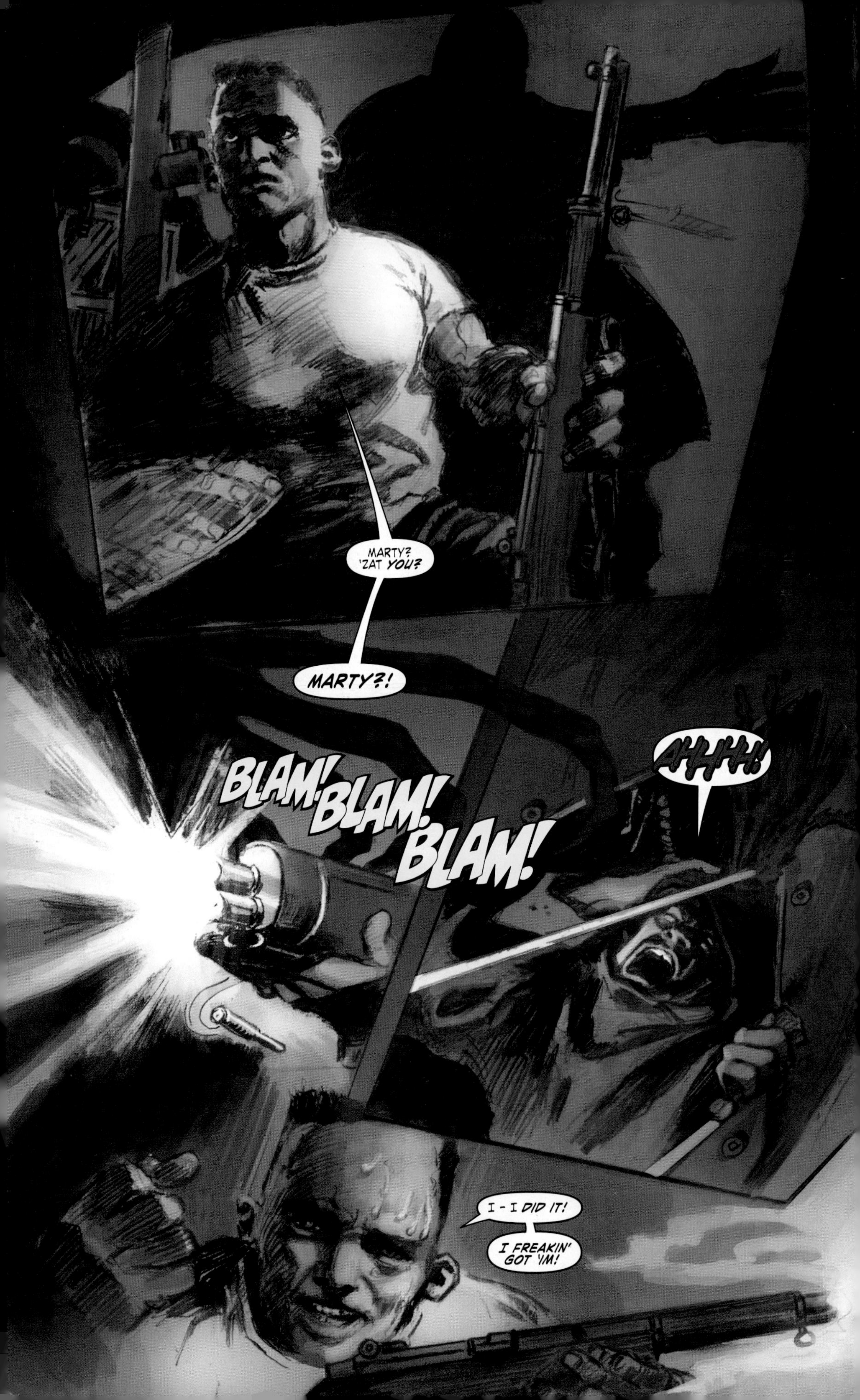

MARTY? 'ZAT YOU?
MARTY?!
BLAM! BLAM! BLAM!
AHHHH!
I - I DID IT!
I FREAKIN' GOT 'IM!

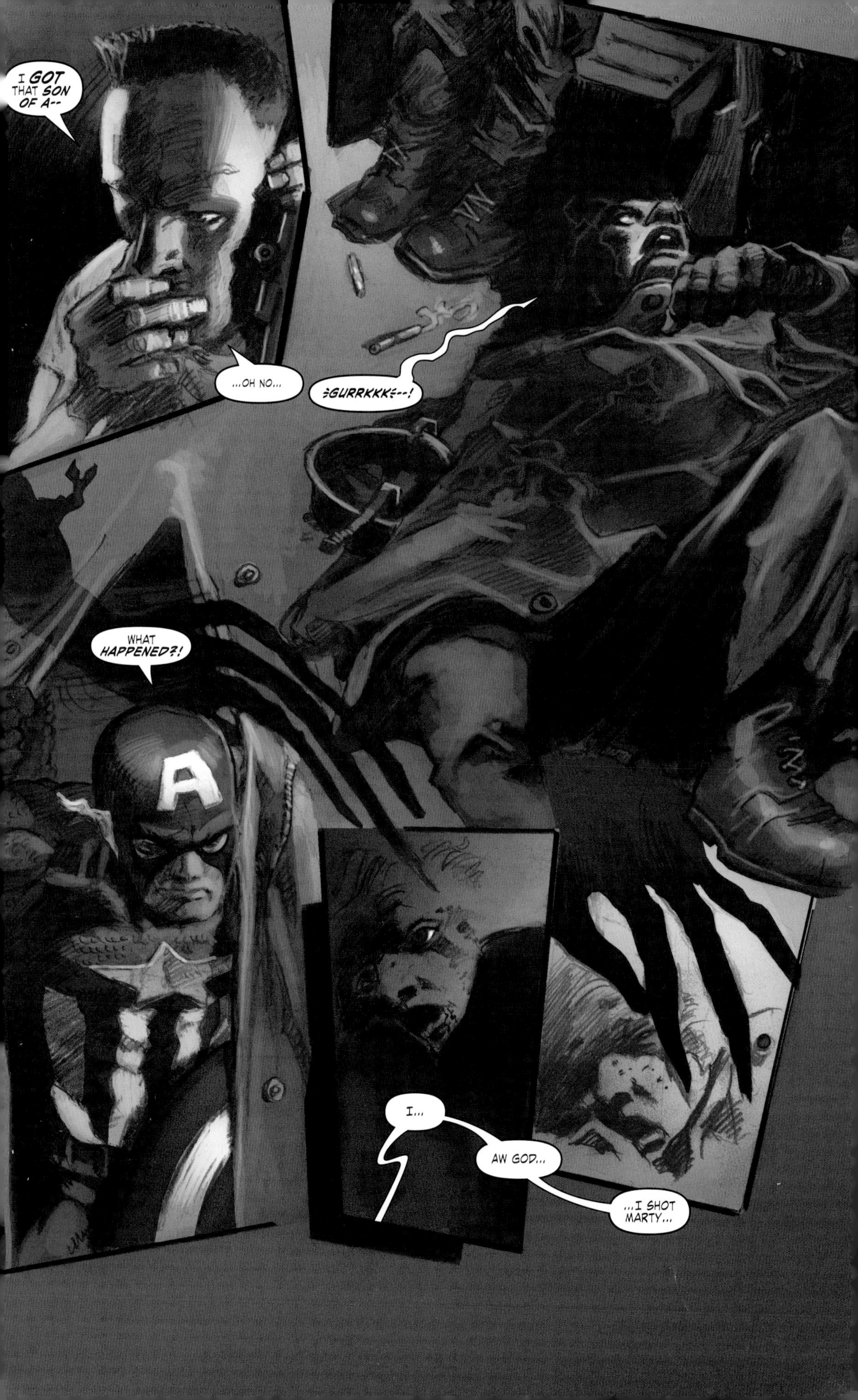
I GOT THAT SON OF A--
...OH NO...
GURRKKK--!
WHAT HAPPENED?!
I...
AW GOD...
...I SHOT MARTY...

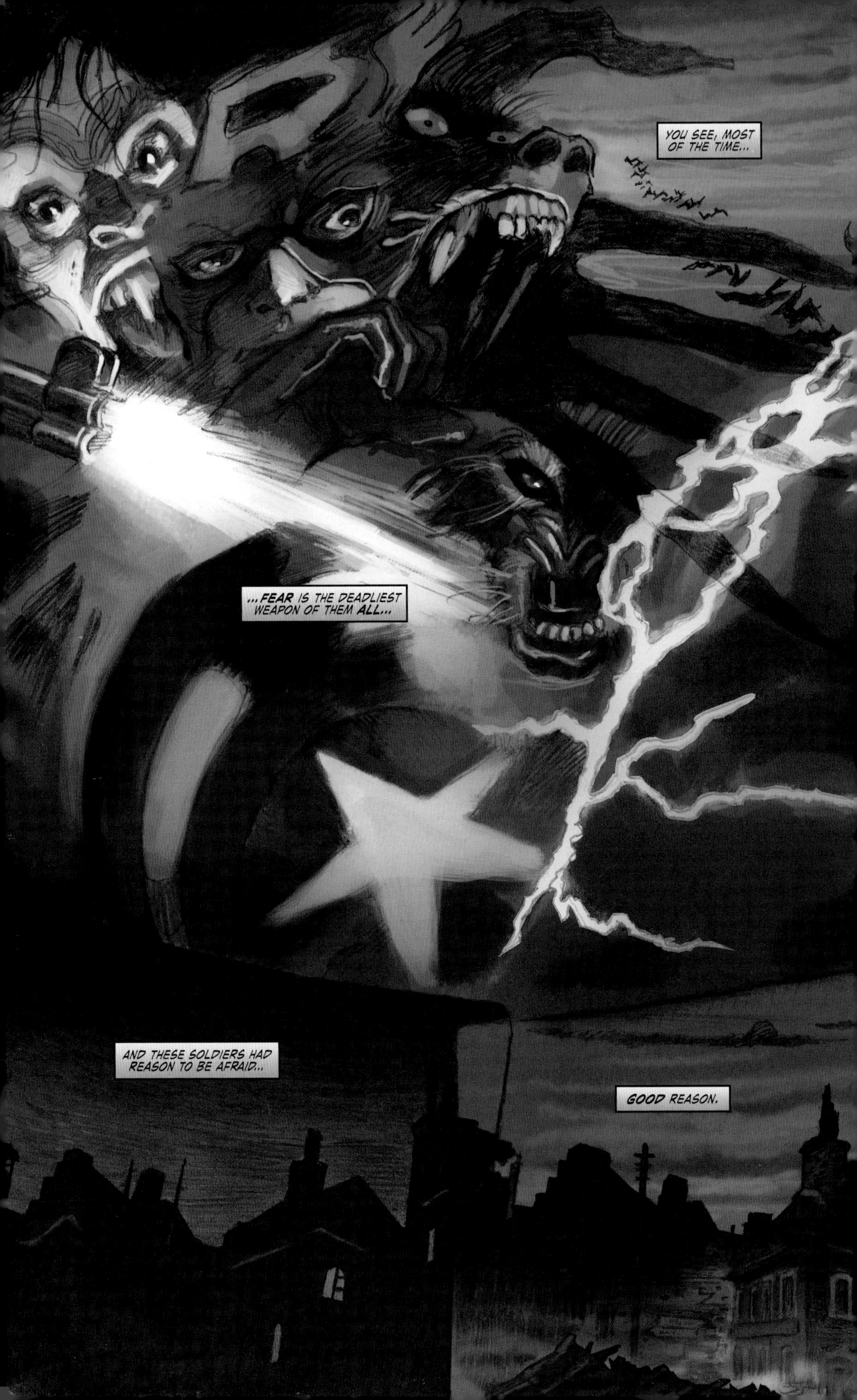
YOU SEE, MOST OF THE TIME...
...FEAR IS THE DEADLIEST WEAPON OF THEM ALL...
AND THESE SOLDIERS HAD REASON TO BE AFRAID...
GOOD REASON.

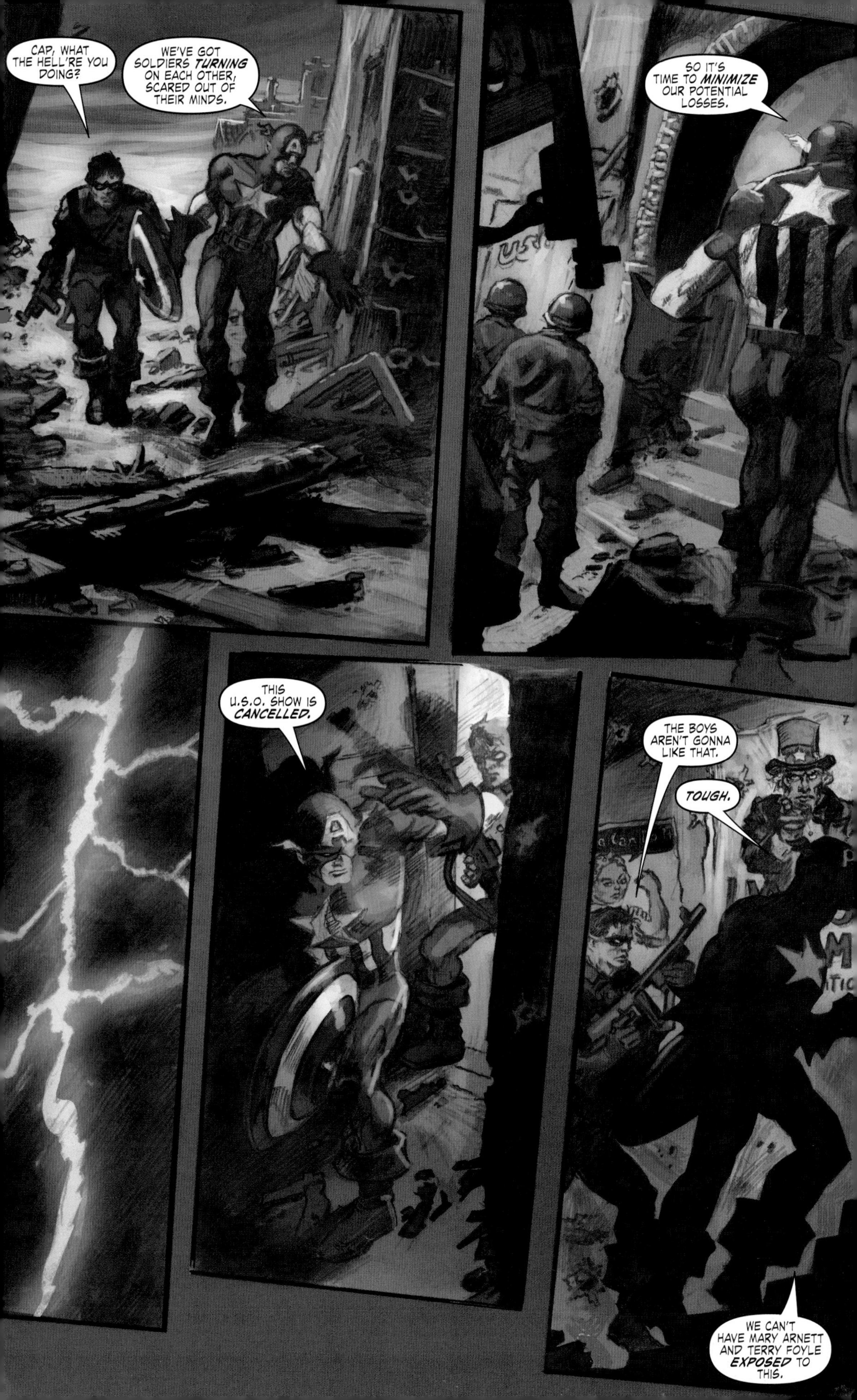
CAP, WHAT THE HELL'RE YOU DOING?
WE'VE GOT SOLDIERS TURNING ON EACH OTHER, SCARED OUT OF THEIR MINDS.
SO IT'S TIME TO MINIMIZE OUR POTENTIAL LOSSES.
THIS U.S.O. SHOW IS CANCELLED.
THE BOYS AREN'T GONNA LIKE THAT.
TOUGH.
WE CAN'T HAVE MARY ARNETT AND TERRY FOYLE EXPOSED TO THIS.

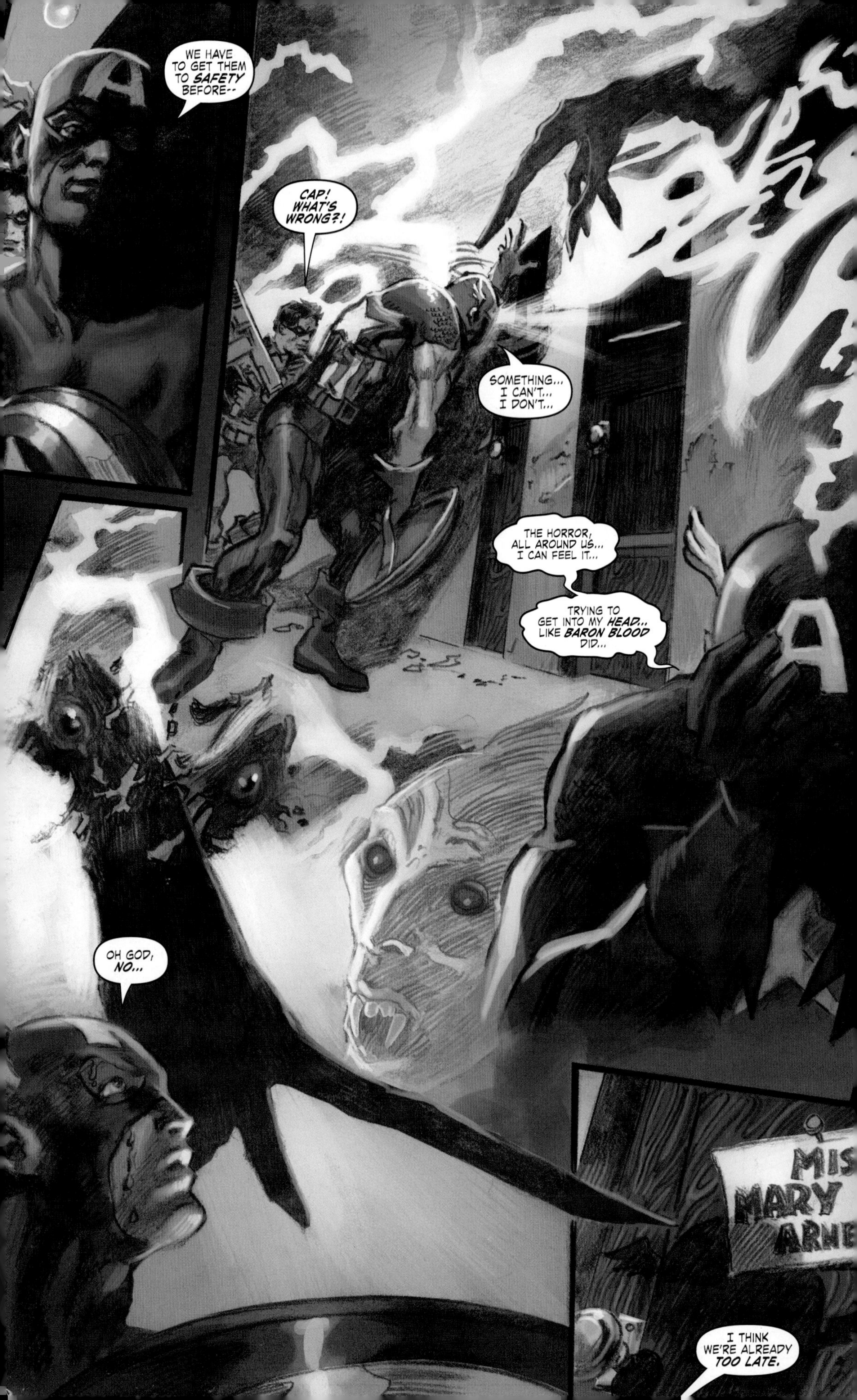
WE HAVE TO GET THEM TO SAFETY BEFORE--
CAP! WHAT'S WRONG?!
SOMETHING... I CAN'T... I DON'T...
THE HORROR, ALL AROUND US... I CAN FEEL IT...
TRYING TO GET INTO MY HEAD... LIKE BARON BLOOD DID...
OH GOD, NO...
MISS MARY ARNE
I THINK WE'RE ALREADY TOO LATE.

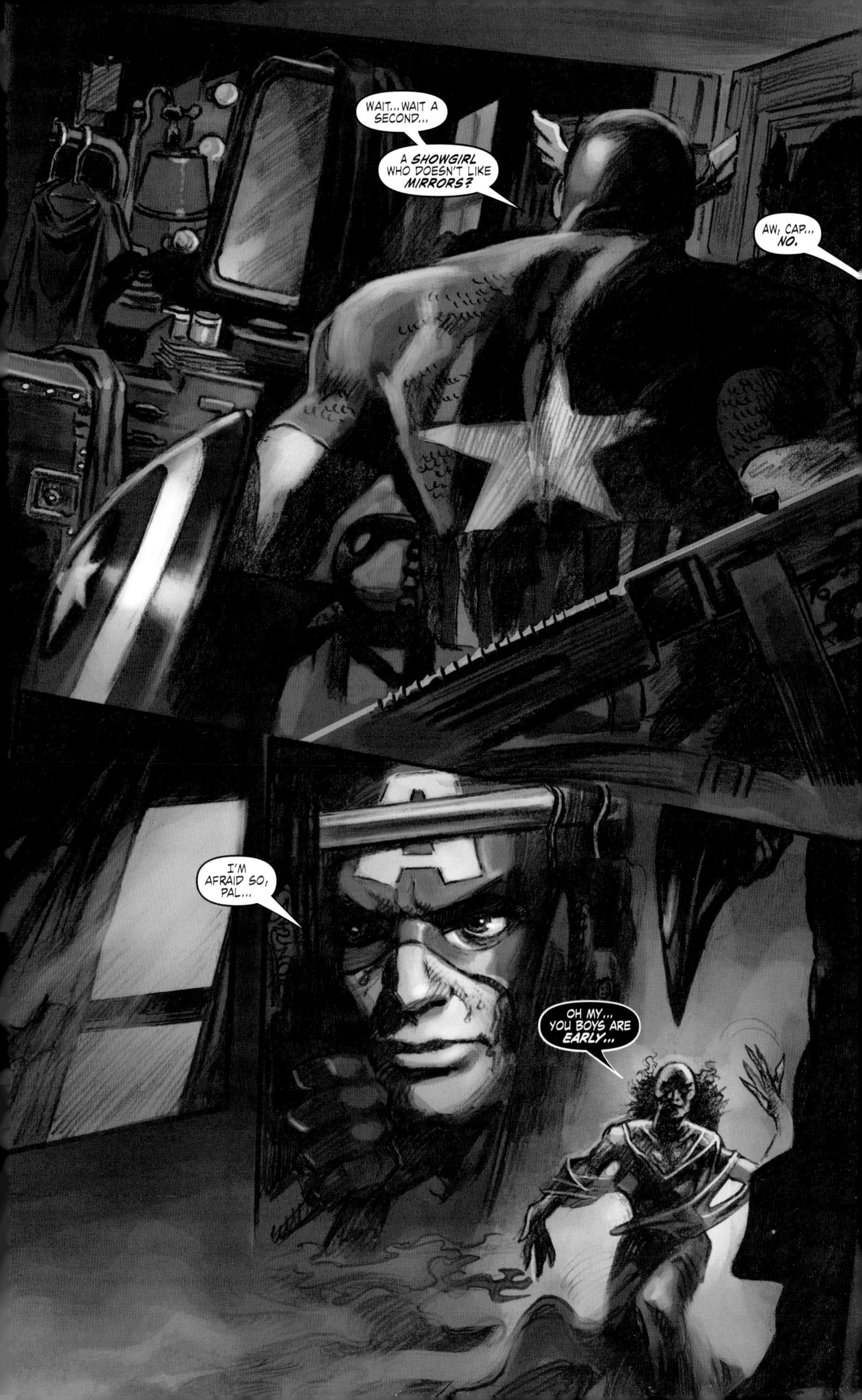
WAIT...WAIT A SECOND...
A SHOWGIRL WHO DOESN'T LIKE MIRRORS?
AW, CAP... NO.
I'M AFRAID SO, PAL...
OH MY... YOU BOYS ARE EARLY...

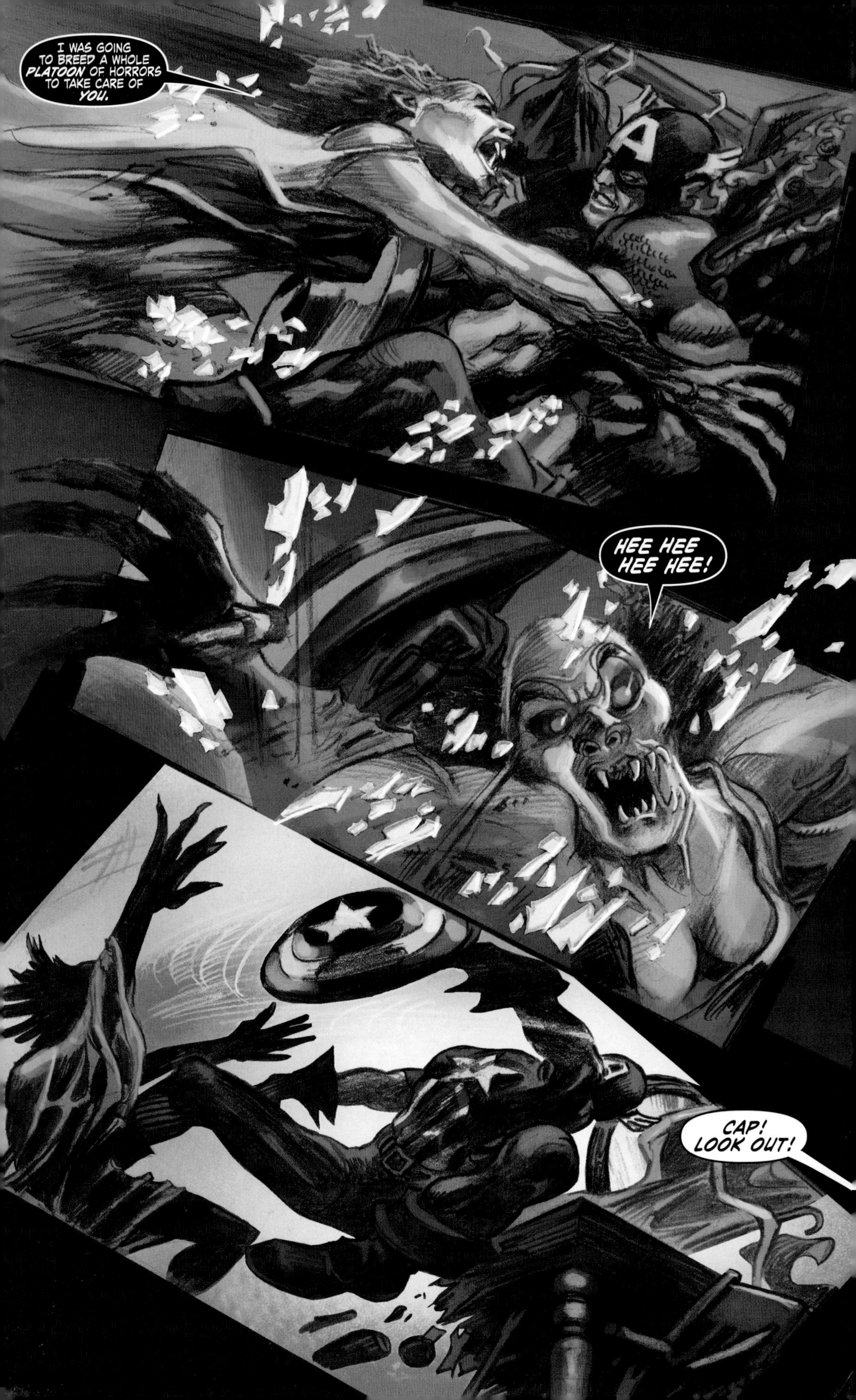
I WAS GOING TO BREED A WHOLE PLATOON OF HORRORS TO TAKE CARE OF YOU.
HEE HEE HEE HEE!
CAP! LOOK OUT!

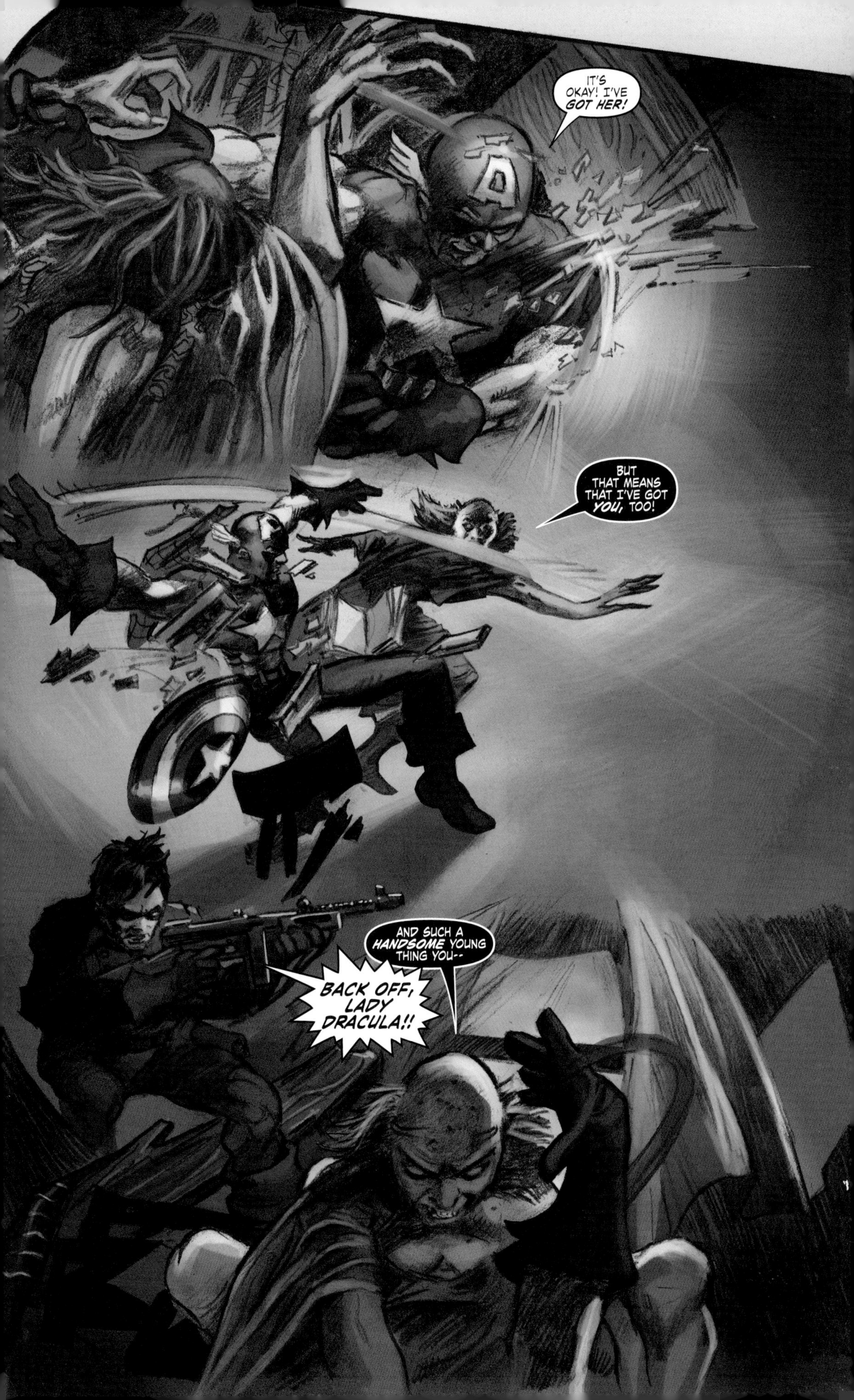
IT'S OKAY! I'VE GOT HER!
BUT THAT MEANS THAT I'VE GOT YOU, TOO!
AND SUCH A HANDSOME YOUNG THING YOU--
BACK OFF, LADY DRACULA!!

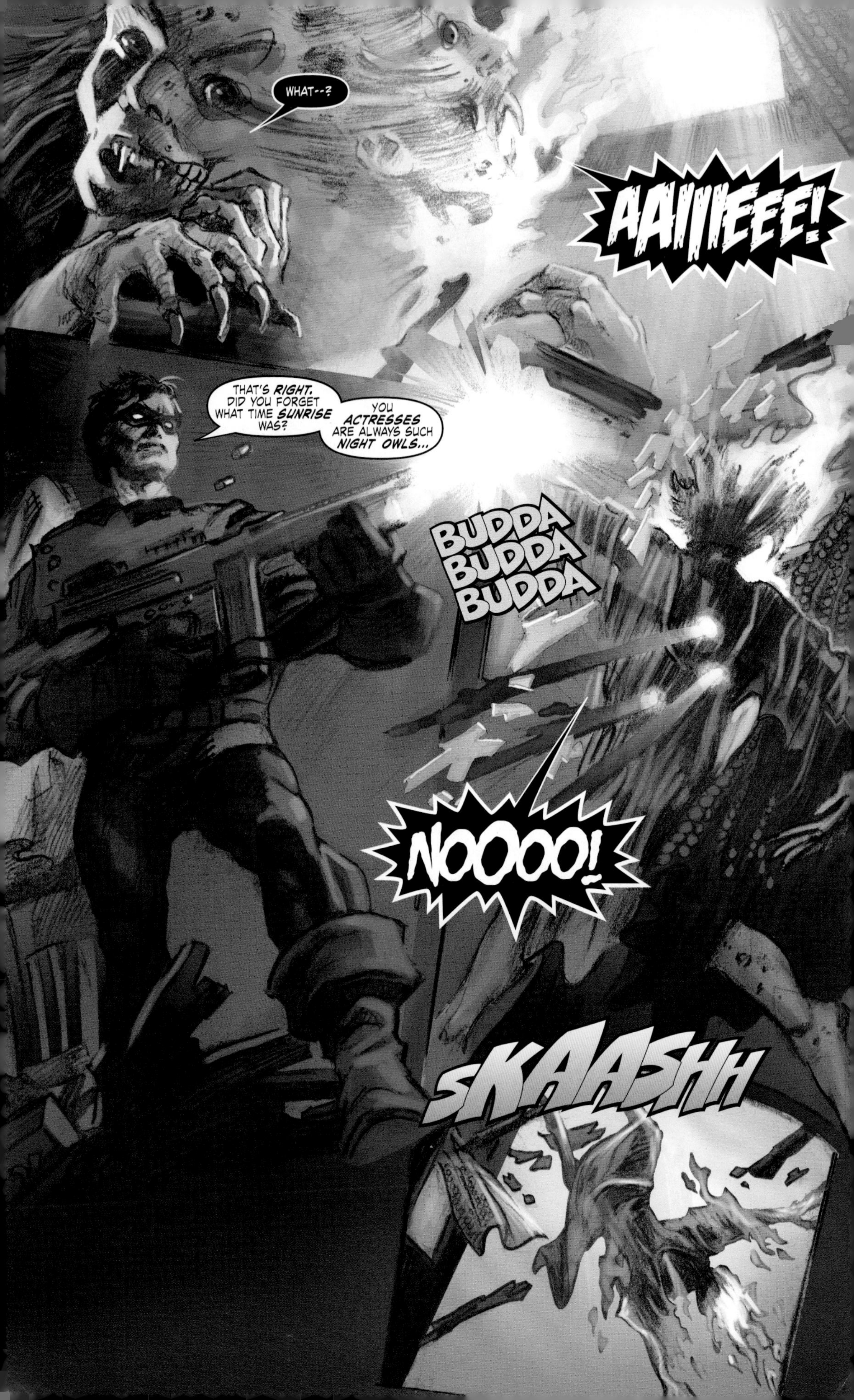
WHAT--?
AAIIIEEE!
THAT'S RIGHT. DID YOU FORGET WHAT TIME SUNRISE WAS?
YOU ACTRESSES ARE ALWAYS SUCH NIGHT OWLS...
BUDDA BUDDA BUDDA
NOOOO!
sKAASHH

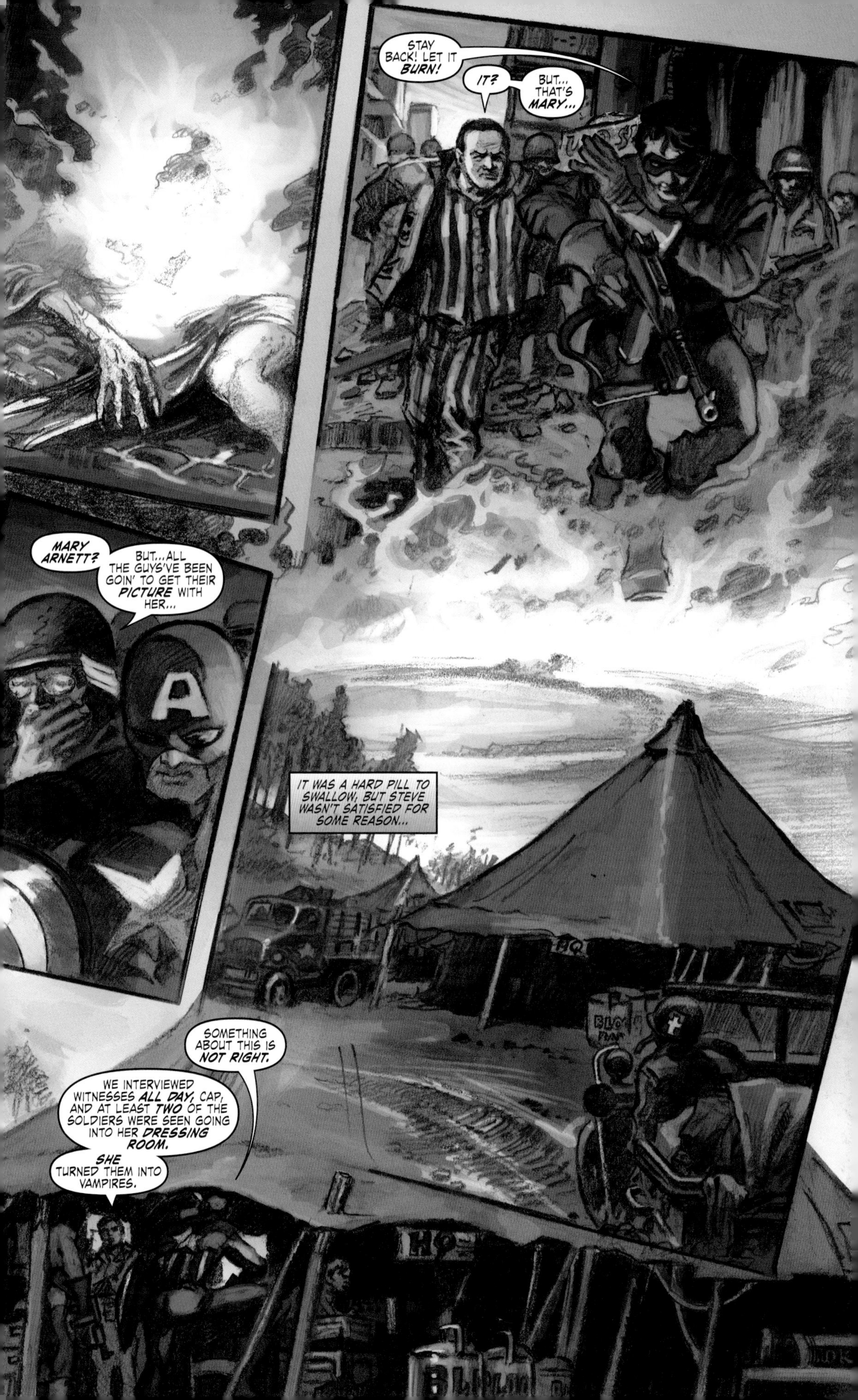
STAY BACK! LET IT BURN!
IT?
BUT... THAT'S MARY...
MARY ARNETT?
BUT...ALL THE GUYS'VE BEEN GOIN' TO GET THEIR PICTURE WITH HER...
IT WAS A HARD PILL TO SWALLOW, BUT STEVE WASN'T SATISFIED FOR SOME REASON...
SOMETHING ABOUT THIS IS NOT RIGHT.
WE INTERVIEWED WITNESSES ALL DAY, CAP, AND AT LEAST TWO OF THE SOLDIERS WERE SEEN GOING INTO HER DRESSING ROOM.
SHE TURNED THEM INTO VAMPIRES.
HQ

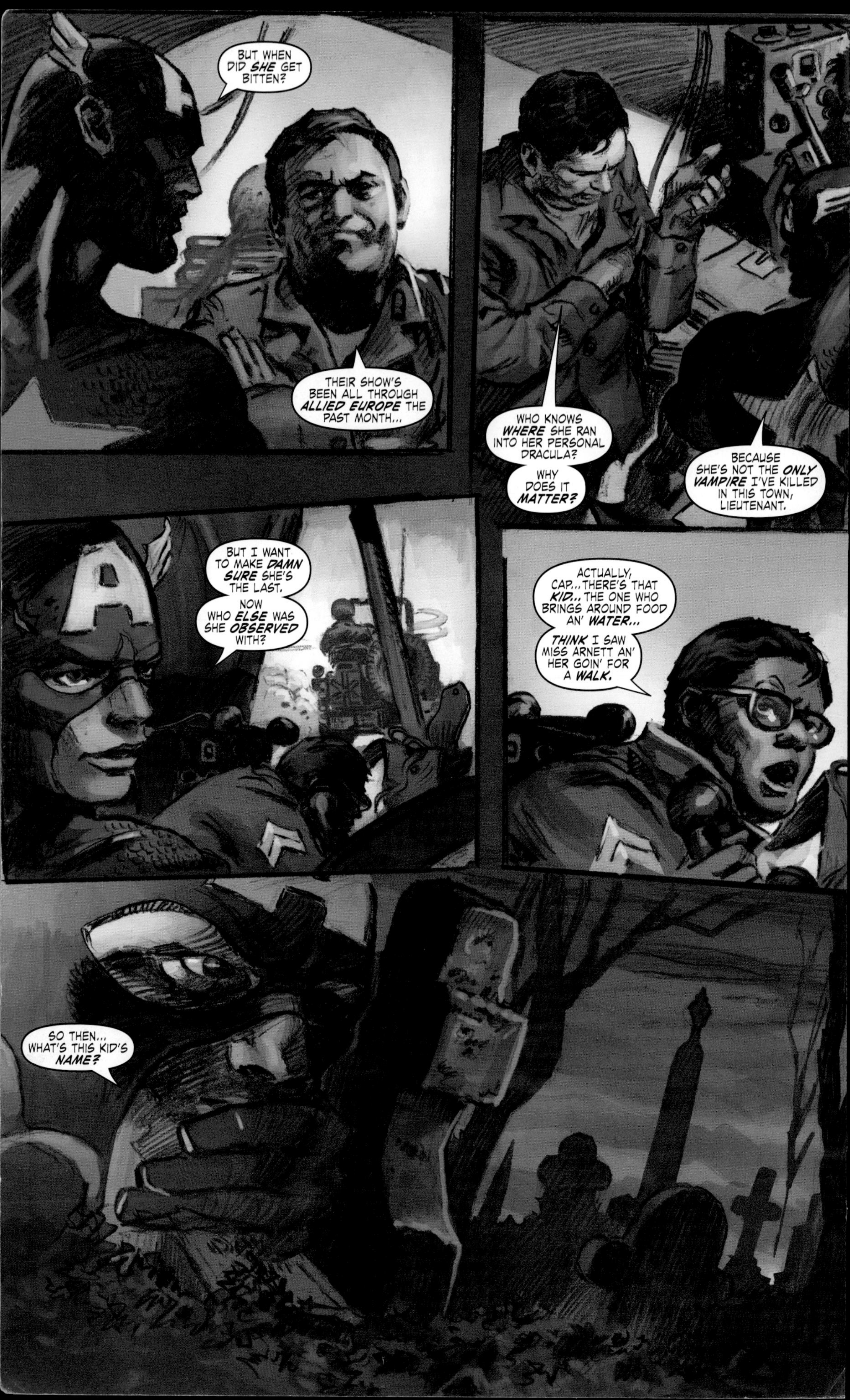
BUT WHEN DID SHE GET BITTEN?
THEIR SHOW'S BEEN ALL THROUGH ALLIED EUROPE THE PAST MONTH...
WHO KNOWS WHERE SHE RAN INTO HER PERSONAL DRACULA?
WHY DOES IT MATTER?
BECAUSE SHE'S NOT THE ONLY VAMPIRE I'VE KILLED IN THIS TOWN, LIEUTENANT.
BUT I WANT TO MAKE DAMN SURE SHE'S THE LAST.
NOW WHO ELSE WAS SHE OBSERVED WITH?
ACTUALLY, CAP... THERE'S THAT KID... THE ONE WHO BRINGS AROUND FOOD AN' WATER...
THINK I SAW MISS ARNETT AN' HER GOIN' FOR A WALK.
SO THEN... WHAT'S THIS KID'S NAME?

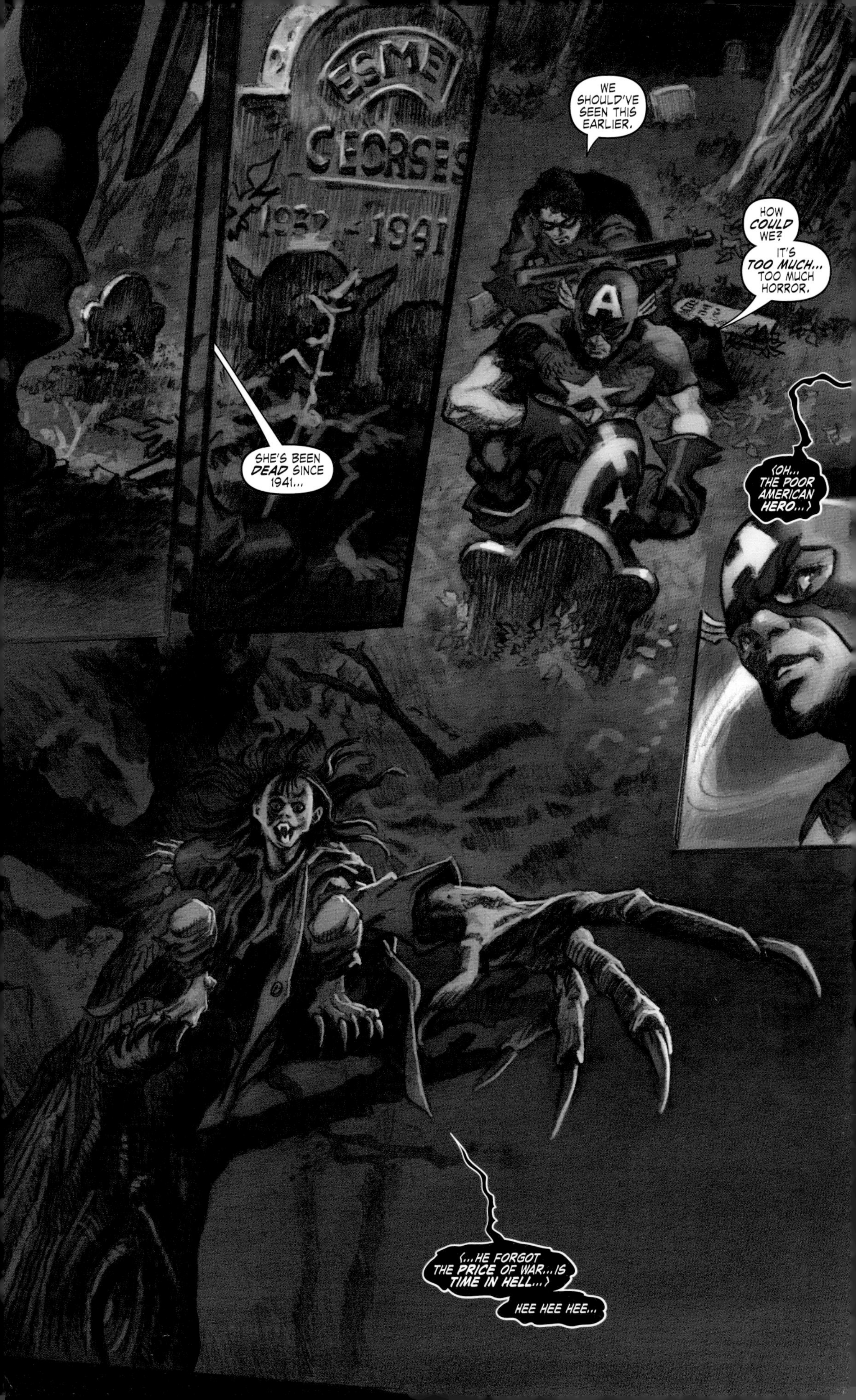
ESME
GEORGES
1932 - 1941
SHE'S BEEN DEAD SINCE 1941...
WE SHOULD'VE SEEN THIS EARLIER.
HOW COULD WE?
IT'S TOO MUCH... TOO MUCH HORROR.
(OH... THE POOR AMERICAN HERO...)
(...HE FORGOT THE PRICE OF WAR...IS TIME IN HELL...)
HEE HEE HEE...

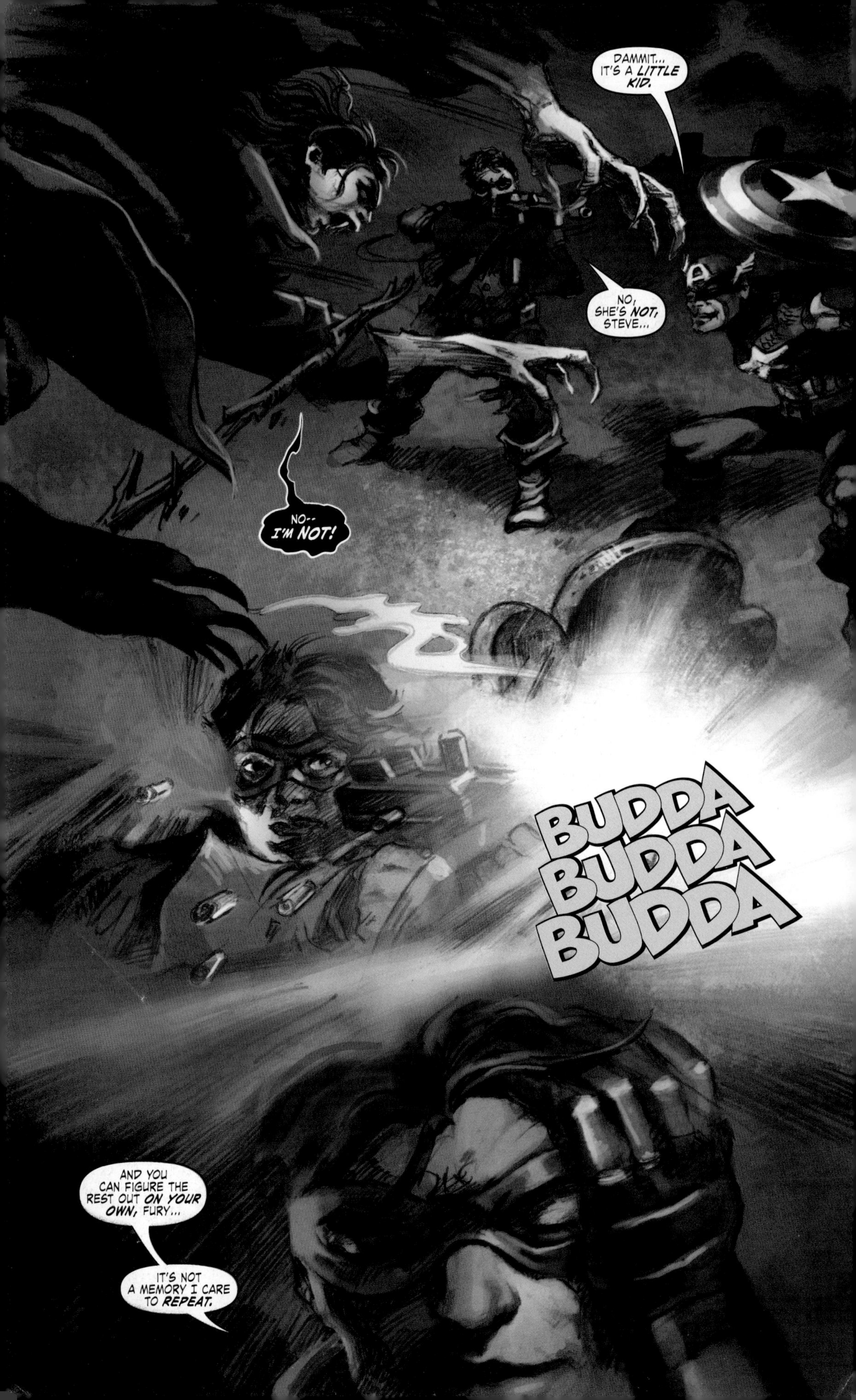
DAMMIT... IT'S A *LITTLE KID.*
NO, SHE'S *NOT,* STEVE...
NO-- *I'M NOT!*
BUDDA BUDDA BUDDA
AND YOU CAN FIGURE THE REST OUT *ON YOUR OWN,* FURY...
IT'S NOT A MEMORY I CARE TO *REPEAT.*

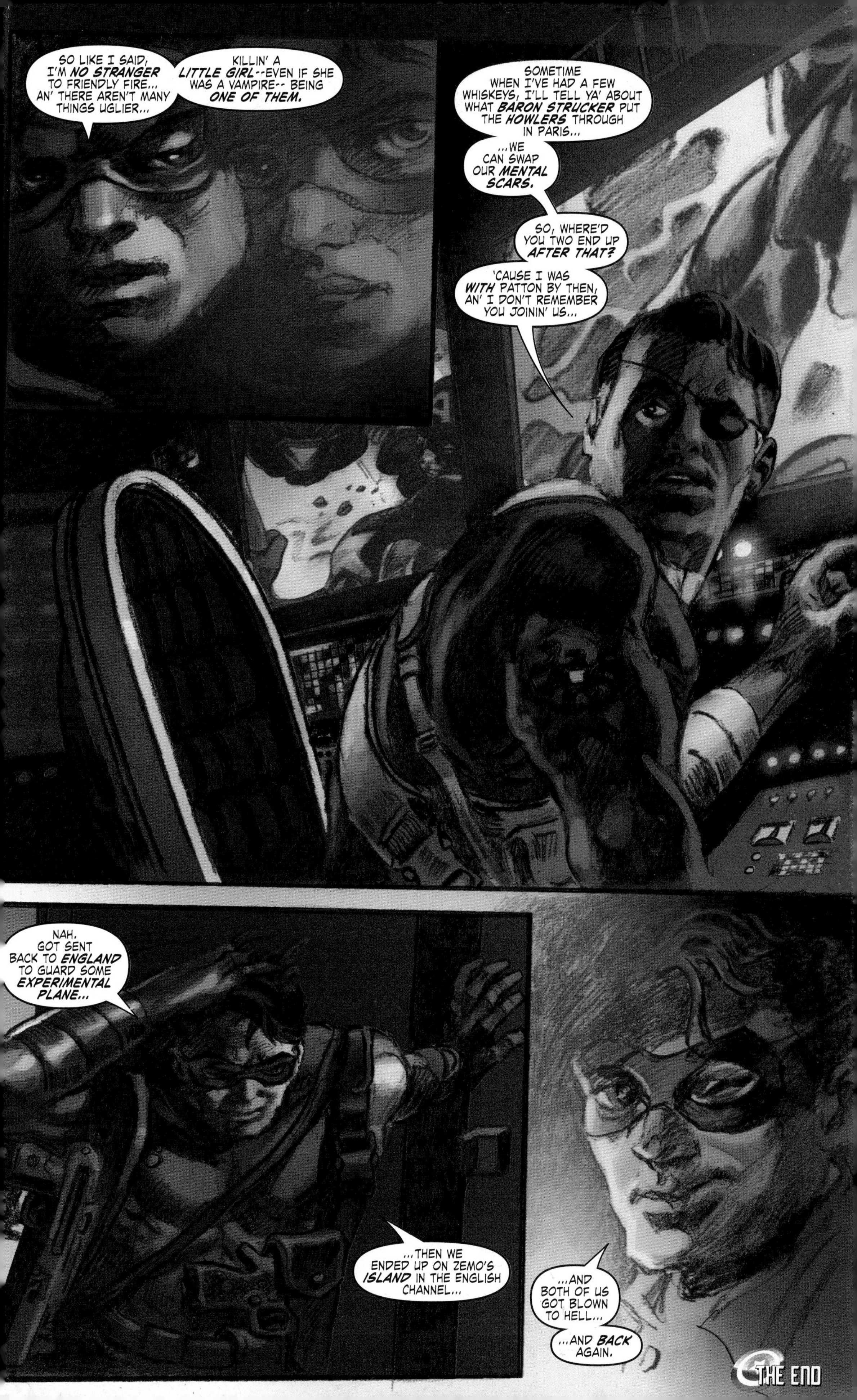
SO LIKE I SAID, I'M NO STRANGER TO FRIENDLY FIRE... AN' THERE AREN'T MANY THINGS UGLIER...
KILLIN' A LITTLE GIRL--EVEN IF SHE WAS A VAMPIRE-- BEING ONE OF THEM.
SOMETIME WHEN I'VE HAD A FEW WHISKEYS, I'LL TELL YA' ABOUT WHAT BARON STRUCKER PUT THE HOWLERS THROUGH IN PARIS...
...WE CAN SWAP OUR MENTAL SCARS.
SO, WHERE'D YOU TWO END UP AFTER THAT?
'CAUSE I WAS WITH PATTON BY THEN, AN' I DON'T REMEMBER YOU JOININ' US...
NAH. GOT SENT BACK TO ENGLAND TO GUARD SOME EXPERIMENTAL PLANE...
...THEN WE ENDED UP ON ZEMO'S ISLAND IN THE ENGLISH CHANNEL...
...AND BOTH OF US GOT BLOWN TO HELL...
...AND BACK AGAIN.
THE END

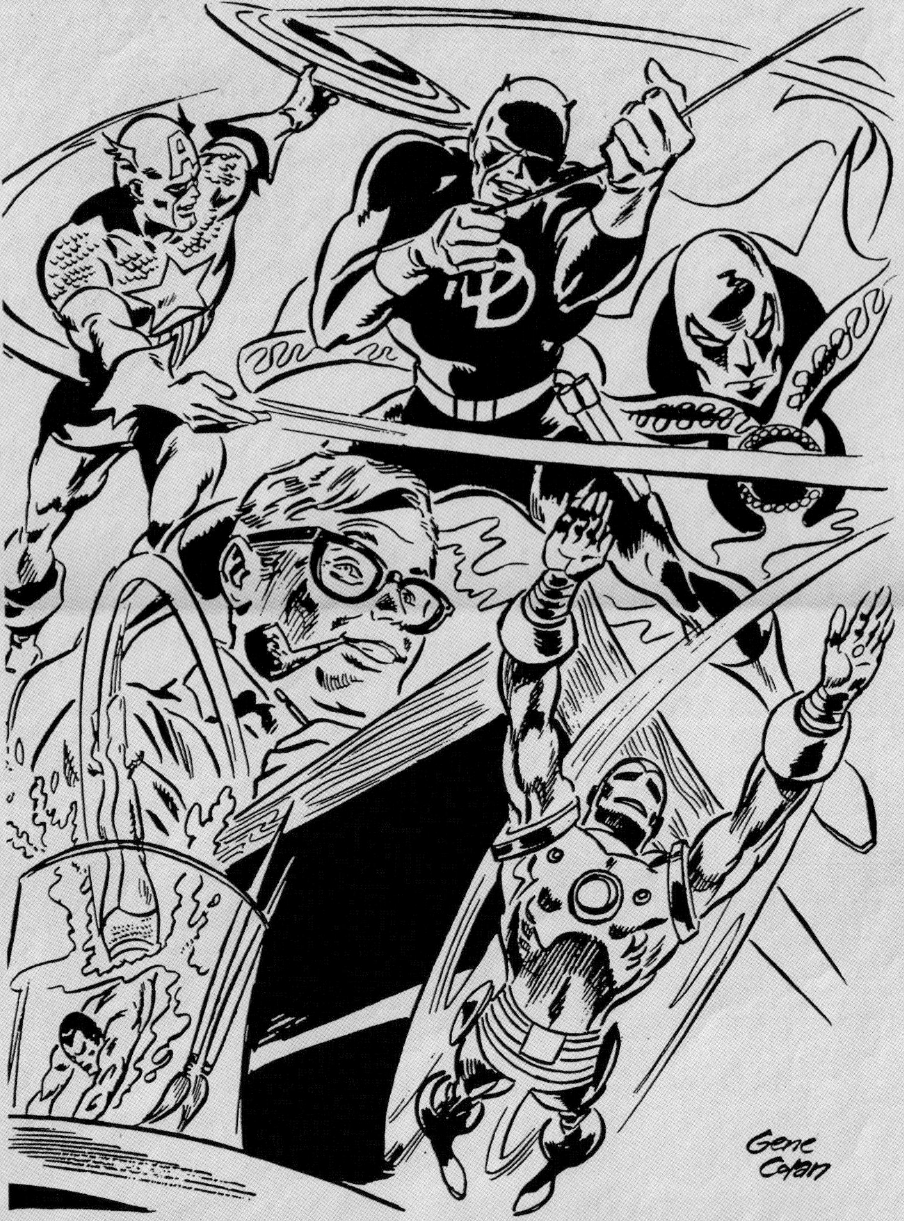
Gene Colan

OUR SPECIAL GUEST ARTIST THIS MONTH IS AS MUCH A LIVING LEGEND AS CAPTAIN AMERICA HIMSELF.

GENE "THE DEAN" COLAN, HAS A HISTORY WITH THE SENTINEL OF LIBERTY THAT EXTENDS BACK TO THE GOLDEN AGE OF COMICS. (GENE DREW THE COVER TO THE VERY LAST ISSUE OF CAPTAIN AMERICA PUBLISHED IN THE 1940S.)

AN UNDISPUTED MASTER OF THE COMIC BOOK FORM, GENE IS BEST REMEMBERED FOR HIS CHARACTER-DEFINING RUNS ON DAREDEVIL, IRON MAN, SUB-MARINER, TOMB OF DRACULA, DR. STRANGE AND HOWARD THE DUCK.

MORE AN ILLUSTRATOR THAN A CARTOONIST, GENE PIONEERED AN APPROACH TO DRAWING COMICS THAT'S COME TO BE KNOWN AS "PAINTING WITH A PENCIL" AND EXPANDED THE FRONTIERS OF WHAT COMIC BOOK ART COULD LOOK LIKE.

WE MEMBERS OF THE MODERN-DAY MARVEL BULLPEN SALUTE GENE COLAN AND HIS TREMENDOUS ACCOMPLISHMENTS OVER HIS STUNNING SIX-DECADE CAREER.

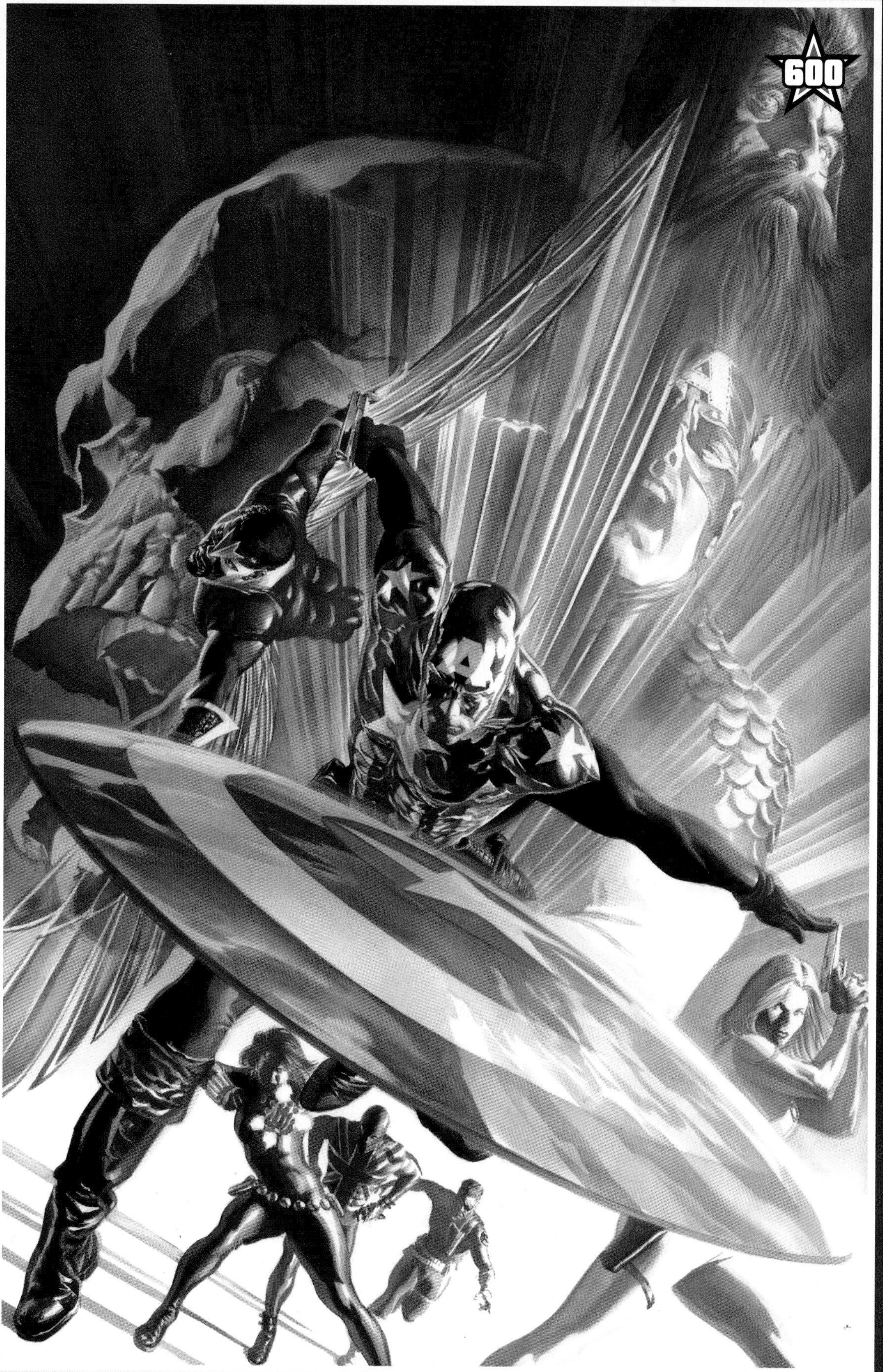
600

VARIANT BY ALEX ROSS

601 CCH

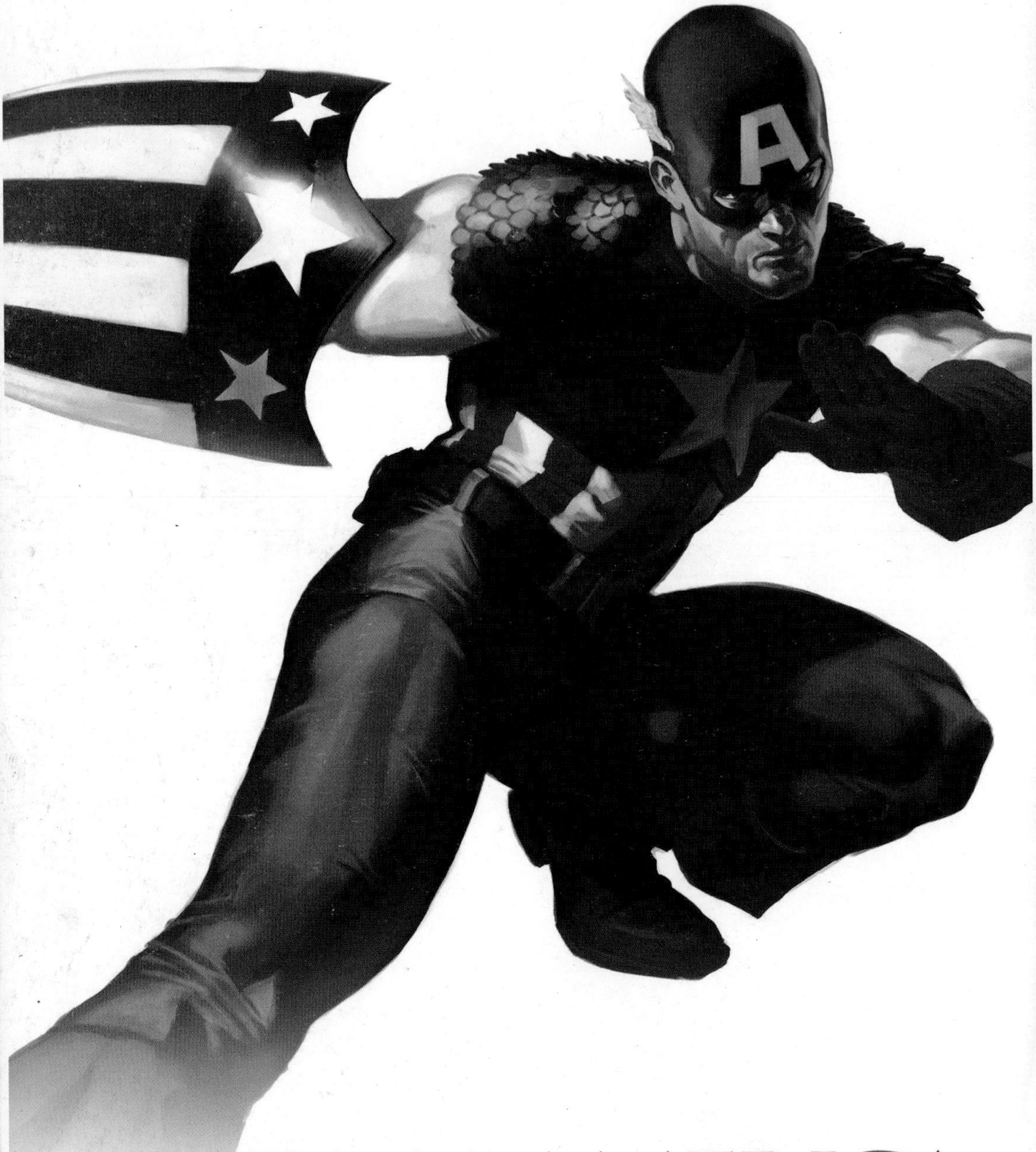

CAPTAIN AMERICA

EST. 1941

70TH ANNIVERSARY VARIANT BY MARKO DJURDJEVIC